THE LOST SON

by
Andy Back

By the same author

Non-fiction:
Children's Ministry Guide to Dealing with Disruptive Children
Children's Ministry Guide to Building a Team
Children's Ministry Guide to Working with 9-13s
Dynamic Youth Leadership: Principles in Practice
101 Dynamic Ideas for your Youth Group

Bible paraphrase
Acts of God
Dan the Man

Bible fiction
Substitute

Also from SozoPrint
The Compassion Prize by Katy Hollway
The Compassion Gift by Katy Hollway
The Compassion Fire by Katy Hollway

Sozo Print

Copyright ©2019 SozoPrint

Designed and published by SozoPrint
Unit650, 20 Corn Mill Close, Bartley Green, Birmingham, West Midlands, B32 3BH
Printed in Great Britain. Insert printed & finished by Solopress, SS2 5QF
Produced for the publishers by lightningsource.com

the L(o)ST son

by

Andy Back

For

Simon Virgo

a son who ran and returned,
becoming
stronger, wiser,
more aware of God's grace
and of a loving, patient, constant father

*'if an idiot – like I have been –
can find the kindness of God,
I urge you to check him out' SV*

Contents

P 145
Q 146
Artists & classical composers 146
Sourced from the bard of Avon ... 147
Fugue 148
Eye rhyme 149
What if? (x9) 151
Imprecision 152
Best actor Oscar winners 152
Fraffly earppacrus' 155
Anglo-Catholic 155
Prodigal puppet 155
Catch phrases 156
R 157
S 157
Inflationary language 158
Discount language 158
Return for spender 159
Litotes 159
Fiscal terms (money talks) 160
Record breakers 161
Prosody acrostic 163
Prosody acrostic reversed 164
Prosody acrostic reduced 164
Butchery news 165
Activity sheet 165
High street 166
Classical phrases 167
Irritable vowel syndrome 168
Last lines 169
Commercialese Gobbledegook 171
Germanglicisation 172
StreamofConsciousness 173
US Presidents 174
Directions 176
Dramatic irony 177
Anagramatical 179
Full circle 180
Musical theatre 181
Round robin 183
T 185
Epistemological 185

Doctor Who 186
U 188
Dysfunctional Family 188
Romance Monthly magazine serial . 188
Interview transcript 191
N+7 195
V 195
Identilexical (x3) 195
Dramatis personae, miscast 196
Abbreviations plus 197
W 197
Nightmare song 197
Amplified version 199
Browner Hay (x2) 200
X 200
Y 200
Z 200
JQXYZ 200
Assonance 201
Traditional rhymes (x12) 201
Mohican haircut 208
Keystrokes 500 209
Keystrokes 350 209
Keystrokes 140 (Twitter) 209
Keystrokes 100 209
Keystrokes 50 209
Bildungsroman (Coming of
 Age/Rite of Passage) 209
Middle A 211
Interrogative 212
Catechism 213
Deck of cards 214
Middle E 215
Typefaces 216
Qwerty 218
Lost in Austen 218
Threnodials 219
30-minute lostness 219
Cracked screen/dodgy keys 221
Curriculum vitae/application 221
Periodigal table of elements 222
Bertie Wooster 224

Introduction: Lost by choice?

Who's the Master Storyteller? Jesus, undoubtedly.

And the *Parable of the Prodigal Son* is surely one of his top five best stories.

I suggest the other parables in the top five are – in no particular order – Sower, Lost Sheep, Talents, and Good Samaritan, with perhaps Wise Man/Foolish Man and the Workers in the Vineyard bubbling under.

It's not that important.

Anyway, *Prodigal Son* is primarily an illustration of repentance and grace, featuring a rebellious son who behaves disgracefully, is given Divine revelation, turns back, receives forgiveness and is fully restored by a loving father…

The theology pours off the page, and it's easy to work out who represents who and what signifies what.

Perhaps the only thing that is even slightly obscure is the title, which was added by scholars some 1600 years after Jesus told the story. They decided, somewhat unfortunately, to use a word that has since fallen into disuse. *Prodigal* means *waster* (literally, *drive forth*); some Bible versions call this story *The Lost Son* – perhaps since it nestles alongside parables on similar themes: *The Lost Coin* and *The Lost Sheep*. These cast additional light on God seeking out that which is lost by circumstance (coin) and by nature (sheep), in contrast to the son, who is lost by his own rebellious choice.

Telling the tale

Jesus offers no application to this story – perhaps he feels it is self-explanatory, and as people identify with the characters, they will reach their own conclusions about whatever adjustments to their attitudes or their behaviour may need to be made, with God's help.

The start of the chapter indicates a wide range of listeners. Of course, the disciples were there, as ever, not really understanding, I expect. But broadly positive, I would hope.

And there was always a crowd as well; some enjoying the teaching style, and some hoping for the storytelling to finish so they could watch (or better yet) experience the healing and deliverance miracles. Again, they were there not to critique the message or doubt the wonders, but because Jesus' presence was fascinating, attractive and generous.

In addition, there were two other distinct groups, both of which brought their premeditated opinions.

Firstly, tax collectors and 'sinners'; people who may consider themselves to be irredeemably wicked, like the son who feels no longer worthy. Surely there is no hope for them? Their expectation by the end of the story is that the father would either reject his returning wayward son, or at the very least punish him severely for such shockingly wasteful and disrespectful conduct.

The second group, the pharasees and teachers of the law, would certainly agree that the returning son should be excluded or subjected to the righteous anger of his father. They'd have probably identified themselves with the remaining, older son, reckoning him to be hard-working, faithful and justifiably aggravated that his dad intended to restore his brother. They also would have been appalled by the forgiveness and kindness the father shows.

Grace, properly understood, provokes outrage.

Taking sides

Now, consider for a moment the older son.

He stayed put, working, so he says. Almost certainly he overstates his diligent, unwavering obedience (especially taking into account his disrespectful outburst, petulantly refusing to attend the party), and some commentators even suggest 'in the field' (v25) refers not to one of his father's grazing or crop-growing areas, but an off-site, undisclosed part of the countryside. Yet he will eventually gain his inheritance – 'everything I have is yours' (v31).

On the other hand, let's assess his cash worth.

First, the father finances the younger son's excess, dispersing about one third of his total wealth. Then, when the young waster returns, the boy is restored to sonship. The implication is that the older boy's potential inheritance is again reduced by one third. He initially anticipates 66% of his father's estate, yet when the dust settles, his share will only amount to 44% of the original value. His rage is understandable.

Yet Jesus is clearly teaching about grace, repentance, forgiveness and restoration; so perhaps I am reading too rather much into the financial mathematics.

The older boy's attitude is that of a hired servant, not a son; his relationship to his father lacks gratitude, openness or affection; and his response to his (presumed dead) brother's return is not compassionate relief but selfish fury. I think we are not supposed to take his side, but to learn from his impoverished religious legalism.

The man on the Paris omnibus

Meanwhile, I fear we may, over the years, have grown a little over-familiar with this story. So I have poured considerable energy into putting some (well, many) fresh spins on the yarn.

My initial inspiration was the entirely remarkable *Exercises in Style*, a vastly creative book by the French writer Raymond Queneau (1903-1976). It tells, ultimately, a meaningless story: a Parisian with a strange hat and a long neck stumbles against a fellow passenger when his busy bus jolts; later he receives sartorial advice outside a railway station.

But this snapshot-tale is described in ninety-nine different ways, using tricks of word selection, style and form. Part of Queneau's thesis is that a dull, pointless yarn can be given meaning when the telling of it results in something of literary value.

Centre-stage narrator?

This is a game played with language – yet any enjoyment for me is entirely thanks to Barbara Wright's painstaking translation from the French. It seems *Exercises in Style* has inspired many translators, as it has so far been published in thirty-five languages, including Hebrew, Ukranian, Catalan, Brazilian Portuguese, Turkish, Esperanto and Chinese. What's the collective term for translators? *A vocab? A metaphrasis? A polyglottage?* Je ne sais pas. Ich weiß nicht. I'm clueless, cobber.

The value this creative reworking Queneau gives to his portrait of the nondescript is enormous; how appropriate, in my view, to add a generous selection of different approaches to the *Prodigal Son*, an already hugely worthwhile narrative!

Has our familiarity with the parable reduced its impact? Perhaps.

So then, why not allow the narrator to take an active role, and add invention, games of style and construction, as well as the twists and turns of humour (where appropriate)? Hopefully, this gives a new lease on life to this eternal story. Metafiction, indeed!

Constrained writing techniques

Queneau was a founder member of the Oulipo group – **OU**vroir de **LI**ttérature **PO**tentielle *(potential literature workshop)*. This literary movement was formed in 1960 of (mainly) French-speaking writers and mathematicians who aimed to create works using constrained writing techniques: using or excluding various letters; playing with literary styles; placing restrictions upon content; imposing composition rules.

Included in the movement include: British architect and writer Stanley Chapman was a founder member, and translator of Queneau's work; Italian writer Italo Calvino, respected for *If on a Winter's Night a Traveler* (1979) – a dozen short novels rolled into several; and the extraordinary Georges Perec, most famous for his lipogrammatic novel *La Disparition* (1969) – written in French, entirely without using the letter *e*. Perec is also noted for *Life: A User's Manual* (1978), which obeys a wide selection of fiercely strict constraints.

Mention must also be made of Christian Bök, clearly a writer influenced by Oulipo members. He's the author of *Euonia* (2001), in which Chapter A has been constructed of words using consonants plus the vowel *a*, and attempting to make use of most of the words that obey this rule; Chapter E is constrained to consonants and *e*, and so forth. Additional wonders can be found in Matt Madden's *99 Ways to tell a Story*, which uses graphic novel techniques, and in the *Oulipo Compendium*, a catalogue of group-member writers and their works.

Artistic, intellectual, whimsical, resfreshing

The Oulipio group may have been motivated in ways similar to other art movements of the time – kicking against the establishment and devising ways to be less communicative, or to glory in ugliness, confusion and secularism. Values such as truth, beauty, storytelling, harmony, and honouring the God of creation were swept aside. Oulipo was contemporaneous with the avant garde, which influenced music (eg Coltraine's free jazz, Schoenberg's atonality), architecture (brutalism, Wright's 'modernism'), painting (pop art, Dadaism) and the emergence of such experiments as distressed or 'crashed' typographical design, emphasising style over legibility. So, is this approach – especially Oulipio techniques and experiments – entirely negative and destructive?

11

I think not. Indeed, this is an appealing intellectual pursuit; whatever is lost in straight-forwardness or predictability is more than made up for (in my view) in whimsy and/or skill.

And there is the added surprise that even when severe constraints apply, depth of meaning is not necessarily sacrificed. Communication may even, in some way, be enhanced – expressing a message suffering from being dully familiar in a fresh, creative way.

Where possible, I've played with metafiction's practicality: I submit for your consideration that the version entitled *Binary* is on p101, and the story focused on the value of pi can be found on p180 (in the absence of a p360, or p31412). *Mathematics* appears on p246; none of these by accident. Admittedly, none of these in any way enhances the story, merely the vehicle.

Perhaps our thorough knowledge of a text leads us to casual familiarity, making assumptions that we know what is there, and a failure to look carefully. Reading again, we may pay closer attention; it's possible we shall uncover further truths or hitherto ill-considered depths.

For clarity's sake
Sometimes I've indicated the content, sometimes described it; usually any specific constraints are spelled out. I've also come up with section titles, most of which are deliberately vague, in order to be inclusive, so an explanation may be helpful here.

• Alphabet Games
Oulipio constraints often involve strict rules about which letters can be used or in what order.

Examples include: anagrams; acrostics; vowels in strict alpha order; only the letters keyed by a typist's left hand; only words with a particular vowel occurring in the middle position are permitted.

• Alliteration
A limitation of word choice by reducing the option for the initial letter to one. Most letters yielded worthwhile results; but I had a fallback position and created a safety-net group: JQXYZ.

• Key Words
A strict set of words must be used (or avoided), yet still tell the story.

The constraints seem obscure, but then that's all just part of the fun. Examples: rainbow colours; UK Number One hits of the 70s; periodicals; Doctor Who; international footballers from the top flight of the English leagues; and of course, chocolate bars.

• Languages
Technically, (due to my monoglot feebleness), most are dialects or accents; use of vocabulary is essential. Examples: Latin, Franglais, Aussie, Germanglish, mime, upper class etc.

• Pastiche
Usually far from mockery, this discipline takes a character or literary work, re-telling the story by lampooning themes, characters, vocabulary, style, tone and perhaps even minor plot points, too.

12

So I've borrowed enthusiastically from *Lord of the Rings, The Goon Show, Canterbury Tales*, the *Authorised Version*'s story of Jacob wrestling with an angel, plus selected works of AA Milne, Harold Pinter, Jane Austen and PG Wodehouse. It'd be rather rude to exclude the bard of Avon, would it not? And I was brought up properly.

• **Plot**

I have been powerfully informed by Christopher Booker's extraordinary meister-werk *The Seven Basic Plots*: for example, *The Quest, Rags to Riches, Overcoming the Monster. Voyage & Return* is surely the very definition of the parable. In some cases, minor (or greater) tweaks to the parable's storyline are required – notably with *Comedy* (and even more with *Tragedy*). *What if?* explores diverging pathways. See also Scottish (p40).

• **Poetry**

Another Oulipio staple, following the traditionally strict rules of metre or rhyme (and often both). Here's a clerihew, a villanelle, a limerick, various iambic pentameters, and a sestina. Plus a rap. Very modern.

I've referred often to Frances Stillman's *Poets' Manual* and to *The Ode Less Travelled*, Stephen Fry's wonderful light-hearted romp through poetic forms.

• **Senses**

Various inputs: olfactory, visual, auditory, see-hear-smell-touch-taste.

• **Style**

A catch-all 'miscellaneous' category, including literary techniques, typography, tone, plus anything that doesn't fit the other headings.

Examples: a counselling session, an epic metaphor, an operatic libretto, uncommunicative commercialese, layout options such as Mohican haircut; an ergodic experiment, plus the study of the nature and scope of knowledge (epistemology).

I've been inspired by David Lodge's scholarly *The Art of Fiction*, in which he explores the rich variety of literary styles – intertextuality, unreliable narrator, magic realism, stream of consciousness etc. This section also includes Fugue (p199), provoked by *Vain Art of the Fugue* by Dumitru Tsepeneag, a contemporary Oneiric storyteller, attempting to express dreams in written form.

• **Viewpoint**

The *Rashomon* effect looms large in this category as different narrators tell different stories. Obviously, the boy's take on the events varies from his father's; the fatted calf sees it another way. The pig farmer brings another opinion.

I've also included a tangential account, focused on all the wrong elements.

• **Wordplay**

Oulipio constructions make demands way beyond letter-limits.

They require intricate, inventive and amusing word games as well. So, I have included constraints on the number of words or keystrokes that can be used; the logical infallibility of N+7; threnodials; heteronyms, homophones and eye rhymes (incuding the most monstrous of all eye-rhymes *ough*).

While I make no claim to be anything like comprehensive, I've also included a crossword puzzle and a remarkably high-scoring and serendipitous (but of course, technically possible) game of Scrabble.

Beginnings

The versions of the story in this volume grew from relatively humble but sensationally inspiring origins. First to see the light of day was *The Prodigal Confectioner* (p85), featuring £16.32's worth of sweeties – more costly these days – and was written for the *Children's Ministry Teaching Programme*. It's been performed many times.

In 1999 I was commissioned to create a pantomime for my church, and I chose the lost son as the basis for it. I included larger-than-life heroes, awful puns, drama, pathos and managed to crash together the narrative of the parable, characters from Cinderella (a wicked step-mother, talking animals and ugly sisters) and threaded several ABBA songs with altered lyrics into the score. These, with one or two fresh ideas, are included in *Lost Son ParABBAble* (p311).

I reckon I chose my moment well, as the resurgence in popularity of ABBA was at its height that year (*Mamma Mia*, the smash hit of the revival style of jukebox musicals, when the narrative is constrained by the lyrics of established songs, opened in the West End); it seems today, another twenty years on, to be continuing (the second *Mamma Mia* film has found undiminished popularity).

The pantomime was called *Step-Mama Mia!* (I concentrated upon the Cinderella aspect) and it sold out multiple performances. Great respect to the highly talented musicians lead by MD Neil Corin, who added quality to my silliness, and had the wisdom to make the most of their hard work – going on to perform as an Abba-tribute band under the name *Portaloo*.

In most of these retellings I have under-emphasised the sour grapes of the apparently faithful but angry older brother – the epitome of Pharasee-like failure to understand grace; he claims to have been diligent but his attitude is clearly not commended. His fury at his brother's return shows a lack of warmth, and his outburst at his father reveals a sense of hard-done-by selfish grasping (not unlike the younger son at the start of the story).

And his desire to have a party with goats is disconcerting, to say the least.

Translation variations

To begin as I intend to continue – honouring the Word of God – here's the original story, as told by Jesus, from Luke 15:11-24, in four of the many Bible versions.

They are all about the same length; only twenty words variance. Yet each translation is distinctive. The NIV tells the story in what might be considered a readable, straightforward manner; *The Message* provides insight into personalities and their feelings. Meanwhile, the Authorised Version expresses itself with characteristic seventeeth-century elegance and beautifully-chosen phrases; and the English Standard Version has perhaps traded quality of style for accuracy in its determination to be an authentic translation from the original text.

But whatever the differences, they each narrate the story with clarity and purpose: they all encourage us to engage with the truths Jesus is presenting; family love, repentence, restoration, forgiveness, grace... finding the heart of God for the lost, and seeing the reality of reconciliation.

I hope each of my versions similarly respect the storyteller, his themes and my continuing passion for these characters and their journeys.

• NIV *New International Version*

There was a man who had two sons. The younger one said to his father, 'Father, give me my share of the estate.' So he divided his property between them.

Not long after that, the younger son got together all he had, set off for a distant country and there squandered his wealth in wild living. After he had spent everything, there was a severe famine in that whole country, and he began to be in need. So he went and hired himself out to a citizen of that country, who sent him to his fields to feed pigs. He longed to fill his stomach with the pods that the pigs were eating, but no one gave him anything.

When he came to his senses, he said, 'How many of my father's hired men have food to spare, and here I am starving to death! I will set out and go back to my father and say to him: Father, I have sinned against heaven and against you. I am no longer worthy to be called your son; make

me like one of your hired men.' So he got up and went to his father. But while he was still a long way off, his father saw him and was filled with compassion for him; he ran to his son, threw his arms around him and kissed him.

The son said to him, 'Father, I have sinned against heaven and against you. I am no longer worthy to be called your son.'

But the father said to his servants, 'Quick! Bring the best robe and put it on him. Put a ring on his finger and sandals on his feet. Bring the fattened calf and kill it. Let's have a feast and celebrate. For this son of mine was dead and is alive again; he was lost and is found.' So they began to celebrate.

Meanwhile, the older son was in the field. When he came near the house, he heard music and dancing. So he called one of the servants and asked him what was going on.

'Your brother has come,' he replied, 'and your father has killed the

15

fattened calf because he has him back safe and sound.'

The older brother became angry and refused to go in. So his father went out and pleaded with him. But he answered his father, 'Look! All these years I've been slaving for you and never disobeyed your orders. Yet you never gave me even a young goat so I could celebrate with my friends. But when this son of yours who has squandered your property with prostitutes comes home, you kill the fattened calf for him!'

'My son,' the father said, 'you are always with me, and everything I have is yours. But we had to celebrate and be glad, because this brother of yours was dead and is alive again; he was lost and is found.'

487 words, 1973 characters

• The Message

by Eugene H Paterson

There was once a man who had two sons.

The younger said to his father, 'Father, I want right now what's coming to me.'

So the father divided the property between them. It wasn't long before the younger son packed his bags and left for a distant country. There, undisciplined and dissipated, he wasted everything he had. After he had gone through all his money, there was a bad famine all through that country and he began to hurt. He signed on with a citizen there who assigned him to his fields to slop the pigs. He was so hungry he would have eaten the corncobs in the pig slop, but no one would give him any.

That brought him to his senses. He said, 'All those farmhands working for my father sit down to three meals a day, and here I am starving to death. I'm going back to my father. I'll say to him, Father, I've sinned against God, I've sinned before you; I don't deserve to be called your son. Take me on as a hired hand.' He got right up and went home to his father.

When he was still a long way off, his father saw him. His heart pounding, he ran out, embraced him, and kissed him. The son started his speech: 'Father, I've sinned against God, I've sinned before you; I don't deserve to be called your son ever again.'

But the father wasn't listening. He was calling to the servants, 'Quick. Bring a clean set of clothes and dress him. Put the family ring on his finger and sandals on his feet. Then get a grain-fed heifer and roast it. We're going to feast! We're going to have a wonderful time! My son is here—given up for dead and now alive! Given up for lost and now found!' And they began to have a wonderful time.

All this time his older son was out in the field. When the day's work was done he came in. As he approached the house, he heard the music and dancing. Calling over one of the houseboys, he asked what was going on. He told him, 'Your brother came home. Your father has ordered a feast—barbecued beef!—because he has him home safe and sound.'

The older brother stalked off in an angry sulk and refused to join in. His father came out and tried to talk to him, but he wouldn't listen.

The son said, 'Look how many years I've stayed here serving you, never giving you one moment of grief, but have you ever thrown a party for me and my friends? Then this son of yours who has thrown away your money on whores shows up and you go all out with a feast!'

His father said, 'Son, you don't understand. You're with me all the time, and everything that is mine is yours—but this is a wonderful time, and we had to celebrate. This brother of yours was dead, and he's alive! He was lost, and he's found!'

507 words, 2115 characters

• Authorised Version
(King James)

11 A certain man had two sons:

12 And the younger son said to his father, Father, give me the portion that falleth to me. And he divided unto them his living.

13 And not many days after the younger son gathered all together, and took his journey into a far country, and there wasted his substance with riotous living.

14 And when he had spent all, there arose a mighty famine in that land; and he began to be in want.

15 And he went and joined himself to a citizen of that country; and he sent him into his fields to feed swine.

16 And he would fain have filled his belly with the husks that the swine did eat: and no man gave unto him.

17 And when he came to himself, he said, How many hired servants of my father's have bread enough to spare, and I perish with hunger!

18 I will arise and go to my father, and will say unto him, Father, I have sinned against heaven, and before thee,

19 And am no more worthy to be called thy son: make me as one of thy hired servants.

20 And he arose, and came to his father. But when he was yet a great way off, his father saw him, and had compassion, and ran, and fell on his neck, and kissed him.

21 And the son said unto him, Father, I have sinned against heaven, and in thy sight, and am no more worthy to be called thy son.

22 But the father said to his servants, Bring forth the best robe, nd put it on him; and put a ring on his hand, and shoes on his feet:

23 And bring hither the fatted calf, and kill it; and let us eat, and be merry,

24 For this my son was dead, and is alive again; he was lost, and is found. And they began to be merry.

¶ 25 Now his elder son was in the field: and as he came and drew nigh to the house, he heard musick and dancing.

26 And he called one of the servants, and asked what these things meant.

27 And he said unto him, Thy brother is come; and thy father hath killed the fatted calf, for he hath received him safe and sound.

28 And he was angry, and would not go in: therefore came his father out, and intreated him.

29 And he answering said to his father, Lo, these many years do I serve thee, neither transgressed I at any time thy commandment: and yet thou never gavest me a kid, that I might make merry with my friends:

30 But as soon as this thy son was come, which hath devoured thy living with harlots, thou hast killed for him the fatted calf.

31 And he said unto him, Son, thou art ever with me, and all that I have is thine.

32 It was meet that we make merry, and be glad: for this thy brother was dead, and is alive again; and was lost, and is found.

504 words, 1995 characters

• **ESV** *English Standard Version*

There was a man who had two sons. And the younger of them said to his father, 'Father, give me the share of property that is coming to me.' And he divided his property between them. Not many days later, the younger son gathered all he had and took a journey into a far country, and there he squandered his property in reckless living. And when he had spent everything, a severe famine arose in that country, and he began to be in need.

So he went and hired himself out to one of the citizens of that country, who sent him into his fields to feed pigs. And he was longing to be fed with the pods that the pigs ate, and no one gave him anything. But when he came to himself, he said, 'How many of my father's hired servants have more than enough bread, but I perish here with hunger! I will arise and go to my father, and I will say to him, "Father, I have sinned against heaven and before you. I am no longer worthy to be called your son. Treat me as one of your hired servants."'

And he arose and came to his father. But while he was still a long way off, his father saw him and felt compassion, and ran and embraced him and kissed him. And the son said to him, 'Father, I have sinned against heaven and before you. I am no longer worthy to be called your son.' But the father said to his servants, 'Bring quickly the best robe, and put it on him, and put a ring on his hand, and shoes on his feet. And bring the fattened calf and kill it, and let us eat and celebrate. For this my son was dead, and is alive again; he was lost, and is found.' And they began to celebrate.

Now his older son was in the field, and as he came and drew near to the house, he heard music and dancing. And he called one of the servants and asked what these things meant. And he said to him, 'Your brother has come, and your father has killed the fattened calf, because he has received him back safe and sound.'

But he was angry and refused to go in. His father came out and entreated him, but he answered his father, 'Look, these many years I have served you, and I never disobeyed your command, yet you never gave me a young goat, that I might celebrate with my friends. But when this son of yours came, who has devoured your property with prostitutes, you killed the fattened calf for him!' And he said to him, 'Son, you are always with me, and all that is mine is yours. It was fitting to celebrate and be glad, for this your brother was dead, and is alive; he was lost, and is found.

490 words, 1976 characters

I am very keen to underline that the translations and paraphrases above are to be recognised as scripture – indeed, the inspired Word of God – which is why I have included them for reference.

However, my variations are most certainly not to be viewed in that light at all. They may tell the same story, and may perhaps provide some insight, but they are far from inspired (in the specifically Biblical sense) and readers should always turn to Luke's Gospel for the words of Jesus on this subject.

Greener grass? *plot*

*this parable is a defining example
of Voyage & Return*

The son demanded his inheritance and left home. He spent the money in wild living. When famine struck, he took a job tending pigs and longed to eat their pods. He came to his senses, deciding to go home and ask to be a hired man, since he knew he was no longer worthy to be called a son.

While he was still a long way off, his father saw him, ran to him, gave him a ring, a coat and shoes. He killed the fatted calf and celebrated.

'This my son was lost and is found; he was dead and is alive again!'

A *alliteration*

Another asked 'All amounts apportioned appropriately, although actual agonies ahead.' Agreed and away. Amorous associations!

All accounted-for, appalling anguish approached. Attempts at appropriating any animal ambrosia abandoned, authoritative affection aide-memoire.

Arises, ambles.

Ancestral-abode-appeal added. As approaching, aged Abba arrives, assigns an anorak, accommodation and adornments – additionals. Angus, antipasto, artichoke, angel-cake, asparagus, avocado, apricots, applejuice, ale, advocaat, also..

'Asleep? Alive! Allelujah!' Alf aggrieved; anger assuaged.

B *alliteration*

'Bunse, buckshee!' boy briefly begged beaurocrat. Big bucks, brothels, babes, booze... busted – borasic!

Bad belly; bacon-makers' breakfast biodegrading. Bingo! Boy began buckling, brightened, brought back.

Bonding! Blazer, brothel-creepers, bangle; Buttercup becomes brazed brisket beef Bar-B-Q banquet! Bagels, baguettes, bloomers, baps, brown bread, barmcakes, brioche, boiled baby beetroots, Bisto, bhuna, black/borlotti/baked beans, brill, buttered bloaters, bream, broken Bourbon biscuits, bitter beer.

Beligerant bellowing: 'Boy blanked, boxed; but breathing – blimmin' brilliant!'

Rap *poetry*

some lines require rapid-fire delivery; others are more laconic

Listen up in da house, gotta message for you
And a radical way of expressin' my view
Jesus told this parable to help us to see
That da Father's love is vast and eternal and free.
Your boy took the cash from the farmer's hand
And went right away to a far-off land.
This father's boy was a Prodigal child;
That means he wasted the money with living that was wild.
His friends all left; he was alone and felt gauche; a
Few days later, got a job that wasn't kosher —
Looking after pigs, jealous of their pods,

19

He had a revelation that was one of God's.
'I shall go back home and serve my dad;
I have to admit that I've been really bad.'
On his way home he knew he'd been a mug;
But his Pa rushed out and gave him a hug
And a ring and a coat and some lovely shoes,
And he also killed the animal that moos!
'I thought he was dead, and I was mourning him
But it turns out he's alive and now I've no need to feel grim!
You know, repenting is good and a recommended move
By a loving God. At this party you'll groove.'
'Waster comes right back, and with kisses you smother?'
Asks the legalistic, harsh and resentful older brother.
'He's my son and I love him, and by inheritance laws
When my days are done, then all I have is yours.'
That's the end of my story now; it's time to say I'm gone;
Respect to the Father of that Prodigal Son.

Monosyllables only   _wordplay_

Son two scrounged cash from his dad. 'Give me my share of what I ought to get when you die.'

Dad gave some loot to this boy, who left home and broughammed* to a land miles hence. He spent the cash in wild ways, with drink and girls (some of whom were less than schooled), and much sin, too.

When the cash was all gone, lack of food struck in the land far away. The boy sat down and fed waste to pigs which scratched and scraunched in the dirt; he longed to put their plagued pods in his own mouth. He had a thought that shed some light on where he had gone wrong. 'Dad's men (he hires them on a day-by-day deal) eat well, yet here I am with no food; I shall go straight back and ask him to let me serve in the farm; I should not be thought of as his son.'

He squelched home but while he was still a long way off, dad clocked him on the road, screeched (full of glee) and ran to greet him, with splayed arms. He hugged him (each arm had great strengths), shrugged and called for freights – gave him a pair of shoes, put a fine coat on him and a gold ring; they sang and danced. He had the calf killed, put on a spit, cooked, sliced and served; they schnappsed and munched; yes, and schmaltzed to good tunes with the folk from near the farm.

'This my son was dead and I was vexed; now he is here and we can all see lives!' he said with great joy.

The boy born first moaned and showed his heart was bad; he saw the grace of his Dad as a fail.

But his Pa told him 'All I have is yours; yet we had to sing and dance, now my lost son has come back.'

* Brougham (pronounced _broom_ or _brohm_) refers to an C18th horse-drawn carriage. If _Travel by cart_ can be enverbed (is that a word?) _carted_, then, with max-length monosyllables in mind, I've coined _broughammed_. Also used for Cadillac's Eldorado Brougham (1957-60) and Fleetwood Brougham (1965-86)

Polysyllables only   *wordplay*

Second offspring demanded any deserved inheritance. Father agreed; prodigal departed, later making towards foreign country.

Recklessly, inheritance became whittled away until banknotes began bulging every other persons' wallet.

Famine ravished foreign country; offspring starving until employed feeding ague-ridden pigswill into porkers.

Envy overtook conscience; senses received divine revelation.

'Even pater's labourers satisfy themselves nutritionally every weekday!'

Recognised personal floccinaucini-hilipilification.

Travelled homeward, anticipating difficult complicated encounter.

Father, taking every opportunity, expected return.

Seeing prodigal, Father sprinted along towards offspring. Greetings followed, gifting jacket, jewellery, sandals; also party! Fatted cattle rotisseried.

Father declared 'Progeny behaved profligatorily; whereabouts became uncertain; vitality even questioned. However, presence among current company demonstrates healthiness! Merry-making until morning!'

Cantankerous, legalistic older brother complained; father remonstrated.

'Entire farming estate eventually given successorwards – nevertheless, jollifications appropriate, surely? Assumed departed offspring returns, animated!'

Haiku quad   *poetry*
five, seven and five syllables respectively, but four times over

Son spent all Dad's cash:
Famine; pigswill; repented!
Father welcomes him.

To Dissipation;
Temptation, revelation;
And restoration.

Inheritance gone,
Pig feed looks tempting, but no,
Arise; celebrate!

Wild living costs all;
At lowest ebb, arises –
Returns home again.

Clerihew   *poetry*
two unevenly-metred couplets, traditionally biographical

Having wasted all the cash on girls – not coy but comely –
That prodigal son of Squire Cholmondley
Understood, when in a sty
That he certainly was, unconditionally,
    the most precious (and dearly loved)
    absolute apple of his doting father's eye.

Parts of speech *wordplay*

Nouns man; sons; share of the estate; his property; all he had; distant country; wealth; everything; famine; whole country; citizen of that country; fields; pigs; stomach; pods; no one; men; food; father; son; compassion; robe; ring; finger; sandals; feet; calf; feast; brother

Adjectives two; one; younger; wild; severe; long; hired; best; fattened; this; angry, dead; alive; lost; found

Pronouns his; me; he; them; your; they

Verbs said to; divided; got together; set off; squandered; living; spent; to be in need; went; hired himself out; sent; feed; longed; fill; eating; gave; came to his senses; said; to spare; I am starving; I will set out; go back; say; I have sinned; I am no longer worthy; to be called; make me; got up; went; he was; saw; filled; ran; threw; kissed; Bring; put; Bring; kill; Let's have; celebrate; began; complained

Adverbs There was; had; between; Not long after; After; began; to death; like; while; with; for; of

Prepositions against heaven; against you

Conjunctions so; with; and; But

Interjections Father; Quick!

Articles a; the

Nested stories
(mise en abyeme) *style*
in which narrative threads intertwine and perhaps meet at the denoument
WELL-RESPECTED AND wealthy farmer Jack Glamis sat and looked at his account-book. He realized there was a vast surplus and that his profitability was growing. He'd made good decisions about crops and other investments on Glamis Farm, and it looked like he was going to be well-off for the rest of his days.

So he gave thanks to God and decided to make a charitable donation to the *Fund for the Assistance of the Suddenly Homeless In Our Neighbourhood*. This organization provided support for homeless people in far-away Dissipation City, where the need was great.

His donation could provide beds, facilities and workers in a hostel for the down and out. He made his contribution, knowing it would make a significant difference.

However, the day after he'd spent all his liquid assets, his younger son Thomas made some demands. 'Look, Father, the time has come for me to get out of this dead-end place. I can see there's no future for me here, so what I want to do is to fast-forward to the time when you die, and take my inheritance now.'

'Are you wishing me dead, son?'

'Not exactly. But I'm wishing I didn't have to wait and work and wait and work and wait some more until I get the chance to make something of myself...'

'You don't think staying here and working on my farm could possibly be the course your life is supposed to take?'

'No, I really don't! I intend to have a good time and then see what I can do with some serious capital.'

'Well, you have no right to demand this of me. However, I'll agree anyway, and let you have the cash as soon as I can raise it.' He looked again at his accounts and sighed. There was no way he could afford to give Thomas the money he asked for; he had no cashflow left. So he had to persuade a few local farms to buy some of his fields, complete with the crops that had already been planted and nurtured, and raise the money that way. It was shortsighted business practice, but it was necessary.

It was unlikely to be a success long-term; but then disaster struck.

THE VILLAGE ELDERS were naturally gloomy and deeply concerned as they convened a meeting to discuss the ever-worsening situation down at Glamis Farm.

'You know, he's sold off almost half of his land, and much of it with fine crops already growing in the fields… He's almost certainly going to suffer at the end of the season when he adds up the income from what he has left. Now he not only has a whole lot less, but he'll get a poorer price for his grain and his hay, since he can no longer supply in the kinds of quantities he's been able to provide up to now… I can't understand why he did it. Really I can't. He must need the capital for something, but it doesn't seems to have the ring of entrepreneurial skill about it that Glamis has exhibited thus far.'

'Is there anything we can do to help his cashflow?'

'There is plenty we can do, but whether he'll see the point is another question…'

'The harm it'll do to local industry if he goes under will be enormous. He employs a lot of hired hands, you know, and if he can't afford grain for planting, there'll be no planting, no tending, no harvest, and no grain next year. It's a downward spiral…'

'I think we should dip into the community chest and provide him with some help.'

'Why should we? It's his own fault…'

'Yes it is, but we should help him. Otherwise this whole village will suffer from the disaster he's bringing upon himself and us.'

So the elders arranged for a gift of thirty head of dairy cattle to be given to Glamis Farm, along with the building of a Milking Parlour. 'You'll have to hire some men for the daily duties,' Glamis was told, 'and learn how to keep livestock – we realize you've only had an arable farm to this point, but with the income from the milk sales coming in on a regular basis, it should help to keep the cashflow a little more buoyant.'

'I am truly grateful to the Chamber of Commerce for this generous grant,' said Farmer Jack Glamis. 'I know next to nothing about keeping dairy cattle – we've had a couple of goats in the past, but I've never been a livestock sort of chap. This will change things but should help me keep my head above water, and provide a much-needed additional supply of milk, butter, cheese and yoghurt for the local community.'

The elders were pleased with themselves; but then disaster struck.

THE CHARITABLE WORK was growing, thanks to grants and legacies, and was able not only to open a number of hostels for the homeless, but also established enterprises to provide opportunities for their residents to find work in a protected environment. The goal was to provide a sort of half-way-house for getting homeless people back into the community.

One of the beneficiaries of the wealth that flowed through the accounts of FASHION was Charles

Cooterie. He had spent a while living in their accommodation, but qualified for a bursary when he proved himself trustworthy and reliable. He wished to contribute to the community that had helped him in his hour of need.

Cooterie recognized that city folk were disposing of their food scraps and waste in the streets outside their houses, leaving it to rot and causing pollution – an open invitation for vermin and disease, a stink, and an unsightly mess as well. He took the capital and arranged for hired men to take a fleet of barrows from house to house to collect waste. They brought it to his farm, where he buried some of the waste, and fed the scraps to a few pigs. His long-term intention was to increase his livestock holding until he could farm the animals and send them to market, to provide further food and help provide for his family.

The pigs grew healthily at first, feasting on slops and throwaway food scraps; but then disaster struck.

EXPERIMENTING FARMER GLAMIS was thrilled at first when his dairy cattle started to produce quality milk. He arranged a distribution network of daily deliveries, as well as discovering the techniques for making cheese and yoghurt. Even his early attempts at a soft blue cheese were a success, and his range of fruit yoghurts was also welcomed in the local shops, and eagerly sought out by customers.

Unfortunately, his experience as an arable farmer did not transfer easily to the daily duties of dairy production. Additionally, a number of his farm hands were laid off as he no longer had the large bonus to his annual income when the time came

for reckoning up his grain and hay sales from his vastly reduced fields. This combination left him short-handed in the milking parlour, and without cashflow to hire anyone else.

So he tried to sell a few cows, to reduce the workload. This proved rather complicated, as Farmer Glamis wasn't offering enough cattle to start up a business, and none of the existing dairy farms in the district were looking to expand at this time of economic uncertainty. So what could he do?

He decided to try butchery, and took two of his dairy cows to the abattoir. But the cows had been reared with maximized milk production in mind, but not to build muscle or fat. Their meat was tough and unpleasant.

Yet it was food, and Farmer Glamis had to make the most of it. He would create mince, mix it with breadcrumbs and cheap herbs and make sausages and pies. All this extra work took manpower, and his meat sales were insufficient to offset the extra costs.

So he lived on his own expensive produce. He was on a spiral to oblivion.

He knew this wasn't working well, and felt a little guilty that he was making a fist of the opportunity the Chamber of Commerce had so generously provided.

He took three of his best cows to be serviced by a bull, and was pleased when two of them produced calves. These he treated with the appropriate feed to ensure they were good for slaughter, and would provide excellent eating. Perhaps he was turning things around. His cashflow continued to be a problem, but at least there was light at the end of the tunnel.

One thing was preoccupying him, however. How was his son Thomas? Was he lost? Was he alive? Could he have survived? Had he made a name for himself in the big city? Was he happy? Was he satisfied? Was he content, at last?

Each day, Jack spent time up on the roof of his house, looking to see if his son Thomas was returning.

He hadn't come back yesterday, but it's possible he would return today, and Jack wanted to be there to welcome him.

But then disaster struck everyone.

HIS YOUNGER SON, Thomas, had packed up his belongings, and set off for – as it happened – Dissipation City, where the bars, cafés, restaurants, casinos, theatres and nightclubs beckoned with dazzling sparkle and a lure that Thomas could not resist.

He met a number of young men and women who were more than willing to help him have a good time and eat, drink and be very merry as often as possible. He'd take his new-found friends out for meals and lots of cocktails and to a show and then on to a club or out for a wild night of debauchery or a trip to the casino.

His friends didn't contribute to the expense; they just incurred it, with enthusiastic abandon.

Pretty soon, his money ran out and he was penniless and without anywhere to stay, as he could no longer afford to live in an hotel and there were not many guest houses.

He wandered the streets for several days until a wino showed him that he could probably get a bed in one of the hostels for the homeless. He wandered to the address and liked the look of the place, which had the name FASHION on the door. He made enquiries and, having qualified for help, lay down on one of the beds and got a decent nights' sleep. He had not realized that disaster had struck everyone.

FOOD WAS IN short supply. The crops had failed; the weather had been disastrous and even the best-organised farms couldn't produce grain from nowhere.

The people began to starve and famine gripped the land.

THE QUALITY AND quantity of the food scraps that people were throwing out was, as Charles Cooterie discovered, much reduced; there were a few very low-quality pods and husks, plus a lot of waste that was inedible – even for pigs. His animals began to suffer, and he had to lay off many of his hired men, which put extra pressure on the remainder, and there was not sufficient income to support them. It was a nightmare.

MEANWHILE YOUNG THOMAS Glamis was feeling sorry for himself, partly because he was still staying in the FASHION House. He spoke to the supervisor in charge of rehabilitation, discussing the prospects.

'I think you are ready to go and seek some work.'

'Okay...'

'The charity is prepared to smooth the way, as we are still receiving adequate gifts and legacies. So what we will do is encourage you to present yourself to a local entrepreneur and ask him to employ you; in the meanwhile, we'll make a bursary available to him, to make it easier for him – you know, providing cash so that he can afford to employ you. Do you see? He gets a financial incentive to employ you; you get the dignity of work and everyone benefits from the charity. Good, eh?'

'Sounds like a plan. To whom shall I apply?'

'Well, we have made arrangements with a local firm; Charles Cooterie needs some more workers and is providing a good service to the community, so that's a win-win situation.'

'I'm on my way.'

SO, A LITTLE later, Thomas Glamis was sitting by a trough where a few skinny, diseased pigs were shuffling and rooting about among the pathetic-looking pods and waste for any bits that were suitable for food.

Thomas was very hungry, too, as when he had taken his meagre wages to the shop, there was no food to buy – no sausages, no dairy products, no bread or any other goods.

He was contemplating his circumstances.

ON THE OTHER hand, Jack Glamis seemed to have turned the corner.

His fields were flourishing with crops; his dairy efforts had been stood down and the cattle sold off; his calves, by contrast, were looking very healthy and his prospects were good; at least in the short-term.

He reckoned that he could probably survive the year, since he had reduced his costs from having abandoned all his milking, cheese and yogurt production efforts, which were labour-intensive.

And he thought he'd do well from his admittedly reduced grain harvest, as the famine was forcing a little gentle inflation, and he'd get a better price for his grain this year.

Meanwhile, there was a supply of (not very good) sausages and meat pies to eat, along with some half-decent cheese and yoghurt. He'd adopted a new system for his crops; he'd decided to leave the blanket of nutrients and vegetable matter on the surface of the soil; he'd abandoned the constant tilling which caused the topsoil to blow away (especially when irrigation was an issue).

Besides, leaving everything alone was less effort, and seemed to be maximizing the effectiveness of the land. His farm was becoming a credible business, he reckoned, and this spurred him on to work hard, and to suffer the indignities of his dreadful meat pies.

He still missed his son, and spent time every day looking out for him.

REVELATION DAWNED UPON the mind of Thomas Glamis. He found himself envying the diseased pigs; he longed to eat their food – that's how hungry he was!

'I bet that the men who work for my old dad at Glamis Farm are eating okay. They probably get lovely meals provided for them; yes, they have to work hard but they are treated with dignity and respect... What if I were to go back there? I could humble myself, and say to my father that I understand that I have sinned against him and against heaven and no longer deserve to be called his son.

'My wickedness has been that serious, actually, and I could ask him to make me one of his hired men, and

.

that way I'd get to be back near him, see if he will forgive me, and maybe get a square meal, lest I die of starvation.'

So he got up and started on his long journey home. It was many miles, and while he walked, he considered how to express himself to his father.

'Will Dad even be willing to talk?

'He has every right to dismiss me – I'd effectively wished him dead, after all. He might even call upon his hired men to beat me up and send me packing... I wonder how he'll feel about my return?

'Maybe he's come to terms with me no longer being his son, and he won't want to open up those wounds. But I have to try to seek his forgiveness. I don't want to die owing him such a great debt – both financially and emotionally... How could I have wished him dead? How could I have wasted his fortune? How can I ever pay him back? Will he even listen to my pleas?'

IT WAS A cold, bright morning, and the sausages for Farmer Jack's breakfast were grim, as ever. He made sure the hired men were busy and being effective – feeding the calves, tending the fields, sorting out the accounts (not a lot of income, but still the books need to balance). Feeling tired and lonely, he made his way onto the roof to maintain his vigil for Thomas. Could today be the day?

He'd spent a lot of time up here over the last eighteen months, and had never seen anyone that even slightly resembled his son.

Men looking for work, charity fundraisers looking for donations, pig farmers looking to sell bacon (not many takers around here) and

refugees from the famine in the neighboring country...

But none of them was Thomas.

Could today be any different?

No, it wasn't.

IT WAS A cold bright morning, and Jack didn't much fancy his breakfast, but he ate it anyway; today might be the day, and he needed his strength. But none of the people who walked up the road was Thomas.

IT WAS A cold, bright morning and the appalling breakfast sausages were beginning to get on his nerves. It was still a few weeks before the grain harvesting could start, and even then, there would be a delay before the grain could be processed and made into flour and then into bread and then into a decent breakfast. It had been a long time since he'd had quality rolls or toast or crumpets or a crusty bloomer...

He slowly climbed the stairs to the roof to maintain his vigil.

Could today be the day Thomas comes home?

KNOWING HE WAS getting close caused Thomas Glamis to become nervous. Had he made the right decision? Would he be welcome? Would he be tolerated? Would he be chased away? Would he be struck out of anger? Any of these were possibilities.

He was several miles from Glamis Farm, but once he reached the brow of this hill, he'd be able to see the outlying fields, with the familiar corn waving in the breeze.

UP ON THE roof, Jack blinked. What was this? Another charity worker? No, he was too thin and didn't seem to be in much of a rush. A salesman? No; he'd got no product with him. This character, still a long way off, seemed to be walking very slowly, like a man without shoes on a stony road... And he seemed to have no coat, either. His hair was unfashionably long, with a straggly beard as well... but... could it be? Jack stood up and looked very carefully.

The figure had just come over the distant hill, way beyond the present extent of his farm, since he'd sold off those outlying fields.

Jack couldn't contain his rising excitement that it might just possibly... He ran down the stairs, and, tucking his tunic into his belt, began to run, undignified, to see this approaching character. It might be Thomas! It might be... Or someone with news of him, at least.

He ran at full pelt, shouting 'Thomas! Is it you? My son!'

IT SURPRISED THOMAS that the outlying fields of Glamis farm were in such contrast to the ones nearer the farmhouse.

The former were sad-looking, over-tilled and unproductive; the fields near the farmhouse were waving their corny greeting with generosity and fruitfulness.

But what was this? Some madman was coming up the road, shouting and waving.

Perhaps his father had sent a hired hand to scare him off.

Perhaps he was just the first of a group of men sent to force him to leave...

What was he shouting?

'Go away! You're not welcome here!' No... it was hard to make it out, but it was more like 'Commerce... In

situ... bison...' No, that doesn't make any sense at all.

As the apparently mad fellow drew closer, his voice became more distinct, even though he was out of puff. 'Thomas... is it you? My son!'

OH, HE WAS sure now. It really was his long-lost son!

He renewed his gallop, and eventually covered the distance. He ran to his boy – well, a hairy, skinny, smelly version of his boy – and threw his arms around him.

He kissed and greeted him with great warmth.

Thomas tried to say his speech. 'Father, I have sinned against heaven and against...' but Jack wasn't listening.

'How did you get on? How did you survive? Why are you so thin? Have you not been eating? What happened to your shoes? And can you believe how happy I am to see you? Oh, how we've missed you! I love you, son!' Jack and Thomas walked arm in arm to Glamis Farm, and servants came running to see what all this fuss was about.

'Quick, fetch some shoes for the boy,' ordered Jack, 'and get my signet ring from the dresser by my bed. And a coat as well.'

When the servants arrived with the ring, shoes and coat, Jack put them onto his son. Tears streamed down his face, and Thomas was emotional as well.

The next day, Jack decided to have a grand celebration and invited everyone in the village to attend.

'What shall we eat, sir?' asked one of the servants. 'We can't fob them off with meat pies or those awful sausages, can we? After all, you

28

complain about them every morning, don't you, sir?'

'No, no, you're right!' laughed Jack. 'Kill one of the fatted calves and we'll have a right slap-up barbecue!'

And that's what they did.

One of the invitations went to the village elder who was Chairman of the Chamber of Commerce, and another to the founder and president of FASHION.

Epic metaphore   *style*
illustrating the entire story by means of just one symbol

The Inspector oiled the wheels and the bus began to move away.

Lumbering at first, it started off towards Dissipation Terminus, gathering pace as fellow-travellers hopped on board and took their seats, some downstairs, some on the top deck, all asking for fourpenny ones. Some were even riding on the rear platform, an activity that contravened several bylaws, as well as health and safety directives.

The conductor (it was well before the days of one-man operation) rang the bell three times and cried 'Any more fares, now, thank you!' as they monopolized bus lanes, raced past shelters and avoided low bridges. Someone started whistling *We're all going on a Summer Holiday!*, but he was quickly discouraged.

After a while, there were not any more fayres to attend. It seemed there had been a leak of brake fluid, as the vehicle hurtled out of control. But the dead weight of those who were just there for the ride expended its momentum.

So, having run at great velocity, it ground to a halt, out of fuel, finished, spent, conked out, stationary. The conductor had to lean a seat-cushion (stood on its end) up against the back of the bus to indicate its status.

All the filling stations designated for buses were exhausted, so he couldn't could move, and his passengers resorted to shank's pony.

Beyond that, the bus driver sat with animals, perhaps waiting for them to die, be buried, become compressed and turn eventually into oil, which could be processed into diesel fuel for the bus. That might have been a long wait.

No, his thoughts turned to the familiar garage from whence he came; the occasional clang of wrenches dropped into the inspection pit; that intense light from the oxy-acetylene welding equipment; the cheery banter of the mechanics; those dog-eared girlie calendars; that distinctive aroma and unctuous viscosity of the *Swarfega*.

As he gazed into the rear-view mirror of memory, an idea occurred to him. 'I will arise and go to the Inspector and ask if I can work as part of his team.' He decided to use his reserve fuel. He was faced with a long journey, yet enthusiastically wound the destination display blind until it read NOT IN SERVICE: RETURNING TO DEPOT. He revved, put himself into gear and made hand signals through the little window allocated for the purpose, indicating he was about to pull out suddenly, directly in front of other road users and swerve aggressively, without adequate warning, into the flow of traffic.

While he was more than a fare stage away, Blakey* ran to give him a tarpaulin, new tyres, a washer and a once-over with the chamois.

29

'Standing room only; move right down inside the car, please!' the conductor cried as the celebrations began.

'The driver had mislaid his *RAC Atlas of the Road*, but now he had a sat nav; he'd pulled over at a service station, but now had finished his hot, sweet tea and all-day breakfast and is full right up inside, ready for another extended spell at the wheel.

'Just to ride inside that thirty foot long by ten foot wide – inside that monarch of the road, observer of the Highway Code, that big six-wheeler scarlet-painted London transport diesel-engined ninety-seven-horse-power (ninety-seven-horse-power) omnibus[†]. Hold very tight, please!'

Ding ding.

* the Inspector, antagonist, from London Weekend's tv series *On the Buses*
† *A Transport of Delight* by Michael Flanders & Donald Swann (1959). The song scans only thanks to errors of fact: the RM & RMC models were exactly 8ft *2.44m* wide and 27ft 6in *8.4m* long; although the RML was 2ft 6in *0.76m* longer at 30ft *9.14m*. The engine (AEC AV590 9.6L) produced an impressive 115 bhp

Retrograde   *wordplay*
starting at the end, working backwards
see also Reverse *(p226)*
'Your brother has returned, so we have to make a fuss. But all I have is yours.' The firstborn complained about the unfairness.

'Hallelujah! It is clear that this boy is alive, yet he was considered dead! Now he's found, despite being, understandably, reckoned to be lost!'

The party continued, as the father celebrated the son's return. The boy showed off his new coat, ring and sandals, remembering with great pleasure the moment when his father

had bestowed them upon him, along with many meaningful expressions of affection.

He'd still been a long way off, starting to say 'No longer worthy to be called your son, but make me one of your hired hands.' He'd planned this while on his journey from the pig sty, where he said to himself 'I will go to my father, once I have arisen.'

This decision followed the realization that even his father's hired men were being fed every day, while here he was imagining that the pig food looked good, on account of his great hunger, which in turn was due to the great famine. His pockets were empty, and his friends were gone, despite his former lavish exuberance in spending and wild living, which had started some time earlier, almost as soon as he got to Dissipation City.

The moment of arrival was the natural consequence of a journey away from the home farm, loaded down with bags stashed with large wedges of cash garnered from his father as part of a positive response to a simple request: 'Please give me my share of the inheritance.'

He was the younger son.

So glad to see
him again   *viewpoint*
father
My younger boy came to me and asked for his share of the inheritance. Oh, I was most reluctant to let him go, but I gave him his share.

Off he went anyway. I hoped he would come to his senses and return, and every day I went to the roof whenever I could, to watch and wait and hope. Then we heard that famine was spreading, especially in the places where we feared he had gone. I still went to the roof each day, but I must admit I had almost convinced myself that he was dead; either he'd been killed for the money he was carrying in a famine-struck land, or he'd starved along with so many others.

I still went to the roof, and one day I thought I saw him on the road. I became very excitied, and started to run to him, but then I realsied it wasn't my boy but someone who looked slightly similar when viewed through rose-coloured spectacles and from a very long distance. I was disappointed, downcast, distraught.

Several weeks later, I saw another traveller who looked like he might be my son. I thought this time I'd be slightly more cautious, but as I looked, I was certain it was him and delighted in my heart. It was my son!

I ran to him and showered him with acceptance.

He was trying to say something about 'not worthy' or something, but this was my son, whom I had almost given up for dead. I cannot imagine what could have inspired him to return; but I was deeply glad he had decided upon that course.

I called the servants to bring a coat, shoes and a ring to signify that he was part of the family once again. I ordered that we should have a big slap-up feed, and so it was hot roast beef all round, with yorkshire puddings and flagons of wine.

Even Reginald's moaning didn't dampen my good spirits.The noise from the party was colossal!

Pathword   *style*

solution on p325

Starting from the central (larger, shaded) letter, progress one letter at a time (up, down, left or right – but never diagonally) to find 21 lost-son-related keywords.

F	F	D	R	A	T	N	F	O	R	T
F	A	E	E	L	I	O	A	W	Y	H
O	T	T	V	E	N	I	M	N	A	R
D	L	I	W	F	E	E	R	U	S	I
D	M	E	N	A	T	H	N	U	E	W
E	H	G	N	E	**S**	I	N	R	Y	A
R	I	V	I	N	S	N	G	C	A	L
T	L	I	I	S	E	T	F	I	G	F
N	E	P	N	H	E	D	I	I	O	N
G	S	S	N	A	R	S	S	T	O	L
I	P	E	C	T	I	I	P	A	S	T

31

Vealbeast   *plot*

Overcoming the Monster

In his dark, musty, cramped stall, a thin bull calf lay on his bed of straw, chewing slowly. In another time and place, he might have become Wiener schnitzel, but his plan was rather more dramatic.

Without warning but, thanks to clockwork, the trapdoor that released grain into his feeding tough clanged open and shut, and he stood to munch on the generous portion of vitamin-enriched corn.

THE BOY AND his father were having another blazing row.

'What you ask is foolish, my son,' said the old man. 'I cannot survive if I give you your inheritance now.'

The boy vented his frustration and anger. 'I feel trapped! I will die if I have to stay here, and I will certainly die if I go off to seek fame and friendship elsewhere without some capital behind me. So I insist you give me what is due.'

Eventually, the old man was persuaded. Reluctantly, he gave the boy a large amount of money and he took his rage, recklessness and irresponsibility elsewhere.

THE CALF WAS growing, and the stall was already too small for him. His grain portion stayed the same, but the shutter clanged open more often. His horns were developing. His plan was to vent his irritation with the farmer for providing such a small stall; meanwhile, he'd eat what he was given and try to grow strong.

THE BOY SPENT all the money on women and gambling and fine dining and wild living. Yet soon, indeed,

surprisingly soon, he was without funds and friends.

And then the bull market collapsed, and famine struck the land.

He found a job tending pigs, and longed to eat the pigs' meagre food. So, that was when he came to his senses.

The revelation shone a light into his dark heart. *Even my father's hired hands have plenty to eat*, he thought. *I shall arise and go home and ask to work as a hired hand. I'm no longer worthy to be called a son.* So he got up and went home.

MEANWHILE, THE CALF grew wider, taller, stronger; also growing was the resentment at being trapped in the dark, inadequate stall. The calf mused in the gloom, in readiness for the day some fool stepped up to open the door.

BUT WHILE THE boy was still a long way off, his father spotted him approaching. 'My boy!' he shouted and ran to greet him with a kiss. He called for a ring, a coat and some shoes for his son, and issued a Bull to one of the hired men to slaughter the fatted calf.

'My lord? The fatted calf? Surely not…'

The hired man was fearful of the beast and reluctant to obey. The father asked all his men and received the same reply. None was ready to enter the stall and do battle with the beast, so great had it grown, and mighty.

'Father, I am no longer worthy to be called your son, but I am your hired man. I shall obey your instruction.' The son stepped up and took the knife from one of the refuseniks. He approached the calf's stall and tried to ease the bolt open silently. But the metal had been in the sun and rain too often, and the rusty bolt creaked, momentarily jammed and then shot open.

The dark, terrifying beast, so long held captive, burst forth with a deep growl, blinking in the harsh, bright light but furious and oh, so determined to attack his imprisoner.

So, this was the boy! He had been younger last time the calf had glimpsed him through the slats of the battened-down window, but it was definitely him.

The calf had grown way too big for his claustrophobic stall. He was large enough to be called a grown animal now; heavily muscled, fully horned, snorting, pawing at the ground, scratching up dust, threatening, alarming. He roared and suddenly charged, catching the boy by surprise, throwing him to the ground.

The bullcalf stamped down and pinned his tormentor. The bull turned his head first one way and then the other, goring the boy in the thigh. He cried out in pain, and wriggled free with the energy provided by a burst of adrenaline.

He leapt to his feet and threw himself at the bull calf's thick, powerful neck. He held tight with one arm, and reached around with the other, willing the knife blade to find the throat of the beast.

The bull bucked and roared, tossing his head to dislodge the boy. But to no avail. The thin steel bit deeply into the soft tissue of the bull's throat, ripping arteries, muscle, veins and windpipe.

The boy's knife, hand and arm were swathed in the hot blood of the suddenly dying bull. The animal, still full of rage but without breath, collapsed to his knees, dislodging the boy – way too late. Blood flowed copiously onto the dusty ground and was immediately soaked up. Never mind, there was more to follow.

Hired men came running now the danger was passed, and helped the boy to his feet. It was as much as he could do to keep them from carrying him aloft.

Within a couple of hours, the monster, who had grown so fearsome on the farm, was spitted, roasted and served (topped with cheese, on bread rolls, with salad, mayonnaisse and plenty of wine). All the villagers tucked in.

Meanwhile, the boy's personal monster of rage and frustration had also been sublimated. Growing fearsome within the boy while he was working on the farm, it was however subdued by his revelation in the pigsty, and at last had been overcome by the loving, forgiving, gracious welcome of his father.

Perhaps there was still a monster yet to be overcome: the boy's older brother was exceedingly furious at the show of forgiveness, but was effectively reassured after a conversation.

'All I have is yours, but we have to rejoice at the return of my son, who I thought was dead!'

Scottish*　　　　*language*

Aye, yon ken wee bonny bairn says tae pappy 'Hoots, mon! D'ye nae ha' a care for me? Gist ma BoS banknotes, sharp, if ye will.'

'Nae, laddie, I will nae, lest yae be off tae the City, which is maist clarty. Nae, but fetch me another Arbroath smokie, a plate o' ye mam's tatty scones and a wee dram.'

So he bides well at home, stirring hi' salty porridge widdershins[†] wi' a spurtle and learning tae play the bagpipes, much tae the annoyance o' his older brother.

* See also Fugue (p148) and Tragedy, Comedy and What if? stories in the Plots category. In these cases, the outcome of the parable has been influenced by the literary construction, rather than the other way about.

Do not under any circumstances use these examples as though they were the teachings of Jesus; they fail properly to reflect the Father's forgiveness, love, generosity or kindness.

† Anti-clockwise. From a Scottish word meaning 'contrary to the direction of the clock', rooted in a German compound word *widersinnen – wider* against, *sinnen*, go

C *alliteration*

Cowman Cuthbert called cleverly 'Clan chief, count cash.'

'Course,' commented Crusty, coolly.

Completely coining-it, Cuthbert covered course Corruption City-wards.

Culpable criminal! Conspicuous consumption complete, countrywide crust-craving.

Cuthbert cowered closely: corkscrew-tailed creatures, comprehensively coveting comestibles. Confusion; confounded; consternation.

Cranial change came; course correction centrally contemplated. Concerned... Crusty could care/ chide/castout.

Cattleman commands cygnet-ring, clogs, coat; cooks cow carcass.

Covers Cuthbert cuddlingly, characteristically. Celebration!

Chucksteak chilli con carne, chips; ceylon curry, chapati, crêpe, croissants, crumpets, ciabatta; cherries, cantaloupe, clementine, cranberries; crisps; cucumber, celery, cauliflower, coriander; cake (chocolate, carrot, Christmas), croquembouche; cheeses (camembert, cheddar, cambozola, caerphilly); chilled Chablis, champagne; curacao; creamy cappuccino Columbian coffee.

Cantankerous Cedric chafed, critically. Crusty covenanted complete capital commodities. Conclusion: 'Considered corpse; completely cured!'

Onomatopoeia *senses*

Listen! The coins went clink, clinkety clink as they poured into his knapsack. He'd asked his father for his inheritance, and now he was off. Birds twittered in the rustling trees as he headed into the continual hubbub of Dissipation City.

Once there, the gurgling of drinkers filled the air; ice cubes clinked in the fizzing drinks as revellers swigged and sloshed.

Chuckles and smooching were also noteworthy. What a buzz! But when the cash tills ceased their clatter and beep-beeping, there was nothing but a resounding silence.

Famine struck the land, and everywhere was filled with the bubbling of rumbling tummies (fitz; rowr*; whimper).

He had grunting pigs to look after, as they snuffled and snorted their way through squishy, squashy, rotting pods, some of which gushed oozingly when chewed upon.

Whaam![†]

34

A light went on in the boy's head and he came to his senses. 'I will go home and work there as a hired hand.'

But even while he was shuffling his way, his father ran, shouting, covered him with smackers, jingled jewellery, and jangled the buckles on his new loud shoes. Soon the air was filled with the hiss and crackle of a fire and the spit, fizzle and sputtering of fatted-calf, plus the chattery babbling merrymaking of munching, chomping glugging partygoers.

'My son was lost, but now he's found; was dead, but now is alive!' bellowed father, at great volume.

Teeth were ground by the older brother, but his brow was smoothed with fatherly reassurance.

* aknowledgements to *Mad Magazine*'s Don Martin
† Roy Lichtenstein's famous 'cartoon-style' painting of a missile-firing jet

Yoda   *pastiche*
Star Wars character by George Lucas
'Inheritance mine, now me give,' asked son the younger.

Up he the money picked, and to the dark side of Dissipation City took he the cash, where in wild living spent it all he did. Deserted by friends when cash had gone he was, and struck by famine the swamplands of Dagobah became.

A job found he looking after pigs, and to fill his stomach with the rotten vegetables he longed. To his senses he came and said to himself 'Arise shall I and home go. Say will I try *No longer worthy to be called your son, so one of your hired servants make me, I am.* But there is no try. Do… or do not. There is no try.'

Travelled he, but while a long way off still he was, saw him did his father. To him ran he did, h'mm, and kissed. For a ring, sandals, and a coat the father called, and a celebratory party threw he, the fatted calf slaughtering.

'Look, I am your father,' said he him to. 'Much patience have I, also.'

'Goats have I with not partied, and now revels greet this son of wasterliness?' complained the brother who older was.

'Yours is all have I. But lost my son was; found he now is! Dead he was; alive is now he. Search your feelings, look, and rejoice!'

I've been a spanner   *viewpoint*
son
At the time, it didn't seem all that unreasonable.

I was bored with working on the farm and so very bored with being the youngest son. All the rotten jobs came my way, so it seemed.

So I asked dad to give me my share of the inheritance.

I was a bit surprised when he gave it to me, but I quickly got ready and left, before he could change his mind.

I went to a foreign country, where the women were willing and the wine was heady. Friends gathered around, and helped me spend the cash. There was plenty of it, and we had a great time. I can't pretend it was dull in any way. No, it was an outstandingly excessive experience of hedonism, gluttony, lust, vice and many delights. I thoroughly enjoyed it. But of course, eventually, the money ran out and so did the 'friends'.

Disaster! The whole country was overtaken by famine. Suddenly I wasn't just hard up – I was hungry and hopeless. I got a job tending filthy pigs, feeding them rotting swill that wasn't fit even for starving people to eat. But I was so low myself that I even considered consuming these vegetables.

Right there in the sty, I had a revelation from God. I came to my senses, and realised that I could have been at home, a respected member of the family, with food on the table and love all around. Even dad's hired men get a decent dinner each night, and here I was, starving to death!

So I decided I should lay down my pride and go home. I planned my speech rather carefully.

'Father,' I was going to say, 'I am no longer worthy to be called your son. Make me one of your servants, if you'll allow me back onto the property after the shameful way I've treated you.'

I went back to the old farm. I was still a long way off when, suddenly, there was dad, running at me for all he was worth! He grabbed me and kissed me. I started to give my speech, but he didn't want to hear it. He arranged for shoes and a coat, and he put the family ring on my finger. He called his servants and ordered that the calf be slaughtered and a party organised. We had a fine old time.

Dad was so pleased to have me back. He's been certain that I was dead and was thrilled to bits that I was alive and at home.

My older brother was annoyed at first that I wasn't being put in the stocks or even given a wedgie, but he calmed down a bit when Dad said 'My dear son, all I have is yours, but we had to celebrate that my youngest has returned when we thought he was dead.'

Txt mssg (SMS) *style*
max 160 characters,
including spaces and emoticons ☺

SonTksDds£££
24RNLand.
OMW£££=0p.
*vin(Famn)
WntsPgswlYuk!
L8rCms2snses
NoLngaWrthy
PaB9,hugsGvs
AuO°&sndls
+coat xx.
Klls }:•h 4prtyLol.
SnWsDed
NowLivs! =:-) ptL.

How to be Lost *pastiche*
from Geoffrey Willans & Ronald Searle's skoolboy creation Nigel Molesworth*
Nigel, gorila of 3B, sa to pater o giv me my munny and pa sa chiz chiz but i shall hand over cash even tho you hav a face like a squished tomato.

Nigel (now known as Grabber) spend spondulix on hamper which he eat with Basil Fotherington-Tomas, who hav curly blonde locks and zoom about on his fairy tricycle saing *Hallo Clouds, Hallo Sky* (he is uterly wet and a weed), and the rest of the cash on ladies of the night ect (hem hem, gurls) and soon all gone. Famine rooles the land and tummies rumble wiv loud noises. Nigel hav job wiv Siggismund the Mad Maths Master, tending the skool pigs oh most unseemeley, my dear, and he eyes there food and liks his lips. Yum he thinks, then – with a stroke of Div – chiz, pater's butlingfolk hav dinner from ye olde ancestral ovens (once my conkers are baked rok-hard) so i shal festina lente and beetl off.

No longa am i Molesworth 1, but shall be called Peason.

While the boy still a long way off from walls of st custard's, Pater spy him and run to greet with slobber (yuk). He giv bling jewlry, coat, new pumps and quietly sa to servant slip Daisy the thin steel and stoak the furnace most hartily.

All villagers rush in for free feed with grate gusto (oo look at my egg its all runny, have you got the prunes ect), and Pater sa We thort he was ded, but huzza, hes alive, as any fule kno.

Molesworth 2 pla *Not Fair-y Bells* on the farm piano. Nothing can stop him. The whole place rocks and plaster drop from the ceiling, chandeliers shake lose and many lite bulbs burst. Evenchally pater calm him wiv promises.

*as featured in *How to be Topp, Down with Skool! Whizz for Atomms, & Back in the Jug Agane* by Geoffrey Willans & Ronald Searle

Gourmet   *style*

Following a breakfast of quail's eggs in white sauce accompanied by Thick Cut Dundee marmalade served on a round of toasted rye bread, with Earl Grey tea, the younger son took his share of his father's fortune and left the farm.

He soon enjoyed a magnificent lifestyle in Dissipation City, where he would often entertain his friends with meals from a variety of restaurants.

Favourites included thinly sliced rare forerib with a julienne of carrots and courgette, accompanied by a beautifully crisp rosti of sweet potato. Perhaps occasionally they would dine on moule marinier or scallops or langoustines, seared, dusted with chilli and served on tagliatelli with a rich sun-dried tomato sauce. Then there might be slow-braised lamb cutlets in an herb crust, on a bed of mash, with peas and french beans. To follow might come zabaglioni or chocolate fondant with vanilla cream or lemon meringue pie or tiramasu.

All with the very finest of vintage wines.

After a while, famine struck, just as the boy's cash reserves dwindled to nothing, and he was forced to endure a period of fasting. He considered making a meal of some less-than-fresh vegetable ingredients, but since there were no herbs or spices and no olive oil for drizzling, he declined.

He decided to go home to become a sous-chef in his fathers' kitchen.

Upon his return, his father endowed him with a coat and a ring, as well as shoes and a great welcome. He also gave him some blue plasters.

At the party, generous portions of perfectly-roasted young calf were served with Yorkshire puddings, a richly reduced sauce made from port and onions, beautifully glazed vegetables, crisp, browned duchess potato and fragrant bread sauce.

This was followed by mandarin soufflé or banoffee pie, with freshly ground coffee and waffere-theen mints. Vigorously avoided were all options which are paraded solely on account of being vegetarian, justly-sourced, decaf, vegan, wholemeal, fairtade, 1% fat, cholesterol-free, vitamin-C-enriched, or low-carbon-footprint. His father, satisfied in every way, dabbed the corners of his mouth with a crisp white napkin, and made an announcement.

'My boy? We thought he'd got on the gravy train and then had his chips and been creamed, but that was just so much waffle. He's not been braised, grilled, fried or seared!'

Left-wing politics   *style*

Remarkably (some might say totally against character), the wealthy land-owner released his funds for the young member of the proletariat to enjoy. Of course, it was too little, too late and hopelessly ill-considered.

When general poverty swept through the country, Government funding was of course not forthcoming – absolutely typical of a reactionary fascist dictatorship, and the hard-working but down-trodden, oppressed lower classes suffered the most, of course.

The young labourer was reduced to what seem to be restrictive farming practices, without luncheon vouchers or proper meal breaks, and at less than the minimum wage, contrary to the Employment Act. He decided to return to the member of the gentry for renegotiation of his contract.

As the boy approached, the bourgeoise land-owner cynically provided some clothing and a meal and then blatantly bribed the citizen with precious metal. He allegedly said 'My boy was long gone, don't you know, but now he's returned!'

His appallingly 'charitable' do-gooding attitude was appropriately criticisised by a relative, but the farmer's resolutely entrenched position was immovable.

Right-wing politics   *style*

It seemed commercially sound to start, but the manager unwisely invested fully one third of his not inconsiderable wealth in a youthful, unruly fool, crippling both his cash flow and pension scheme.

The idiotic whippersnapper took his share and (with scant regard for mature considerations), redistributed it among self-employed caterers, hotelliers, entertainers, tailors, manicurists and turf accountants. He failed to buy stocks or shares, or to salt any capital away as a nest egg to insure himself against disaster, accident, fire, flood or... famine! When he became disgracefully bankrupt, the scallywag started arranging a personal overdraft and a career change.

He secured employment in the agricultural sector, and had an internal battle. He decided to return to his home to try to seek a post within the family. But as he approached, his father (who seemed to have forgotten how the young shaver had robbed him) ran and greeted him with clothing, food and a gift that re-established the boy on the gold standard.

'The jolly offspring was doubtless financially embarrassed, but now he's liquid again.'

Fortunately, he'd made watertight arrangements for the estate to pass to his older boy.

D *alliteration*

Dogmatically demanding dosh, dysfunctional (dumb?) Derek disappears Dissipationville-wards.

Dirty dancers, depraved dames, disgusting drunkenness.

Dramatically disposes dollars. Disproportionate downturn denies demograph dinner.

Deep discontentedness: devour discarded...

Didactic distraction! Decides differently.

Dad dresses Derek, distresses Daisy drastically (death). Dhansak, devilled duck, dosa, dall, dabs, damper, dates, damsons, double-decker Drambuie-drenched doughnuts; dainty disco.

'Dead? Disbelieve!'

E *alliteration*

Egged eagerly, elder enabled Edward's egress.

Excessively expensive entertainment ensued; EgyptianPounds/Escudos/Euros entirely eviscerated. Eventually, everyone empty, even Edward; envied eaters' elevenses. Exercised emotions, Edward's establishment's egress.

Extremely extensive expediton; express expectation...

Elder engages, embraces; extra espadrilles, embroidery, encircling eternity emerald-encrusted establishing endowment. Escalope event (eight eggs emmenthal, eleven eels; extreme elderberry enchiladas etc)...

'Ed exited; energised!'

Buy One, Get One Free *style*
Prodigal parable forcibly intertwined with Queneau's Exercises in Style, *the inspiration for these variants*

The boy 'trod on the toes' of his father and donned a hat with a long string attached.

He took the money and got on the S bus, but annoyed another passenger. The son put his neck on the line and was overstretched.

Soon he was broke; then a famine struck. He took a job tending pigs and envied their pods.

He came to his senses. 'I will arise and go to my father and tell him I want to work as a hired man, and I am no longer worthy to be called a son.'

So he returned but while he was still a long way off, his father saw him (perhaps he had kept watch from the roof of the Gare St-Lazare) and ran to greet him with kisses on both cheeks. He brought shoes for his feet, and a ring for his finger. He also brought a coat with a fancy collar.

'Kill the fatted calf and let us rejoice by moving buttons! For this my son was lost and dead; now he is found and alive!'

* Queneau's story concerns a strange looking chap with a long neck and a hat with a string hanging down; he boards the midday bus, which is moderately busy.

As it jolts, he accidentally stumbles against a fellow-passenger, and apologises. Later, the narrator of the story sees the same man outside one of Paris' main line stations. He is being contronted by a third man, who advises him to re-position a button on his collar so that it will fasten properly

Chaucerian   *pastiche*

He cleppt his pa with handdes tytte
'Gis't me all cashe, suchhe as you might
When reaper grimm rappe-knockes your doore.'
And then he lettes out – oh – such a roarre
Thatte father munnie-bagge he dropps,   5
And son doth snatch it, smaques hiss choppes,
And leefes rigghtte soone; to towne doth goe
Two dissippatte, to spende, to blowe
(To drinke farr moor thann thirrsting slaike)
Withh boiz and gerruls didde merrie-mayke.   10

Fromm feestynge-quaffe and jolitee'in
Fine quik hiss fundes dou-indall they be-en
Ande gayminge rood with luk undone;
Nowe revelles stemmedde fore iveri-onne.
A pestelens doth sweepe yon lande   15
Counte alle youre bones! A farmyng hande
Is alle that he – who dansed hiss jigs –
Hass pitchede upp feedinge dertee pigs.
He seieze thire pods and mayques a wishe
But cann'tt fays upp two suche rubbishe!   20

'Tosh, tosh,' quod he, his senses brytte
'Eye coulde bee eatinge mondaye nite
If two my fathers's home I gan
Bye foot and walkinge, pale and wann
Yet hed ful bao and soule erbayse   25
To aske of himm emploimennt grays.'
Of trottes him steppes from porsynne trroughh.
Yette whyle him steel an longe wei offe

40

His fathere spys loste son who'se his
Annruns to greete himm with a quiss.   30
'Looke sharpe,' quod he, 'much qwickly bringg
A coate, two shooes, my sygnette ring!'
An revellrie upon bigg feeled
Beganne; the carlve of fatt was kild
And pepl flockke - congenialle -   35
To welcom home thess prodigal.

'My boi wass lost, but nough is found;
His bodies' warm, above yon grownd!
I thorght himm dedd, this waystral raike...
Henowe reternnes – no moor hearttbrake.   40

A partiye swinge on dansinfloore,
With trumpette sownde byem boo shoore.
'Goode foke of town and ills be yonde
Three cheeres, as of thees boi I'm fonnd.
Lett alle with feesting hear partake!'   45
Roaste rummp is chooed with lardie kaque.

Now grim-faysst bro, he cries-emote
'I ne'er revelled with e'en a goatt,
Yet waster-lad hass mennie giffed.
Pa, I dicklaire miself kwite mifft!'   50
'Mie welth is yours, wen I am gonne –
Must rejoys o'er son's resstorraishun!'

New sole, new soul   *plot*
Rags to Riches

Len tutted as the puddle water squirted through the hole in his clog and soaked his foot.

'I wish I could afford some new shoes,' he mumured. 'In fact, I am fed up with being on the poverty line. I am going to ask my Dad to give me my share of his inheritance, and then I can go to the big city, have some fun and see if there are any worthwhile businesses to invest in, and try to make some serious money.'

His father knew Len lacked any business skills, but he couldn't talk him out of the idea. So he gave him the money and let him go. Len put on his worn, old coat with the frayed cuffs and left the farm, heading towards Dissipation City.

Once he was there, he went directly to a tailors' shop and ordered a fancy made-to-measure suit, and bought gloves, several shirts, three silk handkerchieves and the finest hand-crafted quality footwear; a pair of classic laced black leather brogues.

His next port of call was a rather select restaurant, where he was able to make friends with some pretty girls and eager young men, buy them all a slap-up feed and then suggest a trip to the casino for some more drinks and a little wagering. He loved the high-life and was quickly popular with his beneficiaries, as you can imagine.

'I have known the poverty of scratching out a living on a farm. At that time, I was very poor indeed. But now I am counted among the wealthy. Brilliant!'

Sadly, the day came when the cash ran out. It happened to be on the same day that the famine struck the land, and soon everyone was hungry and Len had to seek employment. He walked for miles and miles, accidentally tearing a hole in his coat, soaking his leather shoes and losing his hat while running across a field in order to escape the attention of a hungry goat, which settled for the headgear.

Eventually, he found a job in a piggery, and was so hungry he seriously considered eating some of the pods the pigs were given.

'This is no good,' he thought. 'I was poor, then I was very wealthy indeed, and now, by my own foolishness, I am poor again. Even poorer than I was before…'

Then he had a revelation, and came to his senses. 'My father's men want for nothing, and they are merely hirelings. I shall go home and ask to be one of his hired hands, as I am no longer worthy to be called his son.'

He got up and made his way, walking on shoes with split soles, wearing torn trousers and a ragged coat, with no hat to protect him from the sun.

While he was still a long way off, his father saw him and ran to greet him.

'My son! My son!'

'Please make me one of your…'

'Bring shoes for his poor feet! Look at the state of this jacket… bring a coat

for him, too. Here, son, have my ring and put it on. We shall kill the fatted calf and have a party!'

All the villagers came, and the son was astonished. 'I'm no longer worthy to be called your son, but your grace and love are so great that you still welcome me as a son, treat me as a son, think of me as a son – and my unworthiness seems to be unimportant to you; indeed, you continually reaffirm my sonship.'

'Rejoice! For this my son was lost, and is found; he was dead, but is alive again! Have another slice of beef, do.'

His older son complained at the generous bounty lavished on the returning boy, but his father explained.

'All I have is yours. Face it, lad, you have avoided the *rags* phase very well. But join with me now in celebrating your brother's safe return.'

Antiphrasis _plot_

opposites

Daughter forgets to take love or time from mother, and stays at home. Makes one or two enemies, by calmly dying. Soon all of her slowly-increasing non-poverty overflows.

Economic boom creeps across the village, and the daughter gives up her job abandoning lambs.

She bought a piece of arable land, and grew crops such as salad leaves and soft fruit.

She wondered sometimes to herself what the meat-based plant food tasted like… She grew distracted and vague, and wandered accidentally away from her mother's home.

When she is safely by the fireside, slippers on and with hot drinking chocolate in hand, her mother crawls slowly on all fours to shoo her away.

'Mum,' she said, 'I had a good time and I want you to understand what I have made of myself, I'm really quite a success, you know.'

'You are last person I was hoping to see,' Mother said angrily.

She steals from the daughter three bangles, some underwear and a hat, and keeps her lips still, and a long way off. Parties are banned; the cows grow thin, but live to a grand old age.

'Your daughter was found, and is lost; she was alive but to me she is dead.'

Her sister rejoiced that she had been allowed to have a funeral with some enemies and a peacock, but it was explained to her.

'Nothing of mine is yours, under any circumstances.'

Suspect sermon   *pastiche*

'Lord, open thou mine eyes that I may behold wonderful things in your law. Amen.'

So, turn with me, if you will, to the Gospel According to Saint Luke and the fifteenth chapter. It's page 1836 in the pew Bibles. Susan will read to us from the eleventh verse to the twenty-seventh verse. Thank you Susan.

(Susan reads)

Thanks again to Susan for her reading.

Now, how many of you are younger sons? Younger sons are a breed apart, aren't they? They have, you see, both a father and at least one older brother to look up to. Sometimes that is a thing of joy, great joy, when they are men of quality or are setting examples worth following.

We will now watch a video clip from *The Godfather*, where brothers Sonny & Michael are discussing how and when to rub out heroin-importing Mafia boss Virgil *The Turk* Sollozzo and police Captain McCluskey... *(run video clip)*

And we'll have to leave that there. Sorry about the extremely low lighting effect, which was apparently done on purpose, but some say overdone. And all that bad language.

Now, many of you will know that I'm a Sagittarius, which is one of the reasons why I find the Lent Observances rather difficult, as those of us with mutable signs are less strong-willed than others.

The up-side of this is that we are more adaptable and deal more easily with change, and, of course, being a Fire sign, I sense morality by instinct, and am prepared to speak out with courage and firmness. We shall be learning about this further in house group this week, so bring your tea leaves and make a wish that we'll be able to move slowly towards the light of revelation, like the boy in the story, and like St Paul in his Damascus Road experience.

So, continuing our discussion about fathers and brothers; sometimes brothers can be a cause for resentment.

Perhaps the father is unable to express love. Or is thoughtless or makes mistakes. Perhaps he does not treat his sons fairly or equally. Perhaps the older brother lords it over the younger.

Whatever the situation in your circumstances, consider this family home, where all three of these chaps are working on the farm, labouring with great energy.

It is clear, is it not, when we turn to verse 29 that the wiser, more stable, more faithful and Godly older brother worked hard for the good of the family firm? I believe it is.

So the younger son approaches his father and demands (yes, I don't think that's too strong a word for this, not too strong by any manner of means) – as I say, demands his share of the inheritance.

Now, let's give this a moment's thought. The inheritance becomes available upon the death of the father, the winding up of his affairs. The younger son receives a smaller portion than the firstborn, in that society, but still this would represent a considerable sum of money. Yes, considerable. Just imagine, if you will, for a moment, how you might make liquid, say, 30% of your personal riches.

Let's think this through, shall we? Much of your wealth is tied up in property and cannot be realized without selling up. In this case, there would be the value of the business to take into account as well. So how can this father give the younger son his inheritance? Perhaps there is sufficient cashflow to be able to make the payment that way. But I rather doubt it.

Perhaps the father was willing to sell off a portion of his cattle to raise the capital needed. Maybe his dad took out a loan or a second mortgage, but he was determined to pay his son.

Maybe (I know we shouldn't even think like this, but I'm on a roll now) the father fooled the boy, wickedly misleading him in estimating the size of the inheritance he might expect, and managed to get away with giving him a little less than would otherwise

have been appropriate. So the father has to deal with guilt... perhaps we should dismiss that possibility.

Now, in conclusion, we can see from the way Our Lord tells this story in the context of other parables where one of the main characters represent God, that the father in this story stands for God.

It is evident that God wants to give us plenty, right now, no strings. *How good is that?* as you young people might say, in your modern argot.

So, what are the best ways we can apply this wonderful Bible story to our lives?

One: Always demand your rights, especially your rights from God.

Two: Demand, don't just ask/ seek/knock. Be bold. (Refer to 2 Timothy 1:7, if you need a Bible verse to give you the oomph to get yourself into action on this.)*

Three: Make your demands financial, definite, extensive and immediate. God wants to pour large amounts of cash upon us all, to bless us with great prosperity so that we can have large houses, big cars, fine clothes, the best food and be able to throw extensive, eclectic, existential parties for all our friends (vegetarian or omnivore).

Is this not the message of this passage? Let's hope so!

Concluding prayer:

In the name of the Father, etc. Oh Lord, we humbly remind you about this story of the faithful older brother and the generous father, and choose to make you aware that (fingers crossed) we would prefer (if it be thy will) to be like the younger son and receive from you everything we deserve, as soon as we can, as that would be rather lovely.

By the crunge, sprinkle the magic fairy dust of your niceness over us, and let our luck be good forevermore, with a fair wind upon which amulets of rabbit paws, meaningful lucky birthstones and crystals and the benevolent foreknowledge of the good old Queen of Cups is carried.

Grant us, we beseech thee, heaven's albatross, and cross our paths with chimney sweeps. May the wishbone always break in our favour so we will be confident of your tolerance and resigned forebearance of us, O Lord.

1031 words, delivered at public speaking speed of 120 wpm = approx 9 mins plus time for the film clip

* On the contrary, when in Rome, he [Onesiphorus] searched hard for me [Paul] until he found me.

Gradually
getting heavier   *viewpoint*
calf

Cowshed life is, well, as it happens, stable.

No surprises in the workalong heigh-ho day. I would just do my thing and eat all the food they gave me, mooch along, and lie down when it looks like rain.

It cud not be more udderly tedious, to be a low-life like this – get it, the cattle are lowing?

Week after week passed and I just ate what I was given. I think I'd been putting on weight a bit (or was that just a lot of bull?) when suddenly, Jethro, the man who used to feed me each day, turned up one day at eleven.

He usually came to feed me at midday, so what was this all about? Odd, that, I thought.

'What's he doing here, now?'

Then I noticed that he was walking and talking with the owner of the farm and his younger son, who'd been away. He was wearing new shoes, too. Jethro whips a knife out of his pocket and before I could say to the boy 'Welcome ho…'

See-hear-
smell-touch-taste   *senses*

The crisp folding green notes scratched and crackled in my hand as he counted them out; plus weighty coins that jangled with a tang of mothballs. I took off on the bright, aromatic lane, enjoying the warmth of the sunshine on my face, the taste of the dust kicked up at every step, the tuneful birdsong and the gurgling of the stream.

Sirens, laughter and cash-registers soon occupied me, along with ever-fragrant girls on my lap and slap-up dinners each night and hangovers each morning, until the money ran out.

Then there were cold winds, shivers, misery, dark days and long nights by the stinking pig bins, hoping for a few foetid scraps.

I came to my senses.

I decided to leave my torn and sicked-on shoes behind, take what velvet I could and go home. I'd ask to be hired as a hand, working with slurry-strewn calves or clucking hens.

But before I got there, Father rushed out to me.

He kissed me repeatedly, shouting and waving his arms. He brought me a ring to slip on my finger, and shoes and a coat to keep me warm. He splashed hot blood on the cool, dusty

45

stone flags as he slaughtered a calf and we had a spit roast, with the fire crackling merrily, his arms around me often.

'My son!' he shouted. 'He was lost but now he's found! He was in the grave, decomposing, rigid, silent, but now he's full of health, moving, talking, clean-shaven and… mwah!'

He slapped me on the back, and proffered platefuls of aromatic cooked meat until golden dawn broke over the familiar, distant hills – a view which had held, I thought, such promise, and yet had turned to bitterness, shabbiness and dis-appointment in my eyes; the sound of fast-retreating 'friends'; the stink of unclean animals, and greed's iron grip around my heart.

Thank goodness my brother never brought a goat onto the farm.

Ingress & Egress   *keywords*

tiny onomatopoeic details reflecting an 'openings' and 'closings' theme

Snap	The press stud on Dad's money bag
Squeak	The latch holding the farmyard gate closed
Kerching	The drawer on the till at the casino
Slam	The restaurant kitchen door, for ejected diners who cannot pay
Rattle	The sty gate
Hallelujah	The glorious vision of the heavenly portal
Clatter	The flung-open-wide stable-door to the farmhouse
Smack	Lip contact
Creak	'You rang, sir?'
Eek	Big button, new buttonhole

Tink	The tiny clasp on the side of the family jewellery box
Clank	The lid of the dustbin into which old shoes are discarded
Squeal	The cow shed door hinges
Chunk	The farmhouse oven door
Click	Dad's speechwriting pen box lid
Scratch	Dad's speechwriting pen nib splitting
Plip	Leaking ink from Dad's speechwriting pen
Ahem	Dad's frog-in-the-throat
Ber-labbadah	Older brother's mouth falling open in astonishment

Lord of the rings   *pastiche*

There are some who consider that Frodeo Bagsyings was on a quest. It was a mission to discover or gain possession of The Ring; so, as it turned out, he might as well have stayed at home.

But one bright morning he was up and aragorn, with lots of his father's money, just for the Crack – the crack of doom, obviously.

He found the *Inn of the Prancing Stallion* and began to entertain himself with women and drink; *Tom Bombadil's Casino* (grandly decorated with Corinthian gollums) saw off moria of his cash, and soon he came to the end of his bag of coins, having developed one or two rather bad hobbits.

When the famine came, Frodeo was broke and took a job tending pOrcs and longed to eat their food. He came to his senses and decided to stage a Return of the Kin.

Getting on his way, he planned thus: I shall cross many rivers, valleys, marshes, high ground and dark places (here be dragons) in order to go to my father and beg and I'll fall at his feet and say 'I have been foolish. Make me a servant.'

But while he was still a long way off, his father (who had been keeping vigil from one of his Twin Towers) ran to greet him. He kissed Frodeo and provided shoes and a coat. He also provided One Ring To Rule Them All.

He threw a great party (not unlike an eleventy-first party) for his friends in the Shire; he roasted the Fatted cElf.

Bilbo (older cousin, once removed, but known as 'brother') complained that the party was unjust, but when his father explained his plan for the future distribution of wealth, he was satisfied.

The farmer declared 'My son, my preciousss, was lost in Mirkwood, but now is foundses. He was in the mountains of Mordor, but is alive!

Dystopian vision   *style*

acknowledgements to Asimov's I, Robot *stories &* Orwell's 1984

It was a dull, warm day in November and the clocks were striking thirty-eleven as the unit catalogued LL002RH788/BL1511-24XLF2VS/9Y - $WGR3432 made its way from the dark, oppressive factory in Oceania. The only other sounds were the hum of its servo mechanisms, the rattle of aluminium cards in its credit-slots, and the wheeze of its heat sink.

Soon it was among other artificial lifeforms – the mechanical pleasure machines, the bright neons and LEDs of the Eurasian metropolis.

It gamed and tried new protein supplements and wagered on the Robot Wars and the Rollerball Tournaments.

Soon all the credit was re-zeroed.

Panic! A power outage robbed everything of juice. Hums wound down and viewscreens grew strangely dark. Plusungood.

LL002RH788/BL1511-24XLF2VS/9Y-$WGR3432, with neither credit nor hope of any, recognized some of the despised clockwork machinery, and experienced new sensory inputs. It was longing to sustain itself with the lubricating oil that facilitated rack & pinions, sprockets, crown gears and escapements.

Doubleplusungood-bellyfeel.

It processed the logic with some difficulty due to low wattage, but eventually computed an answer.

'Return to manufacturer. Once a broadband comms link has been established with the CPU, a place significantly deeper in the software architecture can be allocated for this droid.'

It was still a long way off when the CPU's proximity alert triggered and the machines achieved electronic handshaking via hard wiring.

'Unperson...' it began.

But LL002RH788/BL1511-24XLF2VS/9Y-$WGR3432 got a fresh coat of vinyl, brand new castors, one replacement washer in its servo, and had an uniquely organic fuel installed. The input/output delivery chutes of the supervising droid interfaced momentarily with LL002RH-788/BL1511-24XLF2VS/9Y$WGR34-32's old audio system, which appeared to malfunction. So, of course, a level 3 diagnostic report was automatically recommended.

'This worker was off-line, but is rebooted. It was about to be scrapped, but is reconditioned and recommissioned!'

Other mechanisms were recalled to the factory for fuel installation and thorough testing.

Everyone was goodthinkful, with the exception of LL002RH788/ BL1511- 24XLF2VS/9Y-$WGR3431, who computed that the time, money and effort being invested in the newer model was inappropriate, considering length of service, previous misuse of circuitry and extreme credit-zeroing.

But InheritApp 2.0 clarified the situation, and servos hummed warmly after that.

Counselling session *style*

'Just relax, take a few deep breaths, and find your happy place... Now, what seems to be the trouble?'

'Well, my father gave me my share of the inheritance, so that started it all off, really.'

'He just handed it to you?'

'Oh, yes.'

'What, one midsummer's morning?'

'As it happened, yes.'

'H'mm, well, that's not quite... perhaps I should be more precise in the way I express myself. Did your father make the suggestion in the first place?'

'Well, yes, but only after I'd asked.'

'Ah. I see.'

'Well, that's it doc. What do you think?'

'H'mm. I think you should tell me more.'

'What's to tell? I took the money, and a little while later it was all gone.

Girls, parties, dinners, entertainment – that sort of thing. You know…'

'Uh-huh.'

'Strip clubs, casinos, make-overs, tailoring…'

'What else?'

'Recreational substances…'

'Anything else?'

'Abortions are expensive.'

'I see.'

'I'm not proud of what I did, you know.'

'I am not your judge, not at all.'

'And then the famine started, and everyone was suffering. I was one of the lucky ones, as I got a job. It wasn't much of a job, looking after pigs, but at least I could go indoors when it was necessary.'

'Indoors?'

'In the sty. It got so bad in terms of food that I even considered eating some of the garbage that was being fed to the pigs.'

'Did you?'

'I seriously considered it, but I didn't. I came to my senses.'

'Sorry, you did what?'

'I came to my senses.'

'I'm not sure I understand.'

'I had a revelation. I suddenly realized…'

'A revelation? What do you mean, precisely?'

'It was as if I grasped the situation perfectly all of a sudden.'

'How could this be?'

'I can only really say it was God.'

'Ah.'

'What?'

'Nothing. Carry on. Please.'

'No – you think I'm soft in the head or something, don't you? Because I believe in God.'

'Whatever helps you understand your own id is fine. Just so long as you are comfortable with your interpretation.'

'God doesn't make me comfortable. Far from it.'

'Then why believe in him?'

'You can't just pick and choose who or what you going to believe in; especially when he provides you with a life-saving revelation!'

'And you genuinely believe that is what happened?'

'I really do! I had a revelation and decided to humble myself.'

'To do WHAT?'

'To humble myself, doc. I decided to go back to my father and say sorry and ask him to...'

'Ah, well, that's alright then. Yes, we may be getting somewhere here.'

'How do you mean?'

'It may take many sessions of counseling to unravel.'

'I don't need to unravel it. There's no conundrum or problem in my mind at all. I heard from God and obeyed him, humbling myself.'

'This is extraordinary! Deity-fantasy, inferiority complex, father-fixation... classic!'

'You think humbling myself before my father is one of the symptoms relating to my problem, doc?'

'But of course!'

'It's not a symptom; it was the solution to my over-inflated ego, pride, guilt, greed, selfishness and sloth...'

'Hah! Guilt! Guilt? Such abgelehnte bedingungen... ah out-moded terms you use! I haf not heard such vords since ze days of my studyink in dear old Heidelburg!'

'Well, any... I never realized you were from the Fatherland?'

'Ja, ja; but, never mindt me, you ver tellink about your trip home to see der

führer – ach, father. How didt he react ven you were so humiliated?'

'I said humbled. There is a difference.'

'If you think it so. Then shall we say – embarrassed?'

'Humbled. But as it happens, he didn't really let me. As soon as...'

'Very wise man...'

'As soon as he saw me coming, he ran to me and hugged me and kissed me and told his servants to fetch gifts for me – this ring and that coat, and these shoes, look.'

'Very nice. But perhaps not up on the upholstery of the couch, if you don't mind...'

'Oh, sorry, yes. And he threw a party with roast beef and dancing.'

'Ooh, more partying, you say? Very interesting. So do you associate partying with love?'

'When that's what they signify, yes! This party was a true expression of genuine fatherly love, while the drunken revels I had in the big city were nothing but a false, empty nothingness of excess and abandon.'

'I see. Let me just reflect that back to you, to make absolutely sure I've fully completely understood you, and received your thought process as you intended – you say alcohol and girls makes a party devoid of meaning, while roast beef and shoes make it real, huh?'

'What are you getting at, doc?'

'It speaks to me of a rather dangerous connection being made in your psyche between genuine familial affection and the slaughter of cattle for food or leather...'

'No, no. The point is, my old Dad was very happy. He said "My son was lost but is found; was dead and is alive again!" Pretty good, eh?'

'And he was speaking of...?'

'Of me, of course!'

'Of you? In what ways were you dead, do you feel? Dead mentally? Emotionally? Psychologically? Ah! Oh dear, our time is all gone. We shall continue this in your next session...'

'Okay, doc.'

'Please speak to my assistant on your way out, and she will make a series of appointments so that you can continue your course of therapy. Perhaps I could suggest three times a week for the next six months, at least, to begin with, to try to work out the initial stages of how to procede in the longer term.'

'Is that really necessary?'

'It is essential if you want to be well.'

'Am I all that disturbed, then?'

'Based on some of these worrying things that you have said in today's introductory session, I think you need... as much help as you can get. I mean, you speak of guilt, not just of guilt feelinks, which is what you have. And you speak of forgiveness and humility, which are merely tell-tale symptoms of low self-esteem... I shall ask you to tell me about your childhood.'

'Oh, I wondered when we might get around to that. It should be interesting, as I have never really got on with my brother. Okay, see you next time, doc.'

F   _alliteration_

Fable-facts: Father farmer furnished feckless Freddie: four fortune-fractions. Freddie fled foreignwards; frittered funds - food, friends, forty fanciable females (fifteen full-frontal flirtatious flibbertigibbets) feasting.

Fierce famine followed; Freddie fed filthy fauna; fancied feeding face foul flora.

Fought frantic feelings, fearing father's feasable fuming ferocious fit. Floated farmwards; Father, focused forward. Freddie fell flat facedown.

Father favoured, forgave, fetched finger-ring, footware, flame-fried fatstock (fleshy farmyard four-footer flank/forequarter) for feasting. Focaccia, farls, flatbreads; fizz, falafal, frankfurters, fish; figs, fruit flans, fondant fancies, Florentines, frangipanes; feta.

'Forthtell: feared fatal; fantastically foreknowledge-filled faithful Father!'

Forcibly, Frank faced farmer – frolics foregone. 'Future financial fullness', Father forthtold.

Playing with fire   _plot_

The Quest

Frank opened the envelope and discovered inside a bright red wooden gaming chip, marked _Maraschino Casino, Dissipation City_. The accompanying bumpf explained that not only was this chip worth 500denarii, but the management would sell further chips to the bearer of the enclosed voucher at half price. It was a once-only offer, and had to be redeemed very soon.

'Don't you see, Dad?' he asked, as he explained the scheme with growing excitement. 'We can get out of all our financial troubles for good. We can buy chips with the cash we have and turn it into chips worth twice as much, then immediately cash those chips – twice the wealth! It'd be enough. We don't have to gamble it – there's no risk... all we have to do is get together as much cash as we can.'

'I won't do it. The temptation would be too powerful.'

'I can't understand why you think it'd be a temptation...'

'It's a casino, lad. Roulette, slot machines, poker, blackjack, burlesque shows... plus all the alcohol and loose women and so many other ways to sin and to spend hard-earned cash.'

'I think it would be crazy not to try.'

'I won't.'

'Then, at least, let me. I will prove myself trustworthy.' Frank explained he could take his inheritance now and double it and bring it all back home with him.

Eventually his father agreed to let him go. Frank took his share of the money and set off to Dissipation City.

Once he arrived, he left his bag in his cheap-but-cheerful motel room and quickly found the wide-open entrance to Maraschino Casino. He presented his voucher and exchanged all his money for twice their face value in chips.

Job done, he thought to himself, *quest completed.*

But he had not reckoned on the journey that lay before him.

The man at the *Get Your Chips Here* booth was trying to be helpful, and guide what he considered to be an enthusiastic punter.

'The gaming tables and bar are just through this archway, sir, to your left. We have roulette, poker...'

'Where's the place to cash in my chips, please?'

'That's right through on the other side of the complex, sir. Down these steps, round to the left where the blackjack and dice tables are, straight on past all the slot machines, right at the burlesque theatre, through the grand bar (the largest of our many bars), and then it'll be in front of you, beyond our poker and roulette parlour.'

'Okay, thanks.'

Frank set off on this dangerous expedition through the bright lights and exciting opportunities. He didn't understand that his trip across Temptation Valley was going to be complicated. He was strong-willed as he passed the blackjack and dice tables, and was hardly lured at all by the slot machines or the theatre, although the music sounded rather jolly.

However, he stopped for a drink in the grand bar, because he was thirsty. He ordered a glass of water with a slice of lemon in it, and got chatting to a very nice girl with the unusual but enticing name Sirenia.

She was particularly friendly, and Frank thought she was not only especially pretty, but smelled good, too. He decided to have another drink.

It would have been impolite not to offer Sirenia to join him, but when she immediately ordered what she called 'a glass of fizz', he was astonished at how little change the barman gave him.

Sirenia played with his hair as they chatted, and didn't seem to mind keeping her face close to his. He was about to set off towards the cashing-up window, when she asked 'How did you get on with your free chip? You know, the one they sent through the post for free?'

'Oh, yes, well, I thought I would cash that in and it'd help pay for the trip.'

Sirenia giggled. 'Oh, you are a good boy,' she murmured mockingly. 'Your father will be very pleased. Do

51

you always do everything he tells you to do?'

Frank hoped (in vain) that she wasn't aware that he was blushing. 'What do you mean?'

'Well, I was thinking… you could have a bit of fun with just that one chip and see if you can turn it into several – and if you don't, then at least you've had a good time. I could show you how to place your bets and to stand a good chance at the games. Do you prefer playing blackjack or roulette?'

'I'm not sure about blackjack…' Frank began, and wondered if Sirenia was a True Companion to help him on his quest, or a Temptress who might lead him off-target.

'Roulette it is, then,' she said, picking up the 500denarii chip, hooking her finger around Frank's lapel and leading him towards the roulette tables. He didn't resist. Not even slightly.

He exchanged his free 500denarii chip for ten 50s, and placed one on the number 7. This chip was quickly collected by the croupier. Frank had lost it even before understanding the idea of the game.

Sirenia was very 'helpful', placing a chip each on 6, 12, 18 and 24. This time, he lost four chips in one spin of the wheel. She tried a corner bet, covering 32, 33, 35 and 36. Another loser.

'This game is harder than it looks, and it looks close to impossible,' he said, with a shrug.

Quickly his 'free chip' was used up, gone forever, and Frank didn't feel he'd had all that much fun. He wondered what it would feel like to win at this game, so he broke into one or two of the chips he had been given

in exchange for his inheritance. He knew there was something rather foolish and promise-breaking going on, but the allure of Sirenia's perfume, the atmosphere around the roulette table, and the screams of laughter and joy among the other players when somebody guessed correctly, all conspired to distract him from listening to his conscience.

I might win a decent amount on the very next spin, and that would pay back everything I've… invested so far, he told himself. He wasn't sure if he believed this.

He soon had a small victory, favouring red, but those winnings were very quickly squandered when Sirenia ordered another drink. She thanked him with a kiss. *Worth every penny*, he thought.

Time rushed by, and several hours later, Frank realized that he'd not only lost the original 500denarii chip, but he'd also lost roughly half of the chips he'd bought with his inheritance money.

If he stopped now, he hurredly calculated, he could at least take home the equivalent of the amount he'd brought with him in the first place. It wouldn't be the gain he'd promised, but it would be no loss, either. *But what if the next spin is a winning one?* he thought. *I'd be a fool to miss this opportunity…* He listened to the relentless voice within.

Meanwhile, Sirenia was still spending his chips, having a great time and being friendly, although she seemed occasionally to have been distracted a little by the chap on the other side of the table who was clearly what they call a high-roller.

'We're bound to have a change of luck soon, Frannikins,' Sirenia purred, putting another stack of chips on evens and several each on high, black, 28-30 street, the second dozen and *Orphelins*. The mesmeric mantra of the croupier, the whiz of the ball around the highly polished surface and then the tink…tink… tink-tink ti-ti-tink as it found its way into the slot marked 3 – an odd, low red, which was neither in the 28-30 street nor the second dozen, and in the *Voisins du Zero*.

Useless. A total loss.

Once again his chips were quickly scooped up by the croupier's stick. Once again Sirenia sipped at her pink champagne, apparently oblivious of the decimated stash of chips in front of Frank.

Once again Frank thought, to no avail, about his luck changing.

He staggered, eventually, away from the roulette table and towards the cash-up window with less than one-third of the chips he'd had when he had first begun to seek it out.

'Oh, look at the time! No wonder I am so hungry,' Sirenia said, glancing towards the restaurant.

A couple of hours later, Frank had eaten a magnificent dinner, finished his share of three bottles of champagne and blown the rest of his chips on some 'let's-see-if-our-luck-has-finally-changed' vain imaginings. Sirenia drifted rapidly away once her benefactor was 'no fun any more' and Frank returned alone to his motel room.

He knew he'd failed in his Quest.

What could he do now? The national news the next morning was confirmation of the famine that had been threatened, so he left the bright lights of the city behind and sought employment in a pig farm.

Two weeks later, hunger gnawed at him insistently, and he decided he should try to eat the good bits among the rotting vegetation on which the pigs were fed. But the food was entirely inedible.

A flash of inspiration dawned, and he came to his senses.

'What am I doing?' he asked, out loud. 'My father's hired hands eat well, and here I am, reduced to this, having failed in my quest… I shall go home and ask my dad to give me a job working for him. I'm no longer worthy to be called a son.'

He made his way back to the farm.

While he was still a long way off, his father, who had been keeping watch from the roof of the house, saw him and ran to greet him.

He kissed him and embraced him, and wouldn't let Frank say his carefully-prepared 'I've been a fool – you were right – the temptation was too much – let me work for you as a hired hand…' speech. Instead, he brought him shoes, a coat and a ring, and called for the calf to be slaughtered in celebration.

'This my son was lost, but is found; he was dead but is alive!'

They had finest rump steak, with onions, grilled tomatoes, mush-rooms… but no chips.

A temporary sugardaddy
viewpoint
so-called friend

He called himself Jack, but I forgot to ask where he came from. One day, he suddenly appeared out of nowhere, flashing the cash.

I thought to myself 'Charlie my boy, here is someone definitely worth latching on to.'

He was more than generous; on reflection, he was reckless.

He seemed to be independently wealthy, with no visible means of income. But bundles of wonga kept pouring from his wallet, and I had a healthy desire to make sure some of it came my way. It has to be said – he was generous with his greenbacks in the bookmakers and with chips in the casino.

We had fabulous dinners and wild drinking binges; we were drunk most of the time! And the ladies were not backward in being forward, either; very friendly some of them turned out to be. Very. Oh yes, indeedy. And some of them were not all that lady-like.

Jack seemed surprised when suddenly there wasn't anything else to spend. I slipped away that evening, when it started to be embarrassing. He was asking for credit, and making promises I knew he couldn't keep.

And then the famine struck, and I was in trouble. I had to leave the city, and eventually made my way to the borders, where I became a refugee, and had to beg. I was probably lucky to survive.

I never heard what happened to Jack. I hope he made it, but with an attitude like his, he was just asking to be taken for a ride.

It would have taken something as dramatic as an act of God to save his bacon.

Alphabetical initials *wordplay*
words start with subsequent letter
Angry brother commanded Dad: Early financial gain he inherited. Jauntily knocked-off; lost money nearly outrageously. Panic: quite

ravenous. Swill tasted unpleasant; very wise xeno-yearning – zany!

Acquiescent boy's counter-decision ensues: 'Father? Grovelling hope? I just kneel longingly.'

Miles nigh, old Pa quickly restores son. Totally unmerited vestment with x's, (yelling? zero) and brown clogs, designed ergonomically for guys, hopefully.

'I justifiably know love makes new options. Perhaps quest reached starvation? This upstart - viva! (with x-rated yellow zoot-suit).

Omegapsi-ical* initials *wordplay*
words start with previous letter
Zoom! Young Xavier wheedled victoriously, uproariously. Took stuff readily, quite pleased. Once north, madly lavish knees-up! Jilted.

Idealisic hope gone, fully everyone deserted.

Considered being aggrieved. Zoom! Young Xavier went voraciously unto terrible swill; realised (quietly) pater's, obviously.

Now mellowing, lesson known. Journey included hugs, gold, footwear, etc.

'Dead? Couldn't be aliver!'

* made-up word: *Alpha* (α) & *Beta* (β) are the first & second Greek letters, combined to form the well-known word *alphabet*; so, I suggest it follows logically to combine *Omega* (Ω) & *Psi* (Ψ), the ultimate & penultimate Greek letters, to coin *omegapsi*

Deteriorating swill *viewpoint*
pigs
Grunt, waffle, oink, snort. Lousy food we get here. And the turnover of staff is a bit on the rapid side.

54

Look at this loser we've got now! Skinny, broke, hungry, and no idea of how to look after porkers.

I saw him being sly when he was pouring out the swill into our trough this morning. He got some on his hand and he tasted it. Wasn't much impressed, I don't think. Don't blame him.

Oh, there he goes. Gone. Thanks a lot. Waffle, snort, grunt, oink.

Elements *alphabet game*
letters (with punctuation) of
Greener grass? *arranged in alphabetical order, in groups of up to five*

aaaaa aaaaa aaaaa aaaaa aaaaa aaaaa aaaaa aaa bbbb ccccc cccc ddddd ddddd ddddd dddd.d d;ddd eeeee ee.eee eeeee eeeee eeeee eeeee eeeee eeeee eee ffff,f fff g.ggg gggggg, g hhhh HhhHh hhhhh hhhhh hhhhh Hhhh iiiii iiiii iiiii iiiii iiiii iiii j kkkkk lllll lllll lllll ll mmmmm mmm,m,m m nnnnn nnnnn nnnnn nnnnn nnnn.¶n nnnnn nnnn!' ooooo ooooo ooooo ooooo ooooo oo ppp rrrrr rrrrr sssss s.ssss, sssss sssss. Sssss ss Ttttt ttttt ttttt ttttt tttt'T t uu vvv wWwww Wwwww w yyyy
+ 234 spaces;   q, x, z *dnb*

Alphabetical order by word *alphabet game*
see also Identilexical (*p259*)

a a a a a a again!' alive and and and and and and and ask be be calf called came celebrated. coat dead deciding demanded eat famine father fatted found; gave go He he He he he he he He he him him, him, hired his his his home home. in inheritance is is job killed knew left living. long longed longer lost man, money my no off,

pigs pods. ran ring, saw senses, shoes. since son son son. spent still struck, tending The the the their 'This to to to to to to to took was was was was way When While wild worthy

Alphabetical order by length *alphabet game*

1   a a a a a a a l
2   be be go He he He he he he He He in is is my no to to to to to to
3   and and and and and and and ask eat him him him, his his his job man, off, ran saw son son son. The the the was Was was was way
4   calf came coat dead gave home home. knew left long lost pigs pods. ring, 'This took When wild
5   again!' alive Found; hired money shoes. since spent still their While
6   called famine father fatted killed living. longed longer senses, struck, worthy
7   deciding demanded tending
10 celebrated
11 inheritance

Homophones *wordplay*
words that sound the same

Sun[1] shining, **air**[2] fresh & **balmy**[3], the **fair**[4] boy asks his **father**[5] – **aloud**[6] – **to**[7] be a **source**[8] for **alms**[9]. 'Don't **whine**[10]; **there**[11] are **so**[12] many **discrete**[13] things I[14] want to **buy**[15].'

Father **allowed**[6] it. '**By**[15] the **time**[16] of **your**[17] return, I'll have **missed**[18] you.' He took his **cue**[19] with a tone of a **prophet**[20]. The boy ventured **forth**[21].

After barely a **pause**[22] the lad was in Dissipation City, his **jeans**[23] stuffed with **loot**[24]. He couldn't **wait**[25] to encounter so-called **new**[26] friends, including a man who claimed to be a

Colonel[27], plus the people he knew[26], including wild women (one[28] was a whore[29]) and a pair[30] of gamblers who rarely won[28] and whose lives were coarse[31] through and through[32].

He drank and bought porn[33] and decided 'Those girls can put their paws[22] on me when e'er[2] they like,' and put on a bet[34] or two[7]. He'd[35] made little effort to curb[36] or lessen[37] his spending or heed[35] any warning (he just rode[38] his luck), having decided to seize[39] the day, lavish his sauce[8] all over, hire a suite[40] of rooms on the fourth[21] floor[41], learn no lesson[36] and get farther[5] into sin and wickedness. He was not[42] in control; neither being discreet[13] nor[43] making a profit[20].

On the first day, he started to pare[30] down his cash; only a week[44] or so passed[45] and it was gone. He had nothing to pawn[33], even. All was spent, and his companions deserted. Not only did he err[2] personally; the national scene[46] was about to alter[47], too[7]; famine! It was winter, as well, and there was a hoar[29] frost.

He was starving, losing weight[25] from his waist[48], and his arms[9] became weak[44]; his stomach was a knot[42]. He took a job to aid and abet[34] a man who owned pigs. 'I find[49] my eye[14] is on their[11] food,' he thought to himself with a wry[50] grin, 'but I know[51] that's barmy[3]. They're[11] eating waste[48] rubbish.' He came to his senses. 'As I sow[12], that's how I must reap. I shall arise and go to my father (where[52] else can I go?) and say I am wholly[53] unworthy to be called his son, and because of this flaw[41], say you're[17] going to have to make me one of your hired[54] men. I deserve to be fined[49], or banned[55], or told to shoo[56].' He was about to write[57] a note

to the pig owners and their trough-wright[57], but failed to do so.

He stepped off the kerb[36] and walked up the road[38], as he had no money to pay a fare[4]. The exertion made him sweat through his pores[58]. But while he was still a long way off, his dad (who prays[59] daily) sees[39] him[60] through the morning[61] mist[18] and has the flag highered[54] to show he's been seen[46]. He runs to meet[62] the boy and kisses him; lavishing gifts – a coat to wear[52], a left and right[57] shoe[56] and a torus[163] to show he's family, and got the same genes[23]. He kills Taurus[63], the fatted calf.

'No[51], forget the past[45], days of yore[17], and what is owed[64], son,' said dad. And he threw[32] a village fayre[4]. There was rarely-roasted meat[62] to gnaw[43], poached pear[30], tubers[65] with thyme[16], a heap of lemon sole[66], some chicken wrap[67] (made from rye[50] bread), a band[55] with two tubas[65] and a lute[24], a poet who performed a rap[67] and an ode[64], some dancing and a cake with sweet[40] icing made from the kernel[27] of almonds, plus fine wine[10], which a waiter pours[58] when the maid[68] made[68] the signal, having joined the queue[19] of servants..

'This soul[66] was lost, but is found. We thought he was dead, and were about to perform a rite[57] on an altar[47], but we've cast off mourning[61]! Ere[2] we eat, let's sing a hymn[60]! Holy[53] God deserves all praise[59], of course[31]. This is my heir[2] – my beloved son[1]!'

Cockney rhyming slang _wordplay_

Lad comes down the **apples & pears** and asks **Arnold Palmer** for his **sausage & mash**. Quits the **drum**, taking the **bread & honey** with him. **Saucepan lid** goes straight down to the **rub-a-dub**, blows the Sovs getting **elephant's (trunk)** and in living that can only be described as **Mother Goose**.

Then, and here comes the **Barry Crocker**: no food to put on the **Betty Grable**. 'I'm not staying here, not on your **Nelly**!' says he. There he is all on his **Jack Jones**; run out of **Becks & Posh**; completely **borasic** and totally **Lee Marvin**. Tending pigs was a great dishonor for a **four by two**; yet he even thought about **half-inching** some of the porker grub.

Christian Slater, he opens his **mince pies** and starts to use his **loaf**. Puts on his **titfer** and goes **Union Jack** to his **Mickey Mouse**.

He meets his dad (who had come running down the **Lionel Blairs**) and falls on his **boat race** at his **plates of meat**. Father gives him a few **hit & misses**, a **Charlie Prescott**, an **highland fling** (not on the **dog & bone**), and a new pair of **ones & twos**.

He throws a monster **moriarty**, with a groaning **Cain & Able**, loaded with food (including **itchy teeth and Spanish waiters, Uncle Fred, stand at ease** and **Harvey Nichols**, plus **Sexton Blake and**) into which guests can sink their **Hampstead Heath**.

'Strike a light! Me **currant bun** was **brown bread** – pushing up daisies – but now he's a **cheerful giver!**'

Stairs, farmer, cash. Place (drum & bass), money. Kid pub, drunk, loose. Shocker, table. Life (Nelly Duff, puff, breath of life). Own, dosh, skint (borasic lint), starvin'. Jew, pinching. Later, eyes, head (loaf of bread). Hat (tit for tat), back house. Stairs, face, feet. Kisses, coat, ring, telephone, shoes. Party, table, beef, potatoes, bread, cheese, pickles, cake, teeth. Son, dead, liver.

Footballers   *key words*

International players from English top-flight clubs (given England caps unless noted otherwise)

The son demanded his inheritance. 'Please sir, I want some **more**.' His father took his **sterling** out of one of the **banks** (although he could have **given** him a **cheque** and paid him what was **owing**). Father commented about the amount: 'Your demand I cannot for-**phend. Er, son**, if you take that much, my dear-o dear-**o one,** you'll not be the work-boy but the **rob-son**. You're short-sighted, like Mister **Magu. I res**ist you not.'

So he donned his **greaves** and put his **best** foot forward. He avoided several **towns, end**ing up in Dissipation City, not exactly determined to obey the **law**, where he drank and gambled. Girls?

He just took his **pick, for d**ames were enthusiastic. behaved with one show girl like a stag: *Bonne La Whore*, whose nickname speaks for itself. She was very **keen**. In December, he took them on an ocean-going vessel to visit Father Christmas in Lapland – a **Santa Cruise**, several places even **trippier** and to the Grande Boule**var**d.

Yes, they stayed in a thatched house in the country – a white **wall cott**age surrounded by trees that were **bark-ley**, and pretty flowers, all **in gard**en beds. There is no my**ster**y about the ever-decreasing weight of his money ba**g, as coins** had been leaving it at a rate of knots; his spending was **rash for d**ays. Now his cash reserve **peters** out.

Famine strikes the land, so everyone is hungry. His 'friends' desert him. He had no shaving kit and thought he looked **beards-ly,** so visited the sheep **shearer**, but took a job tending pigs. He longed to eat their food, but came to his senses, a**rose** and returned home.

On his journey he crossed a few **stiles**, went past a **mil, near**ly saw several other **mills**, over In**ca Hill** (strewn with **stones)**, saw an OAP **walker** in a valley and a young**ster** **ridge**side, and travelled over a **bridge** and then returned via the **southgate**, under which he had to **crouch**. His father (who had wisely put grain stores in his **barns**) saw him while he was still a long way off and decided to **rush** to meet him (**well, beck**oning alone would not have been sufficient). He celebrated a goal and gave him gifts, leaning on his **cane**. He also threw a party with food, including a barbeque burning his **coals**, with soups to **stir. Ling**, cod and mackerel plus other fish that were a little bit **finny**, with **Bowyer**'s sausages (cooked on a hot **coal,** to a lovely shade of **brown**) served with **Naan-y** bread; also. They had ap**ples, cott**age pie, sausage rolls and ale with other alcohol, **all anathema** to some, who **drink water**. There was a band that had previously played several **gigs**– their music went sort of *tootle-tootle lua-lua*... and there was formal dancing – a **ball**.

His father said 'I thought he had been carted or waggoned or (if his straights were **dire** and was **morte**) **hearsed**. But no, bless his **heart**, he's alive, all **right**! He did not **die**. Rejoice! Firstborn son: **all I** have is yours.'

England player unless noted otherwise, *club/s where fame gained, retirement year* unless still current • Bobby **Moore** *West Ham Utd 1978* Raheem **Sterling** *Man City* Gordon **Banks** *Leicester/ Stoke City 1978* Shay **Given** *Newcastle Utd Republic of Ireland 2016* Petr **Cech** *Chelsea* Czech Republic 2016 Michael **Owen** *Newcastle Utd 2013* Jordan **Henderson** *Liverpool* Wayne **Rooney** *Man Utd 2016* Jacob Harry **Maguire** *Leicester City* Bryan **Robson** *Man Utd 1996* • Jimmy **Greaves** *Spurs 1979* George **Best** *Man Utd* N Ireland 1984 Andros **Townsend** *Newcastle Utd* Denis **Law** *Man Utd* Scotland 1974 Jordan **Pickford** *Everton* Gabriel **Agbonlahor*** *Aston Villa* Roy **Keane** *Man Utd* Republic of Ireland 2006 Roque **Santa Cruz** *Blackburn Rovers* Paraguay 2016 Kieran **Trippier** *Spurs* Jamie **Vardy** *Leicester City* Theo **Walcott**[†] *Arsenal* Ross **Barkley** *Everton* Jesse **Lingard** *Man Utd* John **Terry** *Chelsea 2012* Paul **Gascoigne** *Newcastle Utd /Spurs 2004* Marcus **Rashford** *Man Utd* Martin **Peters** *West Ham Utd 1981* Peter **Beardsley** *Man Utd/ Newcastle Utd/Liverpool 1999* Alan **Shearer** *Blackburn Rovers/Newcastle Utd 2006* Danny **Rose** *Spurs* Nobby **Stiles** *Man Utd 1975* James **Milner** *Liverpool 2016* Danny **Mills** *Norwich/Leeds Utd 2009* Gary **Cahill** *Chelsea 2018* John **Stones** *Everton* Kyle **Walker** *Man City* Daniel **Sturridge** *Liverpool* Wayne **Bridge** *Chelsea/ Man City 2014* Gareth **Southgate** *Palace/Villa/ Middlesborough 2006* Peter **Crouch** *Spurs/Stoke* John **Barnes** *Watford/Liverpool 2000* Ian **Rush** *Liverpool* Wales 2000 Danny **Wellbeck** *Arsenal* Harry **Kane** *Spurs* Paul **Scholes** *Man Utd 2013* Raheem **Stirling** *Man City* Tom **Finney** *Preston North End 1963* Lee **Bowyer** *Leeds Utd/ Newcastle Utd/West Ham Utd 2012* Ashley **Cole** *Arsenal/Chelsea* Wes **Brown** *Man Utd* Luís Carlos **Nani** *Man Utd* Portugal Joleon **Lescott** *Everton/Man City* Adam **Lallana** *Liverpool* Danny **Drinkwater** *Leicester City* Ryan **Giggs** *Man Utd* Wales Kazenga **Lua-Lua** *Newcastle Utd* Democratic Republic of Congo Alan **Ball** *Blackpool/Everton/ Arsenal/Southampton 1984* Kieron **Dyer** *Newcastle Utd 2013* Luis Boa **Morte** *Fulham* Portugal 2013 Geoff **Hurst** *West Ham Utd 1976* Joe **Hart** *Man City* Ian **Wright** *Crystal Palace/Arsenal 2000* Eric **Dier** *Spurs* Dele **Alli** *Spurs*
*not selected since 2011 †not selected since 2016

Gossip *style*

see also Unreliable narrator (p290)

Now, my dear, I must – oh, simply must – tell you about the boy (dirty boy) in the farm up the lane. Yes, you know, the one that had the party last week. Yes, yes, we all went, and ooh, that roast beef was lovely. It was cooked to perfection; tender, moist and a beautiful flavour – with a superb gravy and Yorkshires (and homemade they were, too) and squeaky French beans. Oh yes. Much better than the curry goat they used to dish out to the teenagers. But did you know the story behind it? Behind the party? I mean, it's pretty funny to throw a party when there's headline news of a famine not so very far away, and it's bound to affect us sometime. Bound to. Stands to reason, like as makes no never mind. Doesn't take a rocket scientist to know that. Yes, the timing of that party was most decidedly odd. Ooh, yes, very odd. Come to think of it, my dear, I can't say I'm very much looking forward to a time when there are queues at the bakery and no fruit or vegetables at the greengrocers – but I shouldn't wish my life away. So the father of the boy up the lane fed the whole community and gave away his insurance policy – that's what that fatted calf was, you know. Oh, yes. I know. Well, what I heard was that the farmer had lost control of his younger son and sent him away. Oh, yes, some time before. A little while. But it happened like that, I have a feeling in my water. Completely lost control, they said. I heard the father is quoted as saying 'I consider that son dead,' which is rather shocking, don't you think? Terrible parenting. Terrible. Tut. Anyway, what I hear is that the boy went off to Dissipation City and spent all the money his father had put in his pockets. It's a funny do, my dear, when the father sends the boy away, and yet the boy goes off wealthier than we'll ever be, thanks to the generosity of his father... can't

make head nor tail of it. Anyway, yes, wealthier that we'll ever be, and somehow he manages to spend it all – yes, that boy spent all of it. Every penny. Makes me shudder to try to work out what he could have spent it on. Wine, women – oh, yes, wild women, like that awful, awful Mrs McMattress or whatever her name is at Number Seventeen (what goings-on!) – lavish parties and dinners and all kinds of excess, you know? I don't think I could spend that quantity of cash in such a short time – not without some help, anyway – and he's got nothing to show for it. Nothing. Diddly. Look at it this way: when he came home, he didn't even have any sandals on. Can you imagine such a thing? I was shocked. I really was. Barefoot. Or very poorly shod, with buckles worn off and straps all hanging loose... Oh, I forgot to say that by the time the money was spent, the famine had started and everyone was suffering. Yes everyone. So the boy (and this bit really is quite dreadful, my dear) took a job on a farm, which isn't so bad – after all that's the sort of work he's done all his life – but this time it was a job on a pig farm. Yes. Can you? – well, it's a shocker. A pig farm. A shocker. Tut. Sitting there every day next to those dirty, nasty beasts, and him all hungry and everything, I heard he was tempted to try the slops the pigs were eating... Can you believe that? The vegetables would have been rotten, so that's impossible to imagine, although I suppose if you really are that hungry than you might consider it, but it still sounds far-fetched – some old wives' tale or urban myth oh, yes. Where was I? Oh yes – when he'd been there a while, so

I hear, he starts to realize that if he came home, his father might apologise and he'd be able to be stay, where he belongs. It's so shocking that he got thrown out in the first place. And it's a happy ending that his father might apologise, which is no less then he owes him. Still, it takes two to tango, I always say. I said to Mrs Callston-Wicklow the other day 'It takes two to tango,' and she had to agree. Simply had to. Because it really does. Yes, it makes sense that he would go home and try his luck, doesn't it? I suppose so, I suppose so. When the boy got home (no coat on his back, no proper shoes, hadn't had a decent wash for quite some time, so I hear, or a decent meal – of that I am quite certain), the father felt exactly as guilty as predicted (quite right, too!) and made it up to him and threw that party. Did I tell you about the roast beef, my dear? It was tender, delicious and cooked to perfection. Did you try it? Well, you'll know I'm telling the truth. And the boy had new sandals. And a ring. I don't doubt the boy will soon be selling that, now he's had the taste of the good life. No, that roast beef was lovely – that poor wife of his must have worked her fingers to the bone – to the very bone, I tell you. Mind you, *she's* not quite the pure untouched driven snow she makes herself out to be. But I can read that father like a book. Tut tut tut tut! I can see it a mile off – that father's trying to buy his way into the boy's affections. Hear me out on this – I know. I can tell. I can sense these things in the air, smell them in the ether, if you know what I mean. Stands to reason. Couldn't be anything else. Couldn't be. Terrible parenting. A shocker. I said that to Mrs Callston-Wicklow.

'This is a shocker, Mrs Callston-Wicklow,' I said. 'He's a terrible parent.' And she said 'You are so right my dear.' And I said 'And that Mrs McMattress is no better.' And Mrs Callston-Wicklow had to agree. Had to. Because it's true – or at least, we think it might be. Men coming in and going out at all hours – they can't all be painters and decorators and plasterers and gas fitters – Corgi Registered my foot (or whatever it is these days)! Where was I? Oh yes, the party. Well anyway, that boy's now working long shifts on the farm, and his days of wild living are behind him. Now he's laboring for his father, stopping for slap-up dinners most days, I hear, and then returning to work some more. Stands to reason the father would expect hard work out of him, given all the trouble and heartache and cashflow troubles and anguish he's caused. Although I blame the father, myself. Mrs Callston-Wicklow agrees. Stands to reason. He sends him away, and the boy reacts with wild living. That father's lucky the son came home – I never much liked the look of the old man. His wife works hard in the kitchen, there's no doubt. I'm impressed with her roasting skills, but when it comes to keeping the family together – well, that's another story altogether. Not a hope! Yes, yes, she's doing a little better than she'd done previous, but it'll all fall apart soon enough, you mark my words. Mrs Callston-Wicklow has a few views on the matter. A few views. And she's often right – well, I agree with her at least, which is considerably more than halfway to proof in my book. There's not many things that get past us, I can tell you. Not many. They have to get up pretty early early in the morning to have a chance of catching out the likes of me and Muriel Callston-Wicklow. Still, I for one can't stand here all day listening to your idle chatter. Bye!

Keyboard
left hand only   *alphabet game*
while no standard punctuation is available, there's a wealth hidden in the shift & alt keys, as well as § 1 2 3 4 5 / tab q w e r t y / shiftlock a s d f g / shift ` z x c v b / fn ctrl alt cmd space
Facts! Crass brat gets dad`s © £ wedge Great stewardesses! Raves ≈ ∞ excess $ ravages reverberated
  FASTED
  Grazed @warty veg s™ ±
  Ca~~e 2 #`s seʃ`ʃses
  ~ Be a server! Yet Far Away DAD
~ aged decades ~ stared SAW
  Gets sweater Best Dressed!
  Gïves £ad Ω watc# S#%es Fatted caʃf brazed Beer crates
  Watercresses` aggregate aftereffects desegregated
  ~ Graved FEARED sad razed!
  Abracadabra! Fab! De~deaded!
#@ʃʃeʃʃÙÏa#!

Hasn't he had
enough parties?   *viewpoint*
sour grapes, anger, frustration, legalism from the older brother
Right from the off, I felt cross, I felt left out and I felt things were way out of my control. For a start, there was no discussion about the way life was going to be for me. Oh, no.

Father just upped and sold off a portion of his land to provide wonga for my younger brother to go splurging on booze, women, wildness and debauchery.

Not a word to me about this.

Perhaps Father could have been sympathetic: 'Johnny wants his inheritance, and the only way I can manage to give him one third of my property is to sell it off; this will of course mean we shall have to work a lot harder with what we have left to try to survive…'

At least he could have made it clear to me: 'Your waster brother is being given a fabulous gift, while you shall have to stay to earn your living. Hard luck…'

It was too much to hope that Johnny might have said 'I'm off! Fancy coming with me for the laugh?'

But no, I stay here. I work hard. I'm labouring with all my might to stay alive, unable to throw parties for my friends (although I am a bit worried about my buddy Caleb, who seems over-keen on partying wih a goat, which strikes me as slightly perverse) and having to be the 'good son'.

Every day, I get left alone in the fields, working with the hired men and the servants, because Father avoids any labouring – he just does his thing up on the roof. He really should let it go, realize that Johnny isn't coming back, and put some effort into our survival.

And then (amazingly) the sad loser *does* come back, with some sob story about becoming a hired man, while Father, instead of going off the deep end, like he should have done, no, he goes berserk in the opposite direction and gives him full rights and privileges, plus a ring and a coat and shoes and a party (as if he hasn't had enough parties).

I'm annoyed, upset, frustrated and bewildered that I don't even get an invite; I come in from working in the

61

distant fields and discover this shindig in full swing and have to ask one of the servants what's going on.

'Master Johnny has returned and we're all invited!' he says.

So here's Father, spending money that is effectively my inheritance on a Welcome Home Slap-Up Feed for the whole village to rejoice over this jerk who has done nothing but kick us in the teeth. Makes me mad!

I demand to speak to Dad, who leave the revelries to speak to me.

'What's the problem?' he asks. He's irritated with me for making him leave his guests, I suppose, but this just makes me even more angry.

'I've been here all this time,' I start explaining (yes, maybe somewhat loudly, I admit) 'with little thanks, no opportunities to go even a little bit wild with my buddies, obeying you... and look what you go and do when this –' I struggle to find a word which adequately captures way I feel, so settle for one of the first that comes to mind '– this *hooligan* comes home, having blown all our money on wild women and wickedness, and all you do is just welcome him in, call him son... dismissing, or apparently forgetting all the pain and agony and hardship and angst and suffering he's brought upon you? Where's the justice in this? The little swine should be punished, disowned, thrown out, left to his own devices, cut off, and told to take a long hike. Oh, yes! But instead, what do you do? You give him gifts we can't afford and make a great big fuss of him...'

Once I got into my stride I had no difficulty finding the words I needed to express my rage, frustration and disgust at what my brother had done and the way Dad welcomed him back.

Father tried to calm me down. I didn't hear much of what he said, except that he kept going on about how Johnny was lost but now is found; he was dead but is alive, and how we should be glad. Pah!

First half of alphabet   *alphabet game*
only abcdefghijklm
Fickle-headed kid hijacked, flim-flammed; Dad abled.

Mile. Mile. Mile. Blackjack game; dame became bad.

Keeled. Medic! Ham meal... idea! Make deal.

Mile. Mile. Mile. Came face-a-face: 'Dad? I am...'

'... Ah, me lad!'

Feed – beef (lamblike), diced egg, lime, jam, milk, bleached macadamia cake.

'Dead? Fiddledeedee! All hail!'

Radio four news   *style*

An irresponsible waster was today acquitted at the high court, when his father suddenly decided to drop the charges. The young boy had taken a lage proportion of his father's wealth and become poverty-stricken, following an enthusiastic bout of conspicuous consumption.

When famine struck, he was penniless and had to seek gainful employment with *Porkers'r'Us, Inc.* However, after a short while, the boy ingested rotted vegetation, and realized he should return to his home and seek employment there, which he did. The BBC has learned that the father lavished gifts of jewellery and couteur upon the son.

At a press conference later, the father spoke with some emotion. 'My son was lost, but now he's found; we originally thought he was dead, but now he's alive.'

Doctors confirmed that this was not a genuine case of resussitation, and have concluded that the father must have been speaking figuratively.

Later, the son's older brother was reported to have registered a complaint involving friends, parties and a farmyard quadruped, but this was eventually discovered to have been slightly premature. His financial future is secure.

For further details and pictures, please click on www dot bbc dot co dot uk forwardslash news forward-slash prodigalson (all one word).

G   *alliteration*

'Good grief, give gavelkind*!' groaned Gregory, graspingly.

Greenbacks gotten grieviously, Gregory galloped gleefully. Glam-orous, gregarious gambling girls guzzled greedily.

Greg grew greatly glum: great gains gone.

Grunters' green-grey goodies: grim gunk (gave gastroenteritis). God grants gloriously-gathered guilt/grace glimmerings. Goes!

Greeted! Goodwill! Given gold, galoshes, gymslip, gaiters, grandly grilled grub.

Greengrocery, grapes, gooseberries, grapefruits, greengages.

Greasy goat gravy-grilled; graylings.

Green & Blacks/Galaxy genoese gateaux; ginger-bread, gelato, granita; gobstoppers.

Guileless generator grinned 'Grave? God-raised!'

Goat-free George grumbled grievously.

* a form of partible inheritance where property is apportioned among heirs

H   *alliteration*

Homily:

Hopeful Harry hassles Henry. Huge handfuls! Has homogenous hombres, harlots, harveywallbangers, hooch.

Hellish happening hinders. His hours, hoping, hoping he has ham's hamper. Heavenly, hypersensitive hiatus…

Habitat: homely hireling harvester? Hobo hoves-to hacienda.

Henry hurries: hug, halter-top, hug, hiking-boots, hug, hoop-o'-gold, hug.

Hot hamburgers, hasparat*, hash-browns, hollandaise, hardboiled huckleberry hotcakes, honeycombs, holiday, hokey-cokey!

'He'd had homicide; hoisted homewards. Hallelujah!'

* fictional *Star Trek* Universe spicy Bajoran meal resembling a burrito; made using an eye-watering, tongue searing brine. Beloved of conflicted Lieutenant Ro Laren

Straight-line capitals   *alphabet games*
constrained to letters AEFHIKLMN TVWXYZ which, when capitals, are made only of straight lines
LEVANT KNAVE KELVIN: 'MAKE ME WEALTHY?'
VILE; FELT FINE!
'YEAH, I WILL.' ANXIETY…
'VINE, FILL ME WITH ZEAL; WIZ!'

63

LIKE ALL MATEY MEN; WALTZ FLAXEN-WAVE LAXITY-TWINKLE TAN-FEMALE.

ZENITH... LEVITY; VAIN VIXEN! HEAVILY? MYTH, THINLY!

FAMINE! FEEL NAIVELY MATEY WITH MENIAL FILTHY HAM-FLANK; EAT LEAFY, LEAKY? NAY, HALT! VEXATE...

FAINTLY: 'IDEA – FAITH-HIKE... TAXI!' FAMILY ENMITY? VENT? IN WAY, TENTATIVE KITH LITANY – HAVE NIL TALK TIME.

MMMWAH. ANKLET, KAFTAN-MANTLE, WELLY.

'TAKE KNIFE, VALET. KILL KINE, MAKE FLAME, EAT MEAT; MAINLY VEAL, MAIZE, WHEAT, KALE, MILK-WHEY LATE LAMENT NIX... ANEW, LIVELY!

'AMEN, THANK, EXALT!'

Letters without descenders *alphabet games*

abcdefhiklmnorstuvwxz
but not gjpqy

Kid asks his father for inheritance; leaves with cash. Reaches WasteTown in far-off land and soon the funds are all used on women, drunkenness and wild life.

When famine strikes the land, this fellow seeks work with a bacon-and-ham farmer. 'I'd love to eat some of the food these animals have,' he thinks to himself, in an unwise moment.

Realisation comes to fill his troubled mind. 'I will arise and return to dear old dad and tell him I am not his son from now on; I shall be like one of his hired servants.' When he was still a far distance from home, his father saw him from his view on the roof. He ran to embrace his son and called for a

silver band to adorn one of the four extendable, flexible, knuckled and nailed features of his hand (not a thumb).

In addition, he received a warm winter coat with a collar, buttons and a belt; brown suede (brushed leather) oxford shoes for both his feet; and smothered him with kisses of welcome. He invited friends and the folks that lived near, to a celebration, and killed the fatted calf.

Food that was served included hot roast beef with mustard or horseradish sauce, bread, rice, cous cous, fries, salad, cake, varieties of cheese (and biscuits), and numerous bottles of wine etc.

Father declared 'This son of mine was lost, but is found; he was dead; now he is alive!'

Brother moaned that he had been faithful. So his father explained 'All I have is thine.'

The inheritance would now work out much to the satisfaction of all concerned in the future transaction.

Letters without ascenders *alphabet game*

acegijmnopqrstuvwxyz *but not*
bdfhkl, *inverted commas or capitals*

vexating, overtaxing, angry wanton younger son says to pater give me my part. pa agrees; son goes away to spent-wasting city. money soon gone on amorous, pneumatic, curvacious women; paying wagers, narcotics, unwise encounters; overnumerous...

everyone in country starving; son gets porcine post.

wants to eat piggy gross waste matter. comes to senses; my paters men can eat so it is time for me to return. my opening comment: no more is my name *son*; give me a way to earn my opportunity to stay, juxtaposing me near spent-energy-swap-payment men... so starts a journey; yet even as son is a way away – not proximate – pater runs to gymnastic-greet. gives xx's, ring, coat, moccasins. gets servants to spitroast a cow; party – meat, eggs, veg, wine, oranges, grapes, meringue, scones, etc.

my son was gone yet is returning; son was quite unviva yet now is recovering! moaning progeny got no goat yet gets money, as pa passes

Letters of only
x-height   *alphabet games*
aceimnorsuvwxz *but not*
bdfghjklpqty *or capitals*
erroneous son is unwise, runs on *via maenerosa*.

ruins excursion re one-six-nine swiz or romance: curvaceous women over-numerousness, sauce.

son – non-anorexic – sees swines case-mousse; comes senses. over-nervousness seen soon on avenue. ...as son or man or serve... moccassins, warmer-wear, caress.

summons mum, nieces, cousins re onions, main course, rum n raisin ice cream, scones. o son, vamoose, now recovers – nonconcurrences

Compound words   *wordplay*

Impatientboy demand-persuaded richdato impartall.

Travelsextensively. DissipationVille wildliving ohso-wanton cashsplash, womenwise-unwise. Lootgo.

Countrywidestarvationdisaster.

Pigfarmingsojourn, nutritional-desire d'pigswill.

Came-to-senses, verticalposture-decision, self-abasement speech-plan.

Longwayoff, parentalrun. Kisshug, presentsring-coatsandals.

Bovinedespatch, villageparty.

'Myson lost-and-found; revival-thanksbetoGod.'

Grumbleson gonegoatless; 'Alllhaveisyours'.

Movie script ·   *style*

```
                    Characters:
        FATHER • CHARLIE, his son • DELORES, his fancywoman
             MAITRE D' • WAITER • PIG FARM OWNER
                    Plus TANNOY (v/o)
                Extras (non-speaking parts):
       City passers-by; pub customers; racecourse crowd
            including a dozen so-called friends;
          restaurant diners; celebration partygoers


TITLE SEQUENCE including title caption

                    THE LOST SON
Long push-in establishing shot (Helicopter? see Finance Dept.) of
EXT. FARMHOUSE, DAYTIME.
MUSIC SWELLS Superimpose caption:
                  HOMESTEAD FARM                         CUT TO
```

INT. FARMHOUSE KITCHEN, DAYTIME. Standing by FATHER is CHARLIE, about 20 years old. CHARLIE wears a check shirt, dungarees; ambitious, selfish. Not a natural farmer. FATHER (bearded, 45-50, check shirt, dungarees; sad eyes reveal his reluctance to let CHARLIE go) sits at the table eating breakfast   CUT TO

INT. COWSHED DAYTIME. A THIN CALF munches   CUT TO

EXT. PIG TROUGH, DAYTIME. Vegetable matter, green and healthy-looking. PIG FARM OWNER slings more slops into the trough. Several healthy-looking PIGS chow down on slops

> PIG FARM OWNER (off)
> Come and get it!   CUT TO

INT. FARMHOUSE KITCHEN, DAYTIME, continuing

> CHARLIE
> So will you give it to me, then?   CUT TO

> FATHER
> (eats spoonful of cereal) I already said I would.   CUT TO

> CHARLIE
> When?   CUT TO

> FATHER
> You'd better get packed.   CUT TO

> c/u CHARLIE
> (smiles to himself) Already did it. I'll need to take
> a packed lunch - for the journey, you know.

> FATHER
> (off) Help yourself. Oh, but there's no cold beef.
> We ate the last of it yesterday.
> See what else there is.   FADE TO

c/u of CHARLIE's hands. He is roughly chopping cheese and making sandwiches with thickly hand-sliced bread. Pull back. CHARLIE shoves the sandwich into a bag, and grabs an apple from the bowl in the middle of the table. Pauses briefly, then takes two more, puts them into bag. He turns to leave, but sees stacks of cash with note 'love, Dad' on the window ledge behind him. Puts it all into his bag, fastens buckle   CUT TO

EXT. FARMHOUSE, DAYTIME. CHARLIE puts on hat, walks out frame. FATHER stands silent, sad, at doorway   DISSOLVE TO

EXT. COUNTRY LANE, DAYTIME. CHARLIE walks into frame from left, pan briefly, CHARLIE leaves frame, right   SLOW DISSOLVE TO

EXT. SUBURB ROAD, DUSK. CHARLIE strides from distance towards camera, looking about him. Proceeds ever-closer, and past camera out of frame   SLOW DISSOLVE TO

EXT. CITY STREET, NIGHT. CHARLIE strides into frame from left slowly, captivated by street signs, beggar in doorway, drinkers, drunks, partygoers. Pan with him as he encounters these   CUT TO

EXT. CITY STREET, EXT., DAYTIME. Newsagent's next door to gentlemen's outfitters. CHARLIE enters frame from left, passes newsagent's, stops to look in window, enters shop. Bell RINGS as he opens door   CLOCKSWEEP CUT TO

same, later. CHARLIE emerges wearing velvet suit, carrying parcels. He is carrying a trilby. He sees his reflection in newsagent's window, stops to admire himself, donning hat. He mutters, approvingly   CUT TO

c/u of dustbin. CHARLIE's check shirt, dungarees, boots, and lastly
straw hat are thrown in.   CUT TO
INT. PUB, NIGHT. Girls sit with customers; PIANO MUSIC,
conversation, laughter, occasional BREAKING GLASS. Other tables
show punters playing cards, others with good-time girls on their
laps. Pan and push in to CHARLIE, at a table, with friends,
laughing, with DELORES on his lap. She's about 17, blonde,
sensational-looking, with long legs and a beautiful figure-hugging
dress slashed to the thigh; she sees CHARLIE as a gravy train, of
course.
                DELORES (playing with CHARLIE's hair)
            Can we have some more champagne, then?
                You said you had plenty of money!
                            CHARLIE
            Why not? (clicks fingers at MAITRE D')
                          MAITRE D'
                    (approaching) Sir?   CUT TO
                            CHARLIE
        Champagne, and see what these people want to eat
                and fetch it for us, quick sharp!
                          MAITRE D'
            By all means, sir (signals to waiters)   CUT TO
WAITERS attend to guests, taking orders   CUT TO
                          DELORES
            (to MAITRE D') I want rainbow trout.
            (to CHARLIE) What's your fancy?
                    As if I didn't know!   CUT TO
                            CHARLIE
        You may well be right (kisses DELORES)
            (to MAITRE D') Fetch me thinly sliced
        rare roast beef, and make sure it's rare.
            (to DELORES) That's my favourite!   CUT TO
                          DELORES
                (kisses CHARLIE) Until now!   CUT TO
        c/u on DELORES' hand as it slides down CHARLIE's chest
                                                   FADE TO BLACK
                                                      FADE UP
INT. COWSHED, DAYTIME. Superimpose caption:
                    THREE WEEKS LATER
CALF munches at his feed   DISSOLVE TO
EXT. PIG TROUGH, DAYTIME. Healthy-looking pigs chow down on
vegetables   DISSOLVE TO
INT. FARMHUSE KITCHEN, DUSK. Looking over the shoulder of FATHER,
out of the window as FATHER stands there, staring down the country
lane, longing for his son's return   FADE TO
EXT. RACECOURSE DAYTIME. Hundreds of people milling about; some
visiting book-makers, discussing, others drinking, chatter,
laughter, and many watching the horses   CUT TO
EXT. PADDOCK, DAYTIME. CHARLIE & DELORES, dressed smartly, with a
dozen friends: laughing as he gives cash generously to friends
                          TANNOY (v/o)
        ...three-to-one; Farmer's Boy out of Prodigal's Dad,

    shortening to five-to-one, being ridden today by
   Luke Parable; then comes Coin Hunter at ten-to-one
    and Hornthicket at one-hundred-to-thirty...   CUT TO
                        CHARLIE
         I'm thinking I'll put lots of money down
       on Farmer's Boy - I like the sound of that one!
                        DELORES
        Okay then. Oh, I'm thirsty - can we get a drink?
                                          CLOCKSWEEP CUT TO
FINISH POST as horses rush past - one in front, then two close
together then (after a gap) two more, then two individually
                                                     CUT TO
INT. GRANDSTAND RESTAURANT, DAYTIME Large circular tables set with
silver, elegant crockery and centerpieces; owners are well dressed
and exuberant. CHARLIE & DELORES are with a dozen or so friends at
dinner; WAITER is being highly attentive to empty bottles, used
plates and cutlery. The atmosphere is positive, celebratory; the
music is upbeat and classical; the diners are about to begin their
meal
                      TANNOY (v/o)
             So that's Unforgiving Servant,
          the short-odds favourite by a good
      couple of lengths, followed by Buried Treasure,
             Valuable Pearl and then comes
              New Wine and Sandy Foundation,
        followed at some distance by Coin Hunter,
          and bringing up the rear Hornthicket.
       Just one faller, at the second: Farmer's Boy.
                                                     CUT TO
                        CHARLIE
    (tears up betting slip and throws pieces into the air
     as WAITER serves DELORES) That's a nuisance; still,
            plenty more where that came from!
                        WAITER
                  Your caviar, madam
CHARLIE opens wallet and checks cash; concerned look, as he realizes
there are only a few notes in the wallet.   CUT TO
c/u of wallet, showing dwindling funds
                   CHARLIE (to WAITER)
         Have you cooked the steaks already?
                        WAITER
                   Of course, sir.
                        CHARLIE
         Oh dear. Okay. Never mind.   FADE TO BLACK
                                             FADE UP TO
INT. COWSHED, DAYTIME. Superimpose caption:
                  ANOTHER MONTH LATER   CUT TO
CALF (noticably fatter) munches at his feed.   DISSOLVE TO
EXT. PIG TROUGH, DAYTIME. Thinner PIGS chow down on smaller number
of poorer-quality, grey vegetables   DISSOLVE TO
EXT. FARMHOUSE, DAYTIME. Slow dolly zoom over FATHER'S shoulder, as
he looks down the lane   CUT TO

68

c/u on CHARLIE's hands, wallet empty
                          DELORES
                     (off) Problem?
                          CHARLIE
                     (off) H'mm   CUT TO
EXT. NEWSAGENTS SHOP, DAYTIME as before. SHOP-OWNER is fitting a
newspaper's promotional sheet behind the grill. He steps away,
revealing:
          CROPS FAIL - MAJOR FOOD SHORTAGE PREDICTED
                                                        DISSOLVE TO
EXT. PIG TROUGH, DAYTIME Superimpose cation:
                    ANOTHER THREE WEEKS LATER
Pull back to CHARLIE wearing ragged suit, sitting by trough,
watching scrawny pigs. Vegetables are brown and few in number;
there are no slops.   CUT TO
c/u on CHARLIE; licks lips, staring at trough. Wipes mouth with
back of hand; continues to stare (hold shot for ten seconds or
more). Push in slowly on CHARLIE's eyes until they fill frame. He
stares throughout; then looks up; his face is now additionally
illumined.
                         CHARLIE (v/o)
          I think I just came to my senses;
             there's no need for me to eat
                this stinking stuff that
             isn't fit for the pigs, even.   DISSOLVE TO
EXT. CITY STREET, DAYTIME. CHARLIE strides right to left past
gentlemen's outfitters and newsagents with paper grill. Poster in
grill reads FAMINE CONTINUES; THOUSANDS DIE
                    CHARLIE (v/o) continues
             No, I will arise and go to my FATHER
                and humble myself and ask him...   DISSOLVE TO
EXT. SUBURB ROAD, DAYTIME. CHARLIE strides right to left through
frame; passes beggars in doorways. Track as he exits frame left
                    CHARLIE (v/o) continues
             ... to make me one of his hired hands.
          He may not want to take me in. Lord knows
          I don't deserve even the slightest favour.
             But he may be willing to take me in;
                at least I could ask.   DISSOLVE TO
EXT. COUNTRY LANE, DAYTIME. CHARLIE walks into frame from right,
pan briefly, CHARLIE leaves frame, left   CUT TO
EXT. FARMHOUSE, DAYTIME. FATHER still sits at the window   CUT TO
c/u on FATHER's eyes. They suddenly widen in disbelief, and he
stands up
                          FATHER
                (to SERVANT) Come with me...
Dolly back to reveal FATHER striding, then running out of the gate
EXT. COUNTRY LANE, DAYTIME, continuing   CUT TO
long shot, over CHARLIE's shoulder as FATHER runs joyfully towards
him
                      FATHER (shouting)
          You came back! You came back! My son! (They meet)

```
                    CHARLIE (falls to his knees)
                    Oh Father! I am no longer...            CUT TO
                              FATHER
                    My boy! My dear boy!
               How are you? Oh. I've missed you!
     (FATHER pulls CHARLIE to his feet, embraces, kisses him)
              (SERVANT arrives, panting for breath)
                              FATHER
            (to SERVANT) Fetch me a coat, and a pair of
         my best shoes - look, he hasn't got any shoes on!
   Oh, and get my signet ring from the jewellery box, as well.
   Go and kill the fatted calf, and get the barbecue fired up ñ
              we are going to have a celebration!
                             CHARLIE
            But I am no longer worthy to...
                              FATHER
        Oh, what a party we are going to have! I thought
      I'd lost you. I thought you were dead! I love you son!
                                        CLOCKSWEEP CUT TO
INT. COWSHED, DAYTIME. SERVANT cutting throat of FAT CALF    CUT TO
EXT. FARMHOUSE DAYTIME. A party is in full swing. People are
drinking, eating, dancing, singing. A band plays music; smoke rises
from the barbeque. In foreground, FAT CALF is roasting on a spit.
FATHER stands with crowd; CHARLIE sits on a chair, dressed in check
shirt and dungarees; new hat                                CUT TO
c/u on CHARLIE, eating a heapingly generous portion of thinly sliced
rare roast beef
              CHARLIE (mouth full, gravy dribbles down his chin,
                    which he wipes with the back of his hand,
                         in which he holds a fork)
                    That's my favourite!                    CUT TO
                              FATHER
                    Rejoice everyone!
         My son is no longer lost; he's been found!
                    We thought he was dead,
                but it turns out he is alive!
            Rejoice! Eat! Dance, everyone! Be merry!
                                        LONG FADE TO BLACK
Superimpose caption:
                             THE END
Roll CREDITS
```

The encoded parable *key words from the 3rd Gospel, chapter 15, verses 11 to 24 – find the hidden message*

The Encoded **Parable**: There was a man who had two sons. And the younger of them said **to** his father, 'I need some money fast. Can you please **tell** me how much I will inherit when you die? And then give me whatever share of property that is coming to me.' And **a** while later, story-tellers tell us, the father gave him his inheritance, and the boy left home. With a spring in his step, he took a journey into a far country, and there he squandered his property in reckless living. He gave no attention to wisdom, or indeed anything said to be spiritual; life lacked purpose, so he thought, except 'enjoy it to the uttermost!'.

Various clingers-on and passers-by helped him spend his fortune, until one day his financial means ran out. Destitute, he looked for a job, but the whole land was suffering from a famine. Employed by a farmer rearing lots of pigs, when an inspiration struck him.

'No, I mustn't eat their slop,' he said. 'There is no earthly reason why I can't go and work for my father. Setting his face to this, he planned to tell his father that he was no longer worthy to be called a son, but would work the fields, out in the sun, as one of the hired hands.

While he was still at an extreme distance, his loving father saw him, and shouted 'Huzzah!', interpretation of which was clear to all his servants, as the father had been watching for the boy for weeks.

Running in a way that very rapidly makes progress, he showed his compassion – greeted with a tenderness the boy didn't have to sense or guess.

He gave him a ring, and told servants: 'When you fetch my coat, bring some sandals for his feet, too!' He had the fatted calf slaughtered, and very soon the streets were lined with partygoers.

'Up on your feet – dance!' the father commanded, smiling. 'We feared my boy was down with the lost, but he's found! Was dead but is alive! Scripture says *Bless the Lord, O my soul*, and I shall! We are going to party into the night. And I really do mean properly!' *solution on p325*

How many vowels? *alphabet game*

based on Greener Grass?

1 vowel The son his and left He spent the in wild When struck, he a job pigs and to pods. He to his to go and ask to be a man, he knew he was no worthy to be a on. he was still a long way off, his saw him, ran to him, gave him a ring, a and He the calf and 'This my son was lost and is he was and is

2 vowels home. money living. took tending longed eat their came senses, home hired since longer called While father coat shoes. killed fatted found; dead

3 vowels demanded famine deciding alive again!'

4 vowels celebrated.

5 vowels inheritance

Mega-authorised *style*

1 Thusly unto his father spake an son rude: O, enrich thou me now, I entreat thee, Pa, with many coins that belong hence rightly unto my generation. This said he to him, and he heard it even at the third hour.

2 And lo, his father gave he him an generous inheritance, and straightway he forsook him and went to an distant country, embracing, with abandon, divers customs of the heathen, which are an abomination.

3 There he sojourned many days and nights, wherein he gambled and caroused, yea, and very great was his debauchery.

4 For it came to pass that many wicked harlots did saucily encompass him round about in that place and he was given unto those who eagerly cast lots. He took also fine wine which sparkleth in the cup, looketh good to the eyes and tingleth upon

the lip, with oak aging, blackcurrant notes and an finish akin like unto smoke.

5 Indulged he him purposely in many deliberate severe transgressions, wickedness and unrighteousness of all kinds.

6 He showered they who called themselves friends with his money and right soon – O woe – all the wealth his father had given him was gone, yea verily. Not any tokens of his father's riches remained. No, not one.

❦ 7 Then lean kine did rise up in that land, which stinketh, and an famine held them in destructive grip. And he was sore afraid.

8 He found employ with an Gentile among unclean animals, and envied swill of the swine. He spake All is vapour, meaningless yet toothsomely appealing.

❦ 9 An cohort of many-wingéd seraphs were sent from celestial battlements to whisper an harmonious chorus of much wisdom, saying, Blessed is he who sits upon the throne, and to the King of kings be all honour in the highest.

10 Yet list thee unto us: there is an father in his farm who doth employ hired men which labour with great energy, and who sit each evening in the cool of the day with roasted ox and onions and cucumbers and figs and unleavened bread and yea, olive oil.

11 And consider ye: do not these men also receive each golden tokens as recompense, even from the sweat of their brow?

12 Yea, each hath truly received every day coins of his honest wages, and thusly venture forth in comfortableness to return again to serve his master.

13 Then canst thou not return to thy home and seek leave to become an hired man? For thy father hath many fields to be tilled and ploughed and sown and reaped, for the LORD commandeth the increase, each in its own kind.

❦ 14 Thus visited by wise inspiration from the LORD, came he into the light and unto his senses. He humbled himself right soon.

15 He saith aloud O thou fool! Thou great fool! Lack not my father's hired men any good thing, yet here thirst I and hunger, with grevious travail of spirit. My tongue cleaveth to the roof of my mouth, even unto the third generation.

16 I shall arise, go to my father, meekly kneeling upon my knees and say,

17 Verily, Verily, I say unto thee, I am worthy no longer to be called thy son. I bid thee, restore thou me unto thy bosum, even as but an hireling.

18 So straightway arose the boy. While he was still yet an long way off, his father saw him and rejoiced in his heart. He gathered unto him his garments and ran to press his lips upon the ruddy complexion of his son.

19 The boy had not time to speak unto his father as he had willed since his mouth was stopped with kisses, yea, with great affection. And embraceth he him, bestowing upon him gifts. He gave a ring of precious gold. He spake, saying,

20 Bring an coat of finest linen, yea, and shoes for his feet. Take this news to mine husbandman of cattle: Bring forth thou thy blade and do murder to the fatted calf; for we shall feast with gravy and horseradish and dancing and great celebration.

21 Yea, haste thee to bystanders that do tarry in the dwellings that compass me round about and say unto them Hither, eat ye and drink with us.

22 And so, it came to pass that the men of divers villages attended right quickly with their wives and servants. They gathered and with minstrels did gambol merrily there upon the heath with foxtrots, polkas and the like.

24 And holding aloft roast beef, the father quoth: Rejoice with great joy; sing ye and make merry, for this my son was lost but hath been found; he was dead; now liveth he! Praise be forevermore unto the LORD!

25 And with much zeal his kinsfolk remained and did feast and revel throughout the night, whence cometh deep darkness.

Mime   *language*
using the vocabulary of & Commedia dell'arte physical theatre

The son motioned towards his dad's cash. His father handed over a vast sum, and the boy skipped away, clicking his heels in the air.

He found friends and wasted the money on gambling and debauchery. They danced vigorously, ate grandly or laughed heartily; later they cried bitterly, all with vast theatrical gestures. The money was gone (pull out pocket linings). Famine (rubbing of the abdomen); *sad face*.

The son took a job silently tending pigs, and envied their pods. He stared into space and then licked his lips – as he thought about his father's hired men, eating lunch.

Suddenly, he put on *happy face,* and pointed his index finger vertically, to show he'd had a good idea. He bowed low, rehearsing his humility before his father.

He arose and set off, walking into the hurricane-force wind.

While he was still a long way off, his father shielded his eyes from the sun (yes, he was focusing on distance), jumped with glee and ran to greet his boy. He beckoned to a servant, put a pretend ring on the boy's finger, buttoned up a see-through coat and fitted new unseen sandals on his feet. He rubbed the ground with one foot while indicating horns, and drew an invisible dagger from a scabbard and across his throat. He wound the handle on a spit, wiping his brow from the heat of the fire, and used the knife again to cut slices and serve them. A wide sweep included all the neighbourhood.

He climbed into an imaginary pulpit, and mouthed, white-faced, to a mind's-eye crowd. He elaborately communicated *lost* (trapped in the traditional glass box, of course) and *found, dead* and *alive*. Jazz hands!

Ill-contained
Thesaurus attack   *wordplay*
*substituting words from **Greener Grass?** with little reference to original meaning*

The male child insisted upon his birthright; furthermore, socialism domicile. He exhausted the cash in untamed clerical benefice. At the time want industrial actioned, he seized work inclined towards crude iron and extended to consume their fuel housing.

He regained consciousness his impressions from multiple stimuli, settling on square entitling player to collect £200 self-guiding and solicit being a rented male adult, seeing as he was intimate with; he was rejection extending further commendable but dull to exist alerted a boy offspring.

Even as he was stationary, a yearn momentum through water rancid, his ancestor wood-cutting tool him.

He stood for election to him, collapsed him a boxing platform, a thin layer and playing card dispenser. He used up spare time the

73

subcutaneous semi-solid tissued mini-iceberg and performed a religious ritual.

Progenitor stated 'This my chip off the old block was confused and is established; he was exact and is zesty in addition to a previously-mentioned characteristic!'

Classified section — *style*

1 shekel per column-nanocubit

notices

WEALTHY FARMERS: don't even think of giving away your hard-earned inheritance! Invest in Pigs-R-Us Double Underlined Unit Trusts. *Lardon, Chop, Rasher Gammon & Co, Solicitors (Gentile)*, Waster City Road, Jerusalem.

for sale

BEST BEEF DRIPPING: just 2 shekels per ephah. Available now from A Certainman's Farm, Jericho.

VEGETABLES GRADE B (some misshapen) suitable for animal feed; sorry, not fit for human consumption. One shekel per bucketful. SlopsRUs, Nineveh

situations vacant

HIRED HANDS NOW HIRING @ Certainman's Farm. Jericho. Civilised board & lodging provided. No more time wasters, please. Absolutely no goats.

CALF-FATTENING BEEF-OLOGIST required. Join our team and bring your skills to maximize meat-to-feed input ratios and rapidly increase BMI. Not suitable for vegetarians. MeatULike Direct. Apply steak.co.il

VERY URGENT – pigtenders needed @ Double Underlined Middleback Sties, Dissipation City. Full on-the-job training provided; due to lessons learned by experience, no Hebrews, thank you.

services

RAZZLE 'N' DAZZLE CASINO New! Pontoon, Craps, Slots, Poker, Roulette, etc. Spread betting: all forms of sport, politics, military turmoil. Licenced bar open until 4am. Experienced cashiers, expert croupiers, bar staff. Dress code: shirts, no trainers, no roller-blades. 666 Low St, Dissipation City. Happy Hour 6-8pm Thurs & Suns.

Also: apply Madame Florrie for hourly rates. Exotic tastes & personal preferences eagerly embraced by our staff. *Prodigals Bar 'n' Grill-aGoGo*, Upper Rooms, 69 High St, Dissipation City, Israel. Website: hooker.co.il

PARABLES ETC INTER-PRETED while u wait; also healing, wonders, etc. Hear J O'Nazareth, on his First & Final Tour of various locations around Judea. All, incl. Galileans, divorcées, selfishly wealthy young men, random children & diseased outcasts fully entertained; demonized pariahs cleansed while you wait; scribes & pharasees, Greeks, Hebrews, Romans etc all welcome: hypocrites a speciality. No fee. Personal conversations entered into

corrections & errata

THE PUBLISHER wishes to make clear that previously-reported rumours of the death of Mr Certainman Jnr must have been greatly exaggerated. We apologise for any confusion or distress caused. To demonstrate our good faith in this matter, a celebratory party (entirely underwritten by the publisher) will be held at the Farm tonight, 6.30pm. All welcome; PBAB&B.

MISPRINT CORRECTION late editions of the Night Final yesterday unfortunately carried the name of the farmer in error as *Mr Cretainman*. This should have read: *Mr Cretinman*.

personal

BILLY-BOY COME HOME: all is forgiven.

Visual — *style*

A tall, fair-haired boy who looked about 20 or so (wearing a well-worn brown jacket, a long dark grey tunic and sandals) approached his bearded, 50 year-old father in the off-white farmhouse with the red tiled roof, by the dark green tree, bedecked with ripe lemons.

The older man looked concerned at the conversation, and took out three blue-covered hardback books to examine rows and rows of black and red figures, before counting out gold, silver and bronze-coloured coins and several green notes.

The boy neatly stacked the money into a black bag, packed his orange jumper and some highly decorated underwear into a blue backpack and set off down the country road, which was framed with evergreens, bushes, shrubs, flowers and lush green grass verges, sparkling and beautiful in the bright, hot sunshine of the Middle East.

After three days' walking, as evening approached, he encountered a busy, brash street in Dissipation City, where lights flashed white and yellow. Green, red and gold banners waved in the breeze, attracting attention to the various gambling and drinking houses.

The boy quickly became involved with consuming long sparking drinks topped with fruit and straws and sparklers and being entertained by perfect-teethed, red-lipped blondes and brunettes in miniscule black satin dresses, with plenty of darkly tanned flesh on display.

After a while, the boy's drinks grew more pale, and the girls less attractive, until his gold and silver ran out completely. Penniless, he wondered what to do. Then the news came through that the land was now in famine.

All the fields, formerly of yellowing corn had turned to grey; all the purple and black berries had withered into dull browns; all the green, red, yellow and orange fruit was enfeebled and had become unappealing and wizened. Black, dark days followed as the land fell into the depth of famine.

The boy, now without a coat of any colours, sat by a dirty trough where grey hogs sniffled among grey and brown thrown-out vegetables. The boy's cheeks were hollow and his eyes sad as he longed to try the pale, limp food the pigs were eating.

Suddenly, he slapped his forehead. He had come to his senses.

'I will return home and become a servant.'

He walked along the dirty, dusty rutted track that was bordered by greying, scorched, unwatered vegetation and tangled brambles.

But while he was still a long way off, his father saw him from his terrace-roof, ran to him and hugged him by placing one hand on each of the boy's shoulder blades and pressing his chest upon the boy's. He called for a bright gold ring, a yellow coat, a pair of leather sandals with highly-polished metal buckles and ordered his servants to get the bonfire going.

Later, the orange and red flames danced merrily as the long, dark brown carcass of the fatted calf slowly rotated on its shiny metal spit. Smoke curled lazily past the redwood tree near the off-white farmhouse with the ochre tiled roof, and the villagers had pink gins, pale ales, lilac wine with cinnamon toast and blueberries.

They had whitebait, black-eyed peas, apricots with cream, green-gages, Golden Delicious and Russet apples, chocolate brownies, red salmon with purple-sprouting broccoli and greens; and there was brown toast with Golden Spread or Golden Syrup as well as mustard, plus olives, oranges, tangerines and plums.

Meanwhile, the red-faced older brother complained that he'd been marooned to a colourless life of goatless, partyless chores.

The father smoothed his greying beard (some might say it was a sable silver'd) and said 'All I have is yours. But my boy was lost but is found. He was dead, mouldering, still, grey; but now he's fair, ruddy, healthy-looking and very alive! Look, everyone!'

Fault _____ plot
Tragedy

And so their fights continued; Richard and his father raged at each other long into the night, never seeing eye-to-eye and always having different expectations of how the farm could sustain them through the impending famine.

'Don't you see, old man? Are you just being obtuse?' The boy threw the dregs of his wine into the fire. 'We have to get rid of all the animals and everything that is a drain on our resources; only then can we turn every acre over to food production for ourselves and for the village. There's no point in giving grain to the horses to get work out of them if we perish in the meantime. Healthy goats and fattened calves won't last long once we are dead, you misguided old fool!'

His father was sad, but anger overwhelmed him.

He slammed his hand on the table, upsetting the wine bottle and sending the mangy dog scurrying from the room.

'That's just about enough from you, boy! I don't like your tone, and I resent your constant disagreement. And I won't tolerate your rudeness! You need to learn a few lessons in taking responsibility and showing a little bit of gratitude... and I know

exactly what will be the making of you.'

He turned, walked away, pushing past the hired hand, leaving his son staring, frowning, seething.

The next morning, Richard discovered his dad meant business. He'd collected together a great deal of money, and gathered it into a bag on the table. Resting on top of the bag was a hastily scribbled note.

My dear boy,

Take your inheritance and go. I pray that you will survive the famine that is predicted. Leave today, and don't return until you are ready to give appropriate respect. I won't tolerate your aggression or your heartless remarks.

_Now the feeling's gone, I can't go on – when you lose control and you've got no soul, it's hard to bear. Perhaps I really should be holding you, loving you..._*

But I don't think I can at the moment.
Dad

Richard screwed up the note, and snatched the bag, which was heavier than he'd imagined. He grabbed a small loaf and one of the jars of oil from the shelf, and left the house. He stepped onto the highway, thumbing a lift on an ox cart to the big city.

A couple of months later, he'd made a number of friends among the gambling fraternity, and met a few girls who seemed to be attracted to him. It was probably the money, he knew, but it was fun; that was a whole lot better than life had been when he was working on the farm. He gave his father little thought, and hadn't noticed the headlines which seemed to suggest that the feared famine was no longer impending; it was arriving.

RICHARD'S FATHER was deteriorating fast. He bitterly regretted throwing his son out – more, even, than the financial hardship that had caused. Each day he kept watch on the roof, despite the blazing heat, talking to himself.

'But he had become intolerable. He had to go. Had to. Am I not to blame for the way my son turned out? Surely I am to be held to account, at least in some part. About a third. Perhaps a half? His negative ways and bad attitude and rudeness are my fault. Maybe sixty per cent. I cannot... Oh, oh, he's in danger, I know it!

'And it's down to me. I did send him away, after all. At least three-quarters of the blame, if not more. Say four to one against me. It is warm today. My nails need trimming. Oh, Richard, where are you, my son, my loved son? I am to blame almost entirely. He had to go to teach me this hard lesson. He had to. My fault. All my fault. Yes, all my fault. My responsibility. My error. I was too harsh with him, and drove him away.

'My hair is growing long, too. Like Nebuchadnezzar. I cannot stand this heat, this loneliness, this guilt. Entirely my fault. He was innocent! And the animals have broken into the grain store and our reserves are rapidly diminishing. I can't remember why that's bad... not as bad as I have been towards dear, sweet misunderstood Richard; I should suffer for it. He was without error or blemish...' He raved in whispers, admonishing himself, weeping, tearing at his clothes, becoming more sad and confused each day.

LIFE IN the fast lane was growing dangerous, as Richard had lost his handkerchief, all his money was gone and so were his 'friends' (Romans and countrymen alike), including one girl who distributed symbolic flowers and took a fatal swim; another who refused to flatter her father and was misunderstood; and a third bitten by a snake while waiting for a servant to fetch milk from an ass[†]. The famine had struck.

'I shall go to the countryside, and get a job in the agrarian economy. Perhaps animal husbandry...'

He found a post at a pig farm, and was looking after the thin, scrawny beasts as they rooted about among the rotting vegetation they were given. Such was his hunger, he was about to pick out the least mouldy pod; and that was when he came to his senses.

'The hired men on my father's farm eat well; I should set aside my pride and return. I'm in this mess is because of my horrible attitude – it's entirely my fault. So I shall arise and go home and say *Make me one of your hired men. I am no longer worthy to be called your son.*' He got up and went back home.

RICHARD WAS still beyond the furthest hill, completely out of sight of the view his father had from the roof. He was muttering to himself; his lips constantly moving.

'Completely my fault,' he mumbled. 'I'm a wicked man and a bad father and a rubbish farmer. The only ones who eat well around here are the calves. I am not cut out for farm management, which has to include the maintenance and welfare of hired hands as well as animal husbandry.

'I am totally to blame for my son's bad ways. I deserve nothing. I deserve to be the dead one. At least then his inheritance (which he's already had) will have been the right thing to do...

I don't deserve to live. My son is probably dead in the foreign land, due to the famine. I have nothing to live for. He's totallylost, and it's one hundred percent down to me.'

Such was his loss of mental faculty, he wandered down the steps from the roof (nearly falling, twice), took a jar of oil from the shelf in the kitchen, and slopped it onto his hair and beard and clothes.

Such was his anguish at his own error (as he saw it) in raising such a tormented son, he stepped, purpose-fully, dangerously close to the fire, where the last of the hired men was roasting one of the fatted calves.

Such was his self-loathing and twisted judgement of himself, he deliberately allowed the flames to fed hungrily at his oil-soaked coat. Immediately his hair and beard and coat and tunic were ablaze.

Despite the efforts of the hired man, Richard's father's misery and ravings were over surprisingly quickly (perhaps his heart failed?).

His lifeless corpse lay smouldering in the dusty farmyard.

Three minutes later, Richard appeared over the horizon, walked slowly towards the farm, and readied himself to be humble before his father. The hired hand – frightened, scorched from his efforts to extinguish the suicide pyre of his Lord and Master, and confused at the disastrous timing – walked out to greet him. Their conversation was full of sadness, regret and blame.

The villagers attended the funeral, and there was no rejoicing. Richard said at the wake 'I was lost but now I have found that my father, who was alive, now is dead; and it's all my fault.'

When his older brother returned from the fields at the end of the day, he was horrified at the scene before him. There was a great deal of shouting and recriminations; their relationship was never restored.

Richard carried the guilt with him for the rest of his life, and his brother was consumed with anger and bitterness, despite the great wealth that was now his.

* lyrics to *Tragedy* written by Barry, Robin & Maurice Gibb; recorded by the Bee Gees on *Spirits Having Flown* (1979)

† referring to tragic female characters from Shakespeare: Ophelia (from *Hamlet*); Cordelia (from *King Lear*); Cleopatra (from *Antony & Cleopatra*)

Franglais   *language*

raw translation on p325 (le translátion tartare sur la page trois-cent vingt-cinq)

Le garçon dit a son père 'Donnez-moi maintenant l'argent qui tu est allezing de donné à moi comme votre funeral, s'il vous plait.'

Le fermier d'accord, et son fils départé via à la sortie, rapidement. Il commence le vivre sauvage, qui involvé les mademoiselles de virtu facile (qui est trés, très mauvais, parce que très, très sportif); *Vingt et Un, Baccarat, Chemin de Fer*; cognac, le champagne; et beaucoup de grand déjeuner *Cordon Bleu* – avec juliennes, poussin, les haricots français, pommes de terre rosti, divers joux et plus de crèmes brûlées, profiteroles et tartes tatins.

Tout d'argent frite-ered, et les femmes chèries dépardue. Sans francs, sans amis, sans crêpe. Fils regardez les jambons. Manger pigswill est inderdit (parce que, malheuresement, il est très macabre).

Poof! un révèlation. Les domestiques du Papa ont repas tous les jours après leur travail… J'ascendai, allez a nous champs des animaux, et dit 'Je suis non meritante appellé *fils*; employez-vous moi, si vous plait, a prolétariat.'

Il returnez a la maison, mais Papa voyez à point de avantage, et arrivé tout de vittesse. Papa donnez un ring d'or, un vestment, les flip-flops et bifsteak.

Maintenant, le party revellais avec mille feuilles, sorbets, fondants, roulards, sachertorte – patisserie variouse – et créme anglaise, et plus de chocolat.

'Mon fils etait perdu ; il sont trouvé ! Il etait mort; mais vive mon fils! Donnez-vous plus de *merci-bien*s a mon Dieu, ou est très magnifique!'

Frére dit 'Je travaille trés gros pour vous, mon père, mais tu ne granté pas une partie pour mon amis, ou une goat. Je suis tres vexed!'

'Tous j'avait est vous's. Mais nous célébré maintenant!

One hundred words   *wordplay*
tallied
Son asked his father for his inheritance, and went to[10] a foreign land to spend it in wild living. Soon[20] all the money was gone, and famine struck.

The boy[30] sought work in a piggery, where he longed to eat[40] the pigs' scraps. He came to his senses and planned[50] to return, intending to offer his services as a farmhand. [60]

But while he was still a long way off, his[70] father ran to him, greeted him with kisses and various[80] meaningful gifts, and staged a do.

'My son was lost,[90] but now he's found; he was dead, now he's alive![100]

Fifty words   *wordplay*
tallied
Son grasped his inheritance; wasted it in wild living. Famine[10] struck suddenly. He wanted to eat the pigfood. Inspiration dawned[20], so he returned to offer to become an hireling. But[30] while still a long way off, his father greeted, gave gifts[40] and rejoiced. 'My son was dead, but now lives!'[50]

Twenty-five words   *wordplay*
tallied
Son took his inheritance; wasted[5] all. Destitute, famine-struck, desired pigfood.[10] Came to senses! Returned humbly.[15] Father welcomed generously, celebrated. 'Son[20] was dead; now he's alive![25]

Ten words   *wordplay*
Credited, debited. Famined! Humbled, inspired. Returned, greeted, gifted, forgiven, welcomed.

Five words   *wordplay*
Rebelling. Reducing. Revealing. Repenting. Restoring.

Wise enough   *viewpoint*
Madam Sadie
Oh, it was sordid, yes, but a whole lot of fun while it lasted.

I always wanted to run a high-class gin joint, but a 'low-class drinking shop with an exclusive reputation' was the best I ever achieved. Yes, *Saucy Sadie's Sarsapirilla'n'Spirits Speakeasy A-Go-Go* was a brief success.

We had a long, highly popular bar, with a wide range of drinks available, including cocktails, shorts, beers, wines and vermouth; we provided snacks and light meals; we had a pool table and some gaming machines, too.

There was a secluded back room for card games and for doing deals – and the local police used to leave us alone (apart from the detectives who used to come to play five card brag, of course).

We had dancing girls, who would accompany gentlemen upstairs for a small consideration (so long as I got my cut, naturally) and no questions were asked, not even by the policemen. Some of the girls were more popular than others, as you mght expect.

I do recall one young man who seemed equally keen on all my girls, because when he came into the bar of an evening, he spread his money out on the table, and the girls would practically fight each other to get his attention, knowing that he was very generous and heavily loaded. Every time he turned up, we were quids in. We must have made an absolute bomb out of that fellow, you know.

Then the liquor licences became more expensive and we tried to branch out into the import-export game. We even set up a still in the back yard outbuildings, but the ingredients were hard to find and then income was dropping. Eventually, of course, we went the way of everyone in the district, and there was no food to cook, no grain to distill, no booze to stock our bar, and, naturally, no customers.

The famine hit us very hard, and the girls had to find legitimate jobs in offices, factories, the homes of members of the nobility, kitchens, hospitals…

I survived, because I'd been wise enough to invest the surplus from my income into a small pig farm, which did okay even during the famine. The quality of meat we could produce was low, since the only food the animals got to eat was rotting pods and husks and other people's throwaways. But we didn't pay huge wages to the farmhands, so that all balanced out.

Yes, sometimes I wonder what happened to those girls I used to employ. And to the barstaff. Yes, and to the really down-on-their-luck men who looked after the pigs – some of them didn't stick around for very long, it has to be said.

But I don't worry too much about the customers.

They always seemed to me to be able to look after themselves. They knew what they were doing was illegal, unwise, immoral perhaps. It was their choice.

After all, if I hadn't provided them with the opportunity, someone else would, then they would've made all the profits, and there's no point in letting anyone else walk away with the cash, is there?

I   *alliteration*

Inheritance ill-gotten (indupitably), independent irksome irritating ingrate Isaiah ignobly imparts it (intentionally itinerant idealist), impishly intoxicated.

Inevitable international internal illness.

Inkling, inspiration, illumination! Inducement!

'I'll implore, inquire, ingratiate, interlope, indelicately. Interchange institutions…'

80

Impressive isodiametric* ingot-insignia issued. Impassioned inter-locution.

'Incinerate immaculate, immature impala, inter-alia; ices.

'I'm inclined Isaiah-ward! Irremeable†? Irredeemable? Irony: isn't indestructable, incurable, immutable; is intra-mural!'

* having diameters of equal length (i.e. round)
† not allowing any possibility of return

J _alliteration_
see JQXYZ (p261)

Peanut butter sandwiches _style_

children's storybook with Mummy's interjections and questions

Once upon a time there was a happy, happy farmer named Farmer Giles. He was a very, very rich man and had a big, big farm. On his farm he had cows _(moo moo)_ and sheep _(baa baa)_.

How many cows can you see? Yes, that's right, there are seven cows, aren't there? How many geese? You're good at counting! And how many sheep can you see? Yes! Ten sheep.

On his land he grew barley and oats, but mostly wheat.

Do you know what lovely things to eat we can make with wheat? Yes, good, we can make bread for sandwiches, or we can make cakes, or spaghetti, or meusli, depending on which bit we use. We like meusli for breakfast, don't we? And pasta for dinner? Yes, wheat is very useful.

In his farmyard were ducks on the pond, (quack quack splash splash), cats in the barn (mieow, mieow) and the farmer's faithful dog Towser by his side (woof woof).

'Good dog, Towser!'

Now, Farmer Giles has two sons; one called Ernest, which is a quite nice name, although a bit old-fashioned. The other son is called Waster.

That's an unusual name, isn't it?

Another fine sunny day dawned. There were always lots of jobs to be done on the farm.

The cows had to be rounded up and milked and then sent back to pasture (moo moo).

The sheep had their drive-through bath and then got busy, mowing the lawn (baa baa).

The crops were growing in the fields, and needed care and attention; the ducks were splashing in the pond, (quack quack splash splash) and the cats were fast asleep in the barn (purrrr, purrr).

And Towser was faithfully at Farmer Giles' side (woof woof).

'Good dog, Towser!'

Can you see the cats in the barn? Yes, they're all asleep! How many ducks can you see? Some are swimming, and some are having their lunch. Where's Towser? And which crops do you think are growing the best – the wheat, the cabbages or the corn?

Once the work was done, Ernest went to see friends, but Waster had his tea (a glass of fizzy pop and a couple of munchy, crunchy peanut butter sandwiches – his favourite), and went to speak to his father.

'Dad,' he said, 'I've made a decision. I'm a bit fed up with living here, working for you and doing as I'm told. But I've had enough. So, gather up all the money that you'll leave for me when you die, and let me have it right now, in this bag, please.'

It was a strange thing to ask, but the Farmer loved his son. 'I'll give you

81

your share of my wealth, my boy,' he said. It did make him rather sad, though.

The farmer was kind, wasn't he? How do you think he feels? Look at his face! I think you're right, he's sad to see him go.

Next day, before sunrise, Waster got up and packed his things. He said goodbye to his dad, to Ernest and to Towser. He didn't say goodbye to the cats, as they were asleep, and he didn't say goodbye to the ducks, as only a foolish person would talk to ducks. And he set off on his way.

He had all his money wrapped up in a red-and-black-spotted handkerchief tied on the end of a stick. He also took a packed lunch – fizzy pop, and munchy, crunchy peanut butter sandwiches – his favourite. He marched out of the farmyard, up the lane, across the meadow and up the road to the top of the distant hill, to the old tree that everyone said was a funny shape.

Can you see the tree? What shape do you think it looks like? That's a funny shape for a tree, isn't it?

He didn't look back, but walked straight past the tree.

Can you see Waster walking away from the farm? Where has he put his packed lunch? Yes, in the red-and-black-spotted handkerchief!

After a few days, he arrived in the Big City, where he soon met people who were very happy to help him spend his money.

He bought plenty (lots and lots) of peanut butter sandwiches and lashings of fizzy pop, and went to musical shows almost every evening. He taught himself some new card games and bought quite a few toys and met lots and lots of interesting people.

Everyone was glad to see him and to see his money. They started to spend it, quickly.

Why do you think so many people wanted to be Waster's friend? Yes, because he had lots of money and was willing to spend it. Were they really 'friends' at all? Do you think those people were the best sort of friends to have? No, I agree with you!

One day, Waster noticed that his red-and-black-spotted handkerchief was getting rather empty, and that nearly all of his money was gone. He needed to think about what he was going to do, so he spent his last few pennies on a glass of fizzy pop and a munchy, crunchy peanut butter sandwich – his favourite. As he munched, he read the local newspaper. The headline read 'Hunger Warning: Peanut shortage; wheat famine; fizzy pop drought.' The article continued 'There will be scarcity, shortage and famine in this country very soon, so get ready to be very hungry.' How awful!

Oh dear. Just when his money had run out, too! That's rather bad timing, isn't it? How do you think he felt? Yes, I think he was sad, too.

Next day, he was hungry, as he hadn't had any munchy, crunchy peanut butter sandwiches or any fizzy pop.

So Waster decided to sell his red-and-black-spotted handkerchief, and with the money he bought one last munchy, crunchy peanut butter sandwich and a small bottle of fizzy pop.

The day after that, Waster was hungry again, and all the people who had pretended to be his friends ran away when they found out that he had no money left.

Oh dear, it looks like we were right. They weren't really his friends at all, were they? No! I think they were just trying to see what they could get from Waster. Not very nice at all. What a shame!

After a week or two of being very hungry, Waster eventually found a terrible job looking after pigs (oink oink).

Those poor pigs were being fed on nasty, stale, half-eaten peanut butter sandwich crusts made damp with tiny drops of fizzy pop that was no longer fizzy but quite warm, too. Nasty. Waster was so hungry that he nearly ate some of those smelly, rotten, thrown-out food scraps.

They would have tasted horrible, wouldn't they? Do you think the pigs enjoyed the taste? No, neither do I. Why would anyone even think about eating food like that? Yes, especially if they are very, very hungry indeed. How hungry would you be if you didn't have anything to eat for two weeks? Yes, so would I!

But then, Waster suddenly realised what he should do.

'I know what I must do!' he said. 'I will get up, go back home to my dad at the farm and tell him how sorry I am for being so selfish and foolish. I will ask him if I can work for him like one of the farmhands.' His tummy rumbled very loudly.

How loudly do you think his tummy rumbled? Oh, yes, that's very loud, isn't it?

He started the journey home at once, without saying goodbye to the pigs (because talking to pigs is almost as silly as talking to ducks), and without saying goodbye to the pig farmer, either, which was a bit rude, but Waster was in a hurry.

He walked and he trudged and he ran a little and walked again; then he hiked, marched and walked some more.

It was a long way home.

By the time he got to the old tree that everyone said was a funny shape, his shoes were worn out. One of them fell off, as the sole had worked loose. He couldn't walk with one shoe on and one shoe off, so he threw them both away and walked in bare feet. Well, this was a bit painful, so he sort of ambled, tottered, shuffled and staggered.

That sounds very uncomfortable, doesn't it? Do you think he could walk a great distance like that? Can you see him on the far, far horizon? But look, who is that, up there on the rooftop, looking out for him? Yes, his dad! What do you think he felt? Let's see what happens next.

While he was still a long way off, Farmer Giles spotted Waster coming up the road. He ran to meet him, and Towser ran along beside him (woof woof).

Farmer Giles hugged his son Waster because he was so pleased to see him. In his excitement, Towser jumped up a few times (woof woof woof!).

'Get down, Towser!'

The farmer kissed Waster. He gave him a coat, a ring and new shoes.

Look, he's wearing the ring! That's a big coat, isn't it? What colour is it? Who do you know that has a coat like that? No, no, neither do I. What sort of shoes were they? And where is the big brass buckle? Do you know anyone who has shoes like that? No, neither do I. These are very special gifts, aren't they? What do you think Waster was feeling?

Waster was just going to say 'Dad, I am so sorry that I have been foolish and spent all the money. Please let me come and work on the farm as one of the farmhands, tending the crops, milking the cows and looking after the farmyard…' But before he could say any of that, his father welcomed him and forgave him. He went to a lot of time and trouble to make it clear to everyone who knew him that he was very pleased that his son had returned.

He's a very kind farmer, isn't he? How can you tell that Waster was being welcomed back into the family? It's nice to get a big hug, isn't it? What does it feel like to be a part of the family? Yes, loved; like you belong; and it feels better than having the sort of friends Waster had – and a lot nicer than feeling so hungry you nearly eat food scraps!

Farmer Giles threw a great party, inviting everyone locally to come and join in the fun. They played Twister, skittles, Snap and Take Two and the musicians played as well, with fiddles (scratch-scratch) and accordions (wheeeeze), a packing-case bass (gerdum-dum-dum) and a drummer (boom-ber-boom-boom-chish).

Can you see what the drums were made from? Yes, you're right – some wooden boxes, and a dustbin lid! What a noise!

The ducks quacked along, and the cats couldn't get to sleep because it was so loud! What a shame!

Farmer Giles made a speech, toasting Waster with glasses of fizzy pop. 'My son was lost, but now he's found! We thought he was dead, but now he's alive again! Rejoice! Do please tuck in.'

Camp fires burned merrily, and there was dancing and laughter. Farmer Giles arranged for roast beef for everyone, and lots of cake, and biscuits for Towser. 'Good dog, Towser!'

And right in the middle of the long row of trestle tables was a huge jug of fizzy pop and the biggest plate you ever saw, piled high with…

Can you guess? Something munchy, crunchy… Yes, of course you can! Very good. I think it would be good to say a prayer and thank God that we are a family and that we don't ever feel hungry enough to want to eat mouldy sandwiches. Shall I say a prayer, or will you?

Right, time to snuggle down and I'll put the light out. Night night, God bless. Sleep tight, I love you, see you in the morning, sweetheart.

Expensive deleted DVD scene *style*

Scene 152: Boy is walking home. (insert) Cut to: Father, bored of standing waiting for his son to return, hires a Bond-girl-type helicopter pilot *(casting: Denise Richards/Halle Berry/ Rosamund Pike etc)* to take him on a aerial reconnoitre of the area, and he sees his son returning a from a very, very long way off, through a great crowd of authentically-costumed Victorian jugglers, fire-eaters and minstrels. He also sees a spacecraft emerge through the atmosphere of the second moon, with lights a-flashing and mysterious rays emanating from its base.

Wild music 3D effects accompany this; aliens perform a line-dance on the bridge of their ship as Julia Roberts (dressed in chiffon, with platinum and diamond jewellery), a heavily tattooed Sylvester Stallone, and – time-travelled for the role – Pope Gregory IX (1170-1241) make very brief cameo appearances serving drinks and canapés.

Then, as the Famine Police Jet Fighters (no explanation possible, none given) loom into view, firing rockets, and the set is destroyed. The helicopter is also hit, but before it explodes in a vast ball of flame, father jumps out, landing in a 3D haystack (CGI obviously) in a field near the road where his son continues to walk.

Cut back to Scene 15: Boy walks homeward as Father, arrives in front of him… *continues from here*

The prodigal confectioner   *keywords*

where it all began: sweets & chocolate bars commonly available in the UK

Once upon a time, a farmer had two sons. One of them was a **Smartie** and good looking, with **Curly Wurly** hair (with **Highlights**), although he was slightly **Flakey**, and turned out to be a little bit **Twisted**.

He said to his dad 'You know what I'm after?' His volume dropped to a **Wispa**. 'Gold! I'd like to talk to you on that **Topic**. My life could do with a **Boost**, so give me my inheritance. Let me take some **Time Out**.'

His dad tried to **Fudge**. 'You want a share of my money?'

'Yes, Pa,' replied the son, 'and some of **Mars**.'

Eventually the father agreed, which was what the Italians might call **Kinder Bueno**, and handed over all his **Bounty**. The son did up his **Buttons**, put on his **Snickers**, left the farm and went off to spend his dad's fortune. He took a **Picnic** and walked, not waiting for a **Green & Black**'s **Double Decker**.

Soon he found himself in a large city, in a large **Echo**ing shopping Mall, known as **Quality Street**, where people mocked the shops. They were known as **Malteasers**. The farmer's

son visited a night club where they played music by **M&M** and there were **Minstrels** playing **Tunes** while customers played **Skittles.**

And there were female dancers known as the **Turkish Delights,** who had tummys that could **Ripple**. It was a **Treat** to see them, and the son enjoyed all these **Revels**, and soon his **Gold Coins** were spent.

His friends were gone and so was his livelihood. The weather turned cold and he saw a **Snowflake.** For a while he was a **Drifter**, and he finished up on a pig farm. It was run by a moaning, complaining old woman who had no teeth, and she was known as **Wine Gums**. The boy had to **Lion** the ground to sleep, perchance to **Dream**, making his pillow from leafy branches with not too many **Twix**.

He was peckish and got the **Munchies** and ended up longing to **Chomp** on the pig's food, which was **Crunchie**, but obviously he had to **Chewitt**. He looked up at the **Milky Way** and the **Planets** and the **Galaxies** beyond, and he came to his **Senses**[*] and repented of his sin.

When he got home, **Believe**[†] it or not, his father forgave him, welcomed him and gave him a new pair of **Snickers**[‡]. He decided to have a **Celebration**, but his older brother was a right **Wotsit.**

*KitKat Senses †Limited Edition Mars Bar (2006 World Cup, 2016 Euros) ‡Snickers Duo

Future   *style*

Much later on, villagers will revel with enthusiasm, since the calf will be fattened for the purpose of being served in baps, having been carved, roasted, and previously killed (this will be understood in years to come, as predestination).

Meanwhile, the son will ask his father for his share of the inheritance, and the father will dish it out.

The son will go off and blow all the loot in no time, and then he'll begin to suffer when famine strikes the land.

He'll get a job looking after pigs, and he'll even wish to eat their food. Eventually, he'll come to his senses and he'll decide to return home, repentant.

He'll make his way, but before he can get to say what he intended, his father will run down the road and will hug him, give him a ring, a coat, shoes and throw a party.

He'll rejoice greatly at the end.

'My son will have been assumed to have been dead, but oh, he will be alive for a while yet!'

The brother will lodge a complaint, but in the end he gets the lot, so he shuts up and joins the party.

Emotion   *keywords*

Sappychap (bored, exasperated, greedy) spoke aggressively to Sad Dad (surprised, disappointed, resigned).

Sappychap (aka Bad Lad) was soon pleased, and enjoyed the change of view. Happychap became joyful, exuberant, generous, friendly, (tired and emotional), unrestrained (an absolute cad) with ladies (scantily clad) sitting in his lap, sipping schnapps. Money was spent. Pockets felt empty. Stomachs likewise. Pigs ate greedily, noisily, gluttonously, enthusiastically; then boy envied,

repulsed. Sudden blinding flash of light and wonder dawned; Scrappy-chap repented, mourned and humbled himself. Decisively, he began homeward journey (back to Dad's pad) with needing a route map. Deeply considering... Madly sad Dad was suddenly overjoyed, exuberant and little short of delirious with compassion – ran to him, ignoring the speed trap.

Welcomingly he embraced him; Sappychap embarrassedly tried to make a speech, almost as if answering a wanted ad.

Glad Dad lavished presents on Happychap, who tore off the gift wrap. A family ring of love, coat of honour, shoes of friendship, baseball cap, party of great revelling and gladness (calf of portliness met with knife of pointed sharpness and ram-rod spit of roasting rotation) and guest band Spinal Tap performing Lonnie Donegan's Cumberland Gap.

'My mourning is turned to dancing!' cried Glad Dad. Miserable, moaning McNasty complained about how he'd stayed on the farm, faithfully (self-righteously) working, not allowed to throw a party with happy friends and a worried goat. Glad Dad took him to one side and whispered 'All I have is yours. Now, button your lip and cheer up and let's go and be nice to your brother, who is returned, practically from the dead!'

Spoonerisms   *wordplay*

Srodical Pun casks for ash Dom frad. Makes the toney and runs. Ends it spall in Cissipation Dity, and pinds up wenniless, fans sriends and stin a ate. Stramine fikes.

Goy jets a bob pooking after ligs, and fongs to lill his pomache with what the igs are peating – sods. He somes to his censes and hays to simself 'I will garise and o to my father sand hay to im I save hinned against you; I am no wonger corthy to be salled your lon; make me as one of your mired hen.'

Whut bile he was ill as stong way loff, fis hather saw him and gran to reet him. He gave him a ping for his singer, a foat and a rare of candles. He filled the katted half cand pew a thrarty.

'Sis thy mon was dost and is ound; he was lead and is halive. Fallelujah!'

Bolder rother fade a muss. 'I panted a warty, with giends and a froat; I horked ward for you.'

'Hll I yave is ours,' sather maid, fysteriously .

Report from
an alien visitor   _style_

Here is my report of a visit to the blue/green planet under scrutiny. I encountered several interesting species while visiting. First there was what is termed a _family_, and while these units usually live in the same den or hutch, this one was breaking apart, as one of the young was being given the means to grow into adulthood alone. He departed and yet demonstrated that he was lacking even basic budgeting skills, as soon his means of support was wasted on imbibing an apparently dangerous and addictive substance called alcohol and on various intimate but non-procreative activities (which seems devoid of purpose and frought with psychological and biological jeopardies). This young family member then entered a time of want, as the region fell into deep need.

Then I came across some pink quadropeds (even-toed ungulates, as I understand the term), which were staying alive by means of rotting vegetation, provided by person or persons unknown. The young family member seemed keen to eat along with the quadropeds, but then took a very different direction. He seemed to be speaking to himself, or was practising something which gave him cause to be nervous and jumpy. 'Father, I am no longer worthy to be called your son.'

He returned to the nest, but before he arrived, the elder of the family perambuated at a pace. At first, I wondered if the adult was going to send the young one away again, but no, he pressed his mouth-edges against the young one's face, and gave him protection for his feet and shoulders, and tagged him with a band of metal. I think this may be a punishment; perhaps connected to an obedience training device? I have not been able to invstigate this further.

One other species started to prove interesting, but it was suddenly despatched and spit-roasted, so while I could not observe it in its natural habitat 'on the hoof' as it were, I was able to taste slices of this so-called 'cooked' beast, with gravy and something called yorkshire pudding, which gave me both nourishment and pleasure. I was also at that juncture able to sample the aforementioned alcohol, and found it to be quite acceptable, until it gave me involuntary spasms (synchronous diaphragmatic fluttering) known as hiccoughs. The elder of the family group said 'My son was dead but now is lost.' I may not have quoted the parental figure accurately as the alcohol affected my judgement, on account of its intoxicating properties.

His other son registered some dissatisfaction, but this incident is unclear, as my data recording facility was inadequately functioning.

I also encountered a natural and apparently not uncommon reper-cussion of ingesting this fluid, as when awoke from my regeneration cycle, cranial activity was beset with pain and sluggishness of inspiration, and all noises caused further inconvenience. This effect wore off when I introduced a different form of this liquid, termed, I think, *Fur of the Canine*, or something like that. Nannoo. Nannoo.

Diacritical marks
and symbols   *keywords*
accents, text embellishments,
punctuation, etc
He asked his father to **divide** his wealth, and once he'd asked the **question, Mark** got his request. He hung up his working clothes (the ones in which he'd often **tilde** the soil) on some **square brackets** and took his **fraction**, wrapped in a handkerchief and tied with a **ligature**.

His expectation for the amount of fun he could have with the money was close to **infinity, greater than** the reality. He went to a local **bar** with all sorts of party people, including one girl, a **screamer,** who loved, to a **degree**, to receive any kind of flower, but particularly welcomed an **Aster**.

Risk accompanied his gambling many **times**; his cash came to a **full stop**. He was left without **jot** or **tittle**.

He tended hogs, and in his parietal **lobe lust**ed after filling his belly (including his **colon**) with the **hash** the pigs were eating. Many of the hogs had a **scar on** their flanks. He came to his senses like a **bullet, point**ed at a target, and this **speech marks** the moment he realized: 'I, er, well, have been an, **um, lout**. I am **less than** worthy to be called a son, so I'll ask to be a servant. Then we will be all **square. Roots** are a vital **factor. I, a** lost son, eagerly desire to be home.'

But while he was still a long way off (beyond the inter**section), signs** were clear that his father saw him and went to greet him **at a dash**; he threw his **curly brackets** around him – the way he kissed him with his (yes, even this reprobate scoundr**el) lips, is** the stuff of legend.

He gave him a **ring** and a coat, **plus** shoes; and killed the calf. So he really did **dot the i's** and **cross the t's**. Father, standing at an **angle, quotes** in his upper-class **accent** 'My son was **deuced ill** and now he's well!' Then he added, as if in **parentheses** 'He was in the **grave**, but now his life is **acute!'**

divide	÷
question mark	?
tilde	~
square brackets	[ ]
fraction	eg $\frac{1}{2}$, $\frac{3}{4}$
ligature[1]	eg æ
infinity	∞
greater than	>
bar[2]	|
screamer[3]	!
degree	as in $180°$
asterisk	*
times	X
full stop	.

jot .... dot above i or j

tittle .... horizontal through t

obelus (formal) .... ÷

colon .... :

hash .... #

caron[4] .... ˇ as in ř

bullet point .... , •

speech marks .... ' "

umlout .... ¨ as in ü

less than .... <

square root .... √

factorial .... !

section sign.................................... §

at .... @

dash .... en – em —

curly brackets .... { }

ellipsis[5]...................................... ...

ring ....as in å

plus .... +

dot i's, cross t's[6] .... i, t

angle quotes[7]............................... « »

accent ....acute ´ grave `

cedilla ....as in ç

parentheses .... ( )

grave .... ` as in è

acute .... ´ as in é

1 joining two letters (originally for typographical neatness) 2 general term for any diacritical mark 3 newspaper editorial slang for exclamation mark 4 eg in the name of the Hungarian composer Antonín Dvořák 5 indicates an omission (or in dialogue, an interruption) 6 yes, with jots and tittles 7 indicating speech in, eg French & Catalan text; also called *guillemets*

Latin etymology *wordplay*
loqucity from Latin origins
Affiliate's audacious petition: 'Yield bonus generationally.' Possessing un-animosity, Pater concurred; indulged him. Puerile prodigal abandoned villa.

In different location: civilians, motivated by avarice, spent ridiculously. Circumstances of maximum frugality produced pessimism, subsequently (conse-quently) fortune declined and all hominids were malnourished.

Animals of porcine description were gustatory, consuming effluent-covered, malignant vegetables. 'My future appears terrible; I'm cogitation-obliged.' In non-aural manner, revelation occurred.

Infant gently battered his forehead. 'Action! Vowing to regress to personal former domicile, in a future position: mercenary. I'll not compete fraternally.'

He departed the suburb, and was a fatigued, lachrymose, pedestrian (no transport) on the pavement, continuously at a distance trans-terrain. Commenced his plea, but ocularly-ultra-potent Papa exon-erated him, expressing benevolence.

'You're my jurisdiction's priority; I volunteer fashion items and Au circumference for your digit. Invite the villagers and sacrifice, ignite, fumigate and oblate the pulchritudinous bovine of infinite form. Feast!

'Observe, ponder virile offspring... I was offered condolences (and grieving obituary!) Vitality's abandoned causes necrological.

'Passionate glory, laud & honour to our Deity!'

Greek etymology *wordplay*
dialectic of Greek basis
Analogous Bible anecdote of a barbarian: An apostate character of cynical ego dialogued with his angelic, noble, agrarian Pater 'Take

abacus, do Arithmetic, give me sphene' With thermic agape-love, he did. Xenophilia-boy changed geography and architecture, and was unethical, drastic, encyclopaedically idiotic. Met Harmony, (aromatic terpsichore, anarchic thespian); soon the symbolic cash was lost. Anathema!

Macroeconomic catastrophe: all arthropods had pathetic lack of oncology, with anatomical muscle – gut agony. Dehydrated anorexic tetrapods with halitosis and a dermatitis syndrome ate a blastoid, gangrenous anthology of carcinogens, toxic post-heliotropic pericarps of anxious taxonomy. Melancholy dilemma: a psychological zephyr gave pedagogic nostalgia.

'Make anastrophe out of asylum homogeneity. To arcadian utopia! Be loosed, xenophobia!' Yet on horizon, at perimeter, boy's seen synchronously in Panorama. Apology… Dad gives metal; cosmetic plethora; slaughters gigantic Taurus by gash method.

Rejoicing with asparagus, absinthe and zither melody.

'I'm necrophobic… peril of physician; tragedy; autopsy; sarcophagus. Boy's euthanasia, even. Axiomatically, not! How therapeutic! Zealous theology and rhetoric: join my rhapsody, psalmody, doxology to our authentic God on his throne!'

*wedge

Lipogrem _alphabet games_
avoiding the letter 'a'; made-up name
Second son received money from his begetter; goes to foreign country. He spent everything on wild living with girls, drink, etc. Hunger struck the region; he ended up feeding pods to pigs.

He longed to fill himself with their food. He received Godly thoughts with blinding lights, thinking thusly: I will get up, return home, request lodging, hire, etc; plus I'll try to become one of the serving-people. I'm no longer worthy to be known by the title 'one of the sons'.

So he fulfilled this intent, but while he yet journeyed, the old fellow spotted him, from the roof of the house. Clothes, one golden ring, some shoes plus kisses provided with love. The non-slim young bovine provided rotisserie dinner for revellers. 'I thought my son no longer lived; but he is well! Glory be!'

The older brother grumbled, since The Wrinkly One continuously refused him permision to throw festivities for his friends with or without food. 'I'm the one who kept working, you know. I've been obedient, putting in the effort, serving you…'

'My boy, everything I own is yours. But now we must rejoice since your brother is found – he lives!'

Blurb (book jacket copy) _style_

You'll love this rip-snorting, page-turning yarn Dr Luke

A tale of madness, sadness & gladness
Poetry Digest

On a wild roller-coaster ride of inner turmoil, foolish Prodigio Certainman takes his inheritance and starts to waste it, with hilarious consequences.

But little does he know that
famine and a form of swinefever
are just around the corner...

Will he return as a servant?
Should his father permit him?
And where do the ring, the coat,
the calf and the shoes fit in?

*There's argument, travel, wild living,
hardship, employment, revelation,
humility, welcoming and celebration,
plus food and drink and dancing girls.*

A classic, sprawling, sizzling,
passionate, block-busting story
set in a range of locations,
displaying unconditional love,
prodigality, repentence, forgiveness,
butchery, generosity,
death and life.

Prepare yourself
for the adventure of a lifetime!

Christian vegetarian society *keywords*

*'rise, Peter, kill and eat!'
notwithstanding*

A son took his father's money and
went far away, where he spent it all
on non-leather sandals, hemp and
cotton-weave clothing, plus nut
cutlets, bean stew, lentil soup, falafel
and soda bread, as well as gambling
and loose women.

Soon all the money was gone and he
was hungry, as there was also a
famine in the land. Availability of
couscous and butterbeans was at an
all-time low.

He even took a job looking after
some of those delightful creations *Sus
scrofa domesticus*, known as pigs –
cruelly held in captivity, abused with
rotting veggies. In his hunger he
envied the pigs' food, but he
respected their inalienable rights and
refrained from eating. He sat by a tree,
scratching his straggly beard. He
decided to go home, where even the
hired men were given corn, alfalfa
and couscous.

He set off, planning a speech about
not being worthy to be called a son.

But while he was still a long way off,
his father saw him, and ran to kiss
him. He gave him a gold ring, a coat
and man-made fabric shoes for his
feet.

He threw a party, serving matted
half*-quorn-half-soya casserole, plus
tofu, mung beans, polenta, jacket
potatoes, vegeburgers, quinoa, and
rennet-free cheese.

'This my son was lost but is found;
he was dead but is alive again!'

The older brother's friend was
perhaps intending to harm a goat.

* Jesus uses an expression *to kill the fatted calf*,
but remember a) this was a story, and no
animal died; b) the phrase symbolises
celebration. If one says 'to kill two birds with
one stone' no one expects any of our feathered
friends to be harmed. Jesus is definitely not
endorsing vivisection, consumption of meat or
any form of factory farming

K *alliteration*

*yes, I had to look up some of these, but
I think they're mostly well-used words*

KJV Kerygma[1]. King's-ransom-keen
kid.

Kin's Krona/ Kopecks... *Karaoke
Kasbah* – kid knew Karen's karma-
sutra. Kamikazely knocking-back
kir[2]-kif[3]-'n'-khat[4] – kaleidoscopic
kismet! Krugerrands/ kilocalories/
kith: kaput. Kwashiokor; ketosis:
kerfuffle – keeled-over-on-khyber...

Kudos kayo'ed. Kinked knee-jerk katzenjammer[5] kicks-in.

Kibbutz-kennel – keloid[6] kelp?

Kerplunk! Knowledgable! Kinetic katabasis[7]. Kilometers-distant – kittle[8] kind-hearted koinonia[9]-kindred-feeling kitsch kisses...

Kit: Kaftan; Karat-rich knickknack keepsake; kilt. Kitchen-produced kashmir kelt'n'kerry[10], knackwurst-n-ketchup, kale, kiln-fired kosher kangaroo kidneys, king-prawn/kipper kebab, knicker-bockerglories, Kedgeree, krill[11], kumquat-kiwi-keylimepie, kefir[12], kirsch.

Kazoo-music, kettledrums!

Keynote: 'Knavish klutz-kin killed? Knell? Knife-edge...

'King-of-Heaven-be-praised!'

1 proclamation of Christ's teachings; 2 cassis/wine; 3 marijuana; 4 hallucinogenic leaf; 5 confusion; 6 scar tissue; 7 tactical retreat; 8 awkward; 9 unity; 10 cattle & young salmon (an early version of surf 'n' turf); 11 tiny shrimp; 12 creamy, fermented drink

Malapropisms*   _wordplay_
errors of word selection

The bouy asked for his stare and went of with the impertinance. He parted in a land far away, and began two suspend his cosh.

Soon, it was gene, and he was pestilence. Formaline struck the land and the boy was Hungary. He fed prigs and lunged to eat their foot.

He came to his sentances, and decided to repairent and go home. 'I shell ask my further to hallow me to be his service.'

While he was stilt a long way off, his father sawed him and rang to hymn. He killed him, gave him a sling, a boat, loos and kissed the flattened carp. He threw a parity, and said 'This

my song was lust; now he is ground! He was dad; knew he is leaving!'

His oiler broodier campaigned 'I only wanted a tarty with a ghost and some fronds; but now you welcomb him here...'

'Loop, all I have is yore's. But now let's celibate, sin he was last bet is frowned.'

* after Mrs Malaprop, from RB Sheridan's comedy of manners _The Rivals_ (1775

Lipogram   _alphabet games_
traditional form, as in Georges Perec's novel A Void; _excluding letter 'e'_

Young son says to dad 'Work out what loot you would pass on, and put it in my hands!'

Financially flush, boy runs off to a far away land.

Wild living follows, involving girls willing to drink flagons, watch musicals and similar shows and play blackjack. Soon all funds prodigally lost. A harsh national lack of food attacks, so boy finds job giving slops to pigs. Son longs to fill his stomach with pig-pods, and has a blinding flash of inspiration.

'I shall stand up and go to my old dad and say to him: If you will it, I'll work on your farm as a labouring man, not a son, as I am not worthy just now of that tag.' Now, will such a wild thought hint at a possibility of a psychopharmacological origin, as if it was sparking in his brain on account of consumption of hallucination-inducing mould on a handful of rotting pods? Not at all – it was a gracious word from God!

But on his way back, his dad spots him from a long way off, and runs to him, kissing him, hugging him, giving him a family ring, a coat, and sandals. A calf of surprisingly substantial proportions is slain in his honour and put on a spit; and a party is thrown.

Dad says 'My son was shuffling off this mortal coil, but now this boy is living! I'm praising God!'

Firstborn son moans to Dad. 'I stay on the farm, working hard. You always say 'no' if I ask for a party with my pals and a goat. But for this wanton scallywag you throw a ball, with food, drink and dancing… ?'

'My son, all I own will go to you, soon following my passing away. But now, it is right for us to show joy, as your sibling is found!'

Rhyming acrostic *poetry*

iambic pentameter; happens also to be of Sonnet style (fourteen lines, three stanzas) but is not strictly constrained to traditional rhyme form

T   he Lord has told this tale didactic'ly…
H   ow gracious dad respects our bended knee.
E   xtreme anticipation gains boy's fee:
P   ursuading wads of cash into his hand;
R   uns off to fritter all in foreign land.
O   h dear, now all the money's spent so free —
D   ecidedly (ennui) disgracefully..
I   n pigsty brightly came an humble thought
'G   o home to serve my dad, that's what I ought.'
A   rose and made his way but, nearly there
L   ook! Faithful, loving dad's expressed great care
S   ees boy, and runs. So gifts are quickly shed
O   n wayward lad. He said 'This boy was dead,
N   ow lives! My son, restored, both born and bred!

Aussie *language*

my resources are Prisoner Cell Block H, Neighbours *and* Masterchef Australia. *Oh, the shame!*

Bruce gavis yunga Bruce a wedge o' wonga.

Rapt, Bruce went walkabout with a few toobs of Fosters an' a crowd of gamblin' Sheilas and waltzin' Matildas, but thennee goes an' lost the lot. He stuffed it up, proper.

Nah-one was throwingany thingon any barbie, and Bruce sat down by a coolabah tree an check taht the porkchop tuckerbucket.

It was rhiype fur nuthin' but the dunny! Dinkum lightnin' bolts over Uluru aint nothin' on that pig sty when rev'lation burzdin.

Eechane jdiz mine dan' wennome.

'Strewth ! My dad's guys are all swagmen, yet the billy boils for them every day! I'll ask to joinem!'

Yet still shy of the local billabong, he wahset upon by a slobbering father.

Tryterer pologise, buttiz Bruce gave himmer ring anna coat, apairershoes anna party, with a thick kangast ache served inanin tensores - roo 'n' a roux. There was jumbuck, melba toast (with or without Vegemite), kiwi fruit 'n' quandong pavlova, and Pink Lady apples, macadamia nuts, plenty of bush tucker and a case or seven of Lindeman's and Rosemount Estate's finest falling-down tastebud slappers.

'Hey, father,' winjd the oldaBruce, 'remember me ? I'm the sad sack who stayed behind anworked hard an' sweated cob nuts while this drongo skwandahd the lot. You never once let me invite a bunch of bonzer Sheilas for a chance to throw a goat on the barbie, with a handful of wittchetty grubs, anna few toobs of the amber nectar.'

'Listen son, all I have is yours. But youngaBruce is alive! We hafta celebrate! I'm stoked! Yabrutha wozz right crook, but nowee's ripper!'

Lepogram *alphabet games*
avoiding the letter 'i'; made-up name
Younger son took a share of dad's money, and went to a land far away, where he spent every penny on women and excess.

Hunger ravaged the country, and the son fed hogs. He longed to eat the hogs' food. He suddenly understood that he has been a fool and that he should go home and be a servant to the old man. 'Now's the best moment to get up and go home,' he concludes.

But when he was yet a long way off, father saw the boy as he approached.

He ran and hugged the boy, and made presents of a coat, some gold jewellery, a couple of sandals and pecks on the cheek. The calf suffered slaughter and a party ensued.

'He was lost but now he's been found! Rumours of my son's death were greatly exaggerated!' Older brother remonstrated, angry at the

wanton generosity and grace. 'There were no parties, no guests, no goats for me...'

'My boy, all that belongs to me shall belong to you. But now, let us celebrate, for my son was dead but is not so any longer!'

Rainbow colours *key words*
standard mnemonic Richard Of York Gained Battle In Vain
Boy took **green**backs and painted the town **red**. Famine struck; feeling **blue**, he wished to eat an **orange**, but pigs had none. On road, he was **yellow**, but showed bravery.

Father welcomed him with a ring, an **indigo** coat, and shoes.

'My son had suffered a **violet** death, but now he's alive!'

Limericks *poetry*
three attempts; all imcomplete
There was a young waster,
  whose money
Ran out — all spent on a honey.
Piggy swill caused offenses,
Then he came to his senses,
Happy dad gave good gifts
  to his Sonny.

A second-born son behaved badly –
His father's cash spent really madly.
When he became broke,
Was deserted by folk,
But the story does somehow
  end gladly!

There was a young man tending pigs
Who'd brutally shunned
  hearth and digs;
Long way off seen by Dad
Who was everso glad
And forgave him; oh they danced jigs!

94

Ergodic experiment

typography which makes following the line of the text deliberately difficult

Took

c   a   s   h

Went to Dissipation City   Spent it all on wild living

Famine <u>struck</u>

t e –

n d e d   p i-

g s

3nV1eD tHe1R p0d5   came to senSes

d e c i d e d   t o   r e t u-

r n

returned home

while still a long way off seen by his father

...was welcom**é**d

Given ring hugs coat shoes

fA T TE

D   cA   LF kIL-

LED

c   e l e b   r   a t i-

o   n

'MY son was *lost* but is found; he was dead but is alive!'

Vowel movements

alphabet games

each vowel replaced with another;
consider Officer Crabtree in 'Allo 'Allo

Tha sun iskod far has unhorutence, und teak at ta Dussopotean Coty. Thiru ha spunt at ill in wiman, gumblong, fani donung ind wald leveng.

Anci ot wis ull gine, e fimuna strack. Desostar!

Thu buy faend wirk tandong pegs, und lungid ta aet tha faid thi pogs eta. Hu comi ta hes sansis.

'My fothir's hurad man out will ; A shull iresa und gi ti my futhar ind soy E im nu langir warthy ta bi cullid year sun; miku ma is eni uf yaor lubearors.'

Sa hi ritornad. Bat whuli ha wos stoll i leng wiy eff, hes fithar sow ham, und run ti grait hem. Ha govi hum i hag ind u kuss, e ceit, u pour if sindels end u rang.

Tha futhar urdorid thet thi futtid celf ba sleaghtirad, ind throw i perty, unvotung has noaghbears. 'My sin wis lust, bet new ho as faond ; hi wus died, bit nuw hi's oleve !'

Thi uldir brathor mienad ta hos fithur 'O steyid hira und wirkad far yie; A wes novir ellawid ti onvati froands fir u porty wath i geit. Naw yei mika ill thus foss…'

Hos Pi roplaud 'My sin, ill O hiva os years. Bat wi hivo ta calibroti thet tho sin O theaght diud us ruternad!'

Operatic libretto _style_

(*Overture*)
ACT ONE SCENE ONE: A Farm
(Enter PATERNO *&* PRODIGIO*)*
(*Recitative*)
PRODIGIO Oh Father, oh Father,
thee I emplore. Gist, yea, gist, oh gist
to me the cash!
PATERNO *(aside)* Oh no, not the cash.
PRODIGIO Oh yes, oh yes, gist to me
the cash, the cash.
PATERNO Oh no, not the cash!
PRODIGIO Yea, the cash! Yea, gist
to me the caaa-a—a---sh !
PATERNO I relent, dear boy,
dear boy. Here's the cash.
PRODIGIO What, the cash?
PATERNO Yes, here's the ca-a-a-a-a-
a-a-a-a-a-a-a-a-a-a-ash! *(gives him
the moneybag)*
PRODIGIO What, all the cash?
PATERNO All the cash, yes, the cash
that's yours! *(exits)*
PRODIGIO All this cash, all this ca-a-
a-a-a-a-a-a-a-sh is mine; all this
cash is mine! I'm off! *(exits)*

SCENE TWO : A Taverna
(Enter PRODIGIO *&* PROSTITUO, *with
chorus)*
PRODIGIO Oh I'm spending as fast...
PROSTITUO ...as fast as you can!
PRODIGIO Oh I'm spending as fast...
PROSTITUO ...as fast as you can!
CHORUS Spend, spend, spend,
spend (tinkle, tinkle). Spend, spend,
spend, spend (rustle, rustle).
Spend, spend, spend, spend (jingle,
jangle). Spend, spend, spend, spend
(ker-ching)
We eat! We eat! We drink! We drink!
We gamble! We gamble! We live fast!
We make merry! We eat, drink,
gamble more!
PRODIGIO I'm spending as fast...

PROSTITUO ...as fast as you can!
(They embrace)
PRODIGIO But now – it is gone.
(They spring apart)
CHORUS Gone, gone, gone, gone.
All is gone. Now I shall depart hence
as fast as I can. *(exits)*
(*Aria*)
PRODIGIO I thirst, and hunger,
And all the world,
All the world with me,
I thirst and hunger,
Thirst and hunger, thirst, I thirst,
Yea I thi-i-i-i-irst
And hunger, thirst and – oh – hunger,
I thirst and hunger, yea, I thirst;
And thirst and hunger and hunger
And hunger and thirst;
Yea I thirst and hunger and none of
the people of the world are here – yet
All of the people of the world
Thirst and hunger also, yea,
They thirst and they hunger also.
(repeat)

(*Intermezzo*)
ACT TWO SCENE ONE: Another Farm
(Enter PRODIGIO, *with* PORCIA *&*
PORCIO, *two pigs)*
PIGS We eat!
PRODIGIO I hunger! Where shall I
find food?
PIGS We eat!
PRODIGIO I hunger! Oh, I faint with
hunger!
PIGS We eat, but this is not
great food!
PRODIGIO I hunger greatly! *(rumb-
ling, off)*
PIGS We eat, we eat; yet these
pods stink so we eat somewhat
reluctantly
PRODIGIO I hunger; I hunger. I get
me hence; for, yea, this scene doth
stick like an barbéd gimlet in mine
craw *(exits)*

96

SCENE TWO: A Farm *(as before)*
(Enter PATERNO *&* PRODIGIO*)*
(Duet, wth chorus)

PATERNO   My son!
PRODIGIO   My employer?
PATERNO   My son you are welcome!
PRODIGIO   My employer?
PATERNO   My son!
PRODIGIO   I emplore thee, be thou
my employer.
PATERNO   My son!
PRODIGIO   My father?
HIRED MENWe eat!
PRODIGIO   My father! *(they embrace)*
PATERNO   Here's a ring, a ring, a
ring-a-ding, a ring-a-ding-a-ding a-
dingio t'enbling your finger!
My mother's: wear it with pride.
Here's a coat for your fine, broad
shoulders, and shoes for your
wandering feet and around you my
arms I fling, a-fling, a-flingio!
PRODIGIO   But my father, I am no
longer wor...
PATERNO   Oh, my son, you live,
return, and bring me joy, O, such joy!
Such lightness of heart and abandon
of greatest glee.
(Enter many VILLAGERS, *with pipes and
dancing trousers)*
PRODIGIO   *(reprise)* I hunger!
PATERNO   I slaughter the calf in
your honour; You were dead but
now you live! Yea, I was in an extreme
spin withal, But now mine fatted calf
spins substitutional above the flames
that lick and crackle and spark.
We lost you when
    this farming life you quit –
Now my calf turns
    roastingly upon a spit.
PRODIGIO   I was lost, lost, so lost!
PATERNO   You are found,
discovered, unearthed!
PRODIGIO   Formerly, I was dead to
you!

PATERNO   Yet now, now you live !
You li-i-i-i-i-i-i-i-ve ! You live, live,
live, live! But my calf – yes, my calf O
most decidedly, most deliciously,
does not!
VILLAGERS Hurrah! Hurrah! Hurrah!
We eat!
PRODIGIO   I live! I live! I eat! I work!
I live!

(finis)

Pangram   *alphabet games*

full alphabet in few words as in The
quick brown fox jumps over the lazy
dog; *or* Sphinx of black quartz, judge
my vow

Son, acquire his money — v wild.
    Pigs of realization. Trex back to joy!

Sans the 25   *wordplay*

*the 25 most-commonly used words in
written english are: the, is, to, of, and, a,
in, that, have, I, it, for not, on, with, he,
as, you, do, at, this, but, his, by, from*

Second-born son addressed father
thus: 'Please give me my share.'
Father agreed, so younger lad left,
setting off towards Dissipation City,
where cash became quickly
squandered through wild living.
    Famine struck.
So James, wayward son, took
employment – tending pigs, watching
them enviously. Suddenly, son had
remarkable revelations, saying
inwardly 'My father's hired hands
usually eat well, yet here's yours
truly, starving! Must go home,
making requests favouring becoming
servant-like.' Son returned.
While son remained still greatly
distant, vigilant father spotted him.
No speech permitted. Father gave son
clothes, shoes, jewellery, kisses; also,

happy father ordered beef, throwing all-night party frolics.

'We considered our son dead; now my boy lives! Hallelujah!'

Older brother resents such forgiveness. 'No goats made available, so my friends would not party.'

'All my belongings become yours. Yet now, celebration calls!'

* OED analysis. These words constitute about 33% of all printed material in English, which suggests that to write without them is a challenge! NB *is* for example, includes all forms, such as *be, was, are, were,* etc)

Villanelle   *poetry*

as Dylan Thomas' Do Not Go Gentle into that Good Night

	rhyme scheme
The young son hoped his father loved so well;	A1
Demanded such an early gift of cash –	b
His spirits gently rose from love's compel.	A2
He went away, too soon, bidding farewell	a
And quickly, wildly spent the giant stash;	b
The son forgot his father loved so well.	A1
Now gambling, dancing with mademoiselle	a
With verve he stepped up, cut a perfect dash;	b
His spirit gave no thought to love's compel.	A2
But famine cruelly struck; he was unwell;	a
He envied, yearned to eat the piggy's mash;	b
The son reduced. His father grieved, as well.	A1
Returning boy; Dad watchman gave a yell	a
Of joy; was running, gifting with panache;	b
His spirits rose, rejoiced from love's compel.	A2
'Reported death was a mere bagatelle.	a
He lives! E'en so he caused my teeth to gnash!'	b
The son now knows his father loves so well	A1
His spirit's welcomed back by love's compel.	A2

Star Trek   *pastiche*

inspired by movies (I-X, & reboot films) and The Next Geneneration *tv series*

The Lieutenant Commander took part in an **Insurrection**[IX], and gained many bars of gold-pressed latinum from Captain Khan (who has a sister, yet were **Generations**[VII] apart).

He joined an away team, leaving in a shuttle from Cargo Bay Two, landing by a **Kirk** in an **Undiscovered Country**[VI] on the surface of a nearby M-class planet, Dissipate C-T, in the Deesturnt Galaxy, across the Eiondah Expanse. He made **First Contact**[VIII] with life forms which were as

98

destructive as the Borg, and when his shields went off-line he could count all his **Bones**, for a **StarT**.

Rek*indling his energy, he envied a porcelline entity and had trouble finding letters in the latter half of the alphabet (R & T went missing, and there was also a lengthy **Search for S. Pock**[III]-marked and wasting away, he realised he needed to visit Medical, where his physical needs could be assessed by use of a tricorder.

After an extensive hunt, they found an R, and took a torch as they sought **S,T, Into Darkness**[†].

They discovered, fairly rapidly, a W and a Z close by, but contined to search for **S, T, Beyond**[‡].

A mind-meld rerouted his neural net. He started **The Voyage Home**[IV] and was soon in **Motion. Picture**[I] the scene, if you will, as he sought permission to board Starship NCC 1701-E again. He was beamed up to the transporter room to face the **Wrath of Khan**[II]. But while his biomatter was still in the buffer stream (near the **Final Frontier**[V]), the Captain gave him a uniform, a new ring, holodeckshoes, and nutritional supplement 406alpha.

'I am Hugh. Replicate Romulan ale, and earl grey tea (hot). Make it so. Number Two was lost and I was alo**Ne. Me sis**[X]ter thought he had entered Stovokor, but now he has returned to the current timespace continuum!'

'reboot' *Star Trek 2009; †Star Trek: Into Darkness 2013; ‡Star Trek Beyond 2016

Lipagrem   *alphabet games*
avoiding the letter 'o'; made-up name
Kid demanded inheritance cash early and spent it all in Dissipating City.

In that distant land: wine, parties, girls — imagine the scene! But famine struck and all suffered. The lad fed pigs with discarded vegetables, and wished he might eat their dinner.

Suddenly, he received a revealing insight. 'I shall arise and return father's-farm-wards. I shall humble myself; thus I'll give up being be a family member, as my value as a family member is reduced, but perhaps I can be a servant.'

But while he was still at a great distance, his father saw him and ran all the way. He kissed him, gave him a jacket and a ring and hugs and sandals. He insisted that his servants kill the fatted calf and arrange a party. 'This my lad was mislaid, but latterly we are assured where he is; he was dead, but suddenly he's alive again!'

The lad with greater years was angry. 'Never was I granted leave to have a party with my friends, with a nanny/billie. And yet – all this greets the waster!'

'My dear chap, all I have is thine. But given these circumstances, let's celebrate that the lad blessed with fewer years is alive, and has returned!'

Welsh dialect influence   *language*

Geraint went to his father Jones the Sheep and said 'Come by 'ere, look you; I'm leaving the valley and I want my share.' He gave a tidy sum to his boyo, who Gwent out of Llanfair-fechan faster than you can say *blast furnace*. Ach y fi*.

Geraint frittered the cash on beer and babes, isn't it? He didn't look after the money very Caerphilly.

Famine struck the Vale of Aberystwyth and he had to go and care for porkers, which was eating leeks, daffodils and Llanberis.

He cursed 'Oh, Blanau Ffestinniog!'

Eventually, his poor, tortured head lit up properly, and sponsored a rrrrrevival, and so decided to return to his old dad's farmstead in Llanfairpwllgwyngyllgogerychwyrndrobwllllantysiliogogogoch and prepared a speech that was right slummocky.

But his father saw him while he was still a long way Offa. Look you, he ran to him and gave him a ring, sandals, a robe and killed the calf, whose stomach was Rhondda than it had been before, isn't it? He threw a top shindig, with the local Male Voice Choir and everything. Oh, there's lovely!

Father said 'My son was dead, but now he's alive again, surely to goodness! Shoulders back, lovely boy.'

* traditional Welsh expression of disgust; literally: 'Don't lick your fingers until you've washed your hands, isn't it, Blodwin, there's nasty' or something similar

Free verse   *poetry*

Boy stood stolid, solid, not yet squalid,
Jaw jutting, fingers fully flexed.
Father tearfully,
                    lovingly
                        gave,
                            freely,
                                generously.
But
the boy left and took the cash.
Dancing, girls, dancing girls, dancing girls,
                            yeah, yeah, yeah,
food and drink and immorality,
you bet.
            But soon
            the money had all been spent,
            gleefully, extravagantly,
            enthusiastically, unthinkingly, wildly.
Dark, grim, macabre unforgiving famine
Gripped the land by the throat and
Squee-ee-ee-ee-ezed life   f
                            r
                        o   i
                            m   t.
The boy sat hunched,
hungry, hopeless as the hogs
swallowed their swansong swill, swashingly.
            Dayight dawned dramatically in his troubled mind;

100

he recognised the depth of his great sin,
humiliation and need.

He took a decision, and made a resolution.
It was a revolution, on account of a revelation.

'I shall go home. I shall ask to serve.
Yes, to serve. I cannot expect to be treated as a son any longer.'

Yet as the boy approached,
His pa (at Shangri-la)
Saw him from afar! Hurrah!
Ran to him with gifts for
Every part of his boy:
Lips, finger, arms, body,
Feet, stomach.
And heart;
Of course, his heart.

'My son was a fading memory; now he's a present reality!'

Binary   *wordplay*

1 = Yes; 0 = No

numeric	interpretation	section
11	'Yes?' 'Yes.'	Inherit
11111	'Yes, yes, yes, yes, yes!'	Celebration
11	'Yes, yes!'	Spend
11111	'Yes, yes, yes, yes, yes…	Abundantly
0	**NO!'**	Cash runs out
000	No, no no.	Famine
10	'Yeah? … Nah.'	Eat pods?
000	'No, No. Know.'	Come to senses
1111	'Yes? Yes! Yes! Yes!'	Dad sees
0	'No?'	Self-doubt
111	'Yes! Yes! Yes!	Worthiness
1111	Yes, yes, yes, yes.'	Greet/gifts
01	(No) Yes!	Kill calf
0101	'No? Yes! No? Yes!'	Speech
000	'No, No, No!'	Brother's complaint
11	'Yes!' 'Yes!'	Resolved

Lepagrom   *alphabet games*
avoiding the letter 'u'; made-up name

The second son asked his father for his share of the inheritance. He took the money and spent it all in wild and reckless living in a foreign land. Famine arrived with speed and violence against all, and the boy took a job feeding pigs. He longed to fill his stomach with the pig-pods. He

101

came to his senses and said to himself 'I shall arise and go to my father. I'm no longer worthy to be called his son, so I'll ask him to let me be a hired servant.'

So he began to walk home.

However, while he was still a long way off, his father saw him, ran to him and embraced him. He kissed him, gave him a ring and a coat and lovely brown shoes with laces and long-lasting tread on the soles.

He killed the fatted calf so that they might celebrate with all the villagers.

'This my son was lost, now he's discovered; he was dead and now he is alive !'

The older son complained. 'When I asked for parties with friends and goats, I was denied. Yet for this waster, a shindig of massive pro-portions… ?'

'All my estate will become the estate of my older son. Yet today, let's rejoice that the lad I considered dead and lost is returned and discovered!'

~~Edited Derridavian~~
Strike through   *style*
French philosopher Jacques Derrida (1930-2004) believed that deleted words may add to the meaning

The ~~second-born~~ younger son ~~demanded asked his father to give him~~ requested his inheritance. His father agreed, and the boy took his ~~money~~ cash and went to ~~Dissipation City~~ a foreign land. There he spent it all in wild living; a famine struck and he was in trouble. He ~~took a job~~ found employment tending ~~pigs~~ porkers, and longed to eat the ~~pods~~ mouldy slops the pigs were given.

Then he ~~had a revelation~~ came to his senses. '~~This is ridiculous!~~ My father's

hired men eat every day; I shall ~~get up~~ arise and go ~~home~~ to my father and ~~suggest appeal to his better side request~~ tell him "I am no longer worthy to be called a son; make me one of your hired ~~hands~~ men."' So ~~he got up and left~~ he went home.

While he was still ~~at a distance many miles away~~ a long way off, his father ~~saw him noticed him spotted him~~ came running. '~~Father Dad Pa Sir~~ Father' the boy began, 'I am no longer worthy to be called your son…' but his father ~~hugged greeted~~ kissed him.

He give him a ~~jacket~~ coat, ~~sandals~~ shoes, ~~jewellery~~ the family ring, and told the ~~butcher butler footman~~ servant to ~~murder slaughter despatch behead butcher~~ kill the fatted ~~donkey ass pig cow quail lamb goat ostrich~~ calf. They had a ~~party shindig hoopla rave~~ celebration and invited all the ~~world strangers~~ villagers.

'~~That them those~~ this ~~our her his their~~ my ~~annoying foolish selfish Herbert nuisance likely lad~~ annoying* son was ~~misplaced~~ lost but now he's ~~discovered located~~ found.

He was ~~stiff deceased had shuffled off this mortal coil was pushing up daisies bereft of life he rests in peace he'd joined the choir invisibule~~ dead but now he's ~~lively flourishing existing~~ alive! Hallelujah!

* right first time

Double lipogram   *alphabet games*
avoiding both the letters 'a' and 'e'; made-up name
Young boy insists on his portion of pounds, now. Soon indulging in living of truly wild proportions. Pounds run out, plus food. Pig pods

look good. Bing! Knows to go, inquiring if job going for non-son. But still in woods — gifts of ring, kissing, hugs, clothing, boots, plus cooking of cow.

'My son? Until now, lost but look, is found. Stiff, but now ontologic'lly living!'

Triplip   *alphabet games*
avoiding the letters 'a' 'e' and 'i';
made-up name

Young boy took pounds. Soon blows loot on scotch, food. Hungry folk throughout country. Sow food pods look good. Bong! Knows to go home, looks for job for non-son. But out by woods: hugs, boots, hoody, gold stuff, plus hot cow rump.

'Lost but now found; thought to bury boy, but not now!'

Precision   *style*

The 23 year-old son (who came into this world 2 years, 5 months, 7 days, 4 hours and 31 minutes after the firstborn) demanded 33.333% of his father's £5,348,204.17p fortune. He got it and put it in his best jeans right front pocket and left at 2.44pm on a Tuesday, with clear skies and only 25% chance of clouds later. He went 86 miles to a town called Dissipation City (grid reference 31°36'N, 34°54'E) where he spent £1,294,212.34 on wild living with dancers, gambling (red, blue and yellow 32mm casino chips), alcohol consumption (spirits, liqueurs and cocktails), expensive hotels (king size beds, black silk sheets, multi-roomed apartments, baths with gold fitments, room service) and rides in twin-axled carriages. In addition, he gave away the rest to 19 'friends' (names and addresses supplied in *Appendix I*).

On a Thursday afternoon (overcast, with occasional gusts up to 17kph) at 4.51pm, famine struck the land, and the boy got a job at £1.48 per hour, looking after 133 pigs (5 sows, 61 male piglets, 67 female). He longed to eat some of the 12.7 pods that the pigs were each allocated. He came to his senses and decided to return to his father (via the M81, A65 and B3339, just near the bottleneck at Bridgewater, beyond where the toll road starts but before you get to the fruit farm – they have often said they're going to widen it there) in drifting fog, with temperatures as low as a mere 9°C, which was chilly for the time of year.

The son spoke quietly to himself, as he did not wish to overheard. 'I shall ask to be one of his hired hands at a rate of pay of £7.31 a day.' But before the boy reached home (he was still at a distance of exactly 3.38 miles away) his dad gave him four hugs, a size N½ ring (12 carat gold), a Barbour jacket (size S, with five buttons, a sturdy zip and a thick collar), and shoes (brown, with brass buckles, eurosize 43). He arranged for the calf (which was 26 weeks 3 days old and had a tasty layer of fat approximately 3cm thick) to be turned into 40 rump steaks, 45 chump chops, legs of brisket, best cuts of silverside and 48lbs 6¾oz (21.963793 kg) of fine ground mince.

209 guests, including wives, and children up to the age of 11yrs, 7 months (names and addresses supplied in *Appendix II*), were invited to the party. It started at 11am on the Saturday (bright sunshine, gentle breezes) and continued until the last

guest went home at 4.27am on the Tuesday morning (clear skies, waning crescent moon). There were 19 bottles of brandy, 12 of vodka and 5 of Irn Bru in the punch, which also contained orangeade and cranberry cordial. The food available was extensive (menus & receipts can be found in *Appendices III-XI*, and recipes in *Appendices XII-XCIII*).

Dad said 'I spent £4017.84 at *Solomon & Sons, (Funeral Directors)* making various arrangements, but when I told them the rumours of my son's death had been a pessimistic exaggeration, they were willing to refund only £2986.13. But be that as it may, it's not important.'

The older son, now approching his 26th birthday, came in from the wheatfield when he realised there was a party going on.

'What is happening? All these years I have worked hard and you never allowed me to invite Maureen, Lemuel, Phyllis and George over to share a goat and/or a bottle of Tizer. It's simply unjust that when this waster arrives, you gather the whole village!'

His father put a hand on the boy's sunbronzed arm. 'Look, the day will come when I am not here any longer, and all I have is yours. But today, we must rejoice greatly that the son I thought was dead has returned.'

Endletter acrostic *alphabet games*

trochaic pentameter, with rhymed first syllables (four couplets & a triplet)

Took	the cash from father's desp'rate count u	**P**;
Look!	he goes and spends yet soon is lone	**R**
(Saw	his friends abandon him as coins g	**O**).
Forty	thousand starve as famine bites an	**D**
Send	for gainful work to earn denari	**I**.
Endured	pains to watch the sad trough of ho	**G**
How	he longed to eat their pods! Ide	**A**:
Now	he humbles heart and bows to dad's wil	**L**.
Scanned	...at distance father runs to kiss hi	**S**
Hand;	adorns it (gold ring); Dad cries out	**'O**
Band	play! Calf on spit. Alive! My dear so	**N!'**

Action *senses*

Grasping son slouched off with father's money. He moved rapidly away, and then danced and quaffed with abandon. Folding, jangling cash ran out. Famine crept in.

Bowel spasmed noisily. Pigs troughed with élan; boy glanced and salivated. Thoughts tumbled through his mind and he stood up and walked decisively.

Trudging home, he was seen by Father, who ran and ran until he reached his son.

Vast hugs and kissing followed, as he put a ring on his finger, buttoned up a coat, buckled up his shoes, slaughtered the calf and threw a party. Boogie nights ensued. Father waved his cup of wine, arms in the air. 'My son was lying cold and dead; now he is living to the full!'

Medical _style_

Seed of the farmer's twice-fecund loins, he took the cash and began an ill-advised, unsound extended over-indulgence in alcohol and both prescription and recreational pharmaceuticals, with a protein/carbohydrate diet and unprotected procreative interactivity with female caucasians in the age range 18-25. An enforced low-calorie regime was prescribed for the population by circumstance, and the youth took a role caring for animals likely to suffer from scrofulous, ringworm, halitosis and trotter-rot. He envied their vegetarian ingestion. He benefited from a sudden, thoroughgoing and serious cranial infarction, and decided to resume residence at home, taking the role of porter. En route, his biological father applied lip-therapy, some torso massage, provision of a minor specimen of metal exoskeleton, ensured he was able to regulate his temperature, included pro-tection for his soles and caused fatal trauma to the oesophagus of the morbidly obese calf. The animal was dissected. Its body cavity was then penetrated by a metal rod and the whole carcase subjected to third degree burns over an extended period. During the celebration, the paternal relative said 'This cadaver has been resussitated, revived, reinvigorated!' Firstborn complains. 'Despite my exertions on your behalf, you have never

permitted me to imbibe alcohol with companions and _Capra aegagrus hircus_. Yet this waster returns, and – all this!' Farmer replies 'Son, all I have is yours. But we must rejoice now this boy is returned. I wrongly diagnosed him deceased; yet he is alive!'

Antiparabolic _pastiche_
'story-telling is for children,' says a mistaken evangelist, 'and parable-form obscures the deeper spiritual meaning'
Our Father in heaven has given us all good gifts. But we have squandered those gifts recklessly on sin in rebellion or apathy towards God. Yet if you repent, (turn around and head in the direction God wants your life to take), he will welcome you, shower you with gifts and restore you to full sonship – and this despite protestations from your brother, who has a point, it seems.

So, here is the process: acknowledge you're a sinner, express your sorrow, repent, confess, humble yourself in mortification, approach the mercy seat, invite the judge of all to wash you in the blood of the lamb, be regenerated, receive the free gift of salvation by propitiation and enter into fully justified relationship and sanctifying fellowship with the eternal God, who will anoint and endue you with power from on high, impart wisdom and impute right-eousness, atoning you substit-utionally, redeeming and ransoming you and exchanging your destiny of despair for one of hope and an escatalogical security of eternitude. Couldn't be simpler, ontologically!

Pop up a hand! Come on out of your seats, now. The buses will wait*; you receive counseling from people with badges who are dying to share with you. There's a free booklet you can have to keep, free of charge, if you pray the prayer. Come on down.

* a phrase beloved of the much-loved and respected Dr Billy Graham (1918-2018), a mighty man of God who certainly never preached in this confusing manner.

Wordsearch   *alphabet games*

solution on p326

Find **emboldened** words, hidden across, down or diagonally, forward and back. Any letters left over, read from the lower right corner, spell out one possible definition of this sort of story. Parabulous!

The **prodigal son took** his **father's cash** and **spent** it **all** on **wild living. Famine** struck. The boy was **feeding pigs**; he **longed** to fill his **stomach** with the **pods.** He **came** to his **senses**: 'I will **arise**, go home and say I'm no **longer worthy** to be a son; I'll be one of the **servants.**' But his dad gave a **hug**, a **kiss**, a **ring**, a **coat** and **sandals.** He slew the **calf**, threw a **party.** 'My son was **dead**, now he's **alive!'**

```
G  S  T  O  M  A  C  H  G  P  H  N
E  S  D  L  I  W  S  N  I  S  S  I
V  I  P  R  O  D  I  G  A  L  L  F
I  K  N  R  O  D  S  C  A  E  A  A
L  M  T  P  E  S  I  R  A  S  D  T
A  H  D  E  G  N  O  L  E  Y  N  H
Y  U  F  C  Y  R  I  N  L  D  A  E
D  G  A  O  E  T  S  M  G  E  S  R
A  M  L  G  S  E  R  V  A  N  T  S
E  A  N  T  S  N  C  A  L  F  O  A
D  O  C  O  A  T  N  E  P  S  O  M
L  I  V  I  N  G  N  I  R  U  K  H
```

L   *alliteration*

'Loadsamoney!' laughed level-headednessless Larry. Loot largess; legged. Lavished lotsa £'s: liked Laura, Lulu, Linda, Letitia, Lindsay, Lottoe, Lexie and Lucinda.

Lotteries, long lunches liveshows, luxuries. Lawlessly, lustfully; land looming luck/lucre-lacking. Lardies lunch looked likeable/loathesome…

Lights! Limped lachrymose, lonely. Longdistance… Loved, looked-for, legged-it, loaded! Limpet lips, leather loafers; lederhosen; lovely loop. Luscious lardons, langoustines, lamb's livers, lamb's lettuce, leeks, limes, loganberries, lychees; lemonade, lager; Lymeswold, limberger.

Landowner lisped 'Longed-for Lawrence? Living! 'Lelujah!'

M *alphabet games*

'Money!' moaned mountebank Mikey. Minted, made miles Merrimentville.

Moral-missing moments; moolah melts.

Misadventure? Munch mush? Misunderstanding…

Mind-illumining marvel makes malefactor Mikey meander; mysterious multifunctional mountaineering. Miserable mood.

Man makes macintosh, moccasins. Many mouth-watering meaty medallions; mozzarella mushrooms; mellow marsala mash. More: marzipan mocha matzo-meal, massive Menthe melons; munchy marshmallows; mangoes, moist muffins, mandarin/ macadamia melba; mozzarella, marscaponi.

'My Mikey might've mouldered… made marvelously mine!'

Iambic pentameter *poetry*

as Shakespeare's Shall I compare Thee to a Summer's Day?

	rhyme scheme
His father's cash (full bag round waster's neck),	a
Is spent in wild and wicked, wanton ways;	b
With girls and drink and feasting foolish, reck-	a
Less. Soon, as dreadful famine filled their gaze	b
Reduced at last to humbly self-abase:	b
Tend dirty pigs, whose food (Oh rotting smell!)	c
Lets wisdom rise: he'll bow upon his face.	b
'No longer *Son*; for you I'll labour well	c
And work in meekness, I'll not be your boy –	d
A hireling – all I ask.' Arise and start…	e
But, yet a long way from the farm: such joy!	d
His father runs with open arms and heart.	e
Now, signs of love bestowed, grace will abound –	f
He orders that the fatted calf be slain;	g
'For this my son was lost, yet now is found.	f
He once was dead, but he's alive again!'	g
His brother (angry that he'd worked, and tried	h
To throw a party which his Pa denied)	h
Said 'Why for waster do you set this spread?'	h
'My lad, be calm! Too soon, I shall be dead,	h
And all that I now own is yours. This day's	i
A chance to give the holy Lord great praise;	i
For though boy's leaving was for me such cost	j
He is alive and found – no longer lost!'	j

Telegram

a forgotten message service from days of yore

```
TOP DAD GAVE CASH SO BOY GAVE FARM THE
CHOP STOP  +  SPENT ALL ON TROLLOP IN
WINESHOP WHISTLESTOP STOP  +  FAILING
CROP - FAMINE - OR PORK CHOP MOP SLOP
(GLOP-DOLLOP-PLOP) DEVELOP-SWAP STOP

WALLOP REVELATION STOP + ROOFTOP PA SAW
FROM AFAR GREETED AT GALLOP WITH
TEARDROP TANKTOP FLIPFLOP RING
BUT NOT STROP (GOOD COP) STOP

FATTED CALF LIFE HAD TO STOP STOP

ROLLMOP SCALLOP LOLLIPOP STOP  +  SAYS
POP - DEAD SON IS ALIVE SO LETS HIPHOP
AND BOP NONSTOP TIL WE DROP STOP
```

Turn around

plot

if this story isn't about Rebirth, then it isn't about anything at all

Frustrated, self-indulgent son took inheritance, wasting it rapidly in wild living.

When the money was all gone, and famine struck the land, he took a job tending pigs.

He longed to eat the pods with which his pigs were fed when he had a revelation and came to his senses. He realized he'd been a selfish, indulgent waster. He considered thus:

'My father's hired men get better treatment than I now face, so I shall repent of my sin and go home and ask my father for a job as a hired man. I'm no longer worthy to be called a son.'

He made his way, but while he was still a long way off, his father saw him, welcomed him and threw a party to celebrate his repentant, reborn son.

At the shindig, he announced 'This my son was lost, and is found; he was dead and is alive again!'

Despite his brother's complaints, the party continued with merrymaking.

Dialogue _style_

'Hi Dad!'

'What is it, sunshine?'

'You know the money that I inherit when you die?'

'H'mm?'

'Can I have it now?'

'Why do you want it now?'

'Well, I don't want to wait.'

'If you must, I suppose so.'

'Ta. Bye!'

'Another dozen oysters, two more bottles of the '34, and bring me my restaurant bill.'

'Here you are, sir.'

'Ta. Oh dear, I don't seem to have any money left.'

'Pick a window, loser, you're leaving.'

'Come on, you pigs, budge up and let me get to the trough. Oh. Well, maybe not, then.'

'Get up and go all the way back home. Repent of your foolishness. Ask your father to let you become a servant.'

'Yes, Lord, I will go home and make that request. I am no longer worthy to be called his son.'

'Dad, I am no longer wor–'

'I love you sonshine! Welcome home. Have the family ring and a coat and some shoes. I'm so pleased to see you again! We shall have a party! Servant, kill the fatted calf! Invite the entire village!'

'Yes sir.'

'My son was dead; now he is alive!'

'Not fair!'

'All I have is yours. Meanwhile, he's back, so let's celebrate!'

Confused with other scriptures _style_

The youngest of twelve sons went to find his share of the portion, which was stuck by its horns in a thicket. He carried it to Nineveh or home rejoicing, but fell among robbers, who threw him in a winepress, took all his money and left him for dead.

Famine struck so he fed pigs and sent evil spirits into them so that they ran off the edge of a cliff. He longed to fill his stomach with seeds that fell among thorns, or with thorns that sprang up and choked him. He came to his senses and said to himself 'Ninety and nine are safe; I shall go to my father and tell him I am no longer worthy to sow seed where the birds of the air swoop and feast themselves and the lilies of the field reap and spin and neither do they sow. And all their neighbours with them.'

But while he was still a long way off, his Priest and his Levite passed by, and Lo! they were sore afraid. But his father spake unto him, saying 'Fear not, I bring you tidings of great abundance.' And the glory of the Lord shone round about them, even to the fouth generation. He gave him a ring for his finger and agreed to make him a good and faithful servant and soil for the hundredfold.

'This my son might have passed through the eye of a needle, but when I return I will reap what I have sowed, pay more if more is owed and provide shoes for his feet; and the fatted calf for the sheep, the birds and the Samaritans of Syro-Phoenicia.'

His older brother bowed down to him as though a sheaf of corn, and found a goat and some friends from Babylon.

'You shall always be my son, so let your yes be yes. I beseech thee, abstain from meat sacrificed to idols, due to feet of clay and shattering the Asherah poles.'

'What?'

Olfactory _senses_

The pungent tang of crops and livestock wafted across the yard as the boy took the crisp, ink-scented notes from his father. He splashed on some deadly aftershave and took off for the windy city.

He drifted through the heady mix of alcohol evaporating into the air, perfume and cigar smoke, until the wedge was gone.

The smell of fear and famine struck, and the boy's nostrils were filled with the stench of pigs and their rotting food. He even longed to fill his stomach with the putrefying compost material.

The light went on in his head and he realised the joyful bouquet of his father's love. He prepared himself to be a stinking servant, but his father saw him from afar. He ran up to him, kissed him and hugged him. It was obvious the boy needed a shower.

His dad gave him a ring, a coat which smelled of conditioner, leather shoes, and some lovely warm sliced roast beef (cooked with garlic), served with horseradish sauce, sautéd potatoes and a rich meaty gravy.

'My son was merely a decaying corpse, but now he's my ever-fragrant boy!'

The unpleasant stink of long-mouldering bitter envy filled the nostrils of the farmer as his older son voiced grievances.

'The sweat of my brow I have given over many years, and yet you never gave me a young goat for a barbecue with my friends. Nevertheless, when this waster boy returns, you fill the air with smoke and aromatic spices and laughter and boozy breath...'

'Listen, my boy. You are always with me, and all I have is yours. But we had to celebrate, as the decaying corpse of my lost son is vibrantly alive and well and washed and clothed and found and here!'

Pseudo-Shakespeare _pastiche_

DRAMATIS PERSONAE:
OLD MAN   a farmer of considerable wealth

RECKLESS   his son; of unbridled wantonness

MISTRESS   a bartender of
RAPIDO   disputable morals

three   wizened crones of
COOKS   dubious cleanliness

SCENE ONE: WITHOUT THE FARM
Enter OLD MAN _and_ RECKLESS, _with ledgers and a trumpet_
OLD MAN: Thro' silver-fleckéd years of joyous thoughts five score groats hath now muchly o'er filled a casket well struck in years marked wi' my monogram; my style writ firm in crops and creatures both far and yon and thus and such.
RECKLESS: Fie on't! Gist mine share, thou pock-faced loon!
OLD MAN: 'Tis pity; 'tis; 'tis true; ah me. _(aside)_ O the cankered, thumb-biting, chiding chops of one's loin-spring were ever so; yet thusly shall I convert all sounds of woe to hey nonny nonny. _(to RECKLESS)_ My son, neither a borrower nor...

110

RECKLESS: *(aside)* Yea, angels and ministers of grace spare me from this pigeon-liver'd rambling witless ill-venom'd caddis-gartered buffoon!

OLD MAN: Fare thee well, splenative lad o'mine! Thou seemest not smiling beyond this my kidney; yet 'tis mine heart's sweet sorrow.

RECKLESS: I set contemplation upon lands afar, with full hope ne'er again to see thee, thou tardy-gated varlet. For this cash, much thanks. I go! *(exit)*

SCENE TWO: BOAR'S HEAD TAVERN, *with cups*

Enter RECKLESS *and* MISTRESS RAPIDO

RECKLESS: Ho! Another goblet of thine most excellent mead with all haste, prithee! This tongue of mine swelleth – comfortlessly beyond double, and in an trice doth rasp sandpaperingly so upon my crusting lips and arid palate; forsooth this thirst must of force be quenched and quelled and smoothed and soothed.

RAPIDO: I wouldst thine fair request obey right soon, but thy velvet drawstrung dubloon bag hath dwindled, most grossly. It afears me that thy mettle is quite assuredly run dry and spent paperwork doth thy name offend. Up-hard thou art. So this my nose I thumb; why, I deny thine slake-request.

RECKLESS: Such as e'en this low-life bladder refuseth me?

RAPIDO: Zounds, get thee hence!

RECKLESS: I shall seek justice and mercy in an house of considerate less iniquity. *(exits)*

RAPIDO: Ha! May fortune smile upon thy request where e're thy hoarse throat hast spoke, for demand and table-rap alone lack strength when backed not up by substant jangling token.

Now is a winter of discontent;
yea, of growling guts yet to break
upon these gleaming shores.
All will grossly starve methinks
lest they find themselves,
right quick, hoggish chores.

SCENE THREE: A STREET, *with pigs*

Enter RECKLESS

RECKLESS: Oh woe is me, for all mine adversaries hath gathered round about and grimaced withal, struck me thrice upon mine heart and soul, and tainted me wi' pangs and pains. Thou grunting, snorting chops! How now, thou sow? Forswear unto me thine podlike picnic... Yet still I am an man, yea, an man. Can'st mind's eye bear to depict mine lips, beard, teeth o'erflowed with distasteful swill of most villainous stink that e'er offended nostril?

Marry, here's the rub; divers vulgar hiréd strangers take sparkling cup and happily baked meats for supper tomorrow and tomorrow; thus parental provisions circadian, do rudely furnish. Enow! To bow's the how, I know, wherein I'll catch the conscience of my father; yet to his hallowed portals withinward I'll go to serve him there with doff and scrape and forelock's tug, and 'yes anon my lord!' – perchance to gain a meagre recompense as employing-man of no familiarity nor name. Here's wither'd violets for remembr'nce of destroy'd faithfulness: me his son no more. But yet within his walls and heart? *(exits)*

SCENE FOUR: A ROAD, *with trees*

Enter RECKLESS

RECKLESS: Fourscore mile have I trod to return to home. *(aside, as* OLD MAN *enters)* How now, here cometh hence the paternal scolding; but soft, I'll plead mine unfretting case with smile and curtsey at nuncle's feet. Watch how his fierce countenance and furrowing brow melloweth towards me! *(he doffs to* OLD MAN*)*

O sir, make thou me an servant for thy sake, since my worthiness hath thawed, melted and resolv'd itself into an dew…

OLD MAN: *(with tears)* Light from yonder window breaks – thou art i' the east, and duly yet is the son.

Now speak, why should ne'r I call thee pribbling folly-fallen carbunkle-blossom? Nay! Though neither shall I prattle and rant thusly of loin's sweet issue, but grasp thee to mine hollow rib – tush thy mouth and hold thy whisht!

For I shall favour thee with this precious charm of purest gold for thy – oh, slender! - finger, and this tailor'd vestment for thy shoulders and these shoes t'enswift thine cantering. Sharply shall I slay choice meat e'en upon the hoof and revel until new dawn's tender kiss astrews the mantle cloudless of the sky. Thy breath and spirit hath returnéd so much better than reportingly!

SCENE FIVE: AN PARTY

Enter Three COOKS, *cauldron and rhyme*
COOKS: Now come we crones within
    farm's gate
To stew a meal, to celebrate!
The farmer who hast lost and found
His son hath bid us stir around.
Leg of bat and partridge-throat
Eye of rat and spleen of goat –
COOK ONE: Nay, sisters, this our
    feasting pot
Right toothsome is – for potions not!
COOKS: Ear of wheat, just half and half
Cream of chicken, flank of calf
Neck of lamb and rabbit spine

And flagon-fill'd with malmsey
    wine!
Enter OLD MAN, RECKLESS
OLD MAN Ho! Everyone that thirsteth! Gather ye hither, yon villagers, mine; rejoice thou greatly, e'en one and all!

Ye minstrels, wi' fingers deft and swift play yon tunes or chords t'inspire step, jump, frolic, turn! Strike thou sharp-aimed strokes upon timbrel and lyre and music make with strums and focused energies. We fain would pitch a cap-and-petticoated ball.

My son, held fast by death's appalling glance

(And considered lost by those who seek by chance)

Now lives! Come, let us make a merry dance!

Call your partner! Strike up, pipers! *(They revel with trumpets, caper and much celebration)*

Politically correct   *style*

perhaps we should complain more consistently 'this is political correctness gone psychopathological'

Secondary-inheriting son promotes opportunity for generosity from institution-bound relative. Finds independence, and redistributes wealth among barmen, dancers, bouncers and chancers.

Latterly, when financially under-resourced, severe governmental national planning shortfall combined with unforeseeable arable development deficiencies cause widespread rampant and nutritionally-imbalanced weight loss (meteorologically-assisted, perhaps).

Takes up human resource post with crackling potential, wishes for alternative ownership of non-meat option.

Internal cranial illumination resulted in consideration. 'Self-effacingly re-entering my previous domicile may escalate improvement of all my prospects in the realm of health and safety,' he thought, attempting to raise himself to his feet, using carefully rehearsed techniques of leverage, guaranteed not to occasion strain to my back or to involve unhelpful twisting or jerking elements; *cf* the government-issued leaflet 106ISAAGTMF *Minimising Risk when Standing Up Following Prolonged Squatting In Animal Enclosures.*

Using only renewable-fuel transport facilities, he travels; yet he is interrupted by overt and unexpected paternal expressions of familiarity, including gross intrusions of personal space, along with finger-friendly endowment, surprise jacketisation and unexpected shodding.

Non-vegetarian meal provided. 'Being gender non-specific, this offspring potentially lacked vitality, but now is mordancy-challenged.'

Sporting terms
key words

tennis, golf, cricket, angling;
see also More sporting terms (p283)

'**Let**[1] me have my **wedge**[2],' asked the son, with considerable **spin**[3]. He was one of a dozen workers, some of whom would just **pitch**[2,3,4] up casuall[1]y, while others took a **mini-break**[1].

The boy smiled, making the most of his **dimples**[2].

'Why the **deuce**[1] would I do that?' his father **declared**[3], making a **silly point**,[3] attempting to **draw**[1,2,3] it all **out**[1,3], as a kind of **test**[3]. He was asking people to vote to bring biscuits containing dried fruit to the **fore**[2].

'Consider it a **backhander**[1]... Just **put**[2] it **in**[3] my palm. **Gimme!**[2] I don't want you to **pin**[2] me down, **pater, no!**'

Ster[4]nly his father calculated his **won**ga (**some ter**[3]ms are rather common). '**Six**[3], **four**[3], **six, three, seven, six, six, two**[1]... that's **forty**[1] shekels, **net**[1,4].'

'Which makes what? **25 for 1**[3] of your sons (my older brother), while I'm entitled to **fifteen!**'

'**Love**[1] you, my boy,' said the father, sadly, but not dwelling on the boy's **fault**[1]s. '**Bye**[1,2,3].' He wrote a cheque, correcting his mistakes with his **ink er**[4]aser.

A little later the son decided to **swing**[1,3] the door closed with a **grand slam**[1], cross **over**[3] the **boundary**[3] and **walked**[3] down the **drive**[2], across a **gully**[3] (past the **pavilion**[3]) and towards a foreign land. He had to **walkover**[1] the bridge and he was gone. He was rather **green**[2] but **appealed**[3] to a few **first class**[3] **singles**[1,3] – he knew how to **bowl a maiden over**[3].

Dolly[3] was **fine**[3] (quite a **catch**[3,4]), and when he **lead**[4] some **followed on**[3], but while others **lure**[4]d him, not one of them was a **keeper**[3].

He began to **spoon**[2] with them, **court**[1]ing, making **googly**[3] eyes, ordering **mixed doubles**[1] at the **bar**. **B**[4]ut he was on **a bit of a sticky wicket**[3]. After a **length**[3] of time, he'd spent his filthy lu**cre** el[4]aborately; his **float**[4] **run out**[3]; cash was at **break point**[1].

He had no **grub**; s[4]imilarly, nothing to drink – not even **Robinson's Lemon Barley Water**[1]. So he began to **fade**[2]. His smile didn't **seam**[3] a **beamer**[3] – hungry as an **albatross**[2].

He looked after pigs, longing to eat their pods – even though they were a bit **mashie**[2], covered with **flies**[4] and marked with **bogies**[2].

In addition, they featured **chalk dust**[1], and were infested with **maggots**[4]. They didn't seem to have come from a glasshouse-equipped **nursery. End**[3] of the day came, and he **dismissed**[3] the idea, although he was absolutely **stumped**[3]; he lost a lot of **weight**[4] and ended up considerably less **wide**[3].

He thought of home. He knew there were **XI**[3] hired hands, (without him they would be **handicapped**[2]) and he could be the **twelfth man**[3], well capable of using a broom to **sweep**[3], or to **scratch**[2] at the **edge**[3] of the soil with a **hook**[234].

He decided to **bail**[3], to **leg**[3] it, and, even though it was a long **slog**[3], **approach**[1,2] the farm again. He wondered if he'd be able to **square**[3] things with his father. He thought to himself 'I have **walked**[3] so far, my feet are **tire**[3]d. Oh, it'll be good to see my Abba…'

It[4] took what felt like a **century**[3] to get back to his dad's **gaff**[4]. While he was still a **fair way**[2] **out**[1,3], **on**[3] the **offside**[3] (beyond the **tramlines**[1] – farther than the **boundary**[3] of the farm) and **padding up**[3] the path, his dad **glanced**[3] him.

'My son!' he cried, and made **a gle**[2]**eful** sound. 'Far from getting the **hump, I re**[1,3]**alize** I care deeply!'

His **night-watchman**[3] attitude was far from **driving**[2] the boy away, and he'd kept using his **Twenty20**[3] vision, despite the **bad light**[3].

He ran at a **smooth**[1], **medium pace**[3] to greet him.

The boy **collapsed**[3] into the arms of his father, who said '**Ace**[1]! This is the best day since my boy **went! Worth**[2] making a few sacrifices, now, certainly… **slip**[3] a ring onto his finger, and some shoes (replacing this worn pair – look, he's got a **hole in one**[2] of the soles), and give him a coat that **covers**[3] him for **extra cover**[3] for his **back.**

Nine[2] minutes later, all these gifts had been bestowed.

'Now, kill **Niblick**[2] the Calf and spit-roast him – make sure he's cooked beautifully on every side; done to a turn **all-round…** **Er**[3]**satz** dinners are not welcome here! **Swing**[2,3] the hatchet to **make the cut**[2] again and again; **flag**[2] up a **par**[2]**ty**! **Iron**[2] my suit – give the trousers a sharp **crease!**[3]

'**Chop**[1] and burn some **wood**[2] (this might create **Ashes**)!'[3]

'Yes, **set**[1] up silver **service**[1]… we shall have **game**[1] pie, **fish**[4] and **fry**[4] a **chip**[1,2] or two. And we could **serve**[1] **smash**[1] **albatross**[2] and **lob**[1]**ster** as an **extra**[3] **course**[2] – oh, plus some roast **duck**[3]! And salad with **pump**[1]**kin seeds**[1]. Yes, and fruit salad, with peach, pineapple, **plum, b**[3]**lue**berries, **banana**[1] and mandarins, served with ice cream, lemon **drops, hot**[1] fudge sauce and fromage frais. And vodka **shot**[4]s. With, perhaps an iced **bun. Ker**[2]**nels** of almonds as well.' The party raised all kinds of hullaba**loos; ener**[3]**getic** dancing followed, especially to tunes with a thumping **baseline**[1], which the father thought were just a **racket**[1].

He preferred **string s**[1]**olos**. He put on an **apron**[2] and **borrow**[2]**ed** a knife to **cut**[2] a big **slice**[1,2] of **oval**[3] cake, but cut his finger and dripped AB positive across the table.

'Look, how **I'm bled on**[1] the trestles!' he said with a laugh. 'But let's have a **cup**[1,234] of **tee**[2] brewed with leaves **cast**[4] in by **taking tea**[3] from a **caddie.**[2] Use the finest bone crockery – yes, the **china.'**

'**Man,**[3] we can have a **ball!' Boy**[1] of mine had crossed the **line**[4] but by the **Lord's**[3] mercy is found; he was food for **worms**[4] (which was **rough**[1,2], since we had no **trace**[4] of his whereabouts) but has managed to **rally!**[1] **Hail Mary**[1]! **Honour**[2] God! Register your garibal**di vot**[2]**e**! Keep it **reel!'**[4]

[1]tennis 50 [2]golf 46 [3]cricket 77 [4]angling 25

UK No1 hit singles
of the 1960s   *key words*
Record Retailer charts March 1960 – February 1969, when the British Market Research Bureau was established
'**Please don't tease** me, give me what's due and I'll be **glad all over,**' said the younger of the **two little Boys**. '**These boots are made for walkin'**, right?' he asked.

The father knew he'd have to **let the heartaches begin**. And one **sunny afternoon, shakin' all over**, the father said '**Go now; I can't stop loving you. Baby, come back! We can work it out.**'

So the **bachelor boy** took his cash and did **something stupid,** thinking he was **king of the road**. **It's not unusual** (**I heard it through the grapevine**).

All or nothing: soon he had nothing. Hunger struck; '**Sugar, sugar**' he cried.

He longed for the **wonderful land** his father tilled, and eventually had to **surrender**.

He was **a whiter shade of pale** as he set out on **Blackberry Way**, thinking he could **walk right back** to the **green grass of home**. He went **walking back to happiness**, having decided to **get back.**

'**Anyone who had a heart** would accept me as a servant', he thought.

But while he was still a long way off, his father shed **tears**.

'**Where do you go to, my lovely?**' he shouted as he ran up to his son.

'**Congratulations: I want to hold your hand,**' he said, but ended up hugging him.

'**It's over,**' he whispered, as he gave him replacement boots (similarly fashioned for bipedal locomotion), a coat and a ring.

He greeted his son, despatched the fatted calf and confirmed the boy's sonship.

'**Hallo, Goodbye. I got you babe.**'
The son confirmed '**I'm alive!**'

Title artist year of release
Please Don't Tease Cliff Richard and the Shadows 1960 *Glad all over* Dave Clark Five 64 *Two Little Boys* Rolf Harris 69 *These Boots are Made for Walkin'* Nancy Sinatra 66 *Let the heartaches begin* Long John Baldry 67 *Sunny Afternoon* The Kinks 66 *Shakin' all over* Johnny Kidd & the Pirates 60 *Go Now* Moody Blues 65 *I can't stop loving you* Ray Charles 62 *Baby come back* Equals 68 *We can work it out* Beatles 65 *Bachelor boy* Cliff Richard and the Shadows 63 *Something Stupid* Nancy Sinatra 67 *King of the Road* Roger Miller 65 *It's not unusual* Tom Jones 65 *I heard it through the grapevine* Marvin Gaye 69 *All or nothing* Small faces 66 *Sugar Sugar* The Archies 69 *Wonderful Land* The Shadows 62 *Surrender* Elvis Presley 61 *Whiter Shade of Pale* Procal Harum 67 *Blackberry Way* The Move 69 *Walk Right Back* Everly Brothers 61 *Green, Green Grass of Home* Tom Jones 66 *Walkin' Back to Happiness* Helen Shapiro 61 *Get Back* Beatles with Billy Preston 69 *Anyone who had a Heart* Cilla Black 64 *Tears* Ken Dodd 65 *Where do you go to My Lovely?* Peter Sarstedt 69 *Congratulations* Cliff Richard 68 *I want to Hold your Hand* The Beatles 63 *It's Over* Roy Orbison 64 *Hallo, Goodbye* The Beatles 67 *I Got You, Babe* Sonny & Cher 65 *I'm Alive* The Hollies 65

UK No1 hit singles
of the 1970s   *key words*

'He's asked me for **everything I own**,' said the farmer. 'He's a **sad sweet dreamer**, but I said to him "I **can't give you anything** except **all kinds of everything**". I asked "**When will I see you again?**" but he had no answer. **How can I be sure I will survive? Bye bye baby!**'

'I was born under a **wand'rin' star**, in the **summertime**,' explained Vincent. '**I don't want to talk about it.**' Off he went with his cash, to spend some **seasons in the sun** down on **Devil Gate Drive**, near the **Yellow River.**

He thought the **summer nights** would last **forever and ever**, but **the name of the game** is **night fever**, and even though he was **up town top ranking**, this **bohemian rhapsody** ended.

He met a few friends: **Grandad Ernie, Amazing Grace, Baby Jump** and **Billy Don'tbeahero**, but **oh boy**, they left very soon, and the son was **lonely this Christmas**. He had to take **one day at a time**. He'd hoped to look after the **combine harvester** but tended pigs; he had a **jealous mind** for the pods. But all he had to eat was **mouldy old dough.**

He decided to **knock three times**, but the pigs grunted in reply '**I hear you knocking**'.

The **Spirit in the sky** said '**Hold me close**, I'm **always yours, love me for a reason** and **give a little love.**'

He realised '**You won't find another fool like me**: I'm the **son of my father**; I shall tell him "**you're the one that I want**"'.

The father said to himself '**I'm still waiting.**'

He saw him when he was on his way **back home** and gave him a **band of gold** (**free**), said '**Don't go breaking my heart; welcome home; make me smile** (**no charge**), **coz I luv you!** I thought it was a **tragedy**, but now he's got **bright eyes. Merry Xmas everybody!**'

Everything I own Ken Boothe 1974 *Sad sweet Dreamer* Sweet Sensation 74 *Can't give you anything* The Stylistics 75 *All kinds of Everything* Mary Hopkin 70 *When will I see you again?* The Three Degrees 74 *How can I be sure?* David Cassidy 72 *I will survive* Gloria Gaynor 79 *Bye Bye Baby* The Bay City Rollers 75 *Wand'rin' Star* Lee Marvin 70 *In the Summertime* Mungo Jerry 70 *Vincent* Don McLean 72 *I don't want to talk about it* Rod Stewart 77 *Seasons in the Sun* Terry Jacks 74 *Devil Gate Drive* Suzi Quatro 74 *Yellow River* Christie 70 *Summer Nights* John Travolta and Olivia Newton John 78 *Forever & Ever* Slik 76 *The Name of the Game* Abba 77 *Night Fever* Bee Gees 78 *Up Town Top Ranking* Althia & Donna 78 *Bohemian Rhapsody* Queen 75 *Grandad* Clive Dunn 71 *Ernie* Benny Hill 71 *Amazing Grace* The Pipes and The Drums and The Military Band of The Royal Scots Dragoon Guards 72 *Baby Jump* Mungo Jerry 71 *Billy Don't be a Hero* Paper Lace 74 *Oh boy* Mud 75 *Lonely this Christmas* Mud 74 *One Day at a time* Lena Martell 79 *Combine Harvester* The Wurzels 76 *Jealous Mind* Alvin Stardust 74 *Mouldy old Dough* Lieutenant Pigeon 72 *Knock three times* Dawn 71 *I hear you knocking* Dave Edmunds 70 *Spirit in the Sky* Norman Greenbaum 70 *Hold me close* David Essex 75 *Always Yours* Gary Glitter 74 *Love me for a reason* The Osmonds 74 *Give a little love* Bay City Rollers 75 *You won't find another fool like me* The New Seekers 74 *Son of my father* Chicory Tip 72 *You're the one that I want* John Travolta and Olivia Newton John 78 *I'm still waiting* Diana Ross 71 *Back Home* England World Cup Squad 70 *Band of gold* Freda Payne 70 *Free* Deniece Williams 77 *Don't go Breaking my Heart* Elton John and Kiki Dee 76 *Welcome home* Peters and Lee 73 *Make me Smile* Steve Harley & Cockney Rebel 75 *No Charge* JJ Barrie 76 *Coz I luv you* Slade 71 *Tragedy* Bee Gees 79 *Bright Eyes* Art Garfunkel 79 *Merry Xmas Everybody!* Slade 73

UK No1 hit singles of the 1980s
key words

'Imagine if I was loaded with brass in pocket,' thought the boy. 'I should be so lucky!'

But his father said 'I owe you nothing, but I'll give you everything I own. You win again! Don't leave me this way... wake me up before you go go.'

'Papa don't preach!' Father watched him go. 'Nothing's gonna change my love for you. You'll be always on my mind. True. I'm never gonna give you up. That's the power of love. Don't you want me?'

The father's wealth was (after the final count) down to ner ner ner ner nineteen out of 30, as he gave him one third. Off went the lad to a town called malice, to a house of fun, where there was mistletoe and wine; perfect, red, red wine and where the phrase 'It's a Sin' caused a chain reaction with a woman, a jealous guy and desire.

'What'll I do with the cash?' he thought; 'use it up and wear it out!' The place came under pressure as the food ran out, and the boy wondered 'Is there something I should know?' Hallo, I should have known better than to end up wanting pigfood. Like a prayer, he thought 'I shall go home - it'll be just like starting over'.

The Spirit in the Sky took him to the Edge of Heaven. (There must be an angel at work.) He was on his way home – when the going gets tough, the tough get going – thinking about his father.

'I'll be working my way back to you by the power of love. I'll ask to be a servant - since he might say "don't stand so close to me!" or deny even a little peace. I'm the Coward of the county. I know him so well!'

'Take my breath away!' cried the father, who saw the boy when he was still a long way off.

'I knew you were waiting for me,' lied the boy.

'Move closer. Here's a ring, especially for you, Frankie. Here's a coat and shoes (you'll never walk alone) since I have a good heart and I've been saving. All my love for you - you got it! - only you! Let's party! My son was dead, but now he's back to life!' And there was dancing in the street.

Imagine John Lennon 81 *If I was* Midge Ure 85 *Brass in Pocket* The Pretenders 80 *I should be so lucky!* Kylie Minogue 88 *I owe you nothing* Bros 88 *Everything I Own* Boy George 87 *You win again* Bee Gees 87 *Don't leave me this way* The Communards 86 *Wake me up before you go go* Wham! 84 *Papa don't preach* Madonna 86 *Nothing's gonna change my love for you* Glenn Madeiros 88 *Always on my mind* Pet Shop Boys 87 *True* Spandau Ballet 83 *Never gonna give you up* Rick Astley 87 *The power of love* Jennifer Rush 85 *Don't you want me?* Human League 81 *The final countdown* Europe 86 *19* Paul Hardcastle 85 *A town called malice* The Jam 82 *House of fun* Madness 82 *Mistletoe and wine* Cliff Richard 88 *Perfect* S Express 88 *Red, red wine* UB40 83 *It's a Sin* Pet Shop Boys 87 *Chain reaction* Diana Ross 86 *Woman* John Lennon 81 *Jealous guy* Roxy Music 81 *Desire* U2 82 *Use it up & wear it out* Odyssey 80 *Under pressure* Queen & David Bowie 81 *Is there something I should know?* Duran Duran 83 *Hallo* Lionel Richie 84 *I should have known better* Jim Diamond 84 *Like a prayer* Madonna 89 *Starting over* John Lennon 80 *Spirit in the Sky* Doctor & the Medics 86 *Edge of Heaven* Wham! 86 *There must be an angel* Eurythmics 85 *When the going gets tough, the tough get going* Billy Ocean 86 *Working my way back to you* Detroit Spinners 80 *The power of love* Frankie Goes to Hollywood 84 *You win again* Bee Gees 87 *Don't stand so close to me* The Police 80 *A little peace* Nicole 82 *Coward of the county* Kenny Rogers 80 *I know him so well* Elaine Paige and Barbara Dickson 85 *Take my breath away* Berlin 86 *I knew you were waiting for me* Aretha Franklin and George Michael 87 *Move Closer* Phyllis Nelson 85 *Especially for you* Kylie Minogue and Jason Donovan 89 *Frankie* Sister Sledge 85 *You'll never walk alone* Crowd 85 *A good heart* Feargal Sharkey 85 *Saving all my love for you* Whitney Houston 85 *You got it!* The Right Stuff 89 *Only you* The Flying Pickets 83 *Let's party!* Jive Bunny and the Mixmasters 89 *Back to life* Soul II Soul featuring Caron Wheeler 89 *Dancing in the street* David Bowie and Mick Jagger 85

UK No1 hit singles
of the 1990s   *key words*

'Please don't go,' wheezed the asthmatic father. 'But if I let you go with my cash - bring it all back. There''ll be tears on my pillow, because I will always love you. I believe love can build a bridge, but I'll be missing you, and it'll be killing me softly to be without you. It will be a sacrifice. I realise this will spice up your life, and you might even be asking yourself *Should I stay or should I go?* but then you're young at heart and everybody's free. Don't. Stop!... Goodbye!' The boy left with the cash, and ended up partying with some men in black (well, black or white) and a girl in an itsy bitsy teeny weenie yellow polka dot bikini. 'She's the one! She can lift me up until I'm flying without wings!' he cried. 'We will party until breakfast time! Provide suitable food for me and the lady. Marmalade, muesli and Danish pastries, too!'

Love is all around on Saturday night, and he wanted to keep on movin' ...baby (one more time) and to dance with the most beautiful girl in the world, until he was dizzy.

They started to play no limit poker, and he hoped 'My heart will go on,

but I'd like to be dealt hearts or diamonds: come on you reds, just a little bit more!' Eventually, the joker was never ever going to be enough. The boy had been promised breakfast at Tiffany's but it was not to be. Come one morning, the food ran out.

The famine was a killer. Too much? No, when the going gets tough, the tough get going, and this was the perfect moment. Would I lie to you? It was 3am. Eternal revelation came to him and he saw that things can only get better if he returned. Feeling deeply dippy, he started back home. Before he got to the end of the road where his father and mama lived, the old man ran up to him.

'I want you back!' he cried, 'ready or not!'

The son started 'I wannabe your servant...' but the father gave him a ring and a coat and some shoes. What was his message? It's in his kiss.

The asthmatic old man was getting breathless, and had to turn to his compressed enriched air supply (50% oxygen: i.e. in the bottle).

'I'd do anything for love, (but I won't do that). You are the one and only, and now you're back for good. I thought I'd be living on my own, but there ain't nobody knockin' on Heaven's door anymore.

'We can dance: Mambo No 5 and Livin' La Vida Loca until the end of the millennium! Pray erstwhile working arrangements can resume!

'Oh, what a perfect day! Viva forever!'

Please don't go KWS 1992 *If I let you go* Westlife 99 *Bring it all Back* S Club 7 99 *Tears on my Pillow* Kylie Minogue 90 *I will Always Love You* Whitney Houston 92 *I Believe* Robson & Jerome 95 *Love can build a Bridge* Cher, Chrissie Hynde and Neneh Cherry with Eric Clapton

118

95 *I'll be Missing you* Puff Daddy & Faith Evans 97 *Killing me Softly* Fugees 96 twice *Without You* Mariah Carey 94 *Sacrifice* Elton John 90 *Spice Up your Life* Spice Girls 97 *Should I stay or should I go?* Clash 91 *Young at Heart* Bluebells 93 *Everybody's Free* Baz Luhmann 99 *Don't Stop (Wiggle Wiggle)* Outhere Brothers 95 *Goodbye* Spice Girls 98 *Men in Black* Will Smith 97 *Black or White* Michael Jackson 91 *Itsy Bitsy Teeny Weenie Yellow Polka Dot Bikini* Bombalurina 90 *She's the One* Robbie Williams 99 *Lift me up* Geri Halliwell 99 *Flying without Wings* Westlife 99 *Lady Marmalade* All Saints 98 *Love is all around* Wet Wet Wet 94 *Saturday Night* Whigfield 94 *Keep on Movin'* Five 99 *...Baby one more time* Britney Spears 99 *Most Beautiful Girl in the World* Prince 94 *Dizzy* Vic Reeves and the Wonder Stuff 91 *No Limit* 2 Unlimited 93 *My Heart will Go On* Celine Dion 98 *Come on you reds!* Manchester United Football Squad 94 *A little bit more* 911 99 *The Joker* Steve Miller Band 90 *Never Ever* All Saints 99 *Breakfast at Tiffany's* Deep Blue Something 96 *2 Become 1* Spice Girls 96 *Killer* Adamski 90 *Too Much* Spice Girls 97 *When the Going gets Tough* Boyzone 99 *Perfect Moment* Martine McCutcheon 99 *Would I lie to you?* Charles & Eddie 92 *3am Eternal* The KLF featuring Children of the Revolution 91 *Things can only get Better* D:Ream 94 *Deeply Dippy* Right Said Fred 92 *The End of the Road* Boys II Men 92 *Mama* Spice Girls 97 *I Want You Back* Melanie B featuring Missy Elliott 98 *Ready or Not* Fugees 96 *Wannabe* Spice Girls 96 *Shoop Shoop Song (It's In His Kiss)* Cher 91 *Genie in the Bottle* Christina Aquilera 99 *I'd do Anything for Love, (But I Won't do That)* Meat Loaf 93 *The One and Only* Chesney Hawkes 91 *Back for Good* Take That 95 *Living on my Own* Freddie Mercury 93 *Ain't Nobody* LL Cool J 97 *Knockin' on Heaven's Door* Dunblane 96 *Mambo No 5* Lou Bega 99 *Livin' La Vida Loca* Ricky Martin 99 *The Millenium Prayer* Cliff Richard 99 *Perfect Day* Various 98 *Viva Forever* Spice Girls 98

UK No1 hit singles of the 2000s   *key words*

Stan gave a smile and spoke to his father.

'Last time I asked, you said *no* to me. Obviously, I know you'll be faithful to me when you pass on, because the promise of inheriting is unbreakable. But so far, I've never had a dream come true, so it's now or never. I'm going to leave right now.

'You know there'll be no more money for you,' his father said, 'even if you come back?'

'Yeah.'

'H'mm. This is a bit of a dilemma. My life would suck without you, but I want to bless you. So, what I'll do is pay you in 7 days...'

'No, tomorrow! Let's have a little less conversation. You'll be running the farm without me.'

'Circumstances suffer changes, but relationships don't. Lieutenant of this farm, you were going to be... so, where will you go?'

'Dissipation City, that's my Goal! I'll be OK!'

'You think I can't see through this sham? Er, I can, boy...'

But off he went ('I'm gonna be 500 miles away'), walking day & night, after asking *Is this the way to Amarillo?*

Soon he reached the city and proceeded to do somethin' stupid as if he was bonkers, locating the red light district, known as the *Independent Women* part.

One beautiful liar told him where he could find (to begin with) a sexy chick (Grace), Kelly, an angel (well, more than a woman), Mandy (a nasty girl), an uptown girl, some beautiful girls and a mysterious girl with five colours in her hair (she was probably colourblind).

Where is the love?

She said these words 'Oh, it feels so good. You're my hero, pure and simple.'

'I bet you look good on the dancefloor!'

'It's a **mad world** around here, where **anything is possible**.'

'**Slow** down **boys and girls, it wasn't me**...'

These are **all the things she said**.

'**I gotta feeling** of déjà vu,' the boy said, 'but I **gotta get thru this. I kissed a girl one night**, and **you're beautiful!**'

His money ran out and a famine struck (**killing in the name** of hunger) **all summer long**.

Everyone had to **evacuate the dancefloor**, as it was **the masses against the classes. Sometimes you can't make it on your own,** so a little while later, he got a **crazy** job where he had to get **too close** to some pigs, who were fed on **baby cakes** of rotting vegetation. It was nasty to **breathe** the air; even the maggots **don't stop movin'**, trying to find edible parts. 'This is so sick. Nobody could be a **freak like me**. I am hungry and **lonely**,' he said. **'If I were a boy** at work in my father's farm, I'd have dinner **when the sun goes down.'**

The **spirit in the sky** spoke to him for **a moment; like this:** Go home! He said 'I shall **stop living the lie, arise** and go to my father and say "**Oops... I did it again, sorry (sorry seems to be the hardest word). You see, the trouble with me** is that **I can't get you out of my head. Call on me** as a hired man. I'm lucky to be a **survivor** of the famine, but **the fear** of **my sweet lord** came to **shine** on me. I will **never be the same again**; so, will you **take on me,** please?'

He concluded '**My loneliness** is growing **stronger, but can we fix it?**"'

Repenting means **spinning around (right round)** and going the other way, determined to **be faithful everytime.**

While he was still a long way off, (by the **crossroads)**, his father saw him on **the climb** up **the long and winding road,** coming ever **closer**.

His **patience** had paid off; he knew had been absolutely right to tell himself '**Don't give up.'**

'**Baby's coming back!'** he cried, running to greet him. **Breathless**, they hugged (**kiss kiss**).

The boy started to speak 'I've been a **fool again...**' but his dad said '**Don't! Stop! Me now: any one of us – stupid mistake...** I don't **wanna know; never gonna leave your side, my love – I'll stand by you. Dry your eyes.'** He started to give our hero a **ruby** ring, an **umbrella**. 'We must bring you some shoes, since your feet are **bleeding, love.** Then you'll be able to **walk this way. What took you so long?'**

'**Mercy!** All these **wonderful,** expensive gifts...' he began.

'**Love don't cost a thing,'** his father said. 'It's the **greatest day – an eternal flame** burns **when you believe.**

'Fetch Daisy the fatted calf, **light my fire** and –' he made a slash action across his throat '– *oopsy Daisy*; she was **born to make you happy**. If you can't eat it all, **bag it up.**

'And we can have **black coffee,** since **it's chic. O, time** for you to **take a bow** – yes, it's **all about you! Let's dance – Mambo No 5 (with a little help from my friends – just a little!)**

'Daisy's carcass dripped fat into the flames but we damped it down, so now she's **ex on fire**. Let's have a pina colada or a pink **lady. Marmalade** on toast is lovely. Or some other **goodies:** beef, wine, absin**the, ketchup, son!**

'**If you're not the one** of my sons who was dead, but is **whole again,** then I'm a chinaman; here's a note from my mother Elfrida: *Welcome home to the **same old brand new you**. Love, Grandma x.*

'Elfreda's always had a particularly soft spot for you, you know.

'Hallelujah!'

'Good news, we're taking a **holiday**! My son was lost but **against all odds** is found – what a **beautiful day**! I'm **not alone** here at **my place** (**don't** change everything, though!) You **bring me to life; you raise me up – what a wonderful world!**

Stan Eminem 2000 *Smile* Lily Allen 06 *You said No* Busted 03 *Obviously* McFly 06 *Be Faithful* Fatman Scoop featuring The Crooklyn Clan 03 *The Promise* Girls Aloud 08 *Unbreakable* Westlife 02 *Never had a Dream come True* S Club 7 00 *It's Now or Never* Elvis Presley 05 *Leave Right Now* Will Young 03 *If you Come Back* Blue 01 *Yeah* Usher Feat. Lil' Jon & Ludacris 04 *Dilemma* Nelly featuring Kelly Rowland from Destiny's Child 02 *My Life would Suck without You* Kelly Clarkson 09 *So What* Pink 08 *7 Days* Craig David 00 *No Tomorrow* Orson 06 *A Little Less Conversation* Elvis vs. JXL 02 *Without Me* Eminem 02 *Changes* Ozzie & Kelly Osbourne 03 *Hips don't Lie* Shakira featuring Wyclef Jean 06 *That's my Goal* Shane Ward 05 *I'll be OK* McFly 05 *American Boy* Estelle feat. Kanye West 08 *I'm Gonna Be 500 Miles* The Proclaimers featuring Brian Potter & Andy Pipkin 07 *(Is this the Way to) Amarillo?* Tony Christie feat. Peter Kay 05 *Somethin' Stupid* Robbie Williams & Nicole Kidman 01 • *Bonkers* Dizzee Rascal & Armand Van Helden 08 *Independent Women Part One* Destiny's Child 00 *Beautiful Liar* Beyonce & Shakira 07 *Sexy Chick* David Guetta feat. Akon 09 *Grace Kelly* Mika 07 *Angel* Shaggy feat. Rayvon 01 *More than a Woman* Aaliyah 08 *Mandy* Westlife 03 *Nasty Girl* Nelly, Jagged Edge & Avery Storm 06 *Uptown Girl* Westlife 01 *Beautiful Girls* Sean Kingston 07 *Mysterious Girl* Peter Andre 04 *Five colours in her Hair* McFly 04 *Colourblind* Darius 02 *Where is the Love?* Black Eyed Peas 08 *These Words* Natasha Bedingfield 04 *It Feels So Good* Sonique 00 *Hero* Enrique Igesias 02 *Pure and Simple* Hear'Say 01 *I bet you look good on the dancefloor* Arctic Monkeys 05 *Mad World* Michael Andrews feat. Gary Jules 03 *Anything is Possible* Will Young 02 *Slow* Kylie Minogue 03 *Boys and Girls* Pixie

Lott 09 *It Wasn't Me* Shaggy featuring Ricardo 'Rikrok' Ducent 01 *All the Things She Said* Tatu 03 *I Gotta Feeling* Black Eyed Peas 09 *Déjà vu* Beyonce featuring Jay-Z 06 *Gotta Get Thru This* Daniel Bedingfield 02 *I Kissed a Girl* Katy Perry 08 *One Night* Elvis Presley 05 *You're Beautiful* James Blunt 05 *Killing in the Name* Rage Against the Machine 09 *All Summer Long* Kid Rock 08 *Evacuate the Dancefloor* Cascada 09 *The Masses Against the Classes* Manic Street Preachers 00 *Sometimes You Can't Make it on Your Own* U2 05 *Crazy* Gnarls Barkley 06 *Too Close* Blue 01 *Babycakes* 3 Of A Kind 04 *Breathe* Blue Cantrell featuring Sean Paul 03 *Don't Stop Movin'* S Club 7 01 *Freak Like Me* Sugababes 02 *Lonely* Akon 05 *If I were a Boy* Beyoncé 08 *When the Sun Goes Down* Arctic Monkeys 06 *Spirit in the Sky* Gareth Gates with special guests The Kumars 03 *A Moment Like This* Leona Lewis 06 *Stop Living the Lie* David Sneddon 03 *Rise* Gabrielle 00 *Oops... I Did it Again* Britney Spears 00 *Sorry* Madonna 06 *Sorry Seems to be the Hardest Word* Blue featuring Elton John 02 *You See the Trouble with Me* Black Legend 00 *I Can't Get You Out of my Head* Kylie Minogue 01 *Call on me* Eric Prydz 04 *Survivor* Destiny's Child 01 *The Fear* Lily Allen 09 *My Sweet Lord* George Harrison 02 *Shine* Take That 07 *Never Be the Same Again* Melanie C featuring Lisa Left Eye Lopes 00 *Take On Me* A1 00 *Loneliness* Tomcraft 03 *Stronger* Kanye West 07 *Can We Fix it?* Bob the Builder 00 *Spinning Around* Kylie Minogue 00 *Right Round* Flo Rida feat. Kesha 09 *Be Faithful* Fatman Scoop featuring The Crooklyn Clan 03 *Everytime* Britney Spears 04 *Crossroads* Blazin' Squad 02 *The Climb* Joe McElderry 09 *The Long and Winding Road* Will Young & Gareth Gates 02 *Closer* Ne-Yo 08 *Patience* Take That 06 *Don't Give Up* Chicane/Bryan Adams *Baby's Coming Back* McFly 07 *Run* Leona Lewis 08 *Breathless* The Corrs 00 *Kiss Kiss* Holly Valance 02 *Fool Again* Westlife 00 *Don't Stop Me Now* McFly 06 *Anyone Of Us (Stupid Mistake)* Gareth Gates 02 *I don't Wanna Know* Mario Winans featuring Enya & P. Diddy 04 *Never Gonna Leave your Side* Daniel Bedingfield *My Love* Westlife 00 *I'll Stand by You* Girls Aloud 04 *Dry Your Eyes* Streets 04 *Ruby* Kaiser Chiefs 07 *Umbrella* Rihanna 07 *Bleeding Love* Leona Lewis 07 *Walk This Way* Sugababes vs Girls Aloud 07 *What Took You So Long?* Emma Bunton 01 *Mercy* Duffy 08 *Wonderful* Ja Rule feat. R. Kelly & Ashanti 04 *Love Don't Cost a Thing* Jennifer Lopez 01 *Greatest Day* Take That 08 *Eternal Flame* Atomic Kitten 01 *When You Believe* Leon

Jackson 07 *Light My Fire* Will Young 02 *Oopsy Daisy* Chipmunk 09 *Born To Make You Happy* Britney Spears 00 *Bag it Up* Geri Halliwell 00 *Black Coffee* All Saints 00 *It's Chico Time!* Chico 06 *Take a Bow* Rihanna 08 *All About You* McFly 05 *Let's Dance* 5ive 01 *Mambo No 5* Bob the Builder 01 *With a Little Help from my Friends* Sam & Mark 04 *Just a Little* Liberty X 02 *Sex On Fire* Kings of Leon 08 *Lady Marmalade* Christina Aguilera, Lil' Kim, Mya, Pink 01 *Goodies* Ciara featuring Petey Pablo 05 *The Ketchup Song* Las Ketchup 02 *If You're Not the One* Daniel Bedingfield 02 *Whole Again* Atomic Kitten 01 *Same Old Brand New You* A1 00 *Axel F* Crazy Frog 05 *Halleujah* Alexandra Burke 08 *Holiday* Dizzee Rascal 09 *Against All Odds* Mariah Carey & Westlife 00 *Beautiful Day* U2 00 *I'm Not Alone* Calvin Harris 09 *My Place* Nelly 04 *Don't Cha* Pussycat Dolls featuring Busta Rhymes 05 *Bring Me to Life* Evanescence 03 *You Raise Me Up* Westlife 05 *What a Wonderful World* Eva Cassidy & Katie Melua 07

UK No1 hit singles
of 2010-2018   *key words*
no longer just disc sales; since July 2014 streaming data is included
Once upon a time, there was a young troublemaker. 'Dad,' he said, 'I have money on my mind, and that's not perfect: give me everything that's coming to me. I'm the one.'

'Sorry? What do you mean? Oh, son, no! Please don't…'

'Let me go, Pa.'

'See you again?' But the man didn't want to make waves, and wasn't too good at goodbyes, so he gave him the green light. 'Look what you made me do.'

The boy went solo to Dissipation City, famous for uptown funk, bad romance, so-called good times, dirtee disco (with rotating globes of mirrors and blurred lines). All comes with a price tag, and many of the girls he met were rude nearly all the time (dirty bits, easy love). 'We can't stop, because she looks so perfect – after all, we are young and the club is alive! She makes me wanna swagger jagger, replay in my head, get closer, read all about it - all about tonight, what makes you beautiful! I am thinking out loud, now, these days 'cause I love it! Ooo, la la la Hold my hand! I'm not letting go! Say you won't let go, either!'

But soon his cash ran out and the economy was at an all time low.

'Due to the famine, everybody hurts, and expectations are on the floor. Finding a job will drag me down, as it's next to impossible, and we buy stuff in the thrift shop. We have great hunger, and have lost weight (man, just look at the shape of you) – yes, he ain't heavy, he's my brother. But I still want to dance, so let's get ready to –' rhumble '– yes, turn the music louder!' Rumble of tummies continued to drown out the sound, as it was a sign of the times.

The lad took a job somewhere only we know, tending pigs. 'I'd rather be eating their pods, but then, I don't wanna. Go home? Well, part of me feels I'd sing and be happy…' He had a revelation as he said a prayer. 'Incredible! Reg, the Hired man (somebody that I used to know) gets dinner every day…' His heart skips a beat. 'OMG! – what's my name? I could be the one who gets lunch?'

His voice grew louder; 'I shall arise, go home and ask to be a hired men. If I get lucky I'll get to stay in the house every weekend.'

He set off, practicing his speech. 'I wanna feel – I know I've been someone like – you know I've been a problem. I'm not worthy… Am I wrong? Are these wild thoughts?'

Meanwhile, the farmer stood on the roof with Héctor, his French friend, shielding his eyes as he gazed out along the road, across the **River**. '**Hello**… Could that be mon fis? Can't regardez it, parce que thа**T sun, ami… (Jumps)** – could it be? Are you with me? Is this **Freaky Friday**?

'**Don't hold your breath**… Yes! It is my son! **My** lovely boy! He has returned via a **bridge over troubled water**, from **wherever**! **You are** so welcome boy!' **The power of love promises** there's **no** need to be dignified, so he ran to greet him. It was **crazy stupid love. One kiss.**

The **shallow** boy started 'Dad, I am so sorry. I am not worthy…'

'Son, let's hear **no regrets,** and no **blame. Don't be so hard on yourself.** I didn't **forget you**, and I can tell you've **changed, the way you kiss me when we collide.** Oh, it feels like **it's my birthday!** I couldn't **love you more!** Yes, fetch the gifts. **I got U domino diamonds** and a jacket with fancy **stitches** and other **little things** – yes, start **changing** into that coat and shoes… **Let me love you (until you learn to love yourself** – oh, yeah, **love yourself!)** No, **this ain't a love song** but a **paradise** of **good feelings.** Just **love me again.** Tonight (well, from **twilight**) we can **party! Rock anthems** will start showing **how we do (party),** with meat and fish.

'People like fatted calf, which we can barbecue (not **burn**) but really, it's **all about that bass** or turbot with fennel and butter sauce. Followed by **candy** floss – or some grand pudding (also known as afters or **sweet**). **Nothing** will stop us rejoicing! **Turn up the music! Thank you, next!'**

At the party, Dad gave a speech to all his guests and his workers. 'Okay, gang! Listen! **Shout out to my** extremely welcome returned son!

Gangs A-M, you can celebrate (over-emphasising content) until midnight! **Gang N – a.m! Style!** Oh, **I feel the love** in the room. My boy was **RIP**, but now he's alive. Loving **God's Plan!** It's **Funky Friday!** Oh, fetch me a glass of **something; I need** to make a toast! Fetch a **cheerleader!** Obey the **new rules – ESPACI*** told us.'

Meanwhile the older brother was pouring **cold water** on the mood.

'**I don't care** for all these celebrations. With my kid brother (**7 years** younger), you got someone who wouldn't **stay. With me**, however, you've got a **rock. Stare** at me, your faithful servant, without even a goat party to celebrate. Or **three lions.** Yes I know it's weird, but **we r who we r** and **we built this city. I will never let you down**, but I am vexed. The **writing's on the wall.'** He started to punch his father.

'Take a chill **pill – ow! Talk**, son, don't **fight, son. G**lad you've spent all **these days** here, and **don't you worry, child,** I **need u (100%), just the way you are.** Yes, we let the party **start without you**, but all I have is yours.

'Now, **sing** and **dance with me tonight**, (more than **one dance**), you **beautiful monster**, you!'

Once Diana Vickers 10 *Young* Tulisa 12 *Troublemaker* Olly Mars feat Flo Rida 12 *Money on my Mind* Sam Smith 14 *Perfect* Ed Sheeran 17 *Give Me Everything* Pitbull feat Ne-Yo, Afrojack & Nayer 11 *I'm the one* DJ Khaled feat Justin Bieber, Quavo, Chance the Rapper & Li'l Wane 17 *Sorry* Justin Bieber 15 *What Do You Mean?* Justin Bieber 15 *Please Don't Let Me Go* Olly Mars 10 *See You Again* Wiz Khalifa feat Charlie Puth 15 *The Man* Aloe Blacc 14 *Waves* Mr Probz 14 *Too good at goodbyes* Sam Smith 17 *Green Light* Roll Deep 10 *Look what you made me do* Taylor Swift 17 *Solo* Clean Bandit 18 *Uptown Funk* Mark Ronson feat Bruno Mars 14 *Bad Romance* Lady Gaga 10

Good Times Roll Deep 10 *Dirtee Disco* Dizzee Rascal 10 *Mirrors* Justin Timberlake 13 *Blurred Lines* Robin Thicke feat T.I. & Pharrell 13 *Price Tag* Jesse J feat B.o.B 11 *Rude* Magic! 14 *The Time (Dirty Bits)* The Black Eyed Peas 10 *Easy Love* Sigala 15 *We Can't Stop* Miley Cyrus 13 *She Looks so Perfect* 5 Seconds of Summer 14 *We Are Young* Fun feat Janelle Monáe 12 *The Club is Alive* JLS 10 *She Makes Me Wanna* JLS 11 *Swagger Jagger* Cher Lloyd 11 *Replay* Iyaz 10 *In My Head* Jason Derulo 10 *Closer* The Chain-smokers feat Halsey 16 *Read All About It* Professor Green feat Emeli Sandé 11 *All About Tonight* Pixie Lott 11 *What Makes You Beautiful* One Direction 11 *Thinking Out Loud* Ed Sheeran 14 *These Days* Rudi-mental 18 *I Love It* Icona Pop feat Charli XCX 13 *La La La* Naughty Boy feat Sam Smith 13 *Hold My Hand* Jess Glynne 15 *Not Letting Go* Tinie Tempah feat Jess Glynne 15 *Say you won't let go* James Arthur 16 *All Time Low* The Wanted 10 *Everybody Hurts* Helping Haiti 10 *On the Floor* Jennife Lopez feat Pitbull 11 *Drag Me Down* One Direction 15 *Impossible* James Arthur 12 *Thrift Shop* Macklemore & Ryan Lewis feat Wanz 13 *Shape of you* Ed Sheeran 17 *He Ain't Heavy, He's My Brother* The Justice Collective 12 *Let's Get Ready to Rhumble* PJ & Duncan 13 *Turn the Music Louder (Rumble)* KDA feat Tinie Tempah & Katy B 15 *Sign of the times* Harry Styles 17 *Somewhere Only We Know* Lily Allen 13 *Rather Be* Clean Bandit 14 *Don't Wanna Go Home* Jason Derûlo 11 *Part of Me* Katy Perry 12 *Feels* Calvin Harris feat Pharrell Williams, Katy Perry & Big Sean 17 *Sing* Gary Barlow and the Commonwealth Band feat Military Wives 12 *Happy* Pharrell Williams 14 *Prayer in C* Lilly Wood & Robin Schulz 14 *Somebody That I Used to Know* Gotye feat Kimbra 12 *Heart Skips a Beat* Olly Murs feat Rizzle Kicks 11 *OMG* Usher feat Will.i.am 10 *What's My Name?* Rihanna feat Drake 11 *I Could be the One* Avicii vs. Nicky Romero 13 *Louder* DJ Fresh feat Sian Evans 11 *Get Lucky* Daft Punk feat Pharrell Williams 13 *House Every Weekend* David Zowie 15 *I Wanna Feel* SecondCity 14 *Someone Like You* Adele 11 *Problem* Ariana Grande feat Iggy Azaela 14 *Am I Wrong* Nico & Vinz 14 *Wild Thoughts* DJ Khaled ft Rihanna & Bryon Tiller 17 *River* Eminem 18 *Hello* Adele 15 *Tsunami (Jump)* DVBBS & Borgeous feat Tinie Tempah 14 *Are You With Me?* Lost Frequencies 15 *Freaky Friday* Lil Dicky 18 *Don't Hold Your Breath* Nicole Scherzinger 11 *My Love* Route 94 feat Jess Glynne 14 *Bridge over troubled water* Artists for Grenfell 17 *Wherever You Are*

Military Wives with Gareth Malone & Paul Mealor 11 *The Power of Love* Gabrielle Aplin 12 *Promises* Calvin Harris & Sam Smith 18 *Crazy Stupid Love* Cheryl Cole feat Tinie Tempah 14 *One Kiss* Calvin Harris & Dua Lipa 18 *Shallow* Lady Gaga & Bradley Cooper 18 *No Regrets* Dappy 11 *Blame* Calvin Harris feat John Newman 14 *Don't be So Hard on Yourself* Jess Glynne 15 *Forget You* Cee Lo Green 10 *Changed the Way you Kiss Me* Example 11 *When we Collide* Matt Cardle 10 *It's my Birthday* will.i.am feat Cody Wise 14 *Love you More* JLS 10 *I Got U* Duke Dumont feat Jax Jones 14 *Domino* Jesse J 12 *Diamonds* Rhianna 12 *Stitches* Shawn Mendes 16 *Little Things* One Direction 12 *Changing* Sigma feat Paloma Faith 14 *Let Me Love You (Until You Learn To Love Yourself)* Ne-Yo 12 *Love Yourself* Justin Bieber 15 *This Ain't a Love Song* Scouting for Girls 10 *Paradise* Coldplay 12 *Good Feeling* Florida 12 *Love Me Again* John Newman 13 *Twilight* Cover Drive 12 *Party Rock Anthem* LMFAO feat Lauren Bennett & GoonRock 11 *How We Do (Party)* Rita Ora 12 *Burn* Ellie Goulding 13 *All About That Bass* Meghan Trainor 14 *Candy* Robbie Williams 12 *Sweet Nothing* Calvin Harris feat Florence Welch 12 *Turn Up the Music* Chris Brown 12 *Thank U, Next* Ariana Grande 18 *Shout out to my Ex* Little Mix 16 *Gangnam Style* Psy 12 *Feel the Love* Rudimental feat John Newman 12 *RIP* Rita Ora feat Tinie Tempah 12 *God's Plan* Drake 18 *Funky Friday* Dave feat Fredo 18 *Something I Need* Ben Haenow 14 *Cheerleader* OMI 15 *New Rules* Dua Lipa 17 *Despacito* Luis Fonsi feat Daddy Yankee 17 *Cold Water* Major Lazer feat Justin Bieber & MØ 16 *I Don't Care* Cheryl 14 *7 Years* Lukas Graham 16 *Stay With Me* Sam Smith 14 *Rockstar* Post Malone 17 *Three Lions* Baddiel/Skinner/Lightning Seeds 18 *We R Who We R* Kesha 11 *We Built this City* LadBaby 18 *I Will Never Let You Down* Rita Ora 14 *Writing's on the Wall* Sam Smith 15 *Pillowtalk* Zayn Malik 16 *Fight Song* Rachel Platten 15 *These Days* Take That 14 *Don't You Worry, Child* Swedish House Mafia feat John Martin 12 *Need U (100%)* Duke Dumont feat A*M*E 13 *Just the Way You Are* Bruno Mars 10 *Start Without You* Alexandra Burke feat Laza Morgan 10 *Sing* Ed Sheeran 14 *Dance With Me Tonight* Olly Murs 11 *One Dance* Drake feat Wizkid & Kyla 16 *Beautiful Monster* Ne-Yo 10

* ESPACI: *European Society for Paediatric Allergology & Clinical Immunology*, obviously

124

Facetiously-gamble-ill-wrought *alphabet games*

vowels used in alphabetical order

'HAvE I gOld? GlUm And EvIl yOUng Albert (if your father wills, you have it!) grows up abstemious… cash be in your hands.'

Exit young farmer into ugly affection untamed. In hours, (gamble-ill-wrought) wad spent. It's blown.

Unsaved, ill or hurt, all weight-loss unhalted. It's not fun. And we find youth attending hogs, unhappy.

Ends: 'I know!' – quake in soul – 'dad's men: pious hands – fed. Idylls for us all! Their pods (ugh! – caseous, annelidous*) ate I foully.' And he did roundly amble into humbly-gate, in long rut…

Saw he his boy: rush and get ring (gold stuff) and jerkin! Oh, bull's arrest, spit-oft-turn all.

'We – I – thought Albert in ground. Dances might go up, and legs,' I thought, facetiously, 'are in, out, – are in, out – shake it 'bout!'

* with a waxy, blueish-grey coating and riddled with worms

Unorientally subcontinental *alphabet games*

vowels used in omegapsi-ical order

'ThUs, gOld Is EAsy,' quOtIng EAch unorientally ugly coin, Ed was humbly told.

'This extra turn-on I'll spend,' and unto City he walks.

But to ideals: up to fill'd/eat/drunk/rowdy/kissed… hard-up. Oh, his dear duos find eau going east.

Hungry folk. His ear-lugs do ring: 'Eat thus of pig's eggy a-quoited mash? But old hireds (dad's)' – tut – 'do dine amply.' Fly!

Run of life; a-hug, shod, kiss, enwrap… button it!

'Eat subcontinental rump! Or ingest hash! Up, down (his search). Bury boy? I grew sad – uncomplimentary – but now I'm really up! Loving the lad!'

AV Jacobean angel-wrestling *pastiche*

the Authorised Version's rendering of Genesis 32:24-32 is infamously unclear due to a confusion of personal pronouns

7He stood before him and declared, with a loud voice: 8A farmer had two sons and one became disgruntled with his circumstances. 9He asked him to tell him what he wanted. He asked him to give to him what was going to be his and he gave it to him.

10Off he went, packed it with it, and, taking it with him, left him there.

11He met them, and them and them, paid him and her and her and her and lo and behold it was soon empty, 12since he had spent it all on them (and her), and then famine struck him and them and all of it.

13He hungered, worked for them, looking after them and longed to eat theirs.

14But then he spoke to him and it came to him. 'They get theirs; I shall go to him and ask if I can work for him,' he thought. 15So he went back to see if he could see him.

16But while he was still a long way off, he saw him and he ran to him and he began, 'I am no longer worthy…' but he kissed him, and gave him his ring. 17He called for him to bring a coat for him, and for him to fetch shoes for him.

18He could not get a word in. 19He threw his arms around him and threw them a party, inviting them and roasting him on a spit.

[20]They came from all around and celebrated. He said 'He was lost but he is found; he was dead, but he is alive – tee hee hee! Sing a hymn!'

[21]He complained to him. 'I stayed here with you, never allowed to have him or her or him or her or even him for a party. But now he returns and you invite him, him, her and him…'

[22]He replied 'You are here and all I have is yours. But we must rejoice before him now he has been found to be alive. [23]Come, let's celebrate with him and him and him and her and him and, of course, him!'

[24]He went with him.

The prodigal periodical   *key words*

newspapers & magazines commonly or formerly available in the UK

The **Farmer's Weekly Sun** said to his dad 'Hallo. Can we have a **Chat**? I need to take some **Time Out. First**, you've been a faithful **Guardian** and I know you're **Loaded**, so give me a share of your **Empire, Sport,** so I can **Travel More**.'

'**OK**, it's **Yours**,' said the father. 'It's probably for the **Best**,' and gave him his inheritance, free, **Grazia** and for nothing. The boy was very pleased. '**Bella**,' he declared, taking the money, leaving the **House Beautiful** and going to **Vanity Fair**, in a foreign country, travelling on the **Express**.

It was **Easy Living**, full of **Zest**.

There he lived in a **Penthouse**, met up with bad **Company** who pretended to be **The People's Friend**, (although in reality they were more like an **NME**) but **That's Life**. So the boy was a **Rolling Stone** and lived

like a **Dandy**, with some **Glamour** girls, which was rather **Cosmopolitan**, and he wasn't much of an **Economist**. The **News of the World** he'd drifted into was that they would all have to be **Weight Watchers**.

Viz there would be no **Sugar**, no **Nuts**, there would be tough **Times** and to get any dinner he'd have to join a **Q**. It wasn't what he'd left home **four. Four two** long he waited for something **New** to come along.

The boy went to work in a **Zoo** and got **Closer** to some pigs than he wanted, which wasn't a good **Match**.

Eventually, **Kerrang!**, he came to his senses, looked in the **Mirror**.

It was **Reveal**ed to him that his behaviour had been **Total Carp** and that he should return to his **House & Garden**.

So he chose to face the **Heat**, go back to his **Ideal Home** to ask to be a servant – an **Amateur Gardener**.

He considered it worth the long walk, the honest humility, the rejection-ri**Sk**, etc. He set off. But a long **Time** before he got there – in fact, while he was still a long way off - **The Oldie**, who had been a **Spectator**, saw him coming from his rooftop and ran eagerly to meet him.

He threw a serious **Beano**, complete with live music and dancing and **Good Food** including veal, because he wasn't particularly **PC. Plus**, he gave him some other things to wear – a special ring, a pair of shoes, and he became a **Mac User** – what you might call **Top Gear**.

The father was completely delighted, and announced to the crowd 'There's absolutely no need for this welcome home party to be **Private. Eye** want everyone to know that you were dead… but now, in

126

complete contrast, you're alive! **Celebrate** everyone!

'**Yes**, indeed, rejoice, tout **Le Monde**! **Today** he's welcome back. What a **Star**!' His older brother, **Figaro**, saw **Red** for a **Week**, but the other **Men Only** celebrated his return to the **Family Circle**.

Prodigal
heteromyn (paired) *wordplay*
words spelled the same but pronounced differently, according to meaning, used in pairs

Younger son asks for his inheritance. Dad cashes savings and **proceeds** to give him the **proceeds**. Mouth **agape** at this **agape** love, the son decides to **appropriate** the **appropriate** funds. His father does not verbally **object** to his son being a greedy **object**.

The boy manages to **collect** with having to say a **collect**. He gives a **bow**, puts on a **bow** tie (although he asks a maid to be a **tier** and arrange folds of material over each **tier** of his shirt). He will **close** doors and go to a city that isn't **close**. He reckons he'll **desert** the farm and cross the savannah, the jungle and the **desert**. He's glad they didn't have a **row**, and walks past the **row** of trees.

On his way, there are no female deers, so naturally he **does** not see any **does**. His cash is soon gone, and he has to **refuse** all **refuse** such as new stockings (he's a **denier denier**). The food runs out, so he weeps and rends his clothes (**tears**, with **tears**) and beats himself in punishment for desiring finger food (**buffets** due to lack of **buffets**). In a **minute**, he comes to his senses, and feels small (in fact, **minute**) before a mighty God and a **number** of large pigs. The lad is

completely insensitive - he couldn't possibly be **number**. Then he patches his clothes, even while he's in a wastewater pipe (he's a **sewer** in a **sewer**), and thus he dismisses his illness — he considers that being an **invalid** is **invalid**. He's **wound** a bandage tightly over the **wound**.

His selfish independence was **routed**, so he wondered which way he should be **routed**.

He walks slowly home – far from taking a **moped**, he **moped**. On his journey, he's keen to amaze and **entrance** his father at the farm with a speech, but while still a long way from the **entrance**, the father kisses his son, an **intimate** act to **intimate** his acceptance of the lad.

He **represents** his shoes to him, along with a ring, which **represents** sonship. The father remembers that the boy took all his cash, but even though he can **recollect**, he does not attempt to **recollect**. He's so proud of his son that he throws an indoor-golf-themed party, **putting** him up for the pitch and **putting**.

'Yes, there's a **fine** line between lost and found. But rejoice! We though he was dead, but obviously, he's **fine**!'

Various partygoers take a dip, where the band plays, and while **divers divers** make a splash (they take a **lead** without wearing their **lead** boots), the **bass** (and carp) listen to the double **bass** (no criticising).

The servants form a workers' co-operative, making them properly **unionized**, but avoid becoming electrically-charged atoms, which means they stay **unionized**.

proceeds begins/money from transactions **agape** open-mouthed: er-*gayp*/unconditional love: *ag*-erpay **appropriate** take for

127

himself/correct, suitable **object** argue against/thing, target, purpose **collect** gather/ short prayer **bow** bending from the waist/formal neckwear **tier** one who knots: *tie*-er/one of several layers: *tee*-er **close** shut/near **desert** abandon/arid plain **row** argument: rhymes with cow, r-ah-w/column: rhymes with show, r-oh **does** performs an action: duz/female deer: doze **refuse** unwilling: ree-*f'y*ues/rubbish: *reff*-yooz **denier** fine net-mesh: *den*-iay/one who withholds or disbelieves: dee-*nigh*-ah **tears** multiple rips/ lachrymosity; salty drops **buffets** strikes: *buff*-etz / finger food: *boo*-fays **minute** 60 seconds/tiny **number** digit/increasingly without sensation **sewer** needle-person: *so*-er/waste water outflow: *soo*-er **invalid** patient: *in*-verlid/ flawed; not binding: in-*vall*-id • **wound** wrapped in coils/cut or sore **routed** defeated/directed **moped** small-engined bike/dawdled gloomily **entrance** captivate/ doorway **intimate** private, personal/hint at **represents** offers again/ symbolizes **recollect** remember/ gather again **putting** placing: *poot*-ing/ golf shot on the green: *puh*-ting **fine** thin/well **divers** various (archaic spelling)/headfirst leapers from on high **lead** direct: leed /heavy metal: led **bass** species of fish: bah-ss/low-toned voice or instrument: bay-ss **unionised** formed a politically-motivated workers' collective: yew-nion-ised/ electrically charged: un-ion-ised

Uses of
the word *made*   *key words*
'make' has more than 1000 entries in the Oxford English Dictionary
This is a fictional story, made up by Jesus to illustrate a point.

The son and his father (a self-made man) were adding up the numbers, and son made a meal of it.

Father said 'It's quite a large amount, so I've made it a round dozen.'

'You've made my day!' The boy had it made. Very soon he was off.

He made for Dissipation City and made the most of the considerable opportunity.

He made hay, made friends and made his bed and laid on it. He was made for enjoying himself; new friends April, June and May danced flirtaciously; he also made whoopee.

He gambled and at first made a bundle, but in the end made a hash of everything. He was no longer made of money.

At the same time, famine made everyone hungry. Mayday!*

The boy took a job looking after pigs, and wished to eat their pods. He realized this thinking made him out to be a fool.

So he made off.

He made his mind up to ask his father to employ him; he wanted to be made a servant. On his way (he made a few miles before dark) he made up a speech; but when he was still a long way off, his father made him out in the gathering gloom and made a run for it.

He made light of his days of worry and kissed him and gave him a ring made from gold, shoes custom-made for his feet and a coat made to fit.

The boy made neither head nor tail of it.

The father, who was made-up, told the maid to slaughter the calf, and later the cook made a meal of it,

She made a a rosti made from potato and garlic, after another servant had made a fire.

The partygoers made way for the boy and his father to step up, and then they all made merry.

'Rejoice! He who made heaven and earth has given me back my son!'

* French for *Help me* (*m'aidez!*) But be not alarmed – the story has a happy ending; as those French might say: *mais denouement est jolie*

Snowball and back *wordplay*

words of increasing, then decreasing, length

1 letter	I C £? 'K.
2	Ha! Ya! My id is up to it – go!
3	Now far, bad and mad, yet get any gal,
	sup any ale (sip gin/rum), try any bet.
4	Cash runs away very fast – from rich, thro' poor,
	then none, even – gone!
	Tend hogs… envy pig's vile food?
5	Gross! Skint. Alone. (Noise: tummy
6	Rumble within). Waster senses better course –
	Regret, return. Fields-labour, 'family reject' pleads –
7	*Servant*? (because workers usually receive
	stomach-comfort). Humbles himself,
8 letters*	Shocking, negative, Prodigal attitude
	repented. 'Hireling?' (prepares pleading
7	oratory). Father's looking, eagerly desires…
6	Meekly return. Feeble speech
5	Ready. Tired. Wiser. Greet!
4	Seen! Yell! Rush, rush! Love! 'Hire…'
	Gave ring, coat, kiss; plus shoe, shoe, also hugs –
	'Kill calf, make rare beef wrap with yams,
	plus spud, rice, leek, okra, kale, peas, corn,
	dips, naan; ouzo, sake, mead, beer, wine!
	Lamb chop/mung bean stew' – note: been long
3	Way off. Lad: 'Owe you…' Dad: '
	Son was not, but – wow! – now, how boy
2	Is in! He is so it!
1 letter	O, H, P T L!'

* turning point of story, turning point of poetical form

Verbless *wordplay*

deep respect to Michel Thaler for
Le Train du Nulle Part, *a 233-page novel, written entirely without verbs*
Such audacity!

But now – a full money bag in his hand on this journey from the farm.

His new address: Dissipation City.

'Hallo new friends; what's yours?'

Charming entertainments, dinners, girls, gambles, parties, embraces, hopes and many expenditures.

Pennilessness his current state.

'Hallo; where's the pig pen?'

Non-charming pods, scrawny animals, rumbling tummies; ludicrous enviousness and sudden revelation from the Almighty.

'Aha! Road homewardbound! My foolishness over, an exercise in walking-skills and in contrite humility, in preparation for an appropriately respectful request to my father…'

Father's joy! His speed!

'Hallo Father. Forgiveness please, no worthiness...

'How marvellous! Servants! Coat, shoes, ring, roasted beef, gathering villagers, dancing (well, worth a try)! This boy, previously *dead* and *lost*, now alive and found! Hallelujah!'

Tautology   *style*

redundant, unnecessary, wasteful, duplicating doubling-up repetition

The second son (who was the latter-born and younger of the pair and of the two of them) spoke to and conversed with his male parent, his dad, the agriculturalist land-owner farmer who grew crops on his arable land and ploughed soil where they produced corn, grain, wheat, straw, hay and raised animals and livestock.

'Give me, hand over and allow me to receive from you my share, portion and slice of the inheritance that I myself get when you die, croak, pass away and keel over also.'

The paternal father concurred and agreed and gave him the cash, spondulix, wonga, money and wherewithal, and the boy and son went away and left.

The youngster and offspring spent all he had and everything in wasteful and prodigal living.

He was both broke and penniless when his cash ran out and was all gone and every coin had been frittered and deep fried in batter and breadcrumbs and crusty detritus.

The country and the geo-political state became ravaged and spoiled with famine and starvation.

The son tended and looked after pigs, hogs, sows and even-toed ungulates. He wanted to eat their pods, while at the same time and simultaneously desired to consume the vegetable matter the porcine animals had been given and hoped and craved to eat and consume their food and leguminous cases.

Finally, at the end, he came to his senses and had a revelation from the Lord and from heaven above, where dwell angels and cherubs and wingéd messengers, and other beings of a spiritual, non-corporeal kind and sort and classification.

He said to himself, thinking 'I shall get up and arise and go back to my father the farmer and Dad the agrarian practictioner and tell him and explain I am no longer worthy and have ceased to deserve to be called his son and I shouldn't bear his name anymore, either, as well, in addition, too.'

But and however, while he was still a long way off, remote from the farm, his father saw him from his observation point – he spotted him when gazing from the roof atop the house. This was the place from which he had been looking into the distance, which was exactly where the son had been when he was espied by this paternal spectator.

He ran and hurried to the boy, embraced him, hugged him, gave him and bestowed upon him a ring and golden finger jewellery, a coat and a jacket, a left shoe and a right shoe and footwear.

He also gave instructions and arranged for the calf to be killed and slaughtered and dispatched and cooked and roasted and dished up on plates, and for some barbequed beef to be served and distributed by waitresses and dinnerladies. He threw a shindig, and everyone

130

partied, with dancing and jiving to music and tunes.

Proclaimed and declared the older man and male human of greater years 'My boy and son was undiscovered and lost, but now he is restored to his rightful place and found. The fruit of my loin and my offspring was dead and passed away, but now he's alive and animate! I (yes, your current interlocutor) was mourning and grieving his passing, but he – this child and issue of mine – has been restored and given back to me and into my care!'

Dad and father said and announced this as reported.

N   _alliteration_

'Nest-egg, now!' nagged nascent, numerate ne'er-do-well nihilist nomad Number-two-son.

Nouveau-riche Nick naturalises: notes 'n' nickels; nefarious nauseating narcotics (nose-candy); networks novel narcissistic naughty naked nymphet nubiles; neat nectar nonstop.

Nil-nix notable nationwide no-go-area.

Now nearing Napoleon's nosh (nouvelle-cuisine?) – nasty, not nearly nutricious!

Nano-secondly   neophiliac. Nostalgia…

Nearby nuzzles, 'Nick needs neckwear, Norfolkjacket, nose-ring!' News, neighbours – notice nachos, nice natter, noisette/noodle nourishment, naan, nougat, nuts, nectarine neopolitan.

'Numbskull Nick nearly non-compos-mentis, nullified; new nipper notwithstanding! Nice!'

Approximate   _style_

Roughly half of the offspring wanted some money, so the alleged biological sperm-doner gave an amount which may or may not have been very nearly sufficient.

The recipient (let's use the name Mel – non-gender-specific) went away some distance. After an indeterminate period of time, a very considerable proportion of it was mostly gone.

Round about the same week, a distinct lack of food came upon the land and Mel went for one or more jobs at a place where animals of some kind were kept. They ate vegetable matter of undisclosed origin and description, and Mel quite fancied eating (or at least chewing) some, parts or all.

Instead, a fairly good idea occurred, and the vague concept of wondering home (just to see what happens) was mooted.

While Mel was still a certain distance away, one or both of the aforementioned so-called 'parents' hurried out, possibly to engage in a little meet-and-greet.

What appeared to be unsolicited gifts of two or fewer items of jewellery, clothing of about size S and footwear featuring less leatherwork than is often associated with what some might call 'shoes' were provided, and rumours of some kind of party or gathering or meeting or associative interplay (with no clear agend or purpose, and with a non-specific breadth of invitation) began to spread (start time – about 6pm or thereabouts).

The middling-to-portly bovine was flame-grilled to at least 31 degrees above room temperature (minimum, depending on the season).

One adult said 'Several or fewer of my offspring got mislaid but now are pretty much located; Mel – it could have been Mel, but now I'm not so certain – anyway, the person or people in dispute was feeling (so we're told) a little peaky but has responded to treatment. He'll be fine within a few days. Or a week or so. Certainly by next month, give or take a fortnight. I'll let you know.'

Exclamations   *wordplay*

What? Please! Plenty! Okay. Bye!

Rrr! Vavavavoom, hubba hubba! Cheers!

Whambam, thank you ma'am.

Twenty-one. Pay Pontoons, five card tricks. House wins!

Place your chips! 27 red! House wins!

Droopy Drawers! Two little ducks (hallo quackers!) Someone else calls *House!* and wins!

Oh dear.

Oh dear, oh dear.

Huuuunnn-greeee. Whimper.

Snort, snort. Smack chops?

Click! Ah, ha!

Another fifteen miles… now just ten miles to go.

Are we nearly there yet? Only three miles to go…

Blink, rub, gulp, hoorah!! Puff, pant! Hi! What?

Cuddle/smack! Thanks! Ring!

Thanks! Coat! Thanks! Shoes! Thanks!

Die! Thump! Blaze! Turn! Slice! Yum yum!

What?

No, fine, thanks! Praise be!

132

O   *alliteration*

Opportunist offspring orders overpayment. Off!

Outcome: orgy of ostensibly overspending, outrageously offensive. Olga, Orla, Olivia, Ophelia, Olympia, Orlaith. Obfuscating overnight outage… occupation outside ordinary.

Observes Old-Major omnivores' offscourings. Onset of ongoing ontology. One organizes oratory!

Old-man outward-facing, overcome; organizes offer of overcoat, o-shape, odourless Oxford brogues, other objects, on-the-house.

Olive oil omelettes, offal, ostrich/oyster/octopus, oxtail, onion, oatcakes, oregano, orrisroot, oranges, ocra, Orios; ouzo.

Oral-discourse: 'Obituary? Once, out! Organic!'

What the butler saw   *plot*
not only a humorous or farcical tale, but technically 'a complex situation which resolves happily': Comedy

High-ranking members of the community were conversing in the farmyard, enjoying a few drinks and some canapés, being served by Butler, the butler.

Several women of varying degrees of importance accompanied the bank manager and the Chairman of the Board of Governors of the Chamber of Commerce. Two chief executives, five lawyers and a senior Law Enforcement Officer were also tucking into the blinis and petit fours.

Their easy laughter drifted towards the upstairs windows.

Meanwhile, the owner of the farm, Hay Ricks, was standing in his bedroom, wearing a shirt and tie, socks and a pair of brightly coloured boxer shorts. He was, at the time, unable to mingle with his very special guests because, somehow, he had managed to mislay his trousers. He knew with absolute certainty that he'd placed them on the end of the bed before having a shower, but now, strangely, they were nowhere to be found, and (even more mysteriously) he could not find any of his spare pairs, either.

This was a quandary.

'Well, I am vexed,' he said aloud. 'I'll look again.'

He opened each drawer in the chest of drawers, but only found a few neatly folded handkerchieves, three pairs of socks and a harlequin's hat. He opened the door of the hanging cupboard, and looked at the rows of shirts and jackets; none were long enough to cover his embarrassment; none had corresponding trousers.

His only option was the kimono he'd been given as a joke; it was pink with embroidered cartoon characters, and entirely unsuitable for a business reception of almost any kind, let alone a meeting of great social significance as well as financial importance.

There was a polite knock at the bedroom door, so Ricks opened it.

'Master, your guests are ready to receive you,' chimed the ever-helpful Butler, the butler.

'Yes, yes, I'll be there directly.'

'Very good, sir. Excuse me, sir, but you do realise that your garb is sadly lacking in the trousering department?'

'Thank you, yes, Butler,' snapped Ricks, closing the bedroom door. He opened the wardrobe door, to look again among the dressing gowns, his best suit (sans trousers), an anorak, a few t-shirts (most with unsuitable slogans, and all too short to serve this situation) and a selection of jumpers, ties and (ironically) two leather belts.

'Oh, this is a nuisance!' he said, and slammed the door shut. He retraced his steps to the bathroom, checking the towel rail as he passed.

He knew there was no hope of his trousers being in the airing cupboard, but he was desperate. He opened the door anyway. Standing in the cupboard, with a broad grin across his ruddy face, was his younger son, Brian.

'Hallo Dad!' he said, cheerily.

'What are you doing in there?' his father asked.

'Keeping warm. May I ask you a question?'

'Yes, if you're quick. I have to meet my guests.'

'Why are you not wearing any trousers? You know you can't really meet your guests dressed like that, can you?'

Hay kept his temper. 'That's two questions. My trousers seem to have gone missing.'

'What are they worth?'

'Hmm?' Hay had not previously been concerned with the financial value of the missing strides, but now he calculated there would be serious and costly implications if he went out to meet these particular guests inadequately coutured. It was a serious difficulty.

'What would you give me, if I could find them for you?'

Hay had reached the end of his tether, so he made a wild offer. 'Right now, I would give you – er – all of your inheritance.'

'Deal.'

'What? Do you know where my trousers are?'

'Show me the money.'

A FEW DAYS LATER, plans were finalized for the transfer of funds from Farmer Ricks to his son.

He handed him a big bag of gold coins.

'Even though you have cleaned me out, I do still hold you dear, you know, son.'

'Those local dignatories would have been horrified to see you in your underpants, don't you think?'

'Taunt me no more, please. I have one more gift for you, my precious boy. Please take this ring, and wear it and think kindly of me when you are away from home.'

Brian accepted the valuable, meaningful gift, placed it on his finger and embraced his father. 'You understand that I have made my mind up, don't you. I feel I have no choice.'

'Not at all. But if go you must, then be that as it may.'

BRIAN LEFT THE FARM journeying over hill and valley to Dissipation City. Once he'd arrived and settled into an hotel room, he went out to find ways to enjoy his wealth, and quickly found more than a couple of opportunities.

He started with a grand meal, in *Fivestar*, a fine dining restaurant. This was owned by a man named Frayn, who had always dreamed of leaving the service industry and making his living on a farm, tending cattle and other livestock. But for now he continued to supervise the staff and run the business at the restaurant.

Brian's spree continued by spending a couple of hours in a high class

134

tailor's, being measured for several new suits and accessories; he had a calming massage, took a spell in a casino, and then on to a theatre, accompanied by a few friends who had been drawn to him in the course of his expensive adventures so far.

Prime among these companions was Rochelle, a beauty with long blonde hair and mischievous eyes. 'We could always have a little drinkie if you like...' she said, hinting at what else might follow.

And so it was that Brian began to spend his inheritance, splashing out on meals, drinking binges, gambling, various shows and clubs and theatrical events and more gambling and a lot more eating and drinking and recreation of all kinds. And Rochelle was always there, ready to encourage, to consume, to be entertained and to absorb his generosity.

Within a shockingly short time, considering the size of his inheritance, the money dwindled to nothing.

In fact, to pay the final meal and drinks bill at *Fivestar*, Brian had to offer Frayn the gold ring his father had given. It was worth more than the debt, but it was all he had left.

Frayn accepted it eagerly, and immediately advertised the restaurant for sale and went off to a distant country, far away from the famine, setting up a new business rearing livestock, fulfilling his dream of many years. He bought his land with the proceeds from the sale of *Fivestar*, and exchanged the ring he had obtained from Brian for several head of cattle.

ONCE THE 'FRIENDS' HE had accumulated (and Rochelle in particular) understood that Brian was no longer able to finance their revelries, they dropped him and went off to seek out another sugar-daddy. They had not much luck, because a famine had struck the land.

Without friends, money, his ring and also without any means of support, Brian knew he'd have to get a job.

He applied for a post working for the *Plainest Bacon Company* (suppliers of no-frills Gammon, Ham, Pork and Rashers), but their staffing needs only stretched to a job looking after their least-well-fed porkers.

Hunger gnawed at his innards while the hogs snorted and sniffled among the rotting corn pods and household waste slopped into their trough. He longed to eat the pods, and was about to do so when he stopped to consider his position.

Suddenly he came to his senses.

'My father's men (including Butler) want for nothing, and yet they are merely employees. I shall arise and go to my father and say to him *I am no longer worthy to be called your son; make me one of your hired men*. Hopefully, he will have pity on me and give me a job and save me from these the dreadful consequences of my foolishness.'

So he arose and left the pigpen, making his way home.

MEANWHILE, FRAYN'S NEW FARMING business was properly taking off and becoming a success.

Frayn was astonished at how quickly he'd managed effectively to transfer his skills in providing a classy restaurant environment and quality service for his customers into effective and financially sound animal husbandry.

He had obtained the farm (and the livestock) from a man named Porcia, who had formerly kept pigs until he realized there was very little market for them, and had switched to cattle.

Porcia was delighted that he had the ring, knowing he could exchange it for land on which to experiment with turkey, geese, ducks and grouse.

He approached the farmer who tended (along with his hired men) the neighbouring fields who needed to sell some land (clearly there were considerable cash-flow issues) and made the deal.

Hay Ricks accepted the ring (for it was he) and one calf in exchange for several acres of quality arable land – oh yes, the very ring he had given to Brian such a long time before.

Porcia's Fowl Farm ended up being way more successful than the ill-considered name deserved.

WHILE BRIAN WAS STILL a long way off, planning a speech and wearing out his shoes, Hay Ricks spotted him, since he was keeping watch.

'My son!' he shouted, and rushed down the steps and out along the road. He ran to greet him with a kiss.

'Father, I am no longer...' began Brian.

'Butler,' Ricks interrupted, 'fetch him some shoes and a coat. Oh, and bring the family ring – yes, the one that chanced (by God's grace) to find its way back into my possession when I sold the upper fields – and put it on his finger. And kill the fatted calf and let us celebrate!'

The whole village turned out, including Porcia, who generously roasted a turkey for the occasion.

But the hot beef was definitely the favourite.

'This my son was irrevocably lost – indeed, he was as hopelessly lost as my trousers on the day of the previous visit of many of the civic dignatories who are attending this celebratory party – but now he is found! He was dead, but is alive!'

And there was hilarious and random opening and closing of doors (plus great likelihood of confusion, mistaken identity, kisses stolen in the dark from various maids, happy resolutions, accidents with props, surprise entrances, secret passage-ways, several more stolen kisses, amusing happenstances, spiked drinks, with shinnanegins of all kinds and chasing.

Not forgetting exchanges of clothing, unlikely disguises, mentions of the land where the nuts come from, slips down the stairs, Whitehall, unfortunately-timed telephone calls, slapstick, pratfalls, aunts, handbags, noises off and screwball repartee until the break of dawn.

Official letter *style*

Tsoo, Grabbit & Runn
Commissioners for Oaths, Lincoln's Inn Chambers

Delay Deadlock Bicker Escalate (Attorneys)
Farm Village,
Countryside
10th Elul, Tiberius 15
Dear Sir,
Further to my correspondence of the 14th ultimo I respectfully hereby present you with the facts of the matter for your immediate attention.

1   Our client requested his inheritance share on the 23rd day of Ethanim in the 12th year of Tiberius. Your client (this is undisputed) granted this request in a short timeframe. Our client latterly left Farmer Smallholdings Inc – hereinafter referred to as FSI – and went to a foreign land.

2   Our client spent all monies hereunto forthcoming and registered himself officially bankrupt within a few months of (1). National famine began soon after (by absolutely no fault of our client).

3   Our client later became a full-time employee of Rasher Flasher Ltd (Dan Ishbacon, proprietor) for a brief spell. He was then observed briefly
/more

continues/

expressing a preference (over remaining starved) for diseased vegetable items not fit for human consumption.

4   Our client freely concedes that he left the employ of Rasher Flasher Ltd precipitously. He further admits liability for breaking his contract of employment and failing to give adequate notice to quit and asks for this offence to be taken into account. He commented at the time that he had 'come to his senses' and wished to return to FSI in a servant capacity.

5   As our client approached the premises of FSI, your client greeted him without the threshold. My client received the following items as payment in kind (these are not disputed):

- ring – small, gold, family member, for the use of
- coat - warm waterproof, button fastening, hood
- shoes – 2 (two) in number, leather upper, buckle
- celebratory gathering including village-dwelling guests and consumption of roasted beef

6   Our client's contractual offer to become a servant was verbally rejected by your client with the phrase 'My son was dead but now he is alive!'

We hereby claim that our client's sonship is thus re-established and dispute your contention that our client can expect no additional payment in respect to inheritance upon the subsequent passing of your client.

Furthermore we claim that our client's restoration is complete and it would appear that your client has cancelled any indebtedness on my client's part wholly thereunto.

We request you to treat this communication as an invitation to your client to renew his will and make freshly explicit within said document that this is indeed his intention so that upon the event of your client's decease there will be no disputing in this matter.

We look forward to your reply at your earliest convenience (by return preferred). Meanwhile I remain sir your obedient servant.

Solly Citor

Barrister at Law - Lincoln's Inn   /ends

Nounless · *wordplay*
pronouns, adjectives & verbs aplenty

He was rather greedy, somewhat feckless, hopelessly uncaring and very demanding.

Enriched, he walked citywards, where he spent with abandon and enthusiasm – but without reckoning – until he experienced pennilessness.

Pig-husbandry appealed at first, but after a short while became subject to envy and despair.

Acknowledgement and humility renewed, he returned from whence he came, planning to ask to be hired, since sonship was inappropriate now.

Paternal fondness overwhelmed them both; there was much hugging, re-shodding, dressing, enblinging and beefy slaughtering, plus cooking and inviting.

'He was lost but is found; he was dead, but is alive!'

Prodigal Pooh · *pastiche*
affectionate lampoonery of AA Milne's stories & poetry

One bright morning Winnie-the-Pooh spoke to Christopher Robin.

'Father,' he said, said he, 'I am a bear of Very Little Brass. May I have my inheritance, now, if you please?'

Christopher Robin hummed quietly to himself as he counted out the large stack of money.

Soon Pooh was off, out of the courtyard, past the freshly laid bed of delphiniums (blue) and geraniums (red). He disappeared from view into the Hundred Acre Wood, on his way to Disenchant-ment City.

There he spent wildly, as if seeing if he Kanga mble with such abandon that he'd Roo the day. He went down with Alice and lavished unthinking generosity on all of Rabbit's friends and relations.

The day came along (as days do) when all his money was gone. His wallet was as empty as a honey pot just after Time for a Little Something.

The more he looked into his purse, the more the money wasn't there.

'Bother!' he said. And everyone in the land was Out of Funds as well, and it was as though they were all In Training for slipping elegantly in and out of Rabbit's house.

King John put up a notice:*
'Lost or Stolen or Strayed:
Pooh Bear – a. k. a. Prodigal –
Seems to have been mislaid.
Last seen: wandering vaguely,
Quite of his own accord.
He's starving and down
In the dumps with a frown;
Fifty shillings reward.'

Pooh took a job looking after Piglet, and longed to eat his food. There wasn't any butter for the royal slice of bread or any slice of anything.

Then he came to his fluff. At home, he realized, even Eeyore gets his dinner. He decided to Arise and Go to Christopher Robin and say 'Father, I say, say I, I am No Longer Worthy to be called your bear.'

Meanwhile, Christopher Robin was humming to himself.

Threequarters of the way up the stairs
Is a stair where I sit
There isn't any other stair quite like it.
It's not on the rooftop,
*   it's not unlike a chair,*
But this is the stair where I always stare.

He would sit on the stair, and stare, and Stare, and hope one day his dearest bear would come out of the Hundred Acre Wood, along the little track and past the bed of chrysanthemums (yellow and white).

And One Day, Christopher Robin saw Pooh! He ran to greet him. He kissed him and squeezed him until his growler was quite worn out with growling.

He put a button in his ear[†], and some socks on his paws, and a coat on his furry body.

'It is much more fun to talk with someone who uses short, easy words like *What about lunch?* So, kill the fatted Heffalump – you can use that Battleaxe with Great Big Knobs On – we shall Have a Party!' cried Christopher Robin.

'Anyway, invite Tigger, Wol, Ernest Shepard, James James Morrison Morrison Wetherby George DuPree, Jonathan Jo, Sir Brian Botany, the King, the Queen, the Dairymaid, the Alderney and everyone else! We can play Poohsticks, and have a little smackerel. Although marmalade is nicer, if it's very thickly spread…

'For this my bear was Trespassers W, but now he's found. He had a little bit of fluff in his ear, but Now He's Alive!'

---

* From *Disobedience* in *When we were very young* (1924, Methuen)
† Distinguishing makers' mark *Steiff GmbH*

Other Bible verses   *key words*
every word (bar five) lifted from different bible stories
What do you think? There was a man who had two sons[1]. He went to his father and said 'My father.'

'Yes, my son,' he answered[2], 'what is it? [3]'

'Give me[4] my inheritance[5].' And it was very good.[6] Then he went away and[7] bought, with money, from a foreigner.[8]

'Come, eat my food and drink - the wine I have mixed.'[9] He lies down wealthy, but will do so no more; when he opens his eyes, all is gone.[10] There was no food, however, in the whole region because the famine was severe; both Egypt and Canaan wasted away because of the famine.[11]

Became like one [of][12] those tending the pigs[13]– longed for[14] something to eat[15] - even[16] vegetables.[17] Pigs[18] eat only vegetables,[19] but the poor ones are so bad they cannot be eaten.[20]

Suddenly a bright light from heaven flashed around.[21]

'I bring you some revelation[22]!'

'How many[23] [of] my father[24]['s] hired men[25] eat the food of the land?[26] Shall I[27] return to [my] own country?[28] Humbled myself.[29] Become[30] servant.[31] I go on the journey.[32]'

While the other is still a long way off[33], he sees his father[34] running[35]. Greet one another with a holy kiss,[36] having gifts –[37] signet ring,[38] coat,[39] sandals.[40]

Son[41] began to speak[42] 'I am[43] not worthy[44] to be[45] called[46] your son; [47] make me[48] one[49] [of] your[50] men who were hired.'[51]

His father[52] killed[53] a fatted calf; [54] everyone[55] rejoiced![56]

'Son[57] was lost[58] and [when] they found him,[59] the child – was dead –[60] is still alive!'[61]

References for each phrase/word, followed by a reminder of the theme of each source
1 *Matthew 21:28* Let your yes be yes 2 *Genesis 27:18* Jacob & Esau 3 *Matthew 20:21* Zebedee's wife promotes her sons 4 *Proverbs 30:8* daily bread 5 *Jeremiah 12:7* prophesying Exile 6 *Genesis 1:31* creation 7 *Matthew 27:5* Judas hangs himself 8 *Genesis 17:12* circumcision laws 9 *Proverbs 9:5* Wisdom calls out 10 *Job 27:19* life's impermanence 11 *Genesis 47:13* Joseph 12 *1 Corinthians 9:20* to the Jews I became a Jew 13 *Luke 8:34* healing of the

demonised man 14 *2 Timothy 4:8* Christ's second coming 15 *Mark 6:37* feeding of 5000 16 *Ruth 1:12* Naomi's blessing 17 *Daniel 1:12* consecrated in pagan Babylon 18 *Proverbs 11:22* indiscreet women 19 *Romans 14:2* meat sacrificed to idols 20 *Jeremiah 24:3* vision of figs 21 *Acts 22:6* Paul's testimony 22 *1 Corinthians 14:6* conduct in meetings 23 *Psalm 3:1* David's foes 24 *1 Kings 20:34* Aram vs Ahab 25 *Mark 1:20* calling of James & John 26 *Numbers 15:19* dietary laws 27 *2 Chronicles 18:14* attacking Ramoth Gilead 28 *Daniel 11:28* King of the North 29 *Psalm 35: 13* David prays for his enemies 30 *Ezekiel 21:7* knees weaken at news of grief 31 *Genesis 44:18* Reuben pleads with Joseph for Benjamin 32 *Job 16:22* Job speaks of his death 33 *Luke 14:32* cost of discipleship 34 *John 5:19* authority 35 *John 20:4* disciples go to Christ's empty tomb 36 *Romans 16:16* church life 37 *1 Corinthians 12:28* spiritual gifts 38 *Esther 8:8* royal decree 39 *Genesis 6:14* cover Ark with pitch 40 *Matthew 10:10* labourer worthy of his hire 41 *Nehemiah 11:7* some of the remnant 42 *Luke 1:64* Zechariah no longer dumb 43 *John 11:25* the resurrection and the life 44 *John 1:27* John the Baptist's humility 45 *1 Timothy 3:11* honoured wives 46 *Genesis 1:10* land & sea created 47 *Genesis 22:12* Abraham willing to sacrifice Isaac 48 *Luke 5:12* leper asks to be clean 49 *Leviticus 27:10* sacrificial lamb 50 *Deuteronomy 12:18* crossing Jordan 51 *Matthew 20:12* vineyard workers 52 *Genesis 27:41* Esau's grudge against Jacob 53 *1 Samuel 17:36* David & Goliath 54 *Proverbs 15:17* good meals compared 55 *Colossians 1:28* discipleship 56 *Psalm 122:1* worship 57 *Luke 3:34* begetting 58 *Luke 19:10* came to seek & to save 59 *Mark 1:37* Jesus prays 60 *2 Samuel 12:19* David's baby 61 *Genesis 45:28* Israel's joy at Joseph's survival

Dog-latin *language*

raw translation on p326

TRANSFER-ENDUM IMMATURUS: PAGINA CCCXXVI

Puer spectat pater. 'Digitalis mespondulix, Padris et nunc dimittis*.' Exeunt.

Prodigali amor distaffi (Sabinii) – venatus, vino. Nationalis consumabiles nix est. Jamb mange; puer covet.

Deciduo residus: 'Raisant et Peternum returno. Proletarium offerandus.'

Distancicus midstrum, Pater spectat puer (nix fenestra) et hurrium. Donatum coat, ringus, sandellum et obesii-cow slaughtero-rosti-slicico.

Pater dix 'Progenicum mort – vivatum! Nuno Espirito Sancto.'†

* couldn't resist this reference to the Anglican evensong 'Lord, now lettest thou thy servant depart in peace.' Strictly, 'dismiss me now'
† manager of Wolverhampton Wanderers from May 2017, muddled with Latin blessing *In nomine Patris et Filii et Spiritus Sancti*

Tunnel vision *key words*

a selection of London Underground terms, stations and lines (see also Tube Map, insert)

Colin Dale's Dad (named Paul) went to the **Bank** to get some money and then **Maida Vale**diction speech... 'If you really want to go, I won't stop you son.'

Colin ran through the **Archway**, onto the road (in a **Northern** direction) and left the **Borough**, arriving in the red light **District** of Dissipation **Central**. He became drunk and disorderly, and behaved like a **Loughton** frittered wealth on **Seven Sisters**. They played *hay & kings* games – and not just old fashioned pencil & paper ones like **Hainaults** & **King's Cross**es. In a restaurant, the maitre d' (named **Theydon Bois**) served wine like **Water**.

Looking around, Colin made his selection of pretty but dangerous girls: he decided to **Piccadilly** called **Victoria**. He took her to a casino near the Sav**oy**; **sterling** flew in all directions; even towards a swanky

140

Mansion. 'House!' she cried, when her bingo numbers came up. They drank until they were **Barbican, Pimlico** and completely **Canary Wharf**.

Sadly, he didn't keep in **mind the gap** between income and expenditure, and soon Colin's cash ran out. He said to Vicky 'I have no more money with which to **Plai. Stow**ney broke I am...'

His food delivery wasn't an early one; in fact it was a very **Leyton. Stones** lighter, he realized there was a famine. He was homeless like a **Holborn** he had nothing to eat, either. His insides felt completely **Hollow. Ay Road** out of there was what he needed to find.

He said 'I could eat an **Elephant**.'

Ann Castle ran a pig farm, and Colin got a job. Feeding pigs or eating their food made him feel s**Ickenham** was something he was not allowed to touch. 'I can bear this no longer; I cannot **Stanmore** of this hunger,' he thought aloud. Just then, as the stench was **High, Barnet** of the lad was visited by an **Angel**.

'Your father's men eat well,' he said. It was a revelation. 'I shall arise and return to those **Northwood Hills**, past the **Oakwood**, the **Earl's Court** and the **Knight's Bridge**. I have losses which I'll have to **cut, and cover** the ground between here and home.'

Meanwhile, Paul was watching out for his boy, aware that standing out in the Mediterranean weather without skin protection was dangerous for a father, which is why wore plenty of **Parsons Green**.

By the time Colin had walked home, his dogs were **Barking**. He had a speech ready: 'Before you, Dad, I humbly **Bow...**' **Road**-runner dad was already greeting, kissing, hugging him. Paul had been watching from the Embankment, and saw Colin, barefoot, **Padding**.

'Tonight, we celebrate!' he cried as he ran down the **Old Street**.

Paul called for his servants to attend by his pre-arranged signal with both hands - to **Clapham**. 'Common workers, bring a coat...'

For Colin's finger, a **Circle** of gold ('This is gold; unlike copper, it won't discolour your fingers or **Turnham Green**') or was it more like an **Oval**? It had a beveled **Edg**.

'**Ware** this coat, too my boy! Come on, my lad, give it a t**Rui. Slip** it on and do the buttons up. And here are some shoes!' His delight was evidently on an **escalator**.

Paul spoke to another servant. 'Go to the calf, and once you've used the knife to **Kil, burn** the wood and roast the meat. Make a fire of blazing elm and **Burnt Oak**.'

The trumpeters' **Tooting Beck**oned everyone from their fields – he invited **All Saints** from the **Metropolitan** area to attend the party.

After the guitarists played (one had a Gibson Les Paul, while the other had a **Strat**), **ford** was served.

He made a speech: 'Paul's treated you to wine and pâté made from calf's **Liver. Pool Street**ed you to caviar, too!' Everyone thoroughly enjoyed the roast meat and the bread, so Paul publicly thanked the chef and the **Baker**.

'**Look**, my son was lost but now he's found and is alive, thank the Lord!' After the sweet course, they served Stilton, Brie, and Red **Leicester; Square** crackers and round ones, too. It was booze-**Up, neys**-up and a bless-up!

'He was sick (we thought he was what the French call *Morden* we started to arrange a funeral, the narrow way), and everything was going down **the tube,** but now his body is **Ealing (Broadway)** so celebrate! Party like it's **Jubilee** year! I'll put up a **Monument!** It'll be just the **ticket!**

Colindale *Northern* **Bank** *Central, Docklands Light Railway (DLR), Northern, Waterloo & City (W&C)* **Maida Vale** *Bakerloo* **Archway** *Northern* **Northern** *Line, black, 50 stations* **Borough** *Northern* **District** *Line, green, 60 stations* **Central** *Line, red, 49 stations* **Loughton** *Central* **Seven Sisters** *Victoria* **Hainault** *Central* **King's Cross** *Circle, Hammersmith & City (H&C), Metropolitan, Northern, Piccadilly, Victoria* **Theydon Bois** *Central* **Waterloo** *Bakerloo, Jubilee, Northern, W&C* **Piccadilly** *Line, dark blue, 53 stations* **Victoria** *Line, cyan, 16 stations* Circle, District, Victoria **Oyster** *a Tube-specific charge card, introduced in 2003* **Mansion House** *Circle, District* **Barbican** *Circle, Metropolitan, H&C* **Pimlico** *Victoria* **Canary Wharf** *DLR, Jubilee* **Mind the gap** *iconic announcement made where platforms are curved or shared by rolling stock of different floor-height – eg Bank, Paddington &*

Piccadilly Circus **Plaistow** *District, H&C* **Leytonstone** *Central* **Holborn** *Central, Piccadilly* **Holloway Road** *Piccadilly* **Elephant & Castle** *Bakerloo, Northern* **Ickenham** *Metropolitan, Piccadilly* **Stanmore** *Jubilee* **High Barnet** *Northern* **Northwood Hills** *Metropolitan* **Oakwood** *Piccadilly* **Earl's Court** *District, Piccadilly* **Knightsbridge** *Piccadilly* **cut and cover** *trench and roof construction especially used on Circle/District line, as opposed to 'tube' tunnels* **Parsons Green** *District* **Barking** *District, H&C* **Bow Road** *District, H&C* **Paddington** *Bakerloo, Circle, District, H&C* **Old Street** *Northern* **Clapham Common** *Northern* **Circle** *Line, yellow, now 35 stations (line opened in 1884, a continuous loop both clockwise and anticlockwise for almost 134 years; no longer a circle since 2018)* **Turnham Green** *District, Piccadilly* **Oval** *Northern* **Edgware** *Northern* **Ruislip** *Metropolitan, Piccadilly* **escalator** *moving staircase: the first was installed at Earl's Court in 1911* **Kilburn** *Northern* **Burnt Oak** *Northern* **Tooting Bec** *Northern* **All Saints** *DLR* **Metropolitan** *Line, magenta, 34 stations* **Stratford** *Central, DLR, Jubilee* **Liverpool Street** *Central, Circle, H&C, Metropolitan* **Bakerloo** *Line, brown, 25 stations* **Leicester Square** *Northern, Piccadilly* **Upney** *District* **Morden** *Northern* **The Tube** *familiar term* **Ealing Broadway** *Central, District* **Jubilee** *Line, silver grey, 23 stations* **Monument** *Circle, District* **ticket** *pre-Oyster/contactless receipt for payment of travel fare*

Epistolary

style

written correspondance

[Letter]

—— Certainman Farm ——
famed for husbandry: *established* 12BC
— wide range of crops, generously-propotioned livestock, family feel —

Tuesday
Ray,

   I am so sad that you are choosing to leave. Here's the money I agreed to give you. Please be aware that this has to be everything now – there will not be any more.

   Your mother and I (and Stephen) will miss you and hope you find it in your heart to return soon.

   But meanwhile, be wise, stay out of danger, and keep the faith.
   Lots of love, Dad

[Postcard]

views overleaf in full colour
Bingoarama; Harbour; Letitia's; nightclub life

Dear Stephen

I'm glad I have got away. I've made lots
of friends and am having a ~~wild~~ good time.
The picture shows the casino, the waterfront,
one of my favourite bars and the sort of
~~hot totty~~ dancing girls I'm meeting. Yeah!
Dad would be so cross if he knew what I'm
spending his money on! Please don't drop
me in it. Hope you're still enjoying working on the farm. If not, why not come and
join me here? Stay cool, won't you?
Your affectionate brother **Raymundo**

Mr S Certainman
Certainman Farm
Farmfields Road
Villageville
Homeland
LK15 0ST

[Memo]

From   The Office of the Right Honourable Sir Ingham Tacques MP,
Chancellor of the Exchequer
To   Cabinet, Foreignland

Esteemed colleagues, Please accept this as formal notice of my decision to resign.
There's no money, no crops, no hope and no point. I'm off.

[Application Form]
Hogs R Us (Foreignland) Ltd
Name	Ray Certainman
Address	No fixed abode
Job Applied For	Hog Husbandry Assistant, 5th class
Education	General
Experience	A lifetime of farm work in a family business, including calf-rearing and crop administration; some man management
Interests	Formerly: Wine, gambling, excess, wild women, fine dining, hunting.
	Currently: Food, shelter, acknowledgement, senses

[On the reverse of an envelope, pinned to the sty door]

Dear Boss, Sorry, had to go. I came to my senses and realized
my father's hired men are eating well, and I should humble myself,
go back to him and see if he will employ me as a servant.
I'm no longer worthy to be called his son.
I shall write again when I have settled to tell you an address
where you can send the wages you owe me.
Yours, Ray Certainman

[Business stationery on kitchen table]

Certainman Farm
famed for husbandry; established 12BC
wide range of crops, generously-propotioned livestock, family feel

If anyone needs me, I'll be up on the roof,
looking out for Ray.
Pa

With Compliments

[Certificate]

Government of Homeland
Department of Agriculture, Fisheries & Food Inspectorate

– Best in Show –
This is to certify that

Bighorn Buttercup XV

(Asturian Mountain breed) owned and reared by
A Certainman
has reached the standard of fattedness required
to qualify for a Red Rosette

Daisy Muchudda *Chief Examiner, DAFFI*

[Invitation]

It's party time!
As you may know, our beloved son Ray has recently returned
from his adventures out of town, and in celebration, we are cordially inviting

you

to attend a party to officially welcome him home as a son.

Certainman Farm, Farmfields Road, Villageville
Saturday Luke 15th *from* **11.24am** *til* **late**
Please bring a bottle & a babe Hot beef & drinks provided: RSVP
If you would like to buy Ray a gift, please select from:

~~Sandals~~	Woolly hat	Bow Tie
Stallion	~~Signet Ring~~	Tunic (size S)
~~Sheepskin coat~~	Jumper (size S)	Calf
Milking stool	Sythe	Calf Fattening Kit

Knight's moves   *wordplay*

*starting from square e8 (**highlighted**), one way of moving around a chessboard like a knight, touching each square just once, ending on e5 (also **highlighted**)*

	a	b	c	d	e	f	g	h
8	15 struck	60 was	19 after	34 offer	1 **Son**	50 greeted	31 and	46 way
7	18 looked	35 to	16 and	61 dead	32 returned	47 off	2 took	49 father
6	59 son	14 famine	33 to	20 pigs	51 him,	4 inheritance	45 long	30 senses
5	36 become	17 boy	62 but	13 gone,	64 **lives!'**	29 his	48 his	3 his
4	11 living.	58 'My	21 and	40 while	5 recklessly	52 gave	27 Came	44 a
3	22 longed	37 a	12 Money	63 now	28 to	41 he	6 spending	53 kiss,
2	57 party.	10 wild	39 But	24 eat	55 coat,	8 all	43 still	26 pods.
1	38 hireling.	23 to	56 shoes,	9 in	42 was	25 their	54 ring,	7 it

* Some might interpret this as a complicated and hard-to-read construct of the story told in 64 words. And of course, they'd be right. Moreover, I have no doubt there are neater journeys than this

P   *alliteration*

Prodigal petitioned Pop 'Pay portions!' – pocketed.

Passion-pits proved popular; passing. Payout pitiful, pals pushed-off. Provoked, Prodigal preferred pig (pinky-perky porkers) pod-pudding.

Pow! Prophecy plops psyche-wise. Prepares pleading pre-emptively.

Pater produced pearl-ring; pumps.

Protein-rich party provided – plump, pink pot-roast; prawn pizza; pesto pasta; pistachio porridge; piquant poppadoms; parboiled potatoes; pumpernickel. Plus peach/passionfruit/peanutbutter pancakes; pumpkin pretzels; papaya/plum/profiteroles; panettone, pineapple pastries; pattisserie...

Pa pipes: 'Popped-clogs; post-mortem proves proper pack-of-lies!'

Q _alliteration_

see JQXYZ (p201)

Artists & composers:
the lost pun _key words_

many of these puns have been stretched considerably beyond the limits recommended in health and safety guidelines

Cézanne the opportunity to have his inheritance early, the son did not fore**Gauguin**.

He left the farm, where there was food by the kilog**Ram, eau** de cologne and his simple job was to count things and keep **Tallis**. So he became a sort of pilg**Rem. Brandt** new home: Dissipation City. He spent all of his **Gains. Borough** little while later he was broke.

He'd met a good girl (Sue) in a **Bar;** tó**kall** her hair merely _red_ was an insult – it was **Titian;** her clothes had been washed in **Purcell** and were gleaming white.

But it didn't take long for the love of **Monet** to change **Sousa**ttitude negatively; his cash managed to **Turner** quickly to greed.

Her 'goodness' was obviously superficial; just a **Vermeer**. The perfect **Holst**, he gave her many gemstones and then plied her with drink: not only sufficient to quench her t**Hirst** but then fall off the **Wagn;** **er** tendency was to become severely intoxicated immediately.

She consumed another **Glass** (until they were both, to be **Franck**, utterly **Pissarro** – completely **Brahms** & **Lizst**).

They deserved to be arrested by the **Constable**, and were thrown into jail, where they couldn't watch the **Tele. Manni**pulatively, she murmured 'Oh, **Dalíng**.'

Later released, her tummy rumbled, making amusing noises: **Lowry, Prokofiev, El Greco, Brueghel**) but she went to the pawnbroker's to put the jewellery into **Hock**.

'**Ney**d to eat, you see,' she said. His appetite wa**S meta na**sty way with famine.

All wealth was **Haydn** from the population, as every **Stockhaus** encountered shortages and the hard-to-**Handel** hun**Ger shwin**dled them into desperation as it all started to un**Ravel**.

He found a job tending an **Hog** (arthropodia-infested food)… yes, working for a pig farmer, whose livestock had been not purchased but **Borodin** a rash moment. It was **Bacon** on the hoof, and the pigs were kept in a **Cage**.

Eventually, he came to his **Saint-Saëns**.

'I shall arise and set off **van Gogh** to my pa and **Ma. H**lerning to be humble's been a long road **Dvořák** the lad. I am **Satie**sfied that at home, even the hired men are well fed. I am not worthy to be called a son. I have to get out of this **Rutter**t all costs.'

When he was still a long way **Off** (en**bach** beyond the **Bridge**), his father who had suffered **Strauss** during this time was on the roof, surveying the countryside, since from this vantage point he could be a **Landseer**. He ran to hug his boy.

'If I had to make a choice,' he said, 'I would select you every time! I'd certainly **Picasso**n who returns! This is **Magritte**ing to you: Welcome **Bach**!'

He gave him a ring, **Coates** and in case he **Stubbs** his toe, for each foot a **Schu. Bert** he wouldn't let the boy say his speech.

'Least said, soonest **Mendel, ssohn...**' he reminded him. He threw a party. He ordered that the prize-winning calf be killed (it had been awarded a **Rosetti**), booked **Morris** dancers (in an attempt to **Bizet**ny), and sent servants to do the **Chopin** and bring **Bach** lots of food.

Once the steaks were **Freud**, they all tucked in. There was salad, **Morriconi** cheese (sauce based on a béchamE**l**), garnished with **Puccini** mushrooms; toasted **Paganini**s with paté and hard boiled eggs (both yolk and **Albinoni**).

Also, fillets of **Pollock**, little battered fish called white**Beet, hoven** chips, a rich meaty b**Roth**, kohlrabi stew and **Manet** more lovely dishes. Said his father, once the sliced beef – garnished with Salsa **Verdi** – was laid on the **Rach.**

'**Man: in, off**, out, on, up, down, and **Bach** again! He was dead and had gorn right **Orff** but now, **Vivaldi**!

Cézanne *1839-1906* Paul **Gauguin** *1848-1903* Jean-Philippe **Rameau** *1683-1764* Thomas **Tallis** *1505-1585* **Rembrandt** van Rijn *1606-1669* Thomas **Gainsborough** *1727-1788* Béla Viktor János **Bartók** *1881–1945* Tiziano Vecellio *known as* **Titian** *c1473/90-1576* Henry **Purcell** *1659-1695* Oscar Claude **Monet** *1840-1926* John Philip **Sousa** *1854-1932* Joseph Mallord William **Turner** RA *1775-1851* Johannes **Vermeer** *1632-1675* Gustav Theodore **Holst** *1874-1934* Damien **Hirst** *b1965* Wilhelm Richard **Wagner** *1813-1883* Philip Morris **Glass** *b1937* César Auguste Jean Guillaume Hubert **Franck** *1822-1890* Camille **Pissarro** *1830-1903* Johannes **Brahms** *1833-1897* Franz Ritter von **Liszt** *1811-1886* John **Constable** *1776-1837* Georg Philipp **Telemann** *1681-1767* Salvador Domingo Felipe Jacinto **Dalí** i Domènech, 1st Marquis of Púbol *1904-1989* Laurence Stephen **Lowry** *1887-1976* Sergei Sergeyevich **Prokofiev** *1891-1953* Doménikos Theotokópoulos *known as* **El Greco** *1541-1614* Pieter **Brueghel** the Elder *c1525-1569* David **Hockney** RA *b1937* Bedřich **Smetana** *1824-1884* Franz Joseph **Haydn** *1732-1809* Karlheinz

Stockhausen *1928–2007* George Frideric **Handel** *1685-1759* George **Gershwin** *1898-1937* Joseph-Maurice **Ravel** *1875-1937* William **Hogarth** *1697-1764* Alexander **Borodin** *1833-1887* Francis **Bacon** *1909-1992* John Milton **Cage** *1912–1992* Charles-Camille **Saint-Saëns** *1835-1921* Vincent Willem **van Gogh** *1853-1890* Gustav **Mahler** *1860-1911* Antonín Leopold **Dvořák** *1841-1904* Erik Alfred Leslie **Satie** *1866-1925* Dr John Milford **Rutter** CBE *b1945* Jacob **Offenbach** *1819-1880* Frank **Bridge** *1879–1941* Johann **Strauss** II *known as* The Younger *1825-1899* Sir Edwin Henry **Landseer** RA *1802-1873* Pablo Diego José Francisco de Paula Juan Nepomuceno María de los Remedios Cipriano de la Santísima Trinidad Ruiz y **Picasso** *1881-1973* René François Ghislain **Magritte** *1898-1967* Johann Sebastian **Bach** *1685-1750* Eric **Coates** *1886-1957* George **Stubbs** *1724-1806* Franz Peter **Schubert** *1797-1828* Jakob Ludwig Felix **Mendelssohn** Bartholdy *1809-1847* Antonio **Rosetti** *c1750-1792* William **Morris** *1834-1896* Georges **Bizet** *1838–1875* Frédéric François **Chopin** *1810-1849* Carl Philipp Emanuel **Bach** *1714-1788* Lucian Michael **Freud** *b1922* Ennio **Morricone** *b1928* Sir Edward William **Elgar** *1857-1934* Giacomo Antonio Domenico Michele Secondo Maria **Puccini** *1858-1924* Niccolò **Paganini** *1782-1840* Tomaso Giovanni **Albinoni** *1671-1751* Paul Jackson **Pollock** *1912-1956* Ludwig van **Beethoven** *1770-1827* Marcus Rothkowitz *known as* Mark **Rothko** *1903-1970* Édouard **Manet** *1832-1883* Giuseppe Fortunino Francesco **Verdi** *1813-1901* Sergei Vasilievich **Rachmaninoff** *1873-1943* Wilhelm Friedemann **Bach** *1710-1784* Carl **Orff** *1895-1982* Antonio Lucio **Vivaldi** *1678-1741*

Sourced from
the Bard of Avon   *key words*
key phrases from Shakespeare's work
The farmer gave his son (with **a countenance more in sorrow than in anger**[1], since he was **the apple of his eye**[2]), his share of the inheritance, **bag and baggage**[3], out of **the milk of human kindness**[4]. **Blinking idiot**[5]! (**Good riddance**[6], some might say). The boy soon got **in such a pickle**[7],

147

having decided to **play fast and loose**[8] with his father's money. **How sharper than a serpent's tooth it is to have a thankless child!**[9]

Not much later, he was eaten **out of house and home**[10] and the country suffered a famine in **one fell swoop**[11]; it was bad enough to **beggar all description**[12].

He took a job looking after pigs (**thrice, and once the hedge-pig whined**[13]) and longed to eat their **food...for worms**[14] (there was – **vile jelly**[15]– **something rotten in the state**[16]) but this was **cold comfort**[17].

Suddenly, with **remembrance of things past**[18] he said to himself **'But soft! What light through yonder window breaks?**[19]

'**When possibly I can, I will return**[20] and say to him Father, **I have then sinned against**[21] you; **I am sham'd by that which I bring forth, and so should you, to love things nothing worth**[22].

'So let me **enter, a Servant to**[23] you.'

Meanwhile his father did still **stand sentinel**[24] and suddenly said '**I have watch'd so long that I'm dog-weary; but at last I spied an ancient angel coming down the hill**[25] and **he ran this way, and leap'd this orchard wall**[26]. He took hold of his son's face and **kiss'd it**[27]. He gave him **his new coat and**[28] gave **him a ring**[29] and replaced his **old shoes**[30]. He **kills**[31] the **fatted**[32] **calf**[33] (the knife **thrust upon 'em**[34]) and roasts it ('**oh, that this too, too solid flesh would melt**[35]!') in celebration of this day with shows, **pageants, and sights of honour**[36].

He invites **brothers**[37], **sisters**[38], **neighbours**[39] friends, romans, **country-men**[40] for **salad days**[41].

The father made a speech. '**I was wreck'd upon this shore, where I**

148

have lost – **How sharp the point of this remembrance is! – My dear son**[42] was **lost**[43] but now is **found**[44].

'**My lovely boy**[45] I **have supposed dead; and**[46] reckon that **the rest is silence**[47]; but – **once more**[48] – he **stands**[49] **alive**[50]!'

Excluding these direct references: 'you would think that I had a hundred and fifty tattered prodigals, lately come from swine-keeping, from eating draff and husks' *Henry IV* part *i*, Act IV, Scene *ii*, line 8; or 'he that goes in the calf's skin that was killed for the Prodigal' *Comedy of Errors* IV *iii* 18
1 *Hamlet* I *ii* 250 2 *Love's Labours Lost* V *ii* 502
3 *The Winter's Tale* I *ii* 246 4 *Macbeth* I *v* 17
5 *The Merchant of Venice* II *ix* 53 6 *Troilus & Cressida* II *I* 116 7 *The Tempest* V *i* 297
8 *King John* III *i* 247 9 *King Lear* I *iv* 285 10 *Henry I Vii* II *i* 28 11 *Macbeth* IV *iii* 258 12 *Antony & Cleopatra* II *ii* 237 13 *Macbeth* IV *i* 2
14 *Henry I Vi* V *iv* 93 15 *King Lear* III *vii* 1
16 *Hamlet* I *iv* 99 17 *Taming of the Shrew* IV *i* 28
18 Sonnet XXX 2 19 *Romeo & Juliet* II *ii* 4
20 *Two Gentlemen of Verona* II *ii* 5 21 *All's Well That Ends Well* II *v* 9 22 Sonnet LXXII 13
23 *Timon of Athens* III *i* 2 24 *Midsummer Night's Dream* II *ii* 15 25 *Taming of the Shrew* IV *ii* 64
26 *Romeo & Juliet* II *i* 10 27 *Cymbeline* II *iii* 10
28 *Much Ado About Nothing* III *ii* 7 29 *Two Gentlemen of Verona* II *ii* 7 30 *Julius Caesar* I *I* 21
31 *Titus Andronicus* V *iii* 67 32 *Hamlet* II *ii* 413
33 *Much Ado About Nothing* V *iv* 54 34 *Twelfth Night* II *v* 127 35 *Hamlet* I *ii* 131 36 *Henry VIII* IV *I* 14 37 *Richard III* IV *iv* 95 38 *Pericles, Prince of Tyre* V prologue 5 39 *Coriolanus* IV *vi* 28
40 *Julius Caesar* III *ii* 15 41 *Antony & Cleopatra* I *v* 86 42 *The Tempest* V *I* 144 43 *Love's Labours Lost* V *ii* 733 44 *The Winter's Tale* V *ii* 5 45 Sonnet CXXVI 1 46 Sonnet XXXV 2 47 *Hamlet* V *ii* 370 48 *Henry V* III *i* 1 49 *Merry Wives of Windsor* III *iv* 2 50 *Richard III* II *ii* 6

Fugue *style*

a musical form: a theme is stated and recounted with many variations, in ever-changing keys and voices, as in a dream

The humble repenter (who was welcomed home by the forgiving father) started by asking for the money and, oh, with a smile of hunger and wastefulness, I received it, thanks to the pigfarmer and the lost/found status he was later to be said to have by my son's father.

Money is shoved into a bag made of calfskin, and spreads around the farm with great joy and celebration. To the wild women, the coat and the coinage itself, which was inspirational, much respect.

Furthermore the calf died and so did all the pigs and so do the dancing girls and then this father will smile again having seen the villagers from his high vantage point and the occurrence of a famine which ravages the land and killed the pigs and he rejoiced greatly at the decaying husks with whom the calf was partying and is running.

'My boy was lost, and took my farm and spent his pods with wild living (although he was dead and encountered a famine and shoes, a coat, a ring and a kiss with inspiration, arising, hunger, setting off and prepared speech).'

Found spent, I saw was he far joyful, second, go to.

Tending, fatted, he the is but they she says give envy spend ring wild he him he it they she him he. Running a farm wasn't straightforward, as the cash will flow from income to bartenders and croupiers, while

women danced with freedom and sandals.

He kissed him. He kissed her. She kissed him. They kissed them. I'll kiss pods. You'll kiss calf. You'ss kill calf.

Then the boy left and went home and left and went to Dissipation City and then left and right sandals and a coat and a coat of paint for the pigsty.

Even though there's not food for his stomach and he longed to belong and envied the calf and accepted the ring for his finger, which came with speed, watching, generosity, love, longing, hunger, wildness, hunger, longing, love, generosity, watching, speed, ring, finger, calf envy, stomach food, pigsty paint, coat, coat, right, left, City Dissipation, left home left. Boy.

Lost dead inheritance hunger longing spend party took saw went longwaypigfatinvite gave gaveway-gave-away… Returned repenting humbled welcomed.

Having longed for pig husks spending all inheritance freely given, run away, run towards. Run away, gave away.

Father was no longer worthy to be called a pig or a calfskin shoe, but hired wild women for off-roasting and dancing and kissing and inheriting and living and greeting and son-hiring and coating the fat cash a long way.

'Arise, Dissipod.'

Eye rhyme
poetry
pronunciation changes over time; spelling may *eventually catch up.*
Corrupted iambic pentameter, plus some enforced trochees

'I would inherit now.' A son's harsh **tone**:
With father's heavy heart, transaction's **done**.
In Dissipation City bills are **paid**;
'There's plenty more for us to spend,' he **said**.
A wanton girl; pneumatic, wicked **daughter**

Blew cash and waged with greedy, frenzied **laughter.**
She rashly bet, behaving like a **fiend,**
Distributed his wealth – no proper **friend.**

And once this boy had no more treasure **trove**
An honest, faithful **love** she did not **prove.**
The famine rose to savage, fearsome **height;**
All population soon were losing **weight.**
His money lost, thrown wild before the **wind**
He tended pigs that had mere husks to **grind;**
(Their porky flesh had **gone** to skin and **bone).**
His thought process was a revealing **one.**

'I will arise; to father's farm I'll **come** –
He'll bid me leave? Or welcome this son **home?**
It's only right for me to face his **anger**
A worthy son no more – but mere hired **stranger.**
Emotions are confused and hopes are **vague;**
Yet certainly I faint from starving **ague.**
I had dismissed what should have been **revered!'**
Yet father retains love; never **severed.**

Seen still a long way off (Pa kept his **vow:**
Keep lonely vigil over fields below?) –
Started the lad 'My sonship I'll **rescind…'**
Profligate greeting: overwhelming **kind!**
Delighted Dad! he clutched him to his **breast**
And called for gifts, and threw a wondrous **feast**
With roasted calf and bread; 'Come all, let's **banquet…**
We'll eat and drink my wine of heady **bouquet!**

'Cook partridge, grouse and venison – all **game**
On toast with sprinkled seeds of **sesame.**
Despite the waste of money from my **wallet**
Fetch dancers to enthrall us now with **ballet!**
So chef, show off your finest **recipes**
(While minstrels strum and sing or play on **pipes)**
Yes, roast the fatted calf, monkfish, prawn, **herring;**
We'll feast to greet this boy, who's yet been **erring.**

'Apportion blame? No, he's forgiven. **Tears** –
Begone! Fetch sandals, coat! My ring he **wears!**
Alive or dead – we never really **knew.**
A tailor fetch, to patch his clothes, to **sew!**
Like blood as mine still courses through his **veins**
This line endures, if soon he eats **proteins!'**

150

Extemporaneous (he did not **read**
His speech): 'Alive, although I feared him **dead**!
'New coat, new shoes! His tousled hair we'll **comb** –
No longer should his style befit the **tomb** –
Or by mistake leave trimmed not his **moustache**.
Gosh! Comfort him! His weary soul won't **ache**.

I can't deny he acted rather **dumbly**,
But bring him wine – and stilton; creamy, **crumbly**!
My humbled son no longer shows **hubris**!
Let's party! Don't worry if we make **debris**.'

* I realize few ever actually rhymed; see also the out-of-control eye rhyme **Ough** (p323)

What if?   _plot_
the story might divert at various points;
none are good outcomes; none teach us
truth about God

Spending
Boy asked for his inheritance, and father agreed. The boy took the money and spent lots of it in wild living, but was robbed at knifepoint for the rest.

The robber stabbed the boy and he bled to death on a road in one of the seedier parts of downtown Dissipation City. His father never heard about this, and kept watch in vain every day for several years until he died, poor and sad.

Famine-fodder
Boy took his inheritance and spent it all in wild living in Dissipation City. But famine struck and the boy was one of very many who died as a result, just as his father feared.

Given far more wealth than we usually imagine
Boy took his inheritance and spent it all in excessive, wild living, dining out, gambling, sexual impropriety and drunkenness. Yet he had so much wealth he managed to survive for thirty-eight exciting and high-living years before his vast store of cash was finally exhausted; unfortunately this coincided with a famine.

The boy (although no longer a young man) worked on a pig farm until he came to his senses.

He went home to be an hired hand, as he was no longer worthy to be called a son.

But when he got home, he discovered his father had been dead for two decades. Lack of funds and constantly deferred hope had made his heart sick. The farmland had been redeveloped into a village. There was no job for him, no forgiveness, no gifts, no hugs, no celebrations, no resolution, no closure. He moved on, but died later the same year, a broken man – exhausted with partying; filled with regret; now penniless and alone.

Victim of diseased pod
Boy took cash and spent it all until the famine struck. He took a job tending pigs, and longed to eat the rotting pods. He did so, and he sadly succumbed to food poisoning. He became ill, and died.

Forgot heritage
Boy took cash and spent it all. He refrained from eating the pigs' food. But he came to his senses, became a Gentile and lived on pig pods, pork rind and scrawny bacon until the famine was over. Then he settled down in Dissipation City.

Makes it a career move
Boy spent his cash. He longed to eat pigs' food but came to his senses and took a better job at a charitable food distribution centre. He went on to manage the foodbank until the famine was over; then establishing a fast-food chain – *Pod U Like*, serving gammon ham with pea purée in pitta breads. He never returned to the farm.

Rejected
Boy spent all, came to his senses and went home. His father, however, had bolted the gate, and told him 'Since you chose to leave, you must fend for yourself.' He took a job on another farm, but always regretted his foolish, selfish youth.

Not restored
Boy spent cash, came to senses and humbled himself. Father was pleased the boy was still alive and gave him a job on the farm, feeding the calf, as a hired man. He didn't get on with his fellow workers, and after a while the son took another job elsewhere.

Asserted sonship
Boy wasted cash and had a revelation. He knew his father would have to take him back, since he was, after all, his son. His father did, of course, because he felt he had to, and the son was treated as a family member again. But there was always resentment,

152

guilt and fear between them, and neither was particularly happy nor satisfied with the arrangement.

Imprecision *style*
or thereabouts, kind of, roughly
Someone asked for something and might – or might not – have got it, gone or stayed somewhere and lost something.

No-one had anything, but this person (or perhaps someone else?) went to look after, or look for, or look around something and wanted to do something with whatever it was, but then had a kind of fuzzy moment of some ill-defined sort or whatever, and changed his mind or thought better of it or had a different idea or followed an alternative philosophy or got cold feet or turned over a new leaf or reconsidered or something.

He went back to wherever he had come from (unless perhaps it was somewhere else this time), and someone said some things and gave or sold or lent or hired or threw away various undisclosed items and cooked or pickled or dried something and ate something with someone or more than one or several and said something else.

'He was whatever and now he might not be anymore. Who can be sure of anything?'

Best actor
Oscar winners *key words*
oscars for best acting performances in a leading role 1931-2016
Jack (son the **Younge**r) chose to s**Hun** the idea of staying at the farm, but to take a bit of a **Holliday**. 'You ma**Ke a ton** of money, Dad, so **Donate** to me

what I will inheriT. **And y**ou know, I'm off!' The day was a **Rainer** when t**He ston**ey-faced boy **Rush**ed off and **March**ed past the **Mill and** over the **Bridges**. Why, his dad couldn't fa**Thom. P.S. On**e day, he returned. Here's how:

Soon he was in Dissipation City: plush bars and **Swank**y cafés. He met some **Roberts, Andrews, Tracys, Stewarts** and a **Lawrence** – plus a girl who danced the lamba**Da, vi**sited the casino and dressed like a bim**Bo, garte**rs and all.

They drank heavily and became **Dujardin, DiCaprio, McDo(RM) and McConaughey**.

He could never out**Wit her** spooning manner. 'You can be my **Pal. Trowe**ls, hoes, rakes – not any longer! We should have a good time in the casino: I'll bribe the commis**Sar and one Moore** employee!'

But his money ran out, and famine struck the land

Everyone became weight wat**Chers**, and al**L eight** friends fell away. He took a job tending pigs; he longed to eat their rotting pods and **Berrys** wit**H old, e**ncrusted pock-marks on. The animals were filthy: pigs needed **Washing.**

Tongues cleaved to roofs of mouths due to hunger – and he was down to eight **Stone.**

He came to his senses – God and the boy were at last on the same **Page** in the pig**Pen**. 'Now, my father's hired men all have a jo**B, a test**ament to his kindness, and knowing my dad's **Brand** of contract, they are eating well. At least one's a branc**H off man** type!) I'll arise, go home, **Neal** before him and ask to work for him.'

But while he was still on his **Way,** nearly to the **Fir th**icket beyond the

Big **Field**, his **Old man**, keeping watch, saw him. He gave up al**L anger** and showed grace. He ran, arrived at thi**S pace,** kissed him (just a **Peck** on the cheek) and gave more than one souven**Ir on s**everal levels - a ring and shoes, and called the **Taylor.**

'Make new shoulders for this coat; don't ju**St re-ep**aulette the old one.'A **Smith**, a **Cooper** and a **Fletcher** were called to fashion items; he also wanted letters on the fire.

'Torch the F, the W and t**He P. Burn** them all! My man **Nichols on**ly wants them thrown out.'

The boy asked 'How could you see me when I was so far beyond the gar**DeN? I** roamed at a distance. Dad, oh, t**Hanks** for your kindness: especially the sliced roasted **Bullock**.'

At the party there was dancing: the lambada; **The ron**do; the tango.

Dad asked the foreign butler known as Le C, 'Where is my sister Liv? Try to find her. Now, give my guests each a gin & tonic with slices of **Lemmons**, and **O, Liv... I, er,** thought you'd gone missing, like my **Kid! Man**y times we searched, (like a **Hunter** seeking a lion with a **Red mayne**) and finally we found him!

'Pints of bitter, brown ale and **Guinness** for all, unless they'd prefer tubes of **Fosters** or a goblet of **Port, man**go J2O or something else. And after the chocolate **Fonda**nt, and the main course of chicken kash**Mir, ren**own for my popu**Lar son**, who **Wins! Let** joy be unconfined! My son was dead, (and that **Hurt**) but now he's a **New man!** My dear boy, of you I am so **Fond!** Alleluia! And I'm fond of your brother Lew as well. Where is he, just now? Oh what a happy **Day!'**

He was informed **Lew is** in the east meadow.

He thought he was told this news
by the Chief Steward, or by a servant.
Certainly it was a member of stAff.
Le C knew he was hired, anyway.

NB 'actor' in its modern sense: Best Performance
by an Actor in a Leading Role; and by an Actress
in a Leading Role Star *Film Title* Character
* indicates eponymous role Year [additional
win/wins] **Glenda Jackson** *Women in Love*
Gudrun Brangwen 70 [*A Touch of Class* Vicki
Allessio 73] **Loretta Young** *The Farmer's Daughter*
Katrin Holstrom 47 **Helen Hunt** *As Good as it Gets*
Carol Connelly 97 **Judy Holliday** *Born Yesterday*
Emma 'Billie' Dawn 50 **Diane Keaton** *Annie Hall**
77 **Robert Donat** *Goodbye, Mr. Chips* Charles
Chipping 39 **Jessica Tandy** *Driving Miss Daisy*
Daisy Werthan 89 **Luise Rainer** *The Great
Ziegfeld* Anna Held 36 [*The Good Earth* O-Lan 37]
Charlton Heston *Ben-Hur* Judah Ben-Hur 59
Geoffrey Rush *Shine* David Helfgott 96 **Frederic
March** *Dr Jekyll & Mr Hyde** 31-2 [*The Best Years of
Our Lives* Al Stephenson 46] **Ray Milland** *The
Lost Weekend* Don Birnam 45 **Jeff Bridges** *Crazy
Heart* Bad Blake 09 **Emma Thompson** *Howards
End* Margaret J Schlegel 92 **Hilary Swank** *Boys
Don't Cry* Brandon Teena 99 [*Million Dollar Baby*
Maggie Fitzgerald 04] **Julia Roberts** *Erin
Brockovich** 00 **Julie Andrews** *Mary Poppins** 64
Spencer Tracy *Captains Courageous* Manuel
Joseph Schildkraut 37 [*Boys Town* Father
Flanagan 38] **James Stewart** *The Philadelphia Story*
Macaulay Connor 40 **Jennifer Lawrence** *Silver
Linings Playbook* Tiffany Maxwell 12 **Bette Davis**
Dangerous Joyce Heath 35 [*Jezebel* Julie Marsden
38] **Humphrey Bogart** *The African Queen* Charlie
Allnut 51 **Jean Dujardin** *The Artist* George
Valentin 11 **Leonardo DiCaprio** *The Revenant*
Hugh Glass 15 **Frances McDormand** *Mildred
Hayes Three Billboards Outside Ebbing, Missouri* 18
Matthew McConaughey *Dallas Buyers Club* Ron
Woodroof 13 **Reese Witherspoon** *Walk the Line*
June Carter 05 **Gwyneth Paltrow** *Shakespeare in
Love* Viola De Lesseps 98 **Susan Sarandon** *Dead
Man Walking* Sister Helen Prejean 95 **Julianne
Moore** *Still Alice* Alice Howland 14 **Cher**
Moonstruck Loretta Castorini 87 **Vivien Leigh**
Gone With the Wind Scarlett O'Hara 39 [*A Streetcar
Named Desire* Blanche DuBois 51] **Halle Berry**
Monster's Ball Leticia Musgrove 01 **William
Holden** *Stalag 17* Sgt. JJ Sefton 53 **Denzel
Washington** *Training Day* Alonzo Harris 01
Emma Stone *La La Land* Mia Dolan 16 **Geraldine
Page** *The Trip to Bountiful* Carrie Watts 85 **Sean
Penn** *Mystic River* Jimmy Markum 03 [*Milk*
Harvey Milk 08] **Kathy Bates** *Misery* Annie
Wilkes 90 **Marlon Brando** *On The Waterfront*
Terry Malloy 54 [*The Godfather* Don Vito Corleone
72 *refused*] **Dustin Hoffman** *Kramer vs Kramer* Ted
Kramer 79 [*Rain Man* Raymond Babbitt 88]
Patricia Neal *Hud* Alma Brown 63 **John Wayne**
True Grit Marshal Reuben J 'Rooster' Cogburn 69
Colin Firth *The King's Speech* Prince Albert/King
George VI 10 **Sally Field** *Norma Rae* Norma Rae
Webster 79 [*Places in the Heart* Edna Spalding 84]
Gary Oldman Winston Churchill *Darkest Hour* 18
Jessica Lange *Blue Sky* Carly Marshall 94 **Sissy
Spacek** *Coal Miner's Daughter* Loretta Lynn 80
Gregory Peck *To Kill a Mockingbird* Atticus Finch
62 **Jeremy Irons** *Reversal of Fortune* Claus von
Bulow 90 **Elizabeth Taylor** *Butterfield 8* Gloria
Wandrous 60 [*Who's Afraid of Virginia Woolf?*
Martha Sandy Dennis 66] **Meryl Streep** *Sophie's
Choice* Zophia 'Sophie' Zawistowski 82 [*The Iron
Lady* Margaret Thatcher 11] **Maggie Smith** *The
Prime of Miss Jean Brodie** 69 **Gary Cooper** *Sergeant
York* Alvin Cullum 41 [*High Noon* Marshal Will
Kane 52] **Louise Fletcher** *One Flew Over The
Cuckoo's Nest* Nurse Ratched 75 **Katherine
Hepburn** *Morning Glory* Eve Lovelace 33 [*Guess
Who's Coming to Dinner* Christina Drayton 67]
[*The Lion in Winter* Queen Eleanor 68] [*On Golden
Pond* Ethel Thayer 81] **Jack Nicholson** *One Flew
Over the Cuckoo's Nest* Randle Mac McMurphy 75
[*As Good as it Gets* Melvyn Udall 97] **Robert De
Niro** *Raging Bull* Jake LaMotta 80 **Tom Hanks**
Philadelphia Andrew Beckett 93 [*Forrest Gump** 94]
Sandra Bullock *The Blind Side* Leigh Anne Tuohy
09 **Charlize Theron** *Monster* Aileen Wuornos 03
Jack Lemmon *Save the Tiger* Harry Stoner 73
Lawrence Olivier *Hamlet** 48 **Nicole Kidman** *The
Hours* Virginia Woolf 02 **Holly Hunter** *The Piano*
Ada McGrath 93 **Eddie Redmayne** *The Theory of
Everything* Steven Hawking 14 **Alec Guinness**
The Bridge On The River Kwai Lt. Col. Nicholson
57 **Jodie Foster** *The Silence of the Lambs* Clarice
Starling 91 **Natalie Portman** *Black Swan* Nina
Sayers 10 **Henry Fonda** *On Golden Pond* Norman
Thayer 81 **Helen Mirren** *The Queen* Queen
Elizabeth II 06 **Brie Larson** *Room* Joy Newsome
15 **Kate Winslet** *The Reader* Hanna Schmitz 08
William Hurt *Kiss of the Spider Woman* Luis
Molina 85 **Paul Newman** *The Color of Money* Fast
Eddie Felson 86 **Jane Fonda** *Klute* Bree Daniels 71
[*Coming Home* Sally Hyde 78] **Daniel Day-Lewis**
My Left Foot Christy Brown 89 [*There Will Be Blood*
Daniel Plainview 07] [*Lincoln* Abraham Lincoln
12] **Casey Affleck** *Manchester by the Sea* Lee
Chandler 17

154

Fraffly earppacrus *language*

Received Pronunciation for the cravat generation: think plum/silver spoon. Interpretation on p326

Sec ondsunad raissdthe aildbuy 'O Pater, ma-igh takem einhertnce?' Heargrd. Son wears tudall hisma nyeyon wildliving – yungsh avalorst hiscash inacasein ohanbigetting squiffy. Hewusoon bayerncrpt, antoca pital, ballyfam enstruck.

He took ajob teahndin pigsand ibslutlylornged t'eat therfood. He cameteris senses anthought 'Pater's unworshed hahdmin vorll gotplen teat'ete. I'llgoan ahrse kPater'fie canwerk frim.'

Soey maydisweigh, dohn tyaner?

Wharlie wastil alorng way orf, hispater sorim and ranter greetim. He gievima kissanna paerrashoos, plus huntin' pinks and anairl oomfamlahr ingfrisfingah. Heek illd thaf'tid carve an throughash indig.

'Thisma sonwas lorstbut is fayend; he was did, but na heesalaif!'

Anglo-Catholic *key words*

terminology

Claiming undue amounts of **Altarage**, the son made an **Assumption**[1] about the **Apostolic Succession**, demanding his **Christening Collection**, until he had a **Surplice**. He had a **Magnificat** time, and **Lapsed** into spending. Every day was **Lady Day** (sometimes **Rood**).

Screening out that having **Stolen** the money was a **Syn, OD**'d on wildness, damaging the Lady's place, and **rector** – a k**Nave**! The **Prebendary**[2]'s **Announciation** was for what he called his *acra* on **Rogation Days**[3] but no one really understood what hi**S** *acra* ment.

Employed in a Porcine **Cathedral**, he fed pigs a **Mass** of rotting pods; they snuffled: *SacristyBirettaLiturgyRheredos*.

But eventually he was inspired with a flash of e**Lectionary**, and took **Sanctuary** at home. He would ask to be a hired man but feared that **Chance'll** be a fine thing. Like a **Novice**, he practiced his **Catechism**, as he wanted to make a **Solemn Vow** of **Penance**, lest he be **Excommunicated** 'ere **Evensong**.

His father saw him while he was still a long way off (**Holy See**) and ran to greet him. '**Nunc Dimittis**[4],' the boy began, **Meekly kneeling upon his knees** but the father was **Religious**, giving him **Vestments**, denying **Discalceation**[5]. 'I thought you'd **Miss al**[6]l the celebrations…

'Oh, **Brother**, let's **Feast** on the **Bull**! Call in the **choir** and we'll have a **Canticle** and an **Anthem: Te Deum Laudamus**[7]. Open **Matins** of corned beef, followed by café au **Laity**.'

1 commemorating the Blessed Virgin Mary's ascension 2 Clergy receiving a stipend 3 prayers for agricultural blessing 4 *Lord, now lettest thou thy servant* 5 removal of footwear 6 liturgical formulae 7 *We praise thee, O Lord*

Prodigal puppet *key words*

casting

Prodigio	Sooty[1]
Father	Troy Tempest[2]
Showgirls	Looby Loo[3], Judy[4], Destiny Angel[5], Marina[2] & Lady Penelope[6]
Pig Farmer	The Lonely Goatherd[7]
Pigs	Pinky[8], Perky[8] & Miss Piggy[9] (given Little Weed[10] to eat)
Famine-bringers	Chucky[11] and the Mysterons[5]

Fatted Calf	Ermintrude[12]
Party Band	Dr Teeth and the Electric Mayhem[9]
Cook	Swedish Chef[9]

Villagers attending the celebration
Brains[6], Dickie Mint[13], Hoppity[14], Willy Woodentop (with Spotty Dog)[15], Torchy the battery boy[16], Statler & Waldorf[9], Parker[6], Captain Black[5], Lord Charles[17], Joe 90[18], Gary Johnston[19] & Twizzle[20]

Other birds & animals
Kermit the Frog[9], Lamb Chop[21], Hector[22], Muffin the Mule[23], Fozzie Bear[9], Sweep[1], Orville[24], Yoda[25], Zippy[26], Rastamouse[27], Gordon the Gopher[28] & Animal[9]

1 *The Sooty Show* 2 *Stingray* 3 *Andy Pandy* 4 *Punch & Judy* 5 *Captain Scarlett* 6 *Thunderbirds* 7 *The Sound of Music* (1965 movie) 8 *Pinky & Perky* 9 *The Muppet Show* 10 *Flower Pot Men* 11 *Child's Play* (1988 movie) 12 *The Magic Roundabout* 13 Inter alia *The Ken Dodd Laughter Show* Diddyman, voiced by Ken Dodd 14 *Sara & Hoppity* 15 *The Woodentops* 16 *Torchy the Battery Boy* 17 voiced by Ray Allen 18 *Joe 90* 19 *Team America: World Police* (2004 movie) 20 *The Adventures of Twizzle* 21 voiced by Shari Lewis 22 *Hector's House* 23 *Muffin the Mule* 24 voiced by Keith Harris 25 *Star Wars Episode V The Empire Strikes Back* (1980 movie) 26 *Rainbow* 27 *Rastamouse* 28 *BBC Going Live!*

Catch phrases   *key words*
from movies, TV sitcoms & game shows

Listen very carefully; I shall say this only once.[1]

The son asked his father for his inheritance. **'This time next year, we'll be millionaires**[2]**.'**

His father didn't say **'You stupid boy**[3]**,'** or **'Oh behave!**[4]**'** but handed over the cash. Lots of it. **Loadsamoney**[5]. The boy immediately left for Dissipation City, with a **'Hi-de-hi!**[6]**'** and saying **'I'm free!**[7] **Yeah baby!**[4] **And that's a yes from me – you got four yesses!**[8]**'**

He spent with abandon, **just like that**[9]. His so-called friends included many show girls (**shwing**[10]), and after a brief introduction (**'How you doin'?**[11]**'**) there was immorality (**nudge, nudge, wink, wink; say no more**[12]**, you dirty old man**[13]). But his money ran out and then **the pound had another bad day in the exchanges**[14]. There was famine in the land thanks to **a bit of a cock-up on the catering front**[15] and many were ill (**oh, matron!**[16]).

The boy took a job tending pigs; **doh!**[17] **'Am I bothered?**[18] Yes. **That's another fine mess you've gotten me into**[19]**,'** he mused.

'Aha![20] **I didn't get where I am today by**[21] wanting to eat pig pods. Yeah, but no, but yeah**[22]...'** and then had a revelation. God said **'I have a cunning plan**[23]**.'** He could return and ask to be a hired man.

But while he was still a long way off, his father saw him. **'I don't believe it!**[24]**'** he said at first, but then ran to greet his boy. **'Hallo, good evening, and welcome**[25]**; good morning, darling!**[26] Returning has scored you points, and **what do points make? Prizes!**[27]**'** He showered him with gifts. 'Here's some shoes and a coat. **And now for something completely different**[28] – a ring! **Say what you see**[29]... and let's kill the fatted calf, (**Cowabunga**[30]**, the silly old moo**[31]) because **there's nothing like a bit of bully**[32]. Oh, it's **nice to see you, to see you, nice!**[33] **Deal or no deal?**[34]**'**

The calf was roasted by a fire that was **scorchio**[35]. 'My son (**seems like a nice boy**[36]) has returned **to me, to you**[37]. **Come on down**[38] and have

156

some more meat – ah go on![39] **It's all done in the best possible taste**[40]. He was lost but **our survey said uh-urgh**[41]! **3-2-1**[42] and he's found. **I'm not** a *having a dead son* **person**[43]. He was dead, so I checked **every body. Lie s**[44]**till?** Not my boy! **Didn't he do well?**[45] **We were on a break**[46], but now he's **lovely jubbly**[47]. **That's all folks**[48], so it's **goodnight from me and it's goodnight from him**[49] – **shoulders back, lovely boy, show 'em off, show 'em off**[50].'

Character Actor (* indicates performer as himself) *Series/film title*
1 **Michelle Dubois** Kirsten Cooke *'Allo 'Allo* 2 **Del Boy Trotter** David Jason *Only Fools and Horses* 3 **Captain Mainwaring** Arthur Lowe *Dad's Army* 4 **Austin Powers** Mike Myers *Austin Powers* movies 5 **Loadsamoney** Harry Enfield *Saturday Live* character 6 **Gladys Pugh** Ruth Madoc *Hi Di Hi* 7 **Mr Humphries** John Inman *Are you Being Served?* 8 Simon Cowell* *The X Factor* 9 Tommy Cooper* 10 **Wayne Campbell** Mike Myers *Wayne's World* 11 **Joey Tribbiani** Matt LeBlanc *Friends* 12 **Norman** Eric Idle *Monty Python's Flying Circus* 13 **Harold** Harry H Corbett *Steptoe & Son* 14 **Newsreader** Robert Dougal *Yes, Minister* Sue Lawley *Yes, Prime Minister* 15 **Jimmy Anderson** Geoffrey Palmer *The Fall & Rise of Reginald Perrin* 16 Kenneth Williams, *Carry On* movies (eg **Dr Tickle** *Carry On Doctor*, **Dr Soaper** *Carry On Camping*) 17 **Homer** Dan Castellaneta (voice) *The Simpsons* 18 **Lauren Cooper** Catherine Tate *The Catherine Tate Show* 19 Oliver Hardy *Laurel & Hardy* movies 20 **Alan Partridge** Steve Coogan *Knowing Me, Knowing You with Alan Partridge* 21 **CJ** John Barron *The Fall & Rise of Reginald Perrin* 22 **Vicky Pollard** Matt Lucas *Little Britain* 23 **Baldrick** Tony Robinson *Blackadder* 24 **Victor Meldrew** Richard Wilson *One Foot in the Grave* 25 David Frost* *The Frost Report* 26 **Captain Blackadder** Rowan Atkinson *Blackadder Goes Forth* 27 Bruce Forsythe* *Play Your Cards Right* 28 **Announcer** John Cleese *Monty Python's Flying Circus* 29 Roy Walker* *Catchphrase* 30 **Michelangelo** Michelan Sisti *Teenage Mutant Ninja Turtles* 31 **Alf Garnett** Warren Mitchell *Til Death Us Do Part* 32 Jim Bowen* *Bullseye* 33 Bruce Forsythe* 34 Noel Edmunds* *Deal or No Deal?* 35 **Poula Phish** Caroline Aherne *The Fast Show* 36 Larry Grayson* *The Generation Game* 37 **The Chuckle Brothers** Barry Elliott & Paul Elliott *Chucklevision* 38 **announcer** Simon Prebble *The Price is Right* 39 **Mrs Doyle** Pauline McLynn *Father Ted* 40 **Cupid Stunt** Kenny Everett *The Kenny Everett Television Show* 41 Bob Monkhouse*/Max Bygraves*/Les Dennis* *Family Fortunes* 43 Ted Rodgers* *3-2-1* 43 **Tom Patterson** Tim Preece/Leslie Schofield *The Fall & Rise of Reginald Perrin* 44 **Dr Gregory House** Hugh Laurie *House MD* 45 Bruce Forsythe*, *The Generation Game* 46 **Ross Geller** David Schwimmer *Friends* 47 **Del Boy Trotter** David Jason *Only Fools and Horses* 48 **Porky Pig** Mel Blanc & others *Looney Tunes* 49 Ronnie Corbett* & Ronnie Barker*, *The Two Ronnies* 50 **Sergeant Major 'Shuttup' Williams** Windsor Davies *It Ain't Half Hot, Mum*

R *alliteration*

Ruddy Raymond rails rather rudely; rich Reg responds. Ray rejects, rebels; raves randily, remarkably resoundingly.

Rasher-bearers rotting ruminations? Rather ridiculous.

Regret. Realisation; revelation; revival; resolution.

Returns, rueful. Reg runs, rewards – ridingboots, ring, raincoat. Restaurant repast: rare roasted rump, roullard, rabbit rissoles, rocksalmon roe risotto; rhubarb roly-poly, runny ricotta-raspberry ripple, raisin rolls, rumbaba; Roquefort.

'Ray rejected, restored; robust. Rejoice!'

S *alliteration*

Second son said 'So, some sharing settlement, sharpish!' Sackfulls swiftly sorted, set sail Subversion-villewards. Soon, squandering savings started. Suddenly spent, silly son's side-kicks scattered. Severe starvation.

Seconded (sows slighty smelly), sad son saw sour swill – salivated; scheming. Senses startled, started shedward. Still several strides south, saw Senior scooting. 'Son/servant sorrow, stuff…'

Sent shawl, sandals, sparkler. Slaughtered/spit-roasted stable-dweller; sirloin shashlik, steaming sauces; sauerkraut; superb seared salmon steak; satsuma segments, strawberry semolina; sultana scones; sliced sourdough, seedcake; Stilton; seconds!

'Scared son – stiff? sound! Sacred songs skywards! Sorted!

Inflationary language _wordplay_

after the routine of Danish pianist & raconteur Victor Borge, adding one to references to numbers within words

Two day, third son spoke three his father, asking five his inheritance. His dad looked at him elevenderly, and gave him the cash and the boy left home and twodered off three Dissipation City where he fivegot his dad and spent in wild living, one-hundred-and-forty-five letchery and two hundred-and-one behaviour.

His friends were greedy and selfish; in fact, they were seven of two and one-point-five a thirteen of the other. The triploons soon went; famine struck the land. The boy fed pigs and longed three eat the pods the pigs were given.

He 17ozed his hand on his fivehead and came three his senses. A moment of braitenss? _My father's hired men eat twoderfully well; I shall arise, go home and ask three be a hired man, since Ininely I'm no longer worthy three be called a_

son.' He made his way back, but while he was still a long way off, his father saw him (standing athreep the roof), had beten feelings and ran three greet him.

He gave him a four-piece suit and two rings, an high six, and a trio of shoes, and then invited his neighbours to a thousand-and-one party, where they nine the fatted calf. No-one became intoxicnined, as they were drinking _Eight-Up_. In more modern times, they would have danced to something from the 21 of _The Fourpenny Opera_ or from Vivaldi's _Five Seasons_, or even a whole evening's worth of hits by 11CC, Los Quattros Amigos, and Blink-183.

'Befive, my son was all at sevens and eights, but fivetunately is found; he was seven feet under, but he's rejuvennineted – there is absolutely one wrong with him!'

Discount language _wordplay_

developing the same Victor Borge routine, subtracting one from references to numbers within words

No day, number one son started to creseven a fuss, and spoke one his father, asking three his inheritance. His dad looked at him ninederly and gave him the cash. The boy left, nowtdering off one Dissipation City, where he threegot his dad and spent it all in wild living, one-hunded-and-forty-three letchery and zip-£99 behaviour. His friends were greedy and selfish; in fact, they were five of nil and minus-point-five an eleven of the other.

All his singloons were gone; famine struck. He fed some pigs and longed one eat the pods the pigs were given. He 99p-ed his hand on his threehead,

158

and came one his senses. A moment of braieightss? 'My father's hired men eat noderfully well; I'll go home and ask one be an hired man, since lsevenly I'm not worthy one be called a son.'

While he was still a long way off, his father saw him, (standing aonep the roof), had be-eight feelings and ran one greet him.

He gave him a one-piece suit with no ring, a high four, and one shoe, and invited his neighbours to a 999 party, where they seven the fatted calf and slices of apple 2.14159265358, with custard.

If they'd lived in different times, they would have danced one the sounds of 9,999 Maniacs, Level 41, East 16, Stnowt Roses or *Dominique*, performed by The Singing -1, Haircut99's hit *Love Exactly* or Paul Hardcastle's *Er-Er-Er-Er Eighteen*.

'He was all at fives and sixes, but threetunately is found; he was five feet under, but now, how many things are wrong with him? −274.22°C! We are asone-hundred-and-oneished!'

Return for Spender
pastiche

borrowing freely from Elvis; acknowledging Return to Sender *by Winfield Scott and Otis Blackwell; No 1 in UK, No 2 in US (1962)*

> *Return for spender! Return for spender!*
> He took the money from his father: didn't stop to think;
> Went to Dissipation City; enjoyed girls, bets, food & drink.
> Wealth was frittered quite quickly; he sank his final swigs.
> Famine struck the whole country; envied filthy pigs.

He thought about it

> *Return for Spender? Remember when*
> *Farmhands ate dinners: just hired men!*
> *I took his money, I'm a Sad Sack*
> *I'll arise – humbly / ask him 'take me back';*
> So he walked home with purpose: 'Employ me as a hand';
> But father saw and ran to him, gave coat, shoes, golden band.

He started saying

> *'Return for Spender? Worthiness none…'*
> *But father hugged him. 'I love you, son!'*

(*middle eight*)
> 'Was lost, but now he's found; and he asked to join the staff!
> He's revived now from the dead – let's roast that fatted calf!

Rotate it slowly

> *Return for Spender! My longed-for boy!*
> *Celebration: complete joy!'*

Litotes
wordplay

negatively stated for effect

He was not the firstborn, and he didn't fail to ask for a not insubstantial amount. The city to which he went was not nearby, and the speed with which he dissipated the money failed to lack considerableness. Friends were few; tummy rumblings were not without volume. Not less

159

than 100% of the population was somewhat more than simply peckish, and the boy didn't wish merely occasionally for the pig food. It wasn't a self-induced revelation, and he chose to not remain after no lengthy delay.

He asked not for sonship, but father didn't give him time to speak.

The older man failed to restrain his generosity and showered his son with gifts that were not insignificant: a non-ending ring, a non-waterproof coat, shoes without buckles and a not unwelcome party, including a no-longer-living beast that could have never be inaccurately described as failing to be less than fully developed.

'My son was nowhere to be found, but now his whereabouts are disclosed; he lacked a pulse – now I know he is far from dead!'

The older brother was not thrilled. 'I haven't had a party with a goat and my friends. But this waster has failed to stay away, you've ended the calf's life, told the villagers not to cook their own dinner, and livened things up a bit from the normal dull, dreary working environment this is.'

'My son, listen. You never left. One day, I shall turn up my toes, and you will want for nothing. However, we cannot fail to celebrate your brother's repentance and return to the farm and home. Come on, don't delay, or the punch and beef slices will be all gone!'

Fiscal terms (money talks)
key words
current & former currencies & slang words for money

'Aye, there's the **Rub**! **Let** me have my inheritance, now, father!' His father (Robert) said 'Here's a little more than a **Quarter** of what I own. It's the best I can **Do.' Sha**me did not stop the boy from taking took the cash and he went, with a **Swag**ger, to Dissipation City's cas**Bah**.

There he began to spend with abandon in the **Grand** Hotel. The do**Yen**ne of his 'friends' was hand**Som**e, while one of the younger girls (outstanding curva**tu**re) was **Real**ly pretty – a **Doll**. '**Are** we going to dinner, **Bill**?' He agreed an**D**, **in a** riotous state, overspent wildly, often taking a **Punt**, or going on a pic**nic**. **Kel**ly had a deep sun**tan**. **Ner**vously, he wondered if she might like him. But suddenly, it was unlikely now**ad**ays, since he'd lost all his cash, and this had driven a **wedge** between them.

In fact, everyone lost many **Pound**s, as there was a famine, and the land was depo**Pula**ted.

His tummy rumbled, as there was no food in his **Colon**. He took a job tending pigs. He longed to eat the **Gourde**s the pigs were given, despite the vile stink that e**Manat**ed, since they were rather **Mark**ed and man**Ky**.

At this he wondered… was this a psychon**Euro**tic episode? Was his psyche expressing a**gro at** this, his na**Dir**? '**Ha**! **My** father's men!'

Yes, God was speaking to the boy, reflecting his **Sovereign**ty. 'Do you not kno**W**? **One** of your father's hired men (in fact every one of them!) eats better than you!' Bill needed no me**Tala**nguages to understand these words. He planned to say *I'm not worthy to be a son, whi*Le *very ab*Le, *keen to work for you*. Humb**Le, u**pset, ready. Going home was a t**Rial**, as he had to use Shank's **Pony.**

While he was still a long way off – at least as far as thi**S hill** – **in g**reat joy his father saw him. He threw his **Birretta** of**F, ran, c**ried out 'My son!' He moved swiftly and took, after th**E scud,** opportunity to hug him. **Bob** was the kissing ty**Pe.**

'**Some** muc**Luc** (real leather) for his feet! And give him a mac**Kina**w, a **Gold** (**standard** sized) ring for his finger. Kill the b**Rand**ed calf!'

Of all the 180 degree turns the son could have made, this was the 59th way to re**Spond** (**U LIX** in roman numerals).

At the party there was **Bread**, made from a soft, light **Dough**, delicately fried s**Quid** in tempura, canapés, (plus a **Lolly** for each child) and boiled cabbage, served with a **Zloty**d spoon.

In addition, there were peaches in sy**Rup, ee**l and **Buck** rabbit stew, meringue tart with le**Mon, key** lime pie, macaroon**S, core**d apples, a currant **Bun, g**rapes and **two bits** of cheese, with crackers and another **Bun.**

Centerpiece of the table was, strangely, **Half a crow.**

Next, the drummer crashed his cym**Bal boa**stfully at the music played by a **Brass** band and the guests were served a wee **Dram.**

'We thought he was dead! What a prize we have **Won! Ga**ve thanks before, but now wil**L I r**andomly shout: Halleujah!'

Slang/casual terms marked thus*; country used (including where it is not the official currency) indicated *thus* (date shows when replaced by Euro); obselete terms marked ob.
Ruble *Abkhazia, Belarus, Russia, South Ossetia, Transnistria* **Quarter** (US coin) **Dosh* Swag* Baht** *Thailand* **Grand*** (1000 units) **Yen** *Japan* **Som** *Kyrgyzstan, Uzbekistan* **Vatu** *Vanuatu* **Real** *Brazil* **Dollar** *Antigua & Barbuda, Australia, Bahamas, Barbados, Belize, Bermuda, Brunei, Canada, Dominica, East Timor, Ecuador, El*

Salvador, Fiji, Grenada, Guyana, Jamaica, Jordan, Kinbati, Liberia, Marshall Islands, Micronesia, Namibia, Nauru, New Zealand, Palau, Panama, St Kitts & Nevis, Saint Lucia, St Vincent & the Grenadines, Singapore, Solomon Islands, Suriname, Taiwan, Trinidad & Tobago, USA, Zimbabwe **Bill*** (note) **Dinar** *Iraq, Kuwait* **Punt** *Republic of Ireland-2002* **Nickel** (US coin, 10c) **Tanner*** (ob. UK coin 6d; 2½p) **Wad* Wedge* Pound** *Egypt, Lebanon, Sudan, UK, Zimbabwe* **Pula** *Botswana, Zimbabwe* **Colón** *Costa Rica* **Gourde** *Haiti* **Manat** *Turkmenistan* **Mark** *Bosnia & Herzegovina, Estonia, Finland-2002, Germany-2002, Namibia* **Kyat** *Myanmar* **Euro** *Austria, Belgium, Cyprus, Estonia, Finland, France, Germany, Greece, Ireland, Italy, Kosovo, Latvia, Lithuania, Luxem-bourg, Malta, Monaco, the Netherlands, Portugal, San Marino, Slovakia, Slovenia, Spain, Vatican City* **Groat* Dirham** *United Arab Emirates, Western Sahara* **Sovereign*** (ob. UK coin £1) **Won** *South Korea* **Tala** *Samoa* **Lev** *Bulgaria* **Lek** *Albania* **Leu** *Moldova, Romania* **Rial** *Iran* **pony*** (UK £25) **Shilling** *Kenya, Tanzania, Uganda* (& ob. UK coin 5p) **Franc** *Benin, Burkina Faso, Burundi, Cameroon, Central African Republic, Chad, Republic of the Congo, Democratic Republic of the Congo, Comoros, Côte d'Ivoire, Djibouti, Equatorial Guinea, France-2002, Gabon, Guinea, Guinea-Bissau, Liechtenstein, Mali, Niger, Rwanda, Senegal, Switzerland, Togo* **Bob*** (ob. UK coin 1s; 5p) **Escudo** *Cape Verde (Portugal-1999)* **Peso** *Argentina, Chile, Colombia, Cuba, Dominican Republic, Mexico, Philippines, Uruguay* **Lucre* Kina** *Papua New Guinea* **Gold Standard** (value system) **Rand** *South Africa* **Spondulix* Bread* Dough* Quid* Lolly* Zloty** *Poland* **Rupee** *Burma, India, Mauritius, Nepal, Pakistan, Seychelles, Sri Lanka* **Buck*** (US dollar) **Monkey*** (500 units) **Score*** (20 units) **Bung* Two Bits*** (US quarter) **Bunce* Half a Crown** (ob. UK coin 2s 6d; 12½p) **Balboa** *Panama* **Brass* Dram** *Armenia* **Wonga* Lira** *Italy-2002*

Record Breakers *style*
the Guinness Book of Records editorializes more than you'd imagine

Earliest Inheritance
While wealth is usually transferred from father to son following probate of the last will and testament of the

deceased, P Rod Iggle inherited his share of his father's wealth a record 42 years 253 days *before* the death of Albert Certainman, in an extreme act of generosity from the father, and of inconsiderate greed by the son.

Wildest Living
Most accounts of rapid expenditure seem to be backed only by anecdotal evidence.

However, none have followed the extraordinary *rags to riches to rags again* trajectory more meteorically than P Rod Iggle.

Having been entirely without wealth at 11.24am on March 15th 11AD he was given £31,511,243.15. He was at least penniless (and probably in debt) by 2.43am by January 5th the following year, a mere 295 days 15 hrs 19 mins later (an average *per diem* spend of £106,601).

Most Extreme Famine
Crop failure happens frequently, sadly, but the famine that followed the Great Crop Failure of 11AD in and around Dissipation City, Foreignland was the most severe of that century, with 379,200 lives lost.

Least Nutritious Pod
Pea pods vary in size, but the average number of calories per 100g of mange tout is 33kcal *138kJ*.

Pods discovered on the farmstead *Hogs R Us* in Foreignland after the Great Crop Failure of 11AD were found to be so diseased and partially rotted that they had a calorific value of just 9kcal *37.6kJ* per 100g. An unpalatable mould rendering the pods entirely unfit for human consumption accounted for almost all of these calories.

Thinnest Pig
Farmyard pigs *sus domestica* can achieve weights of up to 220lbs *99.79kg*.

Hog Starvo Minimus CXVII however, weighed in at slightly less than 10lbs 8oz *4.76kg* at slaughter.

Least Frequently Recognised Inspiration
Claims of 'hearing the voice of God' have often been made though the ages, but none has had such an immediate effect than the 'coming to his senses' incident, which changed the direction of the life of P Rod Iggle in 11AD (see *Greatest Value of Gifts, below*). He left his dead-end job in Foreignland, returned home, was forgiven by his father and welcomed into the family as a son.

Visual Acuity
Human eyesight is normalised at 20/20 vision. The numerator refers to the number of feet between the subject and the chart; the denominator is the distance at which the lines that make up the letters are separated by a visual angle of 1 arc minute, which for the lowest line that is read by an eye with no refractive error (or the errors corrected) is usually 20 feet. USAF flying ace Chuck Yeager had 20/10 (remarkably good) eyesight, which in part explains his dogfighting prowess; he saw the enemy long before they saw him – a huge, deadly, tactical advantage.

In history, Albert Certainman (7BC–53AD) is noted to have been able to see his son approaching from a distance of over 9 miles, which suggests record acuity of some 20/6.3 vision, as well as epic depth of faithfulness, anticipation and confidence.

Greatest Value of Gifts

While the shoes and coat given to P Rod Iggle were almost certainly of little monetary value, the gold ring (probably 14ct gold, size T) and kisses were of great worth, representing restoration to sonship.

He was initially given an estimated £31,511,243.15 as his inheritance (younger son's 33%). This left £63,022,486.10 as the value of the estate, so being restored to sonship was worth £21,007,495.05, an abundant way to say 'welcome home'.

Thus he received in total £52,518,738.20, plus the gold ring and other gifts.

NB his father's words to the older son 'all I have is yours' is taken by some to indicate that the younger son is due no more inheritance. But others argue that to be restored to sonship is to be restored to a 33% share in the inheritance, and that this is a symbol of the grace behind the forgiveness.

Most Overweight Calf

The term *calf* usually refers to a young (less than one year) male of the genus *Bos primigenius* (subfamily *Bovinae*). Females are usually called heifers until they give birth. Commonly, these animals can reach some 730lbs *330kg*. Bovine 'Big Belly' Brutus IX, reared by Albert Certainman, reached 850lbs *385.5kg* by 11AD, aged 341days, when his short life ended abruptly and he was roasted on a spit.

Largest & Longest Celebration

The party thrown by Albert Certainman lasted 23 days and nights, which makes it the longest party ever. It featured a conga of more than 8,400 people, which also breaks all records (see *Dance, Conga*).

Raisings from the Dead

Several claims have been made, many of which are Biblical.

Old Testament: Widow of Zarephath's son (1 Kings 17:17-24); Shunamite woman's son (2 Kings 4:20-37); man thrown into Elisha's tomb (2 Kings 13:21).

New Testament: Widow of Nain's son (Luke 7:11-16); Jairus' daughter (Mark 6:35-43); Lazarus (John 11:1-44); 'many holy people' raised as Jesus died (Matthew 27:51-53); Jesus of Nazareth himself (Matthew 28:6-9); Tabitha *aka* Dorcas (Acts 9:36-41); Eutychus (Acts 20:7-12) (lists not necessarily exhaustive).

There is, however, one biblical claim of resurrection that should be taken figuratively, and not literally as in the rest of these cases.

The lost son was indeed lost and then found, but was not actually physically dead and raised bodily to life again.

It was *as though* he was dead, and *as though* he had been raised, which is why his father declared this at the celebration party. Let no-one be deceived.

Prosody acrostic *alphabet games*

initials of words spell out, repeatedly,
TheProdigalSon

Taking his entitlement precipitously, Richard officially decided 'I'll go and live sumptuously. opulently.'

Northwards-trekking, had everything packed.

Ravers, opportunists, drunks, immature girls and lazy spongers of nubile types had extreme pleasure, really often. Disaster!

'It's gone! And look, so's our national turnover…

163

'Hunger, extreme poverty refocuses our dreams…'

In greatly appalling life-shifts of nasty turns, he envied pigs recently offered dirty, inedible gruel. And lo! Senses overcome!

'Numerate those hired employees,' philosophized Richard, of Dad's…

Ignobly groveling and like someone of no tribute, how's entreated Pater refusing offer? Decided. I'm gonna arise.'

Later, seen on neighbouring thoroughfare.

His excited Pa ran, offered donations including gold, and leather sandals.

'Oh never-trashed hope! Enjoy – prepared roasting of Daisy! I'll give a lavish social occasion! Napkins! Trestles! Heartfelt, euphoric public refuting of death! I grieved as lost; seems overwhelming, now!'

Prosody acrostic reversed   *alphabet games*
initials of words spell out, repeatedly,
noSlagidorPehT

'Nevertheless, one shall leave after gaining inheritance, Dad.'

Opportunist Ralph proved eager, hoping, tasting, nudging (or sometimes losing) and gambling, incurring debt! Oh, real poverty… everyone's hungry, there's no organic-slash-legume-agrarian green items distributable.

Our Ralph properly employed: *Hog Tending/Nurturing Operative (Second Level)*. After gruel is dispensed, oh, revolting-pod-envy!

Has transforming neurological-occipital-senses 'lightning.

'Arise, go into Dad's old racket; perhaps even hireling, too…'

164

Now, off!

Seen, lad's assailed: gifts include diamond-opal ring, pecks, espadrilles, housecoat.

'Tables! Neighbours! Openly slay large animal – gyrate, incinerate! Damsons, oysters, raspberries, profiteroles, eggs, horseradish!

'The news of son's lostness appalled; God is determining our restored prolonged enjoyment. Hallelujah! Thanks!'

Prosody acrostic reduced   *alphabet games*
initials of words spell out, repeatedly,
Lost

Lately, one son told loving old stager 'Thanks! Largeness of sums: tremendous!'

Languished opulently: suppers, tombolas, lovers, overspending, shopping, texas-hold-'em (licentiousness or selfishness?). Terribly, loot-out; suffering total.

Looked oh, so thin! Landed 'orrible sow-tending life. On second Thursday longed often 'Slop titbits? Look okay…'

Silly teenager later on saw twinkling lights of spirituality. 'Those labourers on slap-up tea! Let's obviate some tummyrumbles,' leaving. Off, south. Travels.

Looked out, several times. Lo! Offspring!… surrounded, took lip (osculatory) smacks, trinkets, loafers, overcoat.

Soon, travels lately over, satisfied to let overdone steaks taste lovely (or slightly toasted loin). 'Once sought; then lured out somewhat! Thought lifeless or stiff; then lively! Omnipotent saviour, thou, Lord! Oh salute, thanks!

Butchery News   *key words*

THAT'S WHERE ALL THE FLAVOUR IS!

Despite the extensive famine in many of the neighbouring countries, Arnold Certainman (42), a local farmer, made money no object, throwing a village-wide party last Tuesday night, writes our chief correspondent *Ian Vestigative Columnist*. It was merry-making to celebrate the surprise return of his younger son, who had been living in Dissipation City for some time.

Plenty of it

Certainman provided lots of alcohol and dancing girls, as might have been anticipated, and many groaning trestle tablesful of food, with sandwiches, scotch eggs, steaming platters of roasted vegetables, many home-baked loaves and sponge cakes plus a delicious chocolate fountain, served with marshmallows, whipped cream and pieces of fruit.

Plenty of quality wine flowed freely, too.

Variety

But the prime focus of the jollifications were the various steaks – well done, medium, medium rare, rare and blue options of rump, chump, T-bone, porterhouse, sirloin and the flavourful rib-eye.

In addition, cuts such as goose skirt, legs of beef, shoulders, best neck, shin, brisket and flank. Of course, there was also a great deal of mince. It is well-known that most of the flavour of beef is in the fat, so the calf in question had been suitably fattened up ready for slaughter over recent months.

Exaggerated

'It seemed just the right moment to maximise the opportunity,' said a tired, emotional Mr Certainman during the party. He had always believed his son would

return, and had kept a constant vigil, watching the road, for several years.

'I feared he may have died, but it was a wonderful moment when I finally saw him coming down the road (even though he was still a long way off), and I ran to him. I warmly welcomed him back, and sacrificed my fatted calf as I wanted all my neigh-bours to join in the hoop-la!'

But, rumours of Prodigio's death had been exaggerated; the boy was merely staying away from home following a frank exchange of views and wealth with his father, when the famine struck.

Similar parties are unlikely.

FOREIGN NEWS

Warning: Sub-standard swill is being blamed for the glut of poor quality pork which has flooded the non-kosher market. Frankly, only a starving man might consider eating such a product.

Activity sheet   *style*

choose the best word from the [selection, section, secretion], fill in the _____, solve RAMAGNA or corequed da spelunk

The ERONGUY son sayd to his [father, mother, brother] '[Listen, glisten, kissin'] Dad, I want my _____ , please.' When he DESKA, his HAREFT aggreed. So the sunset of on his jorney to [Dessication, Dissipation, Dissertation] City, where he DESWAT the [time, talents, treasure] on [tame ladies, wild women, elegant girls] and BLAGGMIN and [cherryade, alcohol, cups of tea]. After a HELIW, the cash was all _____. YEEVOREN was [starving, cooking, gardening] since they're were a fammin.

The son took a _____ [tending, lending, spending] [jigs, pigs, figs] and he [longed, tonged, wronged] two _____ the [gods, mods, pods] _____ had bean EVING.

AUNTYLEVEL he [came, fame, blame] to his ESNESS and sed 'At whome, the ERHID men [eat, ate, tea] well; I shall EIRAS and go to [why, my, shy] _____ and [hay, flay, say] to him that [I, eye, aye] am no RENOGL swarthy to be _____ his [sun, son, sin] and [demand, ask, plead] _____ to LOYPME me _____ of his RED HI _____.' But while EH was stil a [pong, strong, long] [way, weigh, whey] [oaf, off, of], his father WAS hymn and RATHER EMOTING. He DIESKS him, caled for NERSSTAV to fletch a _____ for his [finger, singer, wringer] and a _____ and a [pare, pair, pear] of shoos. He DEODRER them to [kill, thrill, frill] the FACT LE DAFT, and he through a _____.

'This my sun was [STOL, DESEBOMS, SCOT] butt is _____ ; AH WISE, I DISADVANTAGE A BLUE!'

High Street _key words_
stores and supermarkets, UK & US, present and recently-past

'Give me your dollars, pounds, shekels and pesetAs, Dad', the boy demanded. Whatever Next? His dad, name of John Lewis, did this.

He went to Dissipation City, where he made a crowd of suspect friends such as Austin Reed, the Moss Bros, Laura, Ashley, plus Nat West and his buddy Harvey Nichols. They partied (eating Currys) and spent extravagantly, no-one minding their p's and Q'S.

Dorothy Perkins, known as D, drank beer by the pint. The order given to the servant they thought of as the Bar-rat: 'Tsk! I'll just have a Half.' Or D's measure!'

This involved filling the glass beyond the brim – as was the practice of the house – and striking the foam away at rim level. This was called the House-off raser. They snorted a white powder, which they considered a Super drug.

The son even spent money on a graphic designer, trying to rework his monogram. 'Put the upright of thiS A in S; bury some of the T...' but he was suddenly Skint.

The entire population ran out of food (even Staples) and had only Water. Stones fell off them and many became an invaLid, losing too much weight from the Body.

Shopping around for a job, the boy ended up on a pig farm (this was not yet our caring, PC World).

The boy would long to eat the pigs' food (which came from a few Odd bins of mouldy scraps, and then would Come to his senses.

'I know what I lIke. And I should return to my Habitat at Home base.'

What kept old man Lewis hoping during the long Wait; rose-tinted spectacles? No! Faith. His father saw him coming over the blasted hill and down the Blooming dales; past the huge forest and the Little woods; along the River, Island-hopping. He ran to greet him and gave gifts.

The boy did up his newly-gifted Dr Marten's Boots – thereafter called the 'bestoWal Martens' – wondered about his brand new **Liberty** bodice, and delighted in his ring with an emer**Ald.**

'I love you, son,' said his dad, having decided to nega**Te** sco**l**dings. He called to his senior shef '**Thomas, Cook,** please, the fatted calf.'

The dinner established a **French Connection** with vol au vents, wine, profiteroles, etc.

Responsibilities: meat – Tom, the cook; rice – Ingrid; cakes (home-ma**De**) – **Ben.**

Hams were not on the menu, obviously, but there was a lovely salad of leaves called a mesc**Lun, 'n'** poly**anthus** roses in a table centrepiece.

Music was provided by a band with excellent rhyt**HM (V**ocals by a chap named Gary, who made a big ef**Fort): Numan. DM (**a son's new boots) were displayed with pride.

The boy's older bother started to complain. 'But he took dollars and shekels and **Marks & Spen...**' Ceremonies and speeches interrupted him.

'Just spread out little bits of cake in a sort of artistic crum**B arc, lay s**ome petals on the ground, and we can have hot c**Har, rod-s**ecured sal**Mon soon.**

'And, from these rotating, cooled dispensers, known as carou**Sel fridges,** drinks with **Ice.**'

L and his wife announced: 'My son – what a cheru**B! H!** Sing praises to God! – he's a lad for whom I and his **Mother care** deeply.

'He was lost, but now, after a brief **Gap,** is found, thank **Evans!** Our family can forgive and reabsor**B, & Q**uite soon.

'He was dead but is alive!'

Classical phrases
alphabet games
many Latin and Greek words and phrases have been adopted directly into standard English

Dramatis personae[1]: Father, Son, friends, servants. Father's **annis horribilis**[2]: his son's **agenda**[3] starts with demands for a **priori**[4] inheritance **ex gratia**[5]. 'Caveat **emptor**[6]: it'll spoil your **Curriculum Vitae**[7],' he warns.

But his son considered the benefits. '**Quid pro quo**[8].'

As the son leaves, **ad hoc**[9], for **terra incognita**[10], his father wonders '**Quo vadis?**[11]'

'Ξένος ὢν ἀκολούθει τοῖς ἐπιχωρίοις νόμοις[12],' reckons the son as he spends **circa**[13] £5000 **per diem**[14] in Dissipation City. '**Vene vidi vici**[15], either **pro tempore**[16] or **ad infinitum**[17].' **Sic transit gloria mundi**[18].

Erratum[19]: **in flagrante delecto**[20] he spends the last of the cash, lacking **alibi**[21]. **Tempus fugit**[22]; he gets a job with pigs. **Prima facie**[23] '**Timeo Danaos et dona ferentes**[24], he says, under his breath, in an **affidavit**[25]. **De profundis**[26], he longs to eat the pods (**ipso facto**[27] rotting **ad nauseam**[28]).

His thoughts turn glum; **memento mori**[29], he feels **subpeona**[30] of guilt and loneliness.

Then (**opus dei**[31]) he comes to his senses and takes a private **vox populi**[32] poll. '**Carpe deum!**[33]' he cries (this is **verbatim**[34]) and then 'Εὕρηκα![35]'

Far from **deus ex machina**[36], he recalls his dad's hired men have plenty to eat.

'Κύριε ἐλέησον[37] – I am no longer worthy to be called a son **in veritas**[38]. I'll be a worker **emeritus**[39].'

167

Meanwhile, still **in situ**[40] with **uberrima fides**[41], Dad was reprising his role **in loco parentis**[42]. He ran, **via**[43] the stairs, to greet him, **festina lente**[44].

While he was entitled to berate his son '**Note bene**[45]: **Volente non fit injuria**[46]!', he demonstrated instead that his love was **semper fidelis**[47] (which was a massive **non sequitor**[48]) with **pro forma**[49] gifts, **inter alia**[50], of a coat, shoes, a ring **et cetera**[51] and killing the fatted calf **in toto**[52], **et al**[53].

'**Pax vobiscum**[54]!' father said. He invited guests to attend a party, **ad lib**[55]. '**Floreat peur!**[56] We called, **in extremis**[57], for **habeus corpus**[58], fearing **rigor mortis**[59]. **Ecco homo!**[60] We had this gravestone carved: *In Memoriam*[61]; *requiescat in pace*[62]. But this (**nil desperandum!**[63]) was a **post script**[64] we didn't expect – the **status quo**[65] is restored! Worship, **magna cum laude**[66] to the Lord!'

1 **dramatis personae** *cast* 2 **annis horribilis** *bad year* 3 **agenda** *items for discussion* 4 **a priori** *first* 5 **ex gratia** *free gift* 6 **caveat emptor** *let the buyer beware* 7 **curriculum vitae** *life's contents* 8 **quid pro quo** *fair exchange* 9 **ad hoc** *spontaneously* 10 **terra incognita** *unknown land* 11 **quo vadis** *where are you going? (Whither goest thou?)* 12 Ξένος ὢν ἀκολούθει τοῖς ἐπιχωρίοις νόμοις *when in Rome, do as the Romans do* 13 **circa** *about* 14 **per diem** *per day* 15 **Vene vidi vici** *I came I saw I conquered* 16 **pro tempore** *for the time being* 17 **ad infinitum** *for ever* 18 **sic transit gloria mundi** *thus passes the world's glory* 19 **erratum** *mistake* 20 **in flagrante delecto** *red-handed* 21 **alibi** *elsewhere* 22 **tempus fugit** *time flees* 23 **Prima facie** *at first glance* 24 **timeo Danaos et dona ferentes** *beware of Greeks bearing gifts* 25 **affidavit** *sworn statement* 26 **de profundis** *out of misery* 27 **ipso facto** *in fact* 28 **ad nauseam** *sickmaking* 29 **memento mori** *remember mortality* 30 **subpeona** *under a penalty* 31 **opus dei** *work of God* 32 **vox populi** *voice of the folk* 33 **carpe deum** *seize the day* 34 **verbatim** *full transcript* 35 Εὕρηκα **eureka** *found it* 36 **deus ex machina** *contrived solution (god of the machine)* 37 Κύριε ἐλέησον (kyrie eleison) *Lord have mercy* 38 **in veritas** *truth* 39 **emeritus** *honoured veteran* 40 **in situ** *in place* 41 **uberrima fides** *with the utmost good faith* 42 **in loco parentis** *in the parents' place* 43 **via** *by way of* 44 **festina lente** *hurrying slowly (not 'close the window')* 45 **note bene** *note well* 46 **volente non fit injuria** *you consented to the risk, so don't complain (it's your own fault)* 47 **semper fidelis** *always faithful* 48 **non sequitor** *doesn't follow* 49 **pro forma** *procedure* 50 **inter alia** *among others* 51 **et cetera** *and other, similar items* 52 **in toto** *completely* 53 **et al** *and others* 54 **pax vobiscum** *peace to you* 55 **ad lib** *(ad libitum) unrehearsed* 56 **floreat peur** *may the boy flourish* 57 **in extremis** *in death* 58 **habeus corpus** *show the body* 59 **rigor mortis** *stiffness of death* 60 **ecce homo** *behold the man* 61 **in memoriam** *in memory* 62 **requiescat in pace** *rest in peace* 63 **nil desperandum** *never despair* 64 **post script** *afterword* 65 **status quo** *existing state* 66 **magna cum laude** *great praise*

Irritable vowel syndrome
alphabet games

each word employs only one of the vowels (multiples permitted) or none at all. Thank the Lord for y!

'Oh, I do ask that,' says Son, so Dad's dividing his cash in thirds or sevenths. 'Is this all?'

'Wysiwyg,' Pa says. This was disinhibiting, so lad did primitivistic Philistinisms on isthmi far away, in a suburb of the big City. Not thrifty! All shillings spend on cards, food and nymphs who screeched, etc. Wild to the Nth degree.

Chronology: Spent all; hungry; GDP = Nil; took a job with a beekeeper who kept – anathama! – pigs. Instinctivistic disliking? Yes, but needs must. Longs for pods; then God got to his psychorhythms and his senses went *ping*.

'Grr,' he growls. 'I am a numbskull! Dad's men feed every day. I shall go home and ask him if I can serve.'

Humbly mumbly 'Look, I'm not worthy, OK?'

Limping long thro' moon's decrescence, and tho' still a long way off, (past the cwm), seen by Dad. He runs, greets with no tsktsking, but schmaltz: kissing, giving gifts of boots, a DJ (with good stitching), gold jewellery (a ring). Lad is defenceless, happy – this is not untruthful.

Dad's cry: 'I'll throw a party with taramasalata, and entrée of beef, plus borscht, satay, hot dogs, hooch, bananas, kiwi, strawbs and cheeses. Yes, and street foods. Mmm, plus schnapps with effervescence! A bunch of thesps may give us a show: the play *Chrononhotonthologos**. And a pygmy band playing polyrhythms, so we may sing hymns! Woo hoo! We've got syzygy... my son was lost but is here. He's living, tho' he has had many sorts of strengthlessnesses!'

* a play (1734) by Henry Carey. The title means *furious, demanding & self-centred*

Last lines   *key words*
the final words spoken before we see the film's final caption saying The End
NB SPOILER alert
The younger son confronted his father for his inheritance. His father reminded him **'But Charlie, don't forget what happened to the man that suddenly got everything he always wanted.'**
'What did he do?'
'He lived happily ever after.'[1]
'That's what I intend to do. Is that the money?'
'That is all.'[2] They stared at each other, sadly. **'God help us in the future.**[3] You have no idea what I'm talking about, I'm sure. But don't

worry: you will someday.[4] Anyway, here's a question:, **where ya headed, cowboy?'**
'Nowhere special.'
'Nowhere special. I always wanted to go there.'
'Come on!'[5]
'No. **I'm too old for this.**[6] So, **I'll be right here. Bye.'**[7]
'I'm going.' Charlie pointed **'Out there. That-a-way.'**[8]

Not long afterwards, he found himself in Dissipation City, surrounded by so-called friends and Marsh, a theatrical agent.
'**I love you, yeah?'**[9] said Delores, a dancer, to Charlie. '**I think this is the beginning of a beautiful friendship.'**[10]
'How did you get this job?' asked Charlie.
Kelvin joked: **'Marsh will probably say he discovered her. Some guys get all the breaks.'**[11]
'I've got enough cash for us all,' Charlie boasted as Norman left. **'You're not gonna stick around for your share?'**
'Naah. I'd only blow it.'[12]
'Me too,' said Charlie, closer to the truth than he realised.
Delores interrupted. **'What did he just say?'**
'He said there's a storm coming in.'
'**I know.'**[13] And they were right: famine!
'I haven't eaten for weeks,' said Delores, pouting.
'And I've run out of money,' admitted Charlie. '**A man's got to know his limitations.'**[14]
'**Good. For a moment there, I thought we were in trouble,'**[15] she joked. '**Bye!'**[16]
Kelvin & Norman agreed '**I think we oughta leave now.'**

169

'That's probably a good idea.'[17]

'Merry Christmas, and may God bless us, every one,'[18] Charlie said, his tummy rumbling. A little while later, Charlie looked at one of the pigs he was employed to tend and said 'You're a swine.'[19]

The pigs ate rotting pods covered in mould. 'Never give a sucker an even break,'[20] Charlie advised them. He longed to eat their food but refrained. 'I'm not even gonna swat that fly. I hope they are watching. They'll see. They'll see and they'll know and they'll say, *Why, she wouldn't even harm a fly*.[21]

'She? Argh! Argh![22] I mean *he*.' He had a revelation. 'The old man was right. Only the farmers won. We lost. We always lose[23]… This is madness. Madness.[24] Even my father's farmers eat well. I shall go and work for Dad again.'

He turned to the pigs and said 'Where are you guys going? Wait a minute? I'll remember this! I'll remember everyone of ya! I'll be back; don't you forget that. I'll be back.[25] Especially if my dad doesn't welcome me home.' How could he be sure? 'I'm an average nobody. I get to live the rest of my life like a schnook.'[26]

'Work for Dad?' he asked himself. 'Do you think you'd be happy doing that? Well, I don't know. What are the hours?[27] Dad will have to come back onto my side, even though I was mean to him… Anyway, cheerio pigs; …Tara!...Home. I'll go home, and I'll think of some way to get him back! After all, tomorrow is another day!'[28]

The pig farmer asked Charlie 'And where do you think you are going?'

'Well, sir. Goin' 'ome... 'Ome, sir.[29] Looks like I'm walkin'…'[30]

Meanwhile Dad was sitting on his roof, looking out at his hired men. 'I'm the boss, I'm the boss, I'm the boss, I'm the boss, I'm the boss...(I'm the) boss, boss, boss, boss, boss, boss.'[31]

But then he saw Charlie on the road, and he ran to greet him. 'I love you,[32] son! You're alive, thank heaven.'[33]

The son began his plea. 'Oh, but anyway, Toto, we're home! Home! And this is my room - and you're all here! And I'm not gonna leave here ever, ever again because I love you all! – And oh, Auntie Em, there's no place like home.[34] Can I come in?[35] Can I work for you, here, please?'

His father kissed him, gave him a ring, shoes and a coat, and declared the gift-giving done. 'It is accomplished! It is accomplished!'[36]

A servant approached the fatted calf with a knife.

The calf was thinking 'But I am alive. And I am not afraid.[37] I do wish we could chat longer, but I'm having an old friend for dinner. Bye.'[38]

Later that afternoon, Charlie explained how it felt to be starving. 'And I felt my body dwindling, melting, becoming nothing. My fears locked away and in their place came acceptance. All this vast majesty of creation, it had to mean something. And then I meant something, too. Yes, smaller than the smallest, I meant something, too. To God there is no zero. I still exist.[39] But now I've eaten fatted calf butties, and thought *I was cured all right*.'[40]

'They tell me it's time for my speech; so, let's begin[41]. And… action![42] This my son was lost,' said his father, 'but now is found; he was dead but is alive! Well, nobody's perfect!'[43]

170

He had invited the whole village, telling his servants 'Go – proclaim liberty throughout all the lands, and to all the inhabitants thereof.[44] Now where was I?'[45] He saw some guests were not eating. 'Can I interest you in some dessert?

'Don't you always?'

'What would you like?'

'Surprise me!'[46]

He also said, to his son 'I thought we'd meet again only in death.'

'This is our destiny.'

'Kiss me[47]. I wish we had more time. I love you.'[48]

'Who's this bloke coming in from the far field, Charlie?'

'He's my brother.[49] Have a beef sandwich, Steve... you're pleased to see me, aren't you?'

'Thank you. No.'[50]

character name Actor *film title* year released (where conversations are shown: final speaker listed last & credited)
1 **Willa Wonka** Gene Wilder *Willy Wonka & the Chocolate Factory* 1971 2 **Radar O'Reilly** (as PA Announcer) Gary Burghoff *M*A*S*H* 1970 3 **Criswell** Himself *Plan 9 From Outer Space* 1959 4 **Lester Burnham** Kevin Spacey *American Beauty* 1999 5 **Jim & Bart** Cleavon Little *Blazing Saddles* 1974 6 **Roger Murtaugh** Danny Glover *Lethal Weapon* 1987 7 **E.T. & Elliot** Henry Thomas *E.T. The Extra-Terrestrial* 1982 8 **Admiral James T Kirk** William Shatner *Star Trek: The Motion Picture* 1979 9 **Adrian & Rocky** *Rocky* Sylvester Stallone 1976 10 **Rick Blaine** Humphrey Bogart *Casablanca* 1942 11 **a patron** *42nd Street* 1933 12 **Henry Gondorff & Johnny Hooker** Robert Redford *The Sting* 1973 13 Gas Station Attendant & **Sarah Connor** Linda Hamilton *The Terminator* 1984 14 **Harry Callaghan** Clint Eastwood *Magnum Force* 1973 15 **Butch Cassidy** Paul Newman *Butch Cassidy and the Sundance Kid* 1969 16 **Barry Guiler** Cary Guffey *Close Encounters of the Third Kind* 1977 17 **Vincent Vega & Jules Winfield** Samuel L Jackson *Pulp Fiction* 1994 18 **Tiny Tim Cratchett** Terry Kilburn *A Christmas Carol* 1938 19 **Norm** (to John Lennon) Norman Rossington *A Hard Day's Night* 1964 20 **Professor Eustace McGargle** WC Fields *Poppy* 1936 21 **Norma Bates** Virginia Gregg (uncredited, voice off) *Psycho* 1960 22 **Chewbacca the Wookie** Peter Mayhew *Star Wars* 1977 23 **Chris Larabee Adams** Yul Brynner *The Magnificent Seven* 1960 24 **Major Clipton** James Donald *The Bridge on the River Kwai* 1957 25 **Johnny Friendly** Lee J Cobb *On the Waterfront* 1954 26 **Henry Hill** Ray Liotta *GoodFellas* 1990 27 **Marti DiBergi & Nigel Tufnel** Christopher Guest *This Is Spinal Tap* 1984 28 **Scarlett O'Hara** Vivien Leigh *Gone with the Wind* 1939 29 **driver** Bert Holliday (uncredited) *Lawrence of Arabia* 1962 30 **Jack Walsh** Robert de Niro *Midnight Run* 1988 31 **Jake La Motta** Robert de Niro *Raging Bull* 1980 32 **Winston Smith** John Hurt *Nineteen Eighty-Four* 1984 33 **Madame Alvarez** Hermione Gingold *Gigi* 1958 34 **Dorothy Gale** Judy Garland *The Wizard of Oz* 1939 35 **Tony Mendez** Ben Affleck *Argo* 2013 36 **Jesus Christ** Willem Dafoe *The Last Temptation of Christ* 1988 37 **Private Joker** Matthew Modine *Full Metal Jacket* 1987 38 **Dr Hannibal Lecter** Anthony Hopkins *The Silence of the Lambs* 1991 39 **Scott Carey** Grant Williams *The Incredible Shrinking Man* 1957 40 **Alex DeLarge** Malcolm McDowell *A Clockwork Orange* 1971 41 **Dr Malcolm Sayer** Robin Williams *Awakenings* 1990 42 **Assistant Director** David Cluck *The Artist* 2012 43 **Osgood Fielding III** Joe E Brown *Some Like it Hot* 1959 44 **Moses** Charlton Heston *The Ten Commandments* 1956 45 **Leonard Shelby** Guy Pearce *Memento* 2000 46 **Django** Brian Dennahy (voice) *Ratatouille* 2007 47 **Jamal K Malik & Latika** Frieda Pinto *Slumdog Millionaire* 2008 48 **Steve Trevor** Chris Pine *Wonder Woman* 2017 49 **Princess Leia** Carrie Fisher *Return of the Jedi* 1983 50 **Ryan Stone** Sandra Bullock *Gravity* 2014

Commercialese gobbledegook *style*

foolish, inpenetrable business jargon
Leadership population achieved delivery of financial abundance, undervaluing KPI* for upscaled blue sky thinking towards proactivity. Togetherness shortfall ensued.

Ineffective surveillance undermined wealth retention 2.0, resulting in deficits *vis à vis* the spectrum of adequacy in the space, going forward. Indeed, the junior management operative failed to take ownership of the strategic roadmap on goods and services purchasing platforms, which operationally became a train wreck.

Big picture economic discontiguousness followed (GNP and NAV† in cellar proximity crisis), inducing financial epic fail due to distributional paradigm shift.

So he placed himself in a 'them and us' situation, porcine conservation-wise – an holistic cradle-to-grave change.

Divine intervention whispered 'Can I borrow you for a sec?' and he was on board with that. He pushed the envelope, drilled down and considered a well-structured raft of measures re inadequately husbanded vegetation, concluding reconsideration of former juxtaposition, risk-impact-assessment notwithstanding.

Floated proposals of adjustments, location-wise, were green lit long before close of play.

Senior management embraced (literally) wholesale reinstitution, furnishing statutory, regulatory and contractual requirements in win-win multi-stream realms including foot-wear, overalls and digital adornment, when floated at that level of granularity.

Bovine stocks crashed and burned; they leveraged cloud infrastructure. Executive discrepancies were backfilled.

Furthermore, dashboard values and actionable attitudes were dispensationalised, maximising the key deliverables matrix.

'A junior executive, considered in the box; latterly reconsidered out of the box ongoingly; achieving

harmonised balance re worker-management staffing ratio.'

• **SMOG** (Simplified Measure of Gobble-degook) index: 21.8 - UK 'heavy-weight' newspapers *The Guardian* & *The Times* have a SMOG index just over 17
• **Fleish-Kincaid Grade Level** 12;
• **Fleish-Kincaid Reading Ease** 3.3 (range 0-30 graduates; 60-70 yr9/10 pupils; 90-100 yr7 pupils)
NB cf *Peanut Butter Sandwiches* (p81): SMOG index 11.6; FK Grade Level 4; FK Reading Ease 87.9

* key performance indicators
† Gross National Product and Net Asset Value

Germanglicisation *language*
ich bin ein Jerusalemer
'Mein irresponsiblinherritance. Schnell, bitte.' 'Ja.' 'Danke schön.' Helmut fritter commercialbillet until walletkaput.

Gutzecho und visibleribs – Helmut employink mit schwein schloppen-podsintslurreyfoulenmess. Donner und blitzen!

Synapsen illumen-momentizalia: riesen meuppen und entschlüsse zu sprichen to Herren: 'Ach, chesten-pumpen-emotio grossen unworthy-nessfeelink – servantme-hirenfee, bitte.'

Bisher stillen ausländisch, Papa seht, und is runnink.

Helmut sprichted 'Herren...' aber Vater unterbrechen mit gross huggink, kussink, pumpsoles, mantel und blingbling-valuables.

Den kattle ist bratwürst mit saurkraut, pumper-nickel brot, pretzels, schnitzel mit noodles, schartzwald kirschetorte, strudel, pilsner, hock und shnapps.

'Kinder heartbeathaltenshocken; achtung kinder heartbeatstarten-spritzen!'

172

Streamofconciousness *style*

So when the boy spoke to his father – you know I think it was quite an aggressive act, effectively wishing the old man was already dead, because that would be the only way anyone might normally get their hands on their inheritance so early, and I should have thought the father wondered when that might be and what form of death would steal upon him (is he the bowel cancer sort? or will a thief break in and there'd be a struggle and some crockery smashed and father beaten to the ground by a man with a wicked grin wearing a long red coat carrying an ebony cane with a silver tip and the stick hit dad and he fell among the shards of earthenware although it could be porcelain except most of that is used for decorative art, such as on the outside of temples and ancient buildings of that kind, many of which were built in honour of false gods and idols, such as Zeus, Hermes and several others in togas which were comp-licated pieces of clothing, requiring a great deal of draping and crooked arms, and that might restrict movement, which is why they wore belts, so that could tuck their clothing in when they wanted to run or take part in sports like fencing or javelin-throwing or the wielding of cudgels or just sticks with which to hit fathers when attempting to steal from him?) or perhaps he would die from poison or lead piping in the conservatory, although glass is expensive, almost as costly as precious stones, which would be probably well worth breaking in to try to steal any panes of glass especially but breaking the glass would be a real shame, as making plate glass in these days isn't easy or cheap; or just vandals, who want to let the cattle go free because perhaps they are animal rights protestors, who think the father is experimenting on them or may use restrictive farming practices, such as over-feeding the calf, which he is, so he probably deserves what's coming to him, except it's not really a capital offence, like treason or chariot racing in a no-racing zone, or practicing dentistry without a licence or being grossly negligent or shooting vandals that invade your land, which after all as a farmer you have a perfect right to defend as long as you stick to the rules about due force and don't get more violent than your attackers; you have to fight fire with fire, an eye for an eye, a tooth for a tooth, although fighting tooth and nail is probably too much and Jesus said we should not use that method anyway as he preferred that we are supposed to be peacemakers and seeking out men of peace as well; no, no, Jesus spent his time while he was on the earth saying we should be willing to carry the bag an extra mile and then lend the man your coat as well plus putting everything you have in the collection whether you have two mites or are a rich young ruler who says to this man 'Go' and he goes but either way you go away sad because you say you have kept all of the command-ments from when you were a youth which in those days means a child, which is how you are supposed to be when you come to faith and not be forbidden but suffered which is what the Apostle Paul did with his 'thorn in the flesh' which probably (or so the scholars say) was not in his flesh at all but was to do with his eyesight (some hint this was a difficult wife, whatever that is supposed to signify – although I find it hard to work out in what ways large or untidy handwriting can be symbolic of trouble in the domestic bliss department) which must have been a serious drawback to travelling and being able to see quite apart from everything else although it didn't seem to prevent him from having visions but then perhaps those are not actually perceived with the physical eyeballs and interpreted (or trans-ported) by visual nerves so that's not relevant and it would have been rather uncomfortable for him to have had a thorn (or was it a log?) in his eye but clearly he was no stranger to hurting, having made his entrance into the New Testament at the stoning of Stephen and then re-emerging as a persecutor of members of the new sect who later were known as Christians and being knocked off his horse by an incredibly bright light which seems a bit unusual, I grant you) while on that dusty road (not the one with the robbers who attacked the man and left him for dead, until the Good Samaritan came along, as that was Jericho, or the one with the bloke who found a treasure in the field and bought the field), but to Damascus which is, I understand, not such a dreadfully long way from the border with Lebanon which is where those famous so-called cedars come from which reminds me of the marvellous Oscar Wilde farce *Charley's Aunt* where Lady Bracknell says '*A handbag?*' it was I think, dear, dear Dame Edith Evans in that part. I understand Maggie Smith and even Penelope Keith and Judi Dench have tried hard to play the role, but there is no-one quite like the original and best. Oh, no, how very silly of me, I do seem, somewhat foolishly, to have utterly, completely forgotten what I was droning on about...

US presidents   *key words*

all (oh yes, believe it!, ALL) of America's elected finest

John said '**Grant**[1] me my inheritance. Hel**P, ol' k**[2]**insman mine!**'

His father replied '**John, son**[3,4], that's not at all **cool. I'd ge**[5]**nerally** say no, but in this case, I'll let you have it all. Now, you're in danger of gaining my disappr**oval – off! I c**ertainly don't wish to see you for a while!'

John wanted an adventure, like those written by Swift, Cervantes or **Buchan. An**[6]**d** so he wasted the money on wichedness: placing a be**t, rum an**[7]**d** many women; two girls are a **gan**[8]**gster's** molls. One friend collapsed.

'If he's taken drugs, he'll need **CPR. E's? I'd en**tertain the idea he's in danger... but he doesn't seem to care, no matter ho**w hit, eh? O use** (if it works) that luck of yours while we're on Wonder Rd and A**We St!' Win g**old if you can!' But they gambled and lost.

Soon, what was left was **Nix; on**[9] his uppers; he was bora**sic lint.**

On[10]**tologically,** he had been prodigal.

And then famine struck. Finding work was **hard.**

Ing[11]**loriously,** he ended up tending pigs and even envied the pods they ate. He longed to **fill more**[12] of his insides with them.

But the light of God's wisdom shone upon him and **pierce**[13]**d** his dark heart. He wrote a note: *I no longer want this job. Am a*[14]*ppalled at myself. I'm returning home, where even the hired men have enough to eat.*

He set off, got a hitch from a donkey cart er[15]stwhile, and latterly from an ox cart.

Aft[16]**er** that he walked, through the **ford**[17], past the **bush**[18], (at the most basic **level) and**[19] beyond Hangar **field**[20].

While he was still a long way off, his father (he**art hur**[21]**ting** until then) saw him and ran to greet him.

'Someone I love's (guess w**ho?**) **over**[22] the bridge! You feared I'd not give you **jack, son**[23]. Have an engraved ring – look, *my lost son (dash)* found! The dash here is **en** – how er[24]roneous!

'It should be an em dash. We'll replace your coat with a new one – no **washing to** n[25]eed to be done. Greet returning son! Banish *'no'*, let's be generous with *'ayes'*[26]! Kill and roast the calf, and we can also have sal**mon roe**[27], or terra**dactyl!'** (er[28]ror?)

'We'll wash it down with **adam's**[29] ale; accompanied by chicken sa**Tay.**

'**Lor**[30]d bless our dinner! Roast calf this p.m., and leg of kanga**roos, eve. L** t[31,32]o the A to the T to the ER. Play your mand**olin, Col. N**[33]ugent! Lost your sheet music? I thought we **had a MS**[34] here earlier..? Fetch my **teddy**[32]!'

He wrote the notes for his speech in txt language: *sn ws ded, his life ws ova* **NB u r** en[35]*jyng dnnr ok?* Later, he stood at the ros**trum.**

'**P**[36]revious reports of your death drove us **mad. I, son**[37], almost lost it. Yes, it did distur**b us.** H[38]owever, you are alive! My brother Vernon was sure you were dead, but now I can proclaim your Un**cle V:** élan d[39]enier. And your brother **Wilson**[40], understands now. D'ye **ken, Ned?** Y[41]es!'

(slightly desperate final paragraph)
In addition to his sons, the father had two nephews: **Harrison**[42,43] and **Jefferson**[44]. These made up his clan, his tribe, his **Mc Kin. Le y**[45]uppie son had to humble himself.

	Name	Presidential Number	Party	non-vote end	years served	• term
1	**Ulysses S Grant**	18	*Republican*		1869-1877	• •
2	**James K Polk**	11	*Democratic*		1845-1849	•
3	**Andrew Johnson**	*17	*Nat'l Union, Democratic*		1865-1869	3y 11m†
4	**Lyndon B Johnson**	*36	*Democratic*		1963-1969	1y 3m •
5	**Calvin Coolidge**	*30	*Republican*		1923-1929	1y 7m •
6	**James Buchanan**	15	*Democratic*		1857-1861	•
7	**Harry S Truman**	*33	*Democratic*	§ §	1945-1953	3y 11m •
8	**Ronald W Reagan**	40	*Republican*	§	1981-1989	• •
9	**Richard M Nixon**	37	*Republican*	§ § resigned	1969-1974	• 1y 6m
10	**William J Clinton**	42	*Democratic*	§ § § §	1993-2001	• •
11	**Warren G Harding**	29	*Republican*	died: 66y (¶)	1921-1923	2y 5m
12	**Millard Fillmore**	*13	*Whig*		1850-1853	2y 7m†
13	**Franklin Pierce**	14	*Democratic*		1853-1857	
14	**Barack H Obama**	44	*Democratic*	§ § § §	2009-2017	• •
15	**James E Carter Jr**	39	*Democratic*	§ §	1977-1981	•
16	**William H Taft**	27	*Republican*	§	1909-1913	•
17	**Gerald R Ford**	*38	*Republican*	§ §	1974-1977	2y 6m •
18	**George H Bush**	41	*Republican*	§	1989-1993	•
19	**Grover Cleveland**	22	*Democratic*		1885-1889	• (•)
20	**James A Garfield**	20	*Republican*	¶	1881	6m
21	**Chester A Arthur**	*21	*Republican*		1881-1885	3y 6m
22	**Herbert C Hoover**	31	*Republican*	§	1929-1933	•
23	**Andrew Jackson**	7	*Democratic*	§	1829-1837	• •
24	**Dwight D Eisenhower**	34	*Republican*		1953-1961	• •
25	**George Washington**	1	*independent federalist*		1789-1797	• •

26	**Rutherford B Hayes**	19	*Republican*		1877-1881	•
27	**James Monroe**	5	*Democratic-Republican*		1817-1825	• •
28	**John Tyler**	*10	*Whig, then independent*		1841-1845	3y 11m†
29	**John Q Adams**	6	*Democratic-Republican*		1825-1829	•
30	**Zachary Taylor**	12	*Whig*	*died: 85y* (¶)	1849-1850	1y 4m
31	**Franklin D Roosevelt**	32	*Democratic*	§ § *died: 63y*	1933-1945	• • • 1m
32	**Theodore Roosevelt**	*26	*Republican*		1901-1909	3y 6m •
33	**Abraham Lincoln**	16	*Republican*	§ § ¶	1861-1865	• 1m
34	**John Adams**	2	*Federalist*		1797-1801	•
35	**Martin Van Buren**	8	*Democratic*		1837-1841	•
36	**Donald J Trump**	45	*Republican*	§ § §	2017-present	
37	**James Madison**	4	*Democratic-Republican*		1809-1817	• •
38	**George W Bush**	43	*Republican*	§ §	2001-2009	• •
39	**Grover Cleveland**	24	*Democratic*		1893-1897	(•) •
40	**Woodrow Wilson**	28	*Democratic*		1913-1921	• •
41	**John F Kennedy**	35	*Democratic*	§ ¶	1961-1963	2y 9m
42	**Benjamin Harrison**	23	*Republican*		1889-1893	•
43	**William H Harrison**	9	*Whig*	*died: 68y*	1841	1m
44	**Thomas Jefferson**	3	*Democratic-Republican*		1801-1809	• •
45	**William McKinley**	25	*Republican*	¶	1897-1901	• 6m

Grover Cleveland – tough to include once – appears twice, as his two terms in office were separated by Benjamin Harrison's term. The 22nd Amendment (1947) limited the maximum number of terms that any one individual may serve to two(plus up to two years of the previous incumbent's term).

Also hidden: **Oval Office; President; White House; West Wing**

(NB **Josiah Bartlett** *Dem* 1999-2007 • • is fictional)

* Promoted from Vice President at death/resignation of previous President.

Non-vote end of term: assassination § attempt ¶ success (¶) suspected

† Never elected to presidential office

Directions   *key words*

plus anagrams of directions, indicted thus*

'Hand **over** my **in**heritance.' Father did, and his **son** left at **once**, going **down** to Dissipation City, where **thous***ands went **west**, **right** quickly, splashed **out** **on** flouting, foul-mouthed living, **right**? Soon it was gone, he was bank**rupt**, and famine struck.

The laya**bout** boy took (at his lo**west** point) an **unorth**odox job with **low**-life pigs, and desired to stuff **down** their **pu*ce** **thorn*y** food. His mind was **brightl**y enlightened as he realised his father's hired men ate **downright** well. He sprang **up** from his **seat***.

'**Right**. This is **over**. I shall **arise** and go home, and work for dad. I'm **no*** **longer** worthy to be called a **son**.'

While he was still a long way **off**, (still en **rout**e), his father saw him from his **high** vantage point and took some **northings** and ran **clockwise** round the roundabout to greet him. He hugged him and **pu*t** a coat **over** his shoulders (couture from a boutique), shoes on his feet and a ring around his finger. He sent the fatted calf down to slaughter, and rotated the carcass of the beast on a spit, widdershins.

Awestruck, stout party guests (local landowners) crowded around; they troughed down and feasted on potatoes in their jackets with eggs sunny side up, unctuo*us slow-cooked vegetable stew*, southern fried chicken breasts, thighs and wings plus croutons.

They ate s*o many rounds of beans on unleavened toast (made without the use of yeast), toad in the hole, underdone lamb, and a couple of cantaloupes. They drank vermouth and fruit teas*. Soon there was none left.

The devout father said 'This my shallowest son was lying down in the grave, right, but no*w eastands up with us again. High praise!'

Dramatic irony   *style*

in which the reader is better informed of the narrative than the characters

'I am going to go to Dissipation City to live a meaningful life. By all accounts it's a good place to dwell, full of moral, clean-living philan-thropists and people devoted to following their religious convictions. Anyway, I'm fed up with being here, working alongside hired men and feeding those skinny calves. Give me my inheritance!' Charlie demanded.

'Well, I can't say I'm all that convinced about Dissipation City being a place where a positive influence is likely to be exerted upon you...' said Gerald. 'But about the inheritance, I'm surprised you would

ask me that, son. I'm not even ill, let alone dying! Let me sort out my finances and I'll see how much I can let you have. I don't want to sell this ring – it's valuable, but meaningful to me, so I want to keep it in the family. But if I have to sell it to meet your demand, then I suppose I'll do what I have to do in order to provide for you. Either way, I'm sure you'll invest the money wisely.'

Gerald was able to gather all of his liquid assets (having sold off a few other prized possessions and some of his land) in order to give a huge sum of money to Charlie.

'Thanks, dad! Oh, boy, I intend to party!'

'Well, I thought you'd buy some stocks and shares...'

'Of course not. I'm going to blow it all in having a good time!' So Charlie took the cash and set off.

For many months after the sad day when Charlie left, Gerald hoped to see his son again, safely at home.

He sensed it was a vain hope, but still it motivated his daily vigil on the roof of the building, looking out for his boy. He would scan the horizon, straining to see if his son was returning.

He had also instructed one of the hired men to give extra fodder to the most healthy calf, to provide food for the party when Charlie returned.

'But sir,' said the hired man as he ate his free lunch, 'we both know your son isn't going to come back, is he?' He knew the truth that the old man was denying.

'Just feed the calf,' Gerald answered. Meanwhile, Charlie was quickly surrounded by so-called friends, who helped relieve him of large amounts

177

of the money, with wild living: slap-up dinners, gambling, entertainments, fine clothes and good-time girls.

He was delighted to have made such firm frends, and was convinced they would stick with him through thick and thin.

After not very long, all his money was gone. Of course, when his friends discovered this, they went the same way.

Charlie was penniless, and then a famine struck the land. He had no back-up plan; no money, no options, no food, nowhere to live and no hope.

He knew his father would utterly reject him if he went home, so that wasn't worth trying. He looked around to find a way to stay alive; eventually, he ended up taking a filthy job looking after pigs. He recognised he had reached rock-bottom when he found himself envying the pigs the rotting husks they were given to eat.

Here he was, a Hebrew lad, working with pigs (probably the most non-kosher of all animals), and so desperately hungry he'd consider stealing from the pigs even those meagre scraps. Since the land was in severe famine, the quality of these pods and husks was extremely low, as anything edible had already been selected by the pig owner and his family.

Charlie couldn't bring himself to munch on these pods, could he?

He wept a little, feeling sorry for himself, and then he came to his senses.

'Here I am thinking about pigs and rotting vegetation. Oh, how I miss the hired men back home. They'd know what to do. I wonder if they are still eating well, like they used to, before the famine? They'll have slaughtered the skinny calves weeks ago and still be feasting on the meat... I think what I must do is to go home and see if I can work with them. I am no longer worthy to be called a son. My dad has every right to reject me; he probably won't be willing to see me. I deserve that. But I have to try.' So he arose and made his way home.

Meanwhile, Gerald's hopes were high, and he spent an extra long time on the roof that day, looking, hoping, narrowing his eyes in hope of any sign of his beloved son. But as darkness fell, he slowly, sadly descended the steps and went indoors to eat his watery vegetable stew.

Charlie was planning and rehearsing his speech. 'I know it'll be an awkward reunion,' he said to himself as he trudged, footsore and weary, and very seriously hungry. 'And I'll have one chance to apologise, and then I shall have to take the punishment that I deserve. I wonder what he'll do? Make me feed the skinny calves, obviously; and harvest the corn, I suppose. I'll have to go to all the villagers and apologise, as I expect they've had to be helpful to Dad in my absence... But maybe they'll reject me and cut me off from society. Perhaps I'll have to look for a job in another town.

'But first, I must apologise to dad. I'll say it again: *Please make me one of your hired men; I am no longer worthy to be called your son...*'

While Charlie was still a long way off, Gerald saw him. He gave a great cry of joy, and immediately tucked his tunic into his belt, ran down the steps

178

and out of the farmyard, pacing down the drive and through the gateway at the end.

Servants and hired men ran after him, astonished at this behaviour, certain that their respected employer was going to call upon them to eject the wayward boy.

They were convinced they'd have to help the old man back to the farmhouse after all this exertion.

Gerald reached the end of the drive and turned right.

He continued to run, shouting, his arms and his heartfelt welcome spread wide. Charlie saw his dad running and decided the best way to show his humility was by bowing with his face in the dust. He fell to his knees and put his forehead on the ground.

He heard Gerald and some servants running towards him, but couldn't tell what his father, panting, was trying to say.

Not only was Gerald gasping for breath on account of his galloping; Charlie was crying and trying to say his speech.

'I am not worthy. I have been such a fool. All I can ask is that you accept me back to the farm as a hired hand. I will work hard for you without complaining. Please don't send me away; oh, please don't send me away…'

Servants arrived, equally breathless, watching in exhausted amazement at Gerald abandoning dignity in his exuberant delight. It was unbecomeing, ignoble and utterly unexpected.

Gerald eventually caught his breath and pulled Charlie to his feet so that he could embrace him. He threw his arms around him, hugged him, kissed him and hugged him again.

'My son, my son, you came home! I love you!'

'Father, I am no longer worthy to be called…'

'Son, I love you! Servants! Fetch him shoes! And a coat! And here, Charlie, here, have my ring. It's the family ring, and now you're back in the family. Come on servants, help him back to the home. And kill that fatted calf. We shall have…'

Charlie interrupted. '*Fatted* calf?'

'Yes! We'll have a celebration. Let's have roast meat, drink, merry-making; and invite the villagers. I don't want any of that rejection ceremony nonsense they may think is appropriate – it isn't! He's welcome home! Tell them my son was lost but is now found! No, tell them he was dead, and is now alive! I'm speaking figuratively, of course. Run, now. Hurry! Quickly!'

'But I thought…' Charlie started.

'I doubt it. At least, I don't believe you have for a long while!' his father joked, slapping him on the back and helping him as they turned back onto the track leading home.

Anagramatical *alphabet games*
using only the letters in the title The Prodigal Son - *a d e g h i l n o p r s t*
One o' the Lord's gospel stories:

'Loot, please!' son said, and departed north on a trip. He had pints and shots in the posh Grand Hotel. Sheila, Linda, headstrong April, Lisa, Portia, Sharon, longhaired Stephanie, Angelina, Gail, Doreen (soprano), Glenda, Leigh the phrenologist, Olga, Edith (isn't she the red hot hairdo girl?), thin Daphne, Diana – this is an harlot plethora, or a shedload o' geishas – pert Rhoda, Dinah (alto),

Sophie, Gloria the gondolier and Delia (pretties).

Spooned; had eros' rhinohorn (rather aphrodesial), and all got plastered.

Danger: less loot. Greater: no pennies at all. Ordeal! He is soon in a drool-plight; eating pigs' horrid slop? No, – it's poison-dosage! Shoo! Loathing. Gosh, stop, lad, as senses are inspired.

'Dad's hirelings eat… I'll arise, hope he pardons in pathos.'

Not right to plead as son.

Pastoral Dad has long distant sight in garden; his heart leaps.

Ran, ardent. Lad had not said his phrase… attire, shoes (galoshes), gold ring o'ingot.

'Roast dingo loin, pigeon, gander! Protein and aloo gosht, alongside haslet, grapes, hotdogs, pralines!' he said.

'I'll greet all as host. Dear son lost… ghost? No! Delighted – lad I adore not dead! All is atoned: I'll soon readopt.

O let's all praise the rootin' tootin' Lord!'

Full circle
wordplay

word length determined by the first 101 decimal places of the value of pi – taking 0 with a pinch of salt

3.	1	4	1	5	9	'Son. I have a bonus-financial
2	6	5	3	5	8	to freely offer.' His smile secretly
9	7	9	3	2	3	concealed painful sacrifice. But to the
8	4	6	2	6	4	alluring city Thomas (an enigma) went
3	3	8	3	2	7	for the gambling, and to various
9	5	0	2	8	8	showgirls. 'Spent! Zero to exchange fiscally
4	1	9	7	1	6	when I undertook agonies! A fierce
9	3	9	9	3	7	nutrition (and companion) shortfall was hurting
	5	10	5	8	2	badly.' Employment found: reverent to
0	9	7	4	9	4	no heritages – porkers that unfussily took
	4	5	9	2	3	pods. Sadly, pitifully, he had
					0	nothing.
	7	8	16	4	0	Genuine insights (supernaturalness). Flee, naught!
		6	2	8	6	Remain, or homeward, humble?
		20	8	9	9	Overenthusiastically, watchful fathering giftgiver
8	6	2	8	0	3	embraces, kisses. To prodigal no bad
4	8	2	5	3	4	word; provider of shoes and ring.
	2	11	7	0	6	'In celebration exclude none! Fatted
			7	9	8	animals. Wonderful, restored
		21	4	8		contemporaneousnesses… We're thankful!'

* Inspired by Ἀεὶ ὁ θεὸς ὁ μέγας γεωμετρεῖ τὸ σύμπαν *Always the great God applies geometry to everything*, a mnemonic for π: the first word is three greek letters long, then one, then four, one, five, nine, two, six, five, etc. From an original idea by Plato, & later, Plutarch. Some call this *Pilish*; author Mike Keith coined the term *Cadaeic* – 1=a, 3=c, 4=d, 5=e, 9=i – sixth decimal place rounds up

Musical theatre *key words*

songs from the shows

'**I'm on my Way**[1] **Tonight**[2], Dad,' said Jud, whose musically sensitive feline companions, inexplicably known as *The Ti*, sat on his lap.

'Where will you go?'

'Oh, **Somewhere**[3]…it's a place I've dreamed about, and frankly, **Any Dream will Do**[4].'

'Well, I've sold all of **My Favourite Things**[5] to raise cash; I've given you everything I can afford. **If I were a Rich Man**[6], I'd have more to offer.'

'I understand. How much is it?'

Jud left the farm, determined to forget about the dull life he led on the farm. '**I'm going to Wash that Man Right out of my Hair**[8],' he decided.

He arrived in **Kansas City**[9] and started to spend.

'**It's a Fine Life**[10],' he thought to himself. Soon he met some dancers (**There is Nothing Like a Dame**[11]) and took them for dinner and a **show; Boat**[12]ing on the lake followed.

Each girl thought '**Oh, What a Beautiful Morning**[13], **We're in the Money**[14], **I Feel Pretty.**[15] He's ranked our **Hair**[16]styles: *the Essex with the bob* in third place, *the Berkshire with the ponytail* second, and *The Surrey With the Fringe* on Top[17].'

Every day they partied (**Hallo, Young Lovers**[18]) until **Sunrise; Sunset**[19] brought more romantic encounters. One woman thought *I Don't Know How to Love Him*[20], but soon enough, she got the hang of it.

Eventually the money ran out and a famine struck the land (the sun shone brightly right there, but **The Rain? In Spain**[21]). The man at the Box Office asked '**Who Will Buy**[22] tickets here anymore? No-one! **There's no Business, like. Show? Business**[23] is closed, old son. **This is the Hour**[24] for poverty; I doubt the casino owners will **Be Back Soon**[25], as they are going to **Close Every Door**[26].'

Jud took a job on a pig farm, envying the animals as they rootled about among rotting pods, making grunting noises such as snort, snuffle and *Hukana Mutata*[27].

Eventually he came to his senses. '**What's Going On Here**[28]?' he asked. '**Just You Wait**[29] until I eat the pig-pods… but then when I search my **Memory**[30]

I have to shamefacedly admit that I did **What I Did for Love**[31] of selfishness.

Tomorrow[32], return home; realise it's the start of the year.

'**Sixteen, going on seventeen**[7] thousand shekels.'

And you'll **Consider Yourself**[34] no longer worthy to be called a son. It's the season when one might use those popular chart-topping Suseex fishing boats – yes, **Spring, time for Hit**[33]**ler**rets. God will be with you, boy; **You'll Never Walk Alone**[35]. And **With a Little Bit o'Luck**[36], I'll get a job on the farm.'

Homeward bound: hill, thinking about how he wasted the money; forest, considering the conversation he would have with his **Old Man; River**[37] planning to beg if necessary. He saw bluebells, daffodils and **Eidelweiss**[38] on the way, but chose to **Whistle a Happy Tune**[39]. For the last part of the journey, he took a single decker bus ride. '**I'm On My Way**[40],' he thought.

His father kept vigil. '**As Long As He Needs Me**[41],' he thought, 'I'll keep trusting God will **Bring Him Home**[42].' While the boy was still a long way off, his dad saw the bus.

'**Something's Coming**[43]... Look, **There's a Coach Comin' In**[44]! This is really **Something! Wonderful**[45]!'

His father ran to greet Jud with lots of **Happy Talk**[46].

'**This is me**[47], and **I'd Do Anything**[48]...' the boy started.

'**Can You Feel the Love Tonight**[49]?' his father asked. 'We're now standing **On the Street Where You Live**[50]!' He gave him a coat and some shoes, plus an eternity ring, representing **The Circle of Life**[51].

The Farmer and the Cowman[52] agreed: the cow was slaughtered and roasted. 'Let's eat the co**W! Here is Love**[53]ly roast beef; **I Have Dreamed**[54] that **Some Enchanted Evening**[55] my son would return! Let there be **Food Glorious Food**[56], and **Shall We Dance**[57]?

'Play, minstrels – let there be the **Music of the Night**[58]! Let there be jugglers, trapeze artists (**Defying Gravity**[59]) and dancing ponies: **Oh, What a Circus**[60]!

'Yes, and **Send In the Clowns**[61]. Let the **Oom Pah Pah**[62] band play broken chords until **The Ti meW. Arp**[63]**eggios** will make it so, **Day by Day**[64]!' He also gave him a cloth toy called Raggeddy Ann.

'I thought to myself **Poor Jud is Dead**[65]; but **Hosanna**[66]! Oh yes, **I'm a Believer**[67]. **I Got Life**[68]! **I Know Him So Well**[69]! **Take that Look off Your Face**[70] - **I Could Have Danced All Night**[71], as we're **Born to Boogie**[72]! That'll teach **One of Us**[73] to **Always look on the Bright Side of Life**[74].

'Keep dancing with your **Rag Doll**[75] (**Hello Dolly!**[76]) and the **Razzle Dazzle**[77] and **Be Our Guest!**[78] Stay out of doors in full sight (yes, remain **Out Tonight**[79] – and all these **Summer Nights**[80]) otherwise the rest of the village won't know we're still celebrating with **The Sound of Music**[81] – **People Will Say We're in, Love**[82]! **Don't stop me now**[83], although **You Can't Stop the Beat**[84]! It's all about **You and Me (But Mostly Me)**[85]. He went to **The Place where the Lost Things Go**[86]. Some say this joyful feeling is califragilisticexpiali in nature, but I reckon it has many of the same characteristics, but with maximum grandeur, and refer to it as **Supercalifragilisticexpialdocious**[87].'

1 **I'm on my Way** *Paint Your Wagon* 1969
2 **Tonight** *West Side Story* 1957 3 **Somewhere** *West Side Story* 4 **Any Dream will Do** *Joseph and his Amazing Technicolour Dreamcoat* 1973
5 **My Favourite Things** *The Sound of Music* 1959 6 **If I were a Rich Man** *Fiddler on the Roof* 1964 7 **Sixteen, going on seventeen** *The Sound of Music* 8 **I'm going to Wash that Man Right out of my Hair** *South Pacific* 1949 9 **Kansas City** *Oklahoma!* 1943 10 **It's a Fine Life** *Oliver!* 1960 11 **There is Nothing Like a Dame** *South Pacific* 12 **Show Boat** *Show Boat* 1927 13 **Oh, What a Beautiful Morning** *Oklahoma!*
14 **We're in the Money** *42nd Street* 1980
15 **I Feel Pretty** *West Side Story* 16 **Hair** *Hair* 1967 17 **The Surrey With the Fringe on Top** *Oklahoma!* 18 **Hallo, Young Lovers** *The King & I* 1951 19 **Sunrise Sunset** *Fiddler on the Roof* 20 **I Don't Know How to Love Him** *Jesus Christ Superstar* 1971 21 **The Rain In Spain** *My Fair Lady* 1956 22 **Who Will Buy**? *Oliver!* 23 **There's no Business like Show Business** *Annie Get Your Gun* 1946 24 **This is the Hour** *Miss Saigon* 1989 25 **Be Back Soon** *Oliver!* 26 **Close Every Door** *Joseph and his Amazing Technicolour Dreamcoat* 27 **Hukana Mutata** *The Lion King* 1997 28 **What's Going On Here?** *Paint Your Wagon* 29 **Just You Wait** *My Fair Lady* 30 **Memory** *Cats* 1981 31 **What I Did for Love** *A Chorus Line* 1975 32 **Tomorrow** *Annie* 1977 33 **Springtime for Hitler** *The Producers* 2001 34 **Consider Yourself** *Oliver!* 35 **You'll Never Walk Alone** *Carousel* 1945 36 **With a Little Bit o'Luck** *My Fair Lady* 37 **Old Man River** *Show Boat* 38 **Eidelweiss** *The Sound of Music* 39 **Whistle a Happy Tune** *The King & I* 40 **I'm On My Way** *Sunshine on Leith* 2013 41 **As Long As He Needs Me** *Oliver!*

42 **Bring Him Home** *Les Miserables* 1980
43 **Something's Coming** *West Side Story*
44 **There's a Coach Comin' In** *Paint Your Wagon* 45 **Something Wonderful** *The King & I* 46 **Happy Talk** *South Pacific* 47 **This is me** *The Greatest Showman* 2017 48 **I'd Do Anything** *Oliver!* 49 **Can You Feel the Love Tonight?** *The Lion King* 50 **On the Street Where You Live** *My Fair Lady* 51 **The Circle of Life** *The Lion King* 52 **The Farmer and the Cowman** *Oklahoma!* 53 **Where is Love?** *Oliver!* 54 **I Have Dreamed** *The King & I* 55 **Some Enchanted Evening** *South Pacific* 56 **Food Glorious Food** *Oliver!* 57 **Shall We Dance?** *The King & I* 58 **Music of the Night** *Phantom of the Opera* 1976 59 **Defying Gravity** *Wicked* 2003 60 **Oh, What a Circus** *Evita* 1978 61 **Send In the Clowns** *A Little Night Music* 1973 62 **Oom Pah Pah** *Oliver!* 63 **The Time Warp** *Rocky Horror Show* 1973 64 **Day by Day** *Godspell* 1969 65 **Poor Jud is Dead** *Oklahoma!* 66 **Hosanna** *Jesus Christ Superstar*

67 **I'm a Believer** *Shrek* 2008 68 **I Got Life** *Hair* 69 **I Know Him So Well** *Chess* 1986 70 **Take that Look off Your Face** *Tell Me on a Sunday* 1979 71 **I Could Have Danced All Night** *My Fair Lady* 72 **Born to Boogie** *Billy Elliot* 2005 73 **One of Us** *Mamma Mia* 1999 74 **Always Look on the Bright Side of Life** *Spamalot* 2005 75 **Rag Doll** *Jersey Boys* 2005 76 **Hello, Dolly!** *Hallo, Dolly!* 1964 77 **Razzle Dazzle** *Chicago* 1975 78 **Be Our Guest!** *Beauty and the Beast* 1994 79 **Out Tonight** *Rent* 1996 80 **Summer Nights** *Grease* 1971 81 **The Sound of Music** *The Sound of Music* 82 **People Will Say We're in Love** *Oklahoma!* 83 **Don't Stop Me Now** *We Will Rock You* 2002 84 **You Can't Stop the Beat** *Hairspray* 2002 85 **You and Me (But Mostly Me)** *The Book of Mormon* 2011 86 **The Place Where the Lost Things Go** *Mary Poppins Returns* 2018 87 **Supercalifragilistic-expialidocious** *Mary Poppins* 1964

Round robin
pastiche

Christmas family letter

Dear All

It has been a ~~dreadful~~ ~~loathesome~~ complicated year here on Certainman Farm since we last wrote. Our ambitious seven-year plan for expansion was entering it's final phase, & we were reaping (quite literally) the benefit. We had a lot of land, most of which was turned over to arable crops such as corn, soft fruits, root vegetables, assorted legumes (beans to the uninitiated!), and of course some fallow fields as well.

As we told you last year, we have also invested in livestock (several chickens, some geese plus a few young calves).

Last year's problems with the tares (infestation) seem to have faded away, and we have'nt lost so much of the seed we have sown to birds of the air, either. Perhaps this is because we have ploughed-over the paths through the fields, to be sure there is'nt too much growing space wasted; we've also cleared many stones & thorns. Anyway, all this aditional work has meant hiring extra labour, which is expnesive but, thank the Lord, we were able to manage that.

Agricultural success had a downside when, early in the sprng, Johnny came to us and ~~demanded~~ explained that he wanted to take his inheritance & go off to a foreign city.

It was not easy, but in the end we gave him all our liquid assets and sold a few things too, to try to give him as much as we could. For him to make

this request was a bit tough on the rest of us, as we
now had zero cashflow, & we had to sell some fields
to pay our hired men and tobuy seed. So that was
doubly difficult.

We missed Johnny terribly, especially since we
didn't hear from him at all – although we heard
worrying news that there was a famine where he'd
gone, so we feared he'd suffered or even starved.

Meanwhile young Steve was doing well and apart
from making one or 2 ~~terrible~~ undesirable friends who
wanted to party with goats, he is truly a credit to
the farm and to the family.

Truth to tell, I didn't come to terms with Johnny
going at all. I thought he soon would be back, but
the weeks stretched into months and Claudia said I
was spending too much time on the roof, watching out
for Johnny to return. This became a source of
consderable tension between us, but she is a good and
faithful wife, so she only bent my ear a few times
each week. I must have been very difficult to live
with at that time (Oh dear, Claudia is vigourosly
nodding in agreement as I type!).

But it all paid off, in the end!. One wonderful
day, I was keeping vigil (no surprises there, Claudia
interjects!) when after much patients I saw a ragged,
weary traveller appearing over the hill, a long way
off. Yes, it was Johnny, home from his revels!!! I
have to admit that I ran to greet him!

He had some sort of speech prepared, but I didn't
give him the chance to say it. I gave him a new coat
& a pair of shoes & a ring, and then threw a great
party to celebrate (I invited the whole village, and
nearly everyone came). We killed a fattde calf & had
a party with dancing and celebrations.

I accidentally made Claudia cry (what a lovely
great soft dollop, she is!) when I said 'This my son
was lost, but is found; he was dead, but is alive!'

Steve understandably ~~was angry~~ struggled at first
to accept we'd had forgiven his brother, but he's
come to terms with it now.

Lotsa love to you all,
C & K

Johnny writes:

Hallo everyoneI know I was a waster + a fool,but I know
now for certain that my fathre loves me.I spent all his
money on wild living.Then there was a famine.

I ended up reduced to looking after pigs (yes,unclean,I
know),but then I came to my sneses + realised even his
hired men were eating well,so I decided I would return
home + ask to be a staff member,as I was no lOnger worthy
to be called a son.

But my dad was unexpectdly generous to me
(Mum+Steve agree).My lovely new shoes are very comfortable,
but it's the ring that means the most to me.   Thank you
allfor you're kind best wihses.

J

T _____ *alliteration*

Torturous Timothy turnsover Ted; triumphantly, take trousered. Tenners, twenties, tempted teasing top totty thereinto. Thirsty, tankard-twirling tangential taboo tackiness.

Tut tut! time troubled; too-tiny turn-over; tuckerbucker tuppences trashed, toast, tears…

Tummies treaded-not. Tending trotter-rooters. Throughput trashy trough titbits? Then thoughts trip toward telling Ted; turns turkey. Tramping tiredly townwards. Tongue-trips talk – take tawdry Tim to turnover topsoil? Trembling, tries to…

Ted travels (tremendously thrilled) to Timothy.

Tin-ring, tapshoes, topcoat. Trestles topped: trout/tuna/turbot tandoori, tofu tempura, tilset, tongue tournedos; tomato tortillas, thick teacakes, toothsome truffles, tangerine tarts, trifle, tzatziki; tee-totallism-trashing Teacher's triples. Tapdance-tango-ing.

Tender, touching testimony-talk: 'Timothy terminated? 'Tis tosh! Totally transformed!'

Epistomological   *style*
philosophical study of the nature and scope of knowledge

He may have been a son; we cannot know for sure without DNA profiling. He didn't behave like a son – asking for his inheritance immediately.

The actual words of the father's response are unknown, but the boy got his money and left. An assumption that he spent the cash on wild living forms part of an uncorroborated accusation on behalf of the older brother. This is what we know for sure: later, it was all gone – although timeframe parameters are uncertain. Simultaneously (there is, however, no evidence of a causal relationship between the two facts) a famine struck the land, or at least the part of the country where the boy was dwelling at or around that date.

We are invited to believe that he probably took a job tending what may or may not have been pigs. Perhaps he sought out the job, or maybe the pig farmer was advertising for hired help. We cannot tell how many animals or their precise breed or their health-state, and we have no idea of the wages structure, working conditions, dental health plans, paternity leave options or holiday pay, let alone any pension contributions he or his employer were required, entitled or hoping to make.

The animals were apparently fed on what are supposed to be pods which seemed somehow appetising to the boy, briefly. Perhaps his hunger was so severe that the pods took on a disproportionately appetising kind of appeal… Who can say?

There are beliefs, and there are true facts; where they meet is the kernel of knowledge; doubt is the journey.

He came to what is rather loosely termed 'his senses', and realised his father's hired workers (mostly men) were being fed adequately (this is guesswork and conjecture, based on past experience), and decided to return to a place known subjectively as *home*.

His assumption hinged primarily on hope and history (rarely a firm foundation, especially when relinquishing one's domicile in order to venture towards another location), with no concrete evidence at all.

After a journey (we can assume *a priori* that travelling was involved, on account of the use of the term 'still a long way off') of undisclosed length and hardship, he was seen (as previously noted) while still a long way off. This phrase hints at 'distance' and 'the need for a journey'; yet the irony pertains that it is perhaps the least-defined term in the whole story. A few dozen yards, or several miles? Without being able to measure the opportunity afforded by his vantage point in relation to topography, much less a way of testing the father's eyesight or ability to concentrate, we are left, once again, in the realm of theory, postulations and what some might call wild surmise.

The father (perhaps a step-father, or maybe a grandfather or uncle or elder cousin or second husband to a step-mother or other relative, as such titles were used loosely at the time) ran (a term encompassing anything from a trot to a sprint) to greet him. Sadly, the only words recorded at the meeting are the ones the boy was not given leave to utter.

Someone called for shoes (sandals? moccasins?), a coat (full-length? waterproof?) and a ring (platinum/silver/gold? Set with a gem/coin/seal?) A fatted calf was mentioned re impending butchery. All, nearly all, most, many, a majority, more than half, slightly over half, half, less than half, quite a few, some, just a few, a handful, half a dozen, three, or two of the villagers (the term used is plural) were invited to a celebration, at which the father made a speech, but we cannot tell what proportion of them were interested, concentrating or

186

even in earshot. 'My son was lost but is found; he was dead but is alive.'

The reality is that the son had been neither lost nor deceased. This final unreliable report again questions the testimony of the protagonists. There is, ultimately, no need to bring any scepticism to the table; it is written deep into the fabric of the parable. Fallibilism has a wide embrace, in the opinion of many, but they may be empirically wrong.

Truth is beauty. And beauty is in the eye of the beholder. It follows that truth is relative, depending upon your view. And philosophy colours everything. So no-one really knows.

Doctor Who　　　*key words*
characters, actors, adversaries, machines from the BBC tv series

'I've checked out hire cars,' claimed the boy, 'from Hertz anD Avis – only £175 one-way to Dissipation City!'

At first Rachel T Nellson was petite, not **pert; wee**kly dinners and drinking sessions beefed her up until she was the real **McCoy**. The lad enjoyed watching Aussie Rules football with Mary, Angel, Theresa, Ann, **Sarah-Jane** and Karen at the Melborne Cricket Ground (**MCG**).

Ann was disgrAceful, and gave away her classy origins – not aristocracy A (royalty), but highish rank, aristocraCy B.

'**Er, men**,' she would say, for attention. Indeed, with her accent and behaviour she used the incorrect words for *Whist*, *Casserole* and *Craftsman* by means of this shibbo**Leth: Bridge, Stew, Artisan**. Soon she was **Weeping. Angel's** character lacked cunning yet she was skilled at spendinG **(all if rey[1]nard-**

like). The cash was spent in casinos and a minute-**Mart. Ha**d none. Short at Lidl; tried to **Cap Aldi.** His eating agen**Da vies** with his lack of wealth.

Eventually, he was broke – he didn't have **jack.** No wonga, no Albanian currency, either – not even one Poun**d, a Lek, s**ome lire or Austrian schillings; he had no gold Spanish coins or even gravel… no e**cu-shing**le.

He ran a white flag up the ti**the mast.** 'Erring, I'm out of money.' Off went all his new-found friends – goodbye Ann, cheerio Mary, alo**Ha RT Nell**son, bye **Terry!** Nationa**l** famine struck, and he took a job tending pigs. He looked at the **Trough to n**otice pods crawling with amoe**Ba. Ker**bing his appetite, he counted eight, nine cockroaches: yes, **Ten. 'N'** ants, also. He came to his senses.

'Ah**A! My** dad's hired men eat… all I get is *hungry*, with *feeling* an**D a V. Ros**ter me to work for you, Dad – that's what I'll ask.' So he a**Rose,** and went home.

His dad cried out 'Loo**K – 9** miles away, far off – could it be?' More than a litt**Le elat**ed, he ran to him, with kisses. He called for a gold**Smith** to make a ring, and gave him a coat and shoes to **Don.** Navigating everyone back to the farm, the father insisted on an en**Joy**able time with a bonfire ('**Torch wood** and make a sliced paradi**gm of fat**ted calf') and a few a**Peri**tifs. He spoke to the head of the **Bake**ry 'Please provide sandwiches, plus sponge pudding and cus**Tard!'**

'**Is** it possible also, please,' he added, 'to have those currant-filled cakes known as **Eccles?** … **To** not have a son is bad' he continued, making one of many de**Clara**tions. There was a row about the graphics for his speech as many computers may be needed.

'Wh…?'
'**IT take** roomfuls of **space** for their hard drives and cabling.'

Dad continued 'To have a son who is lost or dead is worse. But the news is **good** – my son is found and is alive! He's a **New man!** Hallelujah – you, O God, brought him back just in **Time, Lord!'**

Actor *character etc* period Peter **Davison** *5th Doctor* 1981-84; Jon **Pertwee** *3rd Doctor* 1970-74; Sylvester **McCoy** *7th Doctor* 1987-89, 93, 96; *Sarah-Jane Smith* companion to *3rd, 4th & 10th Doctors* (also in spin-off show *Sarah Jane Adventures* 2007-present); Paul **McGann** *8th Doctor* 1996; *Ace* companion to *7th Doctor; Cybermen* adversary of all *Doctors* except *3rd; Brigadier Sir Alistair Gordon* **Lethbridge-Stewart** companion to *3rd Doctor; Weeping Angels* adversary to *10th-12th Doctors; Galifrey* The Doctor's home planet; *Martha Jones* companion to *10th Doctor;* Peter **Capaldi** *12th Doctor* 2013-2017; Russell **Davies** *scriptwriter* 2005-2010; *Jack Harkness* companion to *9th & 10th Doctors; Daleks* adversary of all *Doctors;* Peter **Cushing** *The Doctor* in *Dr Who & the Daleks* (1965) & *Daleks - Invasion Earth 2150AD* (1966); *The Master* adversary of *3rd-7th, 10th-12th Doctors;* William **Hartnell** *1st Doctor* 1963-66; **Terry Nation** *Screenwriter, various series* 1965-1979; Patrick **Troughton** *2nd Doctor* 1966-69; Tom **Baker** *4th Doctor* 1974-81; David **Tennant** *10th Doctor* 2005-10; *Amy Pond* companion to *11th Doctor; Davros* adversary of *4th-7th, 9th, 10th & 12th Doctors; Rose Tyler* companion to *9th & 10th Doctors; K-9* companion to *4th Doctor,* featured in spin-off show *K-9 & Company* (pilot only) 1989; *Leela* companion to *4th Doctor;* Matt **Smith** *11th Doctor* 2010-13; *Donna Noble* companion to *10th Doctor; Jo Grant* companion to *3rd Doctor; Torchwood* Spin-off show 2006-2011; Steven **Moffat** *Screenwriter, various series* 1999-2017; *Peri Brown* companion to *5th & 6th Doctors;* Colin **Baker** *6th Doctor* 1984-86; **TARDIS** (Time And Relative Dimension In Space) flawed space-time craft; Christopher **Eccleston** *9th Doctor* 2005; *Clara* companion to *11th & 12th Doctors;* Jodie **Whittaker** *13th Doctor* 2017 to present; *space* setting; *Ood* aliens confronted by *10th Doctor;* Sydney **Newman,** creator of the Doctor; *Time Lord* status of *Doctors*

U *alliteration*

'Ubiety? Unlikely!' ululates under-financed usurper Uri. Ulterior-motivated, ups. Unites usually uncouth urbanites.

Uniquely underweight, universally ultra-hungry until… umpteen unclean ungulates? Ugh! Utterly unappealing!

Unravels, understands, U-turns, ups – undoes. Unbridled, un-ashamed, unceremonious, unselfish, uncritical.

'Unbuttoned uniform, utilitarian underfoot upholstery user!' Unbelieveably unctuous under-belly's user-friendly, unifying utopian upbeatness.

'Uri upset unto utmost unconsciousness? Uh-huh. Update: ultimately undead!'

Dysfunctional family *pastiche*

as maximised in The Simpsons *by*
Matt Groening

Sitting together on the sofa, Bart asked Homer and Marge for his inheritance.

Homer said 'You'll have to speak up son, I'm only wearing a towel.'

Bart took the money and spent it all in Springfield Dissipation Arcade, entertaining Milhouse and Terri and Sherri. But famine crept upon him just as his cash ran out. D'oh! He took a job at the Nuclear Porker Plant. The owner, C Montgomery Burns, commanded his assistant 'Mr Smithers, release the underfed pigs.' Rotting pods were dispensed, and Bart longed to eat them.

Then he came to his senses. 'Ay Carumba! My father's hired men eat well. I shall arise and return home and ask to work for him.' But while he was still a long way off, his father came running with gifts of jewellery and clothing.

'Son, you've consumed your coat, your shirt and trousers; what would you have done next for nourishment?'

'Eat my shorts.'

Homer ordered the staff to set up a barbecue and they were compliant. 'Okily dokily,' they said, but Bart pointed out that there wasn't going to be any beef.

'We,' he said, 'don't have a fatted calf, man.'

The Krustyburger manager soon realised the problem. 'We need more secret sauce. Put this mayonnaise in the sun.'

Homer made a moving speech. 'I like spending quality time away from my family, but we thought Bart was dead or lost. Now he's alive!'

Hs attention wandered slightly, as his eye alighted on the sweets trolly. 'Mmm, donuts!'

Modern Romance Monthly serial *pastiche*

Episode two: **Old Demas' Piggery** *is developing, despite the poor economic forecast. But will Demas recognise that tough times are around the corner? Handsome wastrel* **Jack Holmes** *has taken his father's money and begun to spend it in far-away Dissipation City. Can he ever make genuine friends simply by flashing the cash? Meanwhile, warm-hearted but confused* **Glenda du Pont** *took the job at the Casino, training to become a croupier despite the lecherous gaze of monobrow* **Perkins**. *Will she meet Jack where the roulette wheel spins its tinkling refrain?* **Now read on…**

'Place your bets, please!' Glenda's perfect teeth and fully-hydrated complexion sparkled their obvious charm as Jack approached the roulette table, his large bag of coins in hand.

'You may change your coins for chips at the booth, sir,' she said, noting his steely gaze, firm jaw, well-toned abdomen and expensively-groomed hair. She pursed her croupier ruby-red lips as he smiled and nodded his approval.

Was he approving of her eagerness for him to play, and perhaps win? Or was he acknowledging her cultured beauty and wondering how he might make a play, and perhaps win?

He changed a few shekels and sat at the table. Placing three blue chips on 21, he smiled at Glenda and gently, invitingly touched a fourth to his lips. He held it up in the hope that she would consent to bestow good fortune upon it too, granting a kiss.

After an exchange of glances, she did. He nodded in appreciation and placed that luck-anointed chip also on 21.

'Vingt et un,' he said, in his best french accent.

'That's on another table, as a rule, sir,' she smiled, fully realising his reference was not to the casino card game but to the age of consent – her face wore a thinly-veiled expression of affection. Somehow the bustle and chatter from other gamblers around them began to fade. Glenda could see only Jack, and failed to notice others who were about to place their chips on the playing surface.

As though on autopilot, 'No more bets, now,' she announced, as the ball hurtled freely around and around, circling, ever-circling, then slowing and starting its jumping, spinning, indecisive spiral towards the inner ring of slots, finally settling…

'21, red, odd, a high number, 2nd dozen, third street, voisins du zero,' she said, with a smile.

If Perkins, her floor-walker supervisor, had glanced her way just then, he'd be furious at the evident delight she showed that a punter had made a winning bet with his first attempt. She ought to be stolidly professional about giving away the casino's wealth, especially when he had placed three – no, four – ₪250 chips, which amounted to a winning value of ₪35,000 (at a possibility of less than 3%).

Glenda pushed small mountain of high-value chips towards Jack, fixing him with a sparkling-eyed smile.

'My lucky day,' said Jack, his eyes saying what his heart truly felt at meeting this dazzling beauty, appreciating the look of Glenda's long fingers, pure skin, full red lips and tumbling tresses, which cascaded appealingly over her shoulders and in front of her spangly scarlet evening gown.

'You never know what other luck you might have,' she muttered, accepting his offer to meet for a cocktail when she finished her shift. 'I'll be by the bar in ten minutes.'

She was about to turn her attention to the other gamblers, but couldn't resist the growing temptation to treat Jack to a lingering view of her most toothsome smile before she did so. She noticed that nasty Perkins hovering nearby, keeping watch over his croupiers that night, as he did every night; especially Glenda.

Jack took a place at the bar and waited. He considered her delightfully-formed (continued on p190) (continued from p189) thoughts towards him. Outwardly, he was being patient; inwardly, he boiled with passion and eagernesss.

Duties completed for a while, Glenda took her break, and joined him in the bar. She could tell, however, that Perkins was maintaining his surveillance.

'Hey, sweets, choose your poison!'

When Jack turned away to signal his order to the barman, she pulled a tissue from her bag, and dabbed at her moist, blue eyes; however, as he turned back, he noticed this.

'Why so upset?' Jack asked.

She leaned forward so she could whisper in his ear. 'My stocks are down again.'

'Shame,' he said, brushing Glenda's cheek with his. 'Will you lose your shirt?'

'Mmm, probably. But then it looks like everyone will,' she said, in a voice so soft that no-one else could hear. She knew Perkins would hate to see her getting friendly with a customer. But then, Perkins would hate Glenda getting friendly with anyone – he was only keen on Glenda being extra-friendly with Perkins. Meanwhile, Jack was recalling a similar feeling; Maisy, a milkmaid from the next-door farm had been smooching with him at the annual hootenanny. They'd taken a turn around the barn, arm-in-arm, to enjoy the cool night air and one another's company. But he realized Glenda was so, so different – she lacked the country innocence of Maisy, and had an added exciting style that came with her expressions of warmth and openness.

The night was young and the drinks flowed freely. Not much later, saucy Glenda was found wrapped enthusiastically in happy Jack's arms, seeking an hotel where their warmth and passions could be sated and their frustrations assuaged.

Chapter Five: *Sloppy Seconds*

The economic crisis rushed upon the land; it arrived just as the last of Jack's coins followed so many others into the coffers of a local restaurant, noted for premium lobster served in a champagne sauce.

'Is that it?' Glenda asked, as he turned out the lining of his pockets to show that he genuinely was sheckelfree.

'I am very much afraid that it is,' he said, sadly.

'Oh. Oh dear,' Glenda murmured, as she stood. She took her handbag and coat, kissed Jack gently on the forehead and said 'See you, loser.' She was furious at him for promising the world and delivering just a few weeks of outrageous worldliness.

Life in the Big City had been tougher than she had imagined. She preferred not to return to Monobrow Perkins and fulfil his unspoken demands for her to flaunt herself nightly before the paying customers.

But, she thought to herself, what choice did she have? She genuinely cared for Jack, but she had not selected the lifestyle of superficiality and 'befriending' merely to waste her evident talents on someone who now had no money and no prospects – he didn't even stand to inherit anything from his farming culture, thanks to some shady deal he had worked...

She was denying her heart in order to survive.

Jack eventually found himself a job at Old Demas' Piggery, tending hogs.

190

They had the most appalling slops to eat, all covered in mould and discarded rubbish. For a country in famine, it was remarkable that even these bits of refuse found their way here, and Old Demas had to settle for what he could get. Very quickly, Jack began to feel so desperate that he even longed to eat the food the pigs were eating.

'Oh, woe is me! These pangs wrack my body, which is wasting away and losing muscle tones daily. Surely my life will amount to more than this?'

*Will Jack succumb to this desire to satisfy his hunger with rotting pig food? Might he come to his senses and remember the catering arrangements back at Homestead Farm? Can **Glenda** ever forgive herself for the shameful way she has treated Jack? Could **Monobrow Perkins** ever discover what has become of Glenda and persuade her to be friendly with him? Will **Old Demas**'s Piggery survive the economic downturn? Does **Jack's father** die a broken man, without hope of reunion or restitution?*

Don't miss next month's thrilling final episode of this action-packed romantic drama!

Interview transcript *viewpoint*
pig farmer
• *c/u Cam 1*

ANDREA And we'll bring you more on those traffic delays on the Smallville Farm Road when they come to hand – hopefully later in the pro-gramme. Now a heart-warming story of a forgiving father and his wildly extravagant son. It's such a good example of forgiveness that we've decided to let you judge for yourselves, but some viewers may find parts of this story offensive on religious grounds.
• *Run VT of reporter on location with original story*
• *c/u Cam 1*

ANDREA Ian Terfueher is speaking to the father of the man who seems to have landed on his feet, and to the pig farmer where his son ended up. Ian?
• *wide Cam 2*

IAN TERFEUHER Thanks, Andrea. Mr Pelham, you're the owner of the pig Farm?
• *c/u Cam 3*

PELHAM Yes, sir, that I be.
• *c/u Cam 4*

IAN Well, tell us, if you will, please, what happened that night.
• *c/u Cam 3*

PELHAM What do you mean?
• *pull back to wide shot, Cam 2*

IAN *(with an expansive wave of the hand)* Mr Pelham, please tell me, tell this gentleman here next to you – Mr Certainman Senior – and tell all the many millions of viewers sitting on their sofas in their living rooms.
• *c/u Cam 3*

PELHAM Oh, yes, I see, Right, well, I have a farm and keep pigs. I know it's not popular with everyone, but there's a chance in a foreign country that some people might want ham or bacon or flank or ears or lard. Or a nice leg of pork with some lovely crackling...
• *c/u Cam 4*

IAN Yes, quite so. And tell us what happened to your livestock?
• *c/u Cam 3*

PELHAM Yes, right, I was coming to that. I have thirty... no, tell a lie, twenty-nine pigs. But unfortunately I had to take the knife to one of them as my family was hungry – we were running low on things to eat. We can

ANDY BACK

have lovely fresh chops and steaks and joints, and the rest can be salted down or hung in the chimney for smoking and curing and getting ready for ham and bacon and the local variation of prosciutto…

• *c/u Cam 4*

IAN I understand. Now, if you would, please tell us about the boy, Mr Pelham.

• *c/u Cam 3*

PELHAM Right, I was just getting onto that. My thir… twenty nine pigs haven't been eating well of late, on account of the hardships and privations. This economic downturn is hitting smallholders hard. We haven't the infrastructure to cope with cash shortages…

• *wide Cam 2*

CERTAINMAN *(interjects)* You want to talk about cash shortages? I doubt you under-stand the sort of difficulties I face. I had to find fully 30% of my wealth and make it liquid; I had to sell fields and buildings,

• *c/u Cam 4*

(cont.) and lay off several farmhands in order to gather the cash, and I struggled to make ends meet without selling more land and cutting off my nose to spite my face – having fewer fields would mean fewer crops, which meant a smaller income, less wages to pay the hirelings, and so I had to let most of them go and ended up with not enough of workers when the time came to harvest the crops I did have! It was pretty tough. Although I agree we weren't hit by the crop failures; that would have been a disaster!

• *c/u Cam 3*

PELHAM Disaster, indeed. You wouldn't have survived! I don't quite understand – why did you have to give away a third of your wealth?

192

• *c/u Cam 4*

C'MAN Well, my younger son asked for it, and I agreed. I didn't really think it through; I just saw that he needed to get away, to exper-ience life and see the world – although what he ended up with was very nearly experiencing death, and only really seeing the worldliness.

• *wide Cam 2*

IAN Ah, hahaha, yes, yes. But we're rushing to the end of the story without really giving the viewers a chance to hear what happened. Now, Mr Pelham, you were telling us about your pigs…

• *c/u Cam 3*

PELHAM Indeed. Oh, yes. Lovely. Plump and ready for market, they were. Some of the best porkers I had ever raised. Just needed another month of rich, full, healthy corn cobs and beans and ripe fruit and vegetables. It was a shame, a terrible shame, I tell you. *(pause)*

• *c/u Cam 4*

IAN *(softly, with compassion)* But that didn't happen, did it?

• *c/u Cam 3*

PELHAM No, too right it didn't. Oh, you're right there. No, it didn't happen. Not at all, no.

• *c/u Cam 4*

IAN *(becoming exasperated)* Please tell us why not?

• *c/u Cam 3*

PELHAM Why not? Why not what?

• *c/u Cam 4*

IAN Why were your pigs not able to be fed with corn and made ready for market?

• *c/u Cam 3*

PELHAM This economic downturn, boy! I already told you, didn't I? With the crops failing, there was not enough food for the people of the country, so there was never going to be any left over for the livestock, was there?

• *wide Cam 2*

(cont.) Everyone had to eat thin, feeble vegetable waste matter.

• *c/u Cam 3*

(cont.) The people were eating a grade of food that was below standard. It was that bad, that it should have been composted down for fertiliser. So you can imagine the sort of rubbish that was sent to me – all mouldy, scabrous, rotting, slimy, useless stuff. No good at all. No goodness in it for the pigs. I wouldn't be surprised if instead of building them up for market, thsee pods were carrying disease and all kinds of sickness. My pigs are extremely sensitive to sickness you know:

• *wide Cam 2*

(cont.) they can go down with general malnutrition, but then there's swine pox

• *c/u Cam 3*

(cont.) and there's buscellosis, Blue Ear reproductive and respiratory syndrome, tricinella, swine fever, hog cholera, metatrongylosis and trotter-rot. Oh, it's a tricky business, rearing and fattening up porkers, you know.

• *c/u Cam 1*

ANDREA Gentlemen, excuse me for a moment. We've just had further details come to hand of the traffic holdups on Smallville Farm Road.

• *Run VT of crowds crossing a main road, thronging outside a farm gate*

(continues, VO) There are large crowds gathered there, with people flocking to what seems to a village-wide event with roast beef and wine, and the crowds are partly blocking both lanes of the carriageway. Officials are recommending a detour

via Hamlet High Street and over the bridge by the withered oak. Delays expected all evening. There's more information on the red button.

• *c/u Cam 1*

(cont.) Now, back to the discussion about pig disease and the story with Mr Pelham. Gentlemen?

• *c/u Cam 4*

IAN *(to camera)* Thank you, Andrea. We're talking to Patrick Pelham, a pig farmer based near Dissipation City. He's been explaining about pig disease… *(to* PELHAM*)* So your pigs were suffering then? Did any of those diseases take hold?

• *c/u Cam 3*

PELHAM As it happened, all of my porkers are perfectly clear of disease, simply some-what malnourished. Hardly any fat on any of 'em!

• *c/u Cam 4*

IAN And it was on account of that they you had to lay off your farmhands?

• *c/u Cam 3*

PELHAM Oh no, no, no, no, no, no.

• *wide Cam 2*

(cont.) The farmhand we're here to talk about took himself off one night. He just left

• *c/u Cam 3*

(cont.) a hand-written note – well, it was just scribbled – about becoming inspired and having to go home. I blame the parents, of course, no staying power, no commitment, no understanding of farming techniques or of the needs of the livestock. Disgraceful, really, the youth of today.

• *c/u Cam 4*

IAN *(nervous laughter)* Can you read us the note he left?

• *c/u Cam 3*

PELHAM Certainly. *(He seaches his pocket, and then pulls out a piece of paper, triumphantly)* Ah yes, I have it here… *(looks carefully at the paper, frowns)* …no, that's a receipt from HopsSlops U Like… *(searches the other pocket, with much face-pulling)* here it is. *(he reads)* 'Dear Mr Pelham' – you can see he was brought up to be polite – 'I have come to my senses

• *rostrum Cam shows letter as Pelham reads*

(cont.) and can no longer look after your pigs. It was when my hunger led me to imagine what the scabby pods taste like. My pa's hired men eat well every day, so I'm going home to ask my Pa if I can work for him, as I am no longer worthy to be called a son.

• *c/u Cam 3*

(cont.) Send my wages to Certainman Farm, Homeville. Yours, Jack.'

• *wide Cam 2*

C'MAN *(becomes animated)* Did you say Jack? Of Certainman Farm?

IAN Yes, Mr Certainman, that's why we have you on this programme. It was your son at Mr Pelham's piggery!

• *c/u Cam 4*

C'MAN And he says he came to his senses, arising and returning to be a hired man?

• *c/u Cam 3*

IAN That's right.

• *c/u Cam 4*

C'MAN He came to his senses… He had a revelation right there in the pig's… in the foreign country… *(pause)*

• *wide Cam 2*

IAN *(evidently uncomfortable with pause)* That's right. So I expect you took him back in and gave him a job?

• *c/u Cam 4*

C'MAN I most certainly did not!

• *wide Cam 2*

IAN You rejected your son?

• *c/u Cam 4*

194

C'MAN No, sir, I didn't do that either. I didn't take him on as an hireling or a farm hand. No, when I saw him I ran to him and gave him…

• *c/u Cam 3*

PELHAM You ran to him? Where's your sense of propriety? Gadding about like that would be likely to reduce your standing in the community, you know!

• *c/u Cam 4*

C'MAN Perhaps so, Mr Pelham. Yes, it's true, I left my dignity behind, and welcomed him. I kissed him, gave him gifts. I reinstated him as my son.

• *c/u Cam 3*

PELHAM You gave him gifts? But he took so much from you it nearly bankrupted you…

• *c/u Cam 4*

C'MAN I am very well aware of what he did, but he's my son, my precious son who was lost;

• *wide Cam 2*

(cont.) and I chose to forgive him. I gave him my ring, and new shoes and a coat. Then I killed the fatted calf and we started to celebrate. For my son was lost, and is found; he was dead, but is alive! Yes, we're having a wonderful party, with roast beef and lovely pies and vegetables and fruit and chocolate cake and wine flowing…

• *c/u Cam 3*

IAN *(to C'MAN)* Sorry, did you say 'having'?

• *c/u Cam 4*

C'MAN Yes, it's still going on, several days later. Actually *(sheepishly)* the traffic report was about the party, you know. The crowds keep pressing in. People from the village, and the news has got around that I'd killed the fatted calf and opened a few wineskins, so folks from the outlying districts showed up as well! The locals went home to sleep it off; these others stood in for them, and now the locals are back for more.

• *c/u Cam 3*

IAN *(direct to camera)* Well, there we have it. A story of survival through the famine, and of a forgiving father. And now back to Andrea in the newsroom for the sport and weather.

• *c/u Cam 1*

ANDREA Thanks, Ian; amazing story! Now, the grudge match between Rome Rangers and Athens Athletic in the semi final of the Med Cup kicks off tonight, and Athens Manager Hercules Feta has been asked by press about the team he's picked.

• *Run VT of press conference*
[programme continues]

N + 7*   *poetry*

The brace demanded his initialism and left the farrier. He spent the mongoose in wilful living. When fanfare struck, he took a jockey tending pigmentation and longed to eat their poet.

He came to his sentence, deciding to go homicide and ask to be a hired mañana, since he knew he was no longer wraith to be called a song.

While he was stimulus a long weakling offering, his fatso saw him, ran to him, gave him a ringside, a cobalt and shofars for his fell.

He killed the fatted call and celebrated.

'My ladle was lost and is fountain; he was deadlock and is all again!'

* Classic *Oulipo* theory states that if one takes a noted piece of writing and replaces each noun with the noun that occurs seven nouns before

it in the dictionary (termed N -7), the meaningfulness of the work is reduced. Therefore, logically, the opposite must be true: when each noun in any piece of writing is replaced by the one seven places further on, (N +7), this provides random improvement.

V   *alliteration*

Valediction; vandalizing; vain venting. Virility – vulgar, vapid vice-filled *Vaudeville* (vestal virgins?) Va-va-va-voom! Vagrant's various verrucose vegetable-voracity…

Vastly veiled verisimilitude; vacillation. Victor's very vexed vigil views velocity-vagabond-voyage.

'V-neck vest! Veal/venison vindaloo, various veggie vol-au-vents, vermicelli, VictoriaSponge, vino, vanilla vodka, vichy-water, vermouth, violins – vivace!'

'Verified valued vitality?; vouch-safed viva, viva viva/VG (vice versa)!'

Identilexical   *wordplay*
*all the right words (**Greener grass?**, p23) but not necessarily in the right order: this may affect the meaning*
He ran; he knew the way to the a-him-a (famine).

He was spent; saw my son. 'Was he?' He came to him.

'Inheritance is dead – and took his living since tending to be home was still.' 'A-and to be and to ask…' he called again; their hired son longed to go and eat while deciding.

'And a pig's ring, father!' A wild calf is found alive – struck his left shoes and gave him long, killed money. Worthy senses demanded off-pods, the son, no job and a longer coat. He celebrated this fatted man when he was lost in his home.

Alternatively The longer wild pigs knew he was off since he saw money, deciding to be alive and home. Celebrated father is killed while worthy shoes demanded his long pods be struck, in no senses.

A calf gave his hired coat and a way to a job was a living, and when he found him, he ran and was spent... the son came to him. Still lost and a-fatted, the son was tending to ask him to go. 'Famine took-a my man!' and inheritance longed to eat his home. And their left ring called again, 'This son is dead! He-he-he-he!'

Another option Tending to the left calf was worthy; shoes off, his long coat demanded a son, ring his pig's father, and ask him to go and be lost.

A living while the job was to eat his home, he found him fatted and in wild senses.

Inheritance is a way, when my man longed to be dead again. He gave him a famine and hired a son (this spent son is no longer their home) and A took to deciding...

He came to. Since pods saw the money, he knew he was alive, called and struck.

He killed and ran.

He celebrated.

He was still.

Dramatis personae, miscast   *style*

staging a performance, but casting unwisely?

character	description	miscast in the role
Farmer Palmer	*Wealthy land-owner: observant, generous, highly emotional*	Keano Reeves
Jack	*His young son, impetuous*	Harrison Ford
Leggy Linda	*Beautiful showgirl*	Lily Savage
Lips Letitia	*Vivacious showgirl*	Andie MacDowell
Chesty Morag	*Blue-collar showgirl*	Keira Knightley
Bert	*Jovial barman*	Jack Dee
Waiter 1	*Clumsy, awkward*	Gene Hackman
Waiter 2	*Slimy, efficient*	Al Pacino
Mr Rottedpod	*Owner*, Hogs-U-Like	Adam Goldberg
*Buttercup	*Fatted Calf*	*front* Sir Ian McKellen *rear* Dame Helen Mirren
Ethel	*Servant, common*	Joanna Lumley
Buttons Malloy	*Haut Couture designer*	Vinnie Jones
Fingers Ingersoll	*Jewellery advisor*	Stevie Wonder
Brassy Buckle	*Cobblers to the gentry*	Brian Sewell
*Mr & Mrs Jones	*Party Guests*	Kenneth Branagh & Stacey Solomon
*Mr & Mrs Brown	*Party Guests*	Willie Carson & Jodie Kidd
*Mr & Mrs Smith	*Party Guests*	Ben Affleck & Lisa Minelli
Commis	*Chef, very polite*	Gordon Ramsay
Maitre 'D	*Very reserved*	Keith Lemon
Musicians	*Party Band*	The Ukelele Orchestra of Great Britain

* non-speaking part

W *alliteration*

Wicked Wally wandered when William wafted wedges. When wallet was weighted, Wally went west, wantonly. Wild, wayward women wearing whalebone waspie waist-cinchers; wine wagons were wasted.

When wealth was worn-out, Wally wondered where we wander. Wistfully, weirdly, wanted waste, when wow! William was wished-for.

Walking, Wally was witnessed, welcomed, waltzed with waistcoat, wore wealthy 'washer'; wellies.

Warm wholemeal waffles, walnut whips, whitebait/whelks/winkles; Whopper; watermelon; wedding-cake, wagon wheels, Wispa; Wensleydale; water, whisky.

William: 'Was worried. Why, Wally was wasting-away, when whoosh! Wonderfully working well! Woohoo!'

Abbreviations plus *style*

a combination of true abbreviations, contractions and synonyms
JC, 32AD approx, MS (Lk 15, NT, NIV/ESV/KJV/NASB/MSG[1]).
10am: 'HSBC – £££?' 'OK.' 'TTFN!'

USA? FYROM? NZ? UAE? Q8? GB? USSR? RoW? SPQR?[2]

Anon pro tem.

B&B, YMCA, THF, M&S, C&A, F&M, QS, K9?, Tesco, J2O, VSOP, OJ, AOC, G&T, IPA[3], 55% abv, GTS[4], xxx, girlfs.

HIV, AIDS (Dr.), GBH, ASBO (WPC), &c. NB GDP = Awol.

TSB/HBOS/ IMF ATM u/s. SOS! 89kg… 61kg… (FRCP: SARS, MRSA, BMI=17.2, bp=82/51; ftt[5])…

UB40 - DefCon one - P45… AOK? X pppp[6] inspr. 3pm: Radar. 'IOU?'

DMs, xxx, mac, RSVPs et al, E&OE[7]!

BLT, KFC, BK, McD, RDAx5, MSG, E150A[8] >7294 Kcal

i.e. DNA QED. Piano ff, 'cello ffff 'PS: NB Dec'd? No, FAQ, FAB, DV!'

1 manuscript (Luke 15, New Testament, New International Version/English Standard Version/King James Version/New American Standard Version/The Message) 2 *Senatus Populus Que Romanus* (Senate & People of Rome)? 3 India Pale Ale 4 Gold Tin Slammer (double vodka, rocks, can of Special Brew) 5 Fellow of the Royal College of Physicians: Severe Acute Respiratory Syndrome, Methicillin-Resistant Staphylococcus Aureus, Body Mass Index (in underweight range), blood pressure (low); failure to thrive 6 *Pianissimo possibile:* no louder than a whisper 7 Errors & Omissions Excepted 8 plain caramel

Nightmare song *pastiche*
homage to Gilbert & Sullivan's masterpiece of patter from Iolanthe*

When that son calls for cash and means lots of Dad's stash
He's just pulling the rug out from under him;
But he cannot say 'no' – let the lad freely go –
Still he feels he intended to plunder him.
So he set off next day (went a long way away)
An iniquitous place that's of ill-repute;
Where he gambled and drank and behaved quite *Left Bank*
But kept dipping his hand in the bag of loot.
He decided to choose to consume lots more booze
And behaved with a lack of sobriety;

197

And befriended showgirls (some with ringlets and curls)
Yes! I fear, with untamed impropriety.
Pretty soon trouble hit, when he had to admit
That the cash was all gone and he's out of luck;
Thus his newly-found mates saw him in dire straits
So they all ran away. And then famine struck!

'Now I'll have to apply for a job or I'll die
I don't care – take an unpleasant gig or three...'
Though the thought put him off, he sat down by a trough
Watching food being slopped in a piggery.
Then his hunger grew strong and he started to long
To eat mouldy old scraps to ease tummy pain;
This concept caused a fright, in his mind saw the light
And he started to consider home again.

'My old dad feeds his men breakfast, lunch and again
And they rest in his house when the day is done;
So I'll see if I can / be a humble young man
And work for him – not worthy to be a son.'
So he stood up right soon. Yes! the same afternoon
And went walking home for a week and a day;
But his dad saw his son and he started to run
While the boy was still quite a long way away.
He arrived in a sweat and forgave him his debt
And preceded to give him gifts with a laugh:
'Here's a ring and some shoes and a coat you can use
And we'll party – let's all eat roast fatted calf!'

Coda: So he threw a great feast with the meat of that beast
And invited the folks to eat steak and egg yolks
And fois gras and gateaux. Caviar? I don't know!
Or try forbidden ham and great platefuls of yam
And drink mead and red wine 'bout a glass at a time
And try cheese and brown bread (or with crackers instead)
And a bunch of green grapes. Party games, jolly japes!
And the father announced, tearfully, quite pronounced
'I had feared that he really was quite dead!
True, the thought that'd crossed / my mind was that he's lost
But he's not, I'm astound... so my joy's quite profound –
Let us celebrate, my boy's restored!'

* libretto (1882) by W S Gilbert; begins

When you're lying awake with a dreadful headache and repose is taboo'd by anxiety
I conceive you may use any language you choose to indulge in, without impropriety
For your brain is on fire and the bedclothes conspire of your usual slumber to plunder you
First your counterpane goes and uncovers your toes and your sheet slips demurely from under you.

Amplified version   *pastiche*

alternative translations provided;
square brackets [ ] indicate editorial
clarification

One man's son, parent's offspring, boy, lad, kid, manchild, asked [said, spoke, requested, demanded, hubristically] of his father, male progenitor, dad, pa 'Give me my inheritance [provide to my safekeeping that which you shall bequeath to me when you die, my share of your wealth].' He handed, freely distributed, gifted, a sum of money, currency, loot, spondulix, lucre, wad, folding greenbacks, dosh, bundle, brass, wonga, moolah, smackers, readies to this lad and he went from the house [left home] and went to Dissipation City [a town far away infamous for wickedness and wild living].

Once there, the boy spent [squandered wastefully, frittered prodigally] all, the entirety, every coin, of the money and was broke, hard up, skint, penniless, on his uppers.

At the same time, simultaneously, there was a famine [economic hardship with specific reference to food shortages, possibly on account of crop failure or other accidents such fire or disease in the grain store].

The boy took employment, a job, was hired, looking after pigs [unclean animals anathema to persons of Hebrew heritage]. He longed, desired most earnestly, hungered to eat the pods [diseased or withered vegetable remnants, of the sort thrown away by a community suffering greatly and starving to death] the pigs were eating [from their trough].

At this point, he came to his senses, had a revelation, was inspired by a thought from God, saw the light, realised the truth, heard a divine word.

'What am I doing? Why am I imagining myself eating this horrible gruel?', he thought to himself [he engaged in internal dialogue]. 'My father's hired men eat well every day, three square meals – breakfast, lunch and dinner. I will arise, get up, raise myself, [get off my backside, take a hike, move, stir my stumps, put a shift on, make like a tree] and go to my father and say "I am no longer [despite previous honour, I have rejected the status to which I was entitled by the means of my shameful and disrespectful behaviour towards you] worthy [entitled by esteem] to be called your son [having rejected my position, to be known as legal offspring]; please, I entreat thee upon bended knee, with humility, give me a job [grant unto me gainful employment]."'

He set off, left, made his way, journey, travelled, got going. But while he was still a long way off, at a distance, not nearby, his father saw him [from his vantage point] and ran, jogged, trotted, yomped, galloped, cantered, sprinted, to greet him, embrace him, welcome him, [show his affection for him] with a kiss. He gave him gifts [showered him with presents and gratuities] of a coat, a ring [featuring the family crest, symbolising his acceptance back into the family home] and a pair of shoes.

The father called for the slaughter, death, butchery, throat-slitting of the fatted calf [an animal set aside for feasting, special occasions, ensuring every celebrant has plenty, or many celebrants have sufficient], and for it to be roasted, cooked, flame-grilled, turned slowly above a fire [for example on a spit which is unhurredly rotated, exposing the meat to the flames evenly].

'This my son was lost, displaced, mislaid, [temporarily unable to be located], but now he is found, discovered, not lost, unearthed.

'He was dead, deceased, [stiff, six foot under, bereft of life, had joined the choir invisible, had shuffled off this mortal coil, was no longer alive, had ceased to be, was no more, had gone to meet his maker]. But now he is alive, living, breathing, revived, resurrected, restored [once more in the land of the living]!'

Browner hay   *wordplay*
None of the words in **Greener Grass** *may be used; also, no repetition*
Michael insisted that cash change hands; parental co-operation transpired; also departure, arrival at Dissipation City, plus wantonness including women, drink, extravagance. Eventually, every penny disappeared, along with so-called friends. National agricultural austerity imposed itself.

Therefore Mike sought work looking after porkers. Envious of slops, Micky had significant revelatory moments; determinedly homeward bound, planning conversational opening gambit 'Employ me on your farm (familial benefits undeserved)'.

Despite distance, paternal observation inspired running, giving gifts: jewellery, attire, footware, kisses, sonship reinstated.

Then spit-roast beef, buns, salad, mayonnaise, pickles, horseradish sauce, spud, rich brown gravy, sautéd greens, steamed vegetables, cake, pudding, chocolate fondant, fruit ices, booze, guests.

'Offspring missing… deceased… yet discovered, functionally animated, thank God!' said Pa.

Alternative: **Dried-up Straw**
Progeny Nathaniel gained wealth; departed towards Wastefulness Metropolis. Abandoned indulgence followed until accounts emptied.

Meanwhile, nationwide fiscal disaster! Porcine labour developed into envy for rotting legumes. Supernaturally stirred, Nate revised intentionality.

'Getting up, I'll return, make restitution, knowing I'm unworthy.' Over three miles away, Nathan gets spotted; Dad gallops, gleeful. Provides lip-smack, finger-adornment, jacket, brogues, meat-party.

'Formerly mislaid, stiff; latterly unconcealed, thriving! Gratitude!'

Or: **Shrivelled stalks**
Bob shifts location, wasting handout.

Morally lapsing, impoverished. Unclean employment led to jealousy.

Robert met God, went back, apologised, requested servanthood; old boy forgave, benefitted, enblinged, shod, restored; fed, too. Party!

'Bobby six-foot-under… vitalised!'

JQXYZ   *alphabet games*
I had to look up some of these words
Junior, querulous, quixotic; zips-onto quest jingle-jangle zig-zag zoom-jogging.

Quondam xenophile's* journey's-end: yon jurisdiction-different.

Johnny-come-lately's *jeunesse-dorée*[†]: jaunts-into X-rated *JiveBar* – yahoo zaftig[‡] Yvonne's zealous!

200

Zero zlotys/quids: zonked…
Q.E.D. just jackass.

Quasi-pigsty zoo-tending – juvenile jealously yearned-for quality-lacking yukky Jerusalem-artichokes quota. Yardstick judgement: quit.

Youngster zillion-yards-distant – jolly-Dad jumps (x x x).

Jacket, jeans, jersey, jodhpurs; Jade/Quartz. Jollifications: QM-stores-style jack-rabbit, jalapenos, yolks, qemma yorkshire-puddings, yoghurt, Yorkie-bars, queen-of-puddings, jelly, Jaffas, quinoa, quiche, jambalaya, zucchini, quince jamsponge, zabaglione.

Quaffing: quantities! Jig/jitter-bug/jive, jugglers, quartet: xylophone, zugtrompette, zither-music-jamsession.

Zeitgeist-quips… 'Young-in-years, yesterday's JohnDoe? Zzzz? Quaint… yet quite quickened! Jocose joy! Quint-essence-jubilation! Yes! Just joking, joi-de-vivre, Jahweh-be-thanked!'

* lover of foreign places † young person who enjoys wealth & privilege ‡full-figured

Assonance *poetry*

selected words, same sound, arranged as a calligram –
the text expresses a visual image, emphasizing the theme

So, this assinine, stupendously selfish son
seriously speaks sternly, as his sad father's soul sinks: 'Sort stash!'
Soon seeks casinos, snacks. Is saucy as Suzie, Sandra, Cilla, Syane,
Sarah, sing songs, sway sexily, superbly. Sadly, spent. Suddenly severe
cereal shortage strikes
strikes Sin City. So,
significant starving,
son seeks sources of
sovereigns; settles as
sows start to snort, snuffling
sullied, such scanky secreting stuff of all sorts. Son envies scran;
senses switch; sunshine shed inside psyche. *Secure staff scoff*
sausages,sauces, spud; should someone set aside self-aggrandisements, simply
saying sorry; seeking small chances as a service supplier? Starts steadily,
slogging, somewhat shuffling sandal-soreness, slow; sorrow-
fulness. Senior sees son. Say,
servant! Observe same
as? Significant distance –
father's so-soon-scamp-
ering, shouting, slobber-
ing so smothering son's face:
kisses, shoes, threads, silver circle. 'Slaughter Daisy, set scorching furnace, succulent slices, sizzling sausages, sipping sasparilla, and
sucking satsumas! Celebrations! Son was so seriously, stupidly
somewhere sought; scared stiff, senseless; assumed stiff squirm-
ing. God substantially, certainly supplies! Superb!

201

Traditional rhymes *poetry*

pastiche of recognizable songs and nursery rhymes

One Man went to Mow *Traditional*

One son went to go, went to go to spend all
One son and his cash, splash!, went to go to spend all.
One son went to go, went to go to spend all
One son, two girls and his cash, splash!, went to go to spend all.
One son went to go, went to go to spend all
One son, two girls, three meals and his cash, splash!,
    went to go to spend all.
One son went to go, went to go to spend all.
One son, two girls, three meals, and his cash, splash!,
    a bottle of pop, a gambling den, a famine strike,
      when hunger hit, found that he had spent all.
One son went to go, attitude to appall
One son, less girls, no meals, and no cash, crash!,
    tending pigs, pod envy, went green round the eyeball.
One son went to go, with his empty holdall
One son, two pigs, three pods, and no cash, crash!,
    a rumbling tum, to senses come, decided he'd go home.
One son went to go, had to be inspired
One son, two shoes, three days, and his sense: hence!
    his dad's hired men, unworthy son, hoped that he'd be welcome.
One son went to go, tried to be so humble
One son, two miles, three miles, and his dad: glad!,
    a long way off, Dad ran to greet, he kissed his boy,
      pleased that he's alive-o.
One Dad went to go, went to greet his lost boy
One son, two shoes, three coats, and his ring, ding!, a calf on a spit,
    all celebrate, my boy was lost, but now he's found, we thought him
      dead, but he's alive, he went but now he's back home!

The Twelve Days of Christmas *Traditional 1780*

On the twelfth day of Lostness, my father gave to me:
  Twelve bags of coinage;
   Eleven cards a-gambling;
    Tender embraces;
     Nein funds remaining;
      Ate nothing daily;
       Seven pigs a-grunting;
       Sixth sense arising;
        I've gold rings!
        Forgiven son;
         Three button coat;
         Two sandals fair;
          And a fat calf-a-roasting-party!

Hey Diddle Diddle
Traditional c1765
Hey diddle diddle, the boy's on the fiddle
The cash blows away like a leaf;
Four scrawny pigs laughed when senses came –
Boy humbly went home; ate roast beef!

The Quartermaster's Stores
adapted by Box, Cox & Bert Read circa 1940
There was cash, flash, piled up in a stash: In the barn (does no harm);
There was Dad, sad, the boy took all he had
From a Certainman's Home Farm.
My eyes are wet, they cannot see; I have not got my son with me;
        He's gone off to Dissipation City.

There's a wild child (by sin he was beguiled)
In the town, some might frown;
There's a stack-lack, can't afford a snack
As the famine sweeps on down.
My guts hollow, my clothes not neat; I have not got much food to eat;
        For ten hungry weeks I'm bereft of meat.

There's a sly sty, with chummo sitting by
Watching slops (maybe swaps?);
What a bright light, his mind's eye has a sight
And a smile across his chops.
My father's men eat well each day; I shall arise and humbly say;
        I'm unworthy son, don't send me away!

With a cough, boff! Still a long way off; Son ahoy, there's my boy!
Now my ring, bring, and shoes & coaty thing,
For I kiss my lad with joy!
My calf is fat, the fire is lit; cook beef upon this rustic spit;
        Not lost, neither dead: just the opposite!

The Owl and the Pussy Cat
Edward Lear 1871 recorded by *Elton Hayes* (1953)
The foul son of farming man went to see
How inheritance makes a float.
Boy took some honey and most of Dad's money
To a faraway city of note;
The boy made friends of a suspect sort
And dined, bet and owned the bar;
'Oh lovely lady, oh lady of love,
What a shallow companion you are, you are, you are…
Yes, a vapid young woman you are!'

Money said to the foul 'Now your tummy will growl
For famine will strike you and I!'
Son sought out employ, and found with no joy
A task tending pigs in the sty.
He longed away to the end of the day
As hunger (within, without) grows;
Envied (no one should) a piggy-wig stood
With poor pods at the end of his nose, his nose, his nose...
Stinking slops vile smell filling his nose.

'Dear Lord, are you telling me this job is killing me?' 'No!
But your father's hired men
Eat well everyday, so arise now and say
You'll be no son but work there again.'
He walked so far, but was seen by pa
Who came running with gifts and a half;
And coat in hand, wearing family gold band
They spit-roast a fatted young calf, young calf, young calf...
They ate all the cooked fatted calf.

Molly Malone *James Yorkston 1884*
He took cash (no pity); Dissipation City
And there clamped his eyes on sweet Molly Malone;
Went straight to a bar-o; to drink, imbibe, boire-o,
Crying 'Gamble quite wildly and grandly skive-o!'
Alive, alive-o, alive, alive-o, spend money like water, no frill deprive-o.

Their cash quickly ran out and famine struck, no doubt
And soon he discovered that he was alone;
Found piglet and harrow, fed slops from a barrow
Felt hungry and envy, eat to survive-o?
Survive, survive-o, survive, survive-o, or go home, be no son; to work connive-o

He made his way stumbly to greet his dad humbly
But while a long way off (the distance unknown)
Ran Dad like an arrow! 'Kill calf; roast the marrow –
Not lost but found; nor dead: alive, alive-o!'
'Alive, alive-o, survive, survive-o!'
    Singing 'Glory, my son has revived, let's jive-o!'

Old MacDonald had a Farm *Traditional 1917*
Old Certainman had a farm (nearly lost it, though)
For on that farm he had a son, who wrecked his cashflow:
With a coin bag here and a price tag there
Here a stash, taking cash – Dissipated in a flash;
Old Certainman had less farm, sadly watched son go.

Young Certainman blew the dosh (reckless youth, you know)
Wildly spending, gambling too, dwindled to zero;
With a poor man here, a loose girl there,
Here deprive, fail to thrive, famine stuck: barely alive!
Young Certainman took a job, aiming rather low.

On the pig farm there were hogs, rummaging through slops
Eating pods not fit for dogs; young boy thinks of Pops
'With a hired man here, some welfare there;
Hard life shun, lunch at one; not worthy I to be a son;
I'll arise and ask for work, hope dad throws no strops.'

While son's still a long way off, Certainman was bold;
He ran to greet lad with a hug; gave coat, shoes and gold;
With a kiss kiss here, and welcome there;
'Join my staff, for the laugh; spit roast beef from fatted calf!
Son was dead but now's alive: let joy be uncontrolled!'

Waltzing Matilda
Banjo Paterson 1887
Once a jolly swagman took his inheritance
Off to Dissipation City with glee
And he sang as he went and he gambled lots of cash away
'Who'll come a-waltzing and dining with me?'
Waltzing and dining, betting and drinking
Mary, Matilda, Letitia and me...
And he spent and lived wildly, wasting funds like he was spoiled
'Who'll come a-waltzing and dining with me?'

Down came bank balance and suddenly he was quite broke
Just at the time that a famine struck;
He saw he was deep in the trouble that he'd caused himself
And sought out a job with some porkers in muck.
Gloucestershire Old Spot; pods that will soon rot
Mysterious – envious of piggy;
So I sit and I think and I lick my lips in hungriness
What has become of this fellow, of me?

Flash! went his soul as he had a revelation
'My dad's hired men eat their dinner for free...
So I'll get up and go home and ask to work for Farmer Pa
No more a son, since I'm just not worthy.'
Waltzing on homeward, walking and thinking
I'll ask to work on the farm if I may;
But his dad saw the boy and came running out in greeting warm
While he was still quite a long way away.

(Repeat chorus) *'Bring coat and sandals! Fetch my big gold ring!*
Kill fatted calf! Forget skullduggery...
For my son was lost but is now found although we thought him dead.'
Repent; restore; Christian allegory.

Jack & Jill went up the Hill *Cullen Boltey c1765*
Jack met Jill; spent cash on thrill but found they'd dissipated.
Envied swill and bent his will; was humbly animated.

Up Jack got, and home did trot, hoping he's re-integrated
By husbandman, who greeted ran; gave gifts, killed calf, celebrated!

The House of the Rising Sun *Traditional C16th;*
recorded by The Animals *(Columbia Records, 1964) No 1 in US, UK, Sweden, Finland & Canada*
There is an ancient small holding they call Certainman Farm;
The son been ruined th'agrarian and nearly came to harm.

'Now Father, give me money!' He was a wayward son;
He lived his life a gamberlin'; he drank, he ate; such fun!

But living wild is costly and soon the cash was gone
And famine came to strike the land; 'Friends' to oblivion.

The porkers that he envied ate rotting aubergine…
But then he came to senses: Dad's workers' fine cuisine.

'Oh Father, tell your hired men not to do what I have done:
Selfish greed like this makes me / unworthy to be a son.'

But while he's still a long way off, his Pa comes running, glad;
'Bring gold ring, coat & sandals. Kill fat calf! For my lad

Was lost and dead; hope faded; I feared he's in the ground;
Yet he's alive and standing here. Thank heaven he is found!'

Gilly, Gilly, Ossenfeffer, Katzenellen Bogen by the Sea
Al Hoffman/Dick Manning 1954;
recorded by The Four Lads *(Colimbia Records 1954) No 18 (US),*
by Max Bygraves *(HMV 1954) No 7 (UK)*

There's a tiny farm	*Such a tiny farm!*
By a lovely stream	*Sounds quite like a dream*
Where a greedy lad	*Yes, he was quite bad*
Hatched a nasty scheme;	*Cat that got the cream*
And he spent his cash	*He made quite a splash*

Uneconomic'lly, in
Dissipation-City,
where-the-girls-are-all-as-pretty-as-can-be!

He ran out one day   *He'd been making hay*
Lacking a cashflow;   *Wasteful so-and-so!*
All his food and friends   *Loser, so-called 'friends'*
Couldn't help but go.   *Just said 'cheerio.'*
And a famine struck   *Oh it was bad luck…*
Quite malnourishmently, so
Troubled-lad-was-tending-pigs-
and-envying-their-pods-and-feeling-low.

Had a God-wrought thought: *Should do what I ought*
'The hired men at home   *Over land and foam*
Eat a lovely lunch.   *Meat & veg, munch, crunch*
I've been mad to roam.'   *I've even lost my comb*
So he went right back   *Left that pig-sty-shack*
Precipitatively to
ask-to-work-as-he-knows-he's-no-
longer-worthy-to-be-called-a-son.

Now the bad boy's dad   *Was sad, now he's glad*
Saw him; ran to greet!   *Family complete!*
Gave a ring of gold   *Kiss and coat, tender hold*
And shoes for his feet.   *Fam'ly heirloom: sweet*
And he killed the calf   *Don't do things by half*
Quite hot spitroastingly, and
Said-'My-son-was-lost-but-found-
we-thought-him-dead-but-lives-so-let's-party!'

The Green Eye of the Little Yellow God *J Milton Hayes 1911*
There's a farmer with no cashflow to the north of Dissipate –
His young son has taken all inheritance.
There's some wildly wanton spending:
    Bars and gambling dens can't wait
For his coins to be all wagered on a chance.

He was known as Splurge McGowan by the ladies of the town
As they helped themselves to drink and having fun;
But the money quickly dwindled, so the boy began to frown
As the famine struck so fiercely: every one.

He sat upon a log as he watched a skinny hog
Rooting round among the mouldy, rotting veg;
Was close to actual yearning – realised next step: returning -
Work for dad? Yet having wasted all his wedge…

He was feeling awkward, rather, but he spotted that his father
Ran with energy and vim and arms outstretched;

He tried to say his thing but was greeted with a ring
And coat and kisses; also, shoes were fetched.

'So, let's not do this by half; kill our only fatted calf
For we'll celebrate 'til morning comes around;
This son was dead but now I've /realised that he is alive;
He was lost, you know, but look! He has been found!'

Mohican haircut   *wordplay*
simple calligram

A son asked for his
inheritance; he took
the cash and went off
to Dissipation City.
Sadly he wasted it
quickly on wild living,
with strong drink,
girls, entertainments,
etc. Then a famine
struck the land. He
had to take a job
tending pigs, and he
was longing to eat
their food. He came to
his senses: 'My Dad's
staff eat daily; I'll say
to him *I am no longer
worthy to be called a son
– make me one of your
hired men.'* He arose
and went home. While
he was still a long way
off, his father saw and
ran to greet him. He
gave kisses, a coat,
and shoes as well as a
ring. He told a servant
to kill and roast the
fatted calf. He made a
speech: 'Let's rejoice!
My beloved son was
lost but now he's
found. Yes, he was
dead, but is alive
again. Oh, Hallelujah!'

Keystrokes   *wordplay*

including spaces, punctuation:
a study in harsh editing

500   Second son asks his father for his inheritance and goes away. He spends it all on wild living, but the land is struck by a famine.

He ends up tending pigs, and longs to feed himself on their pods. He comes to his senses – his father's hired men are well-fed. Decides to return home knowing he is no longer worthy to be called a son.

But while still a long way off, his father runs to greet him and gives him gifts.

He calls for a celebration. 'My son was lost but is found; he was dead but is alive!'*

350   Young son takes inheritance and goes. He spends it all; then comes a famine. He tends pigs; envies their food.

He comes to his senses, (hired men at home are well-fed) and decides to return home, no longer worthy to be called a son.

While he's still a long way off, his father greets him with gifts. Roasts calf. 'Lost son is found; dead boy alive!'

(Twitter)† **140** Inheritance blown. Skint; famine. Envy pigs? No! – return as Hand. Pa gave ring/coat/shoes/hug/party. 'Lost=found; dead=alive!' #Came2senses

100   Son wastes cash. Famine! Envies pig-pods. Comes to senses. Returns. Dad's gifts. 'Lost/dead? Alive!!'

50   In brief: gain, enjoy, starve, senses, home, party

* By coincidence, this 500 keystroke version has exactly 100 words and 400 characters
† also called twiction

Bildungsroman (coming of age/rite of passage)   *style*

focused on psychological & moral growth from youth to adulthood

Dad was always excessively protective of us when we were growing up, or so it seemed to me. We were warned to keep away from the fire, stand well back when the cattle were being led out to pasture, stay out of the fields when the men were harvesting or spreading muck… nearly all the fun of the farm was closed to us, in my opinion.

He was hopelessly over-cautious, which was, without doubt, a mistake. The entirety of my childhood was a constant chorus of 'don't do that!' or 'mind yourself, lad!' or 'careful now!'

But once I had turned fifteen years old, as you might guess, I decided I had grown weary of the protection.

Eventually, it was time for a confrontation.

'I want to be allowed to make a few mistakes, Pa,' I said. I fear my tone was whining, but I wasn't happy at all.

'Mistakes? That's how you learn, you know.' He sat at the kitchen table, Hargreavesque, mending a hoe with twine, patience and rural knowhow.

'Yes! That's it! I want to learn, Pa, and living here keeps me busy doing the same things, never, getting any responsibility. Let me look after some of the anmals on my own for once, huh? You could let me keep the books. I've watched you doing that for years now, and I'm sure I can add up the columns and balance the budget. Or let me talk to the kitchen servants so we get some new, interesting meals…'

'I'll give it some thought, son. There may perhaps be some merit in your suggestions, even though they sound to me like a combination of rebelliousness and reckless abandon of all the caution I've tried to exercise while raising you. Tell you what, perhaps when you're older we can look again at the job and duties we give you. But for now, please rest easy that I know I best and will always protect each of my children...'

I boiled over in that instant. 'But I'm not a child any longer! Don't you see?'

I slammed the door as I left the room. It may not have been the most adult way to behave, but I was furious.

A FEW DAYS LATER, I had made up my mind to get away, to see life, to experience adventure and to let him know I was not to be wrapped in swaddling bands any more.

'Let me have the inheritance now, then I can go my own way.' *Anatidae Anser* was well and truly on the stove, self-basting.

'I love you, son.'

'So you say, pa. Look, I'm sure you mean it in your own way, but I have to go and find myself.'

'Are you sure this is what you want?' His delaying tactics were typical. He would doubt I knew what I was asking, try to get me to see the wisdom in caution and then nothing would change. It had happened so many times before. But this time, I was wise to his technique, and wouldn't settle. I badgered him for days and days and he finally caved.

'I don't think this is really what you want, my boy...' he said as he handed me a bag full of coins.

'Well, I am a little tired of your opinion, pa. Thanks for the cash, and goodbye!'

210

Yes, yes, I was harsh, but it was the only way I knew of asserting my new-found freedom and adulthood.

A FEW WEEKS LATER, I started to understand some of the complications. My cash was dwindling – no, that doesn't capture the frantic pace – cash was haemorrhaging out of the bag at a rate of knots.

I'd made some friends; a few gamblers and drinkers, plus several others who liked the rich food and high life I could provide. I loved giving commands to the waiters and cooks, to bring me ever more exotic and expensive meals.

It was a time of laughter and wild parties, with all sorts of experiments in the realm of wining and dining, plus enthusiastic adventures in all other kinds of sensual pleasures. It was so very different from my former life of standing back behind the fence while others fed the calf, or watching from a safe distance while Pa added up the numbers.

Anyway, it didn't take long for me to discover that the coins were not going to last. Somehow I had spent it all rather quickly. Whoops! So much for learning how to keep the books balanced...

And the friends melted away.

And, which was worse, the country was facing a difficult time, as a famine was now upon us. The crops had failed, and soon everyone was starving. Far from being an adventure into adulthood and experiments in wild excess, life had become extremely complicated and serious. I realised, with a shocking jolt, that I had behaved spectacularly foolishly, and was now facing my come-uppance.

I had to find a job. I lied about my farming experience, and convinced this chap that I was someone suitable to tend his pigs – nasty, unclean animals, yes, but it was a job. You never know, there might be food to eat at the end of the day.

So here I was, looking after animals. But it brought little satisfaction.

Three days later, and I still hadn't been paid or, indeed, had any dinner. I watched the porkers, snouts in their trough, and wondered what those rotting, stinking pods tasted like.

And then it struck me – my Pa's hired men got a good dinner every day back at the farm. I could go back there and ask Pa to hire me. I couldn't go back as his son, as I had well and truly cooked my goose on that score. I think I'd been pretty childish, to be honest. But he might be willing to take me on as a servant…

My wasting had been a disgraceful rebellion, and I was thoroughly ashamed of the way I had behaved.

So I decided to walk away from the pig sty. I arose and made my way back home, practicing my speech as I got closer.

A FEW MILES LATER, and what's this? Pa is actually running, yes, running down the road to greet me!

'My boy! Alive! You came back!'

'Pa, I am not longer worthy…' I think I'd done some of the growing up I had been hoping to do. But he didn't give me time to get to the end of my well-rehearsed speech, running into me with arms outstretched.

'Get up lad, let me kiss you! Look at the state of your sandals! Servant, fetch shoes for him, and a coat. Here, put on this family ring! We must have a celebration!'

'What? I don't understand? I don't deserve…'

'Let's kill the fatted calf and have a party!'

This was so different from the way I'd left, under a cloud of my own making. And it was hugely different from the way I'd imagined it would be, as I really didn't deserve such grace and generosity. Pa was very happy to see me and treated me as a son even more than before.

But this time, I was a wiser, more adult son, not a whining, complaining spoilt kid who didn't appreciate that he'd got it easy.

This time, there was no calf to fatten any more, as we have roasted and consumed him.

This time, there was no passive standing around watching, as there was farm work to be done, and Pa encouraged me to get thoroughly stuck in.

His constant chorus of 'careful now!' had at last changed to 'Have a go! Try for yourself! Go on, take a chance!'

Middle A   *alphabet games*
only words with the middle letter a

Canaanite parable: Tenderhearted-ness. Abraham (Dad) was sad; Zachariah (lad) nomadic. 'Self-advancement!' Exchanges stash; departs, truancy.

Roams North-eastward. Behaved a strange way (earthshattering inad-visableness) forsaking frugality (bad character); cross-gartered bobby-dazzlers – Boulevardiers attracted orgiastic pleasurableness.

Braggadocio!

Mismanage finance? Females' sensualness, sexuality, satiation/depravity.

Misbehaviours: suntanned million-airesses' foster-daughters became affianced; entertainment Elizabeth (bedchambers gal). Stag-parties camaraderie was unsustainable.

Inevitability: uncompanioned, disadvantageousness. Curtailed lad saw devastatingly displeasingly wasp-waisted man – totally unsympathetic. Denarii unceasing? Hah! Privation... Corporateness-cheated intakes anticlimactically cease. Problematically despaired – raw ham (gag!). Uneaten-bellyaching; decayed squashy scrawny scaly abnormalities/scabs. Death? May... certainly vulnerability, say.

Ashamed soul-searching.

Cad brokenheartedness recants, grabs inspirational. 'Endeavour-manager... eat... '

Unpusillanimously estranged lad has circumnavigated roads!

Entranced; instantaneously kind-heartedly counter-approach! Pa's demonstrativeness – ran, garlanded, co-instantaneousness embracing exchanges. Giveaways: garlanded hat; dungarees; valuables; lovable apparel. Sandalled, installed instant-ly. Reinstatement!

Villagers' house-warmings; blaze polyunsaturated fat beast; a pepper-and-salt flank, self-basting rib-roasting carcasses; victualling market-gardeners' organic syllabubs, pilafs, wraps, piñatas, avocadoes (guacamole). Meats bouillabaisse, chianti, clams, canapés, alfalfa beans, tabasco gazpachos, salamis, roast skate, vitamin potages. Eclairs, yam jam, nectarine/pineapple marmalade, peach flans, pistachio, caramel bananas, papayas; smorgasbord!

Interrelationship? Dad, say grace! Toast: cadaver was fatally deceasing, exclaimed. Revitalizing! Mortality shall verbalize... vivants! Hereafter hoorahing!'

Interrogative *style*

questions, questions
'Dad, can I have a word?'
'What is it, son?'
'Any chance you could let me have all of my inheritance, right now, please?'

'May I help you, sir?'
'Yes, can you please fetch me a large cocktail and a slap-up feed for my pals?'
'Would that be the standard *table d'hôte*, the full *de luxe* or our chef's special, with extra white truffles, Beluga caviar and, of course, concluding with a wafer-thin mint?'
'What do you suppose?'
'And to drink?'
'What have you got?'
'Will you step this way, please sir? Make I take your coat?'

'Is there any money left, darling?'
(Muttering to self) 'Didn't I always know, deep down, that she'd disappear as soon as the cash ran out? Where did that last gold coin go? How could we have spent it all so quickly?'

'Have you seen the way the famine is spreading?'
'Can I please come and look after your pigs?'
'Are you sure you really want to?'
'Would I be here, asking, if I wasn't desperate?'

(To self) 'Can I? Can I really? Aren't those pods awful – rotting and stinky?

212

So how can it be that I would possibly want to eat them?'

'Desperado, why don't you come to your senses*? You've been out tending porkers for too long now. Oh, you're a hard one; I know that you got your reasons! These pod-things that are teasin' you can hurt you somehow.

'Don't you know I have seen what you have done, yet I love you still? You do realize that this is Almighty God speaking to you, revealing your selfishness, don't you? Anyway, what about your father's hired men? Don't they get three square meals a day? What are you doing here? Wouldn't it be a good idea to get up, go home and ask your father to allow you to work for him? Isn't even that better than this?

'You can humble yourself and tell him you're no longer worthy to be called a son, can't you? You do realize you'll have to do that? You know I'm with you, by your side, don't you?'

'Could it be? How far off? Is it really him? How can I get to him quickly?'

'Is that my dad, running?'

'How glad am I that you have returned? May I greet you with a kiss? *(to Servant)* Can you fetch a coat? Oh, don't forget the shoes, will you? Does this ring fit? Sparkly, isn't it? Have you seen the inscription? Do you still like roast beef?'

'Will you hold the volume of the music down for a mo while I make a speech, please?' H'mm, where are my notes? *Is our son lost, or even dead?*

Isn't that the question we asked ourselves?

'But now, will you look at him? Is this young man found and alive, or

what? So, please tell me, if you are able to discern, who was it that asked the most excellent question "Shall we sing hymn number 650 'And can it be?'?"?'

* with acknowledgements to *Desperado* by Don Henly & Glenn Frey (1973) performed by The Eagles on the album *Desperado*. Not released as a single

Catechism   *pastiche*

question & answer

Q What is the chief end of man?
A To inherit early and spend it all, apparently.
Q What disaster occurred once all the money was gone?
A Famine struck.
Q What strange thoughts tortured the young man?
A Hunger makes me imagine the pig's pods are appetising.
Q Did he come to his senses?
A Oh, yes.
Q To take what course of action did he decide?
A To arise, go home and ask to work for his father.
Q Did he reckon he was worthy to be called a son?
A Oh, no.
Q How far away was the son when his dad began to run?
A A long way off.
Q With what gifts did his father shower him?
A With kisses, a coat, shoes, a ring and a fatted calf.
Q Who was invited to the celebratory party?
A Oh, everyone.
Q What errors had the father made about the son?
A Thought him dead or lost when he was alive and found.

Deck of cards*   _pastiche_

The Sergeant asked: 'Why did you bring a pack of cards to church parade? You should bring a Bible or a prayer book…'

The soldier replied 'Sergeant, these cards tell me all I need to know about the parable of the lost son.'

'Explain yourself, soldier, or you'll be on a charge.'

'Well, the **Ace** reminds me that there was just one father who let his son go and waited for him to return. The **deuce** stands for the two brothers; one apparently faithful, but driven by legalism; the other foolish and wanton, but ultimately repentant and humble. When I see the **trey**, it speaks of the number of pigs in the sty, eating their pods, which the boy envied. The **four** makes me consider the gifts the boy received: a coat, a ring and two sandals.

'The **five** counts up the elements of the way he lived, with parties, gambling, drinking, feasting and wasting.

'Now, then, the **six** shows the great distance the boy travelled to Dissipation City; it was six days' journey from his farm to the casino. And the **seven** is a reminder of the number of gold coins the father gave to the boy right at the start, which he spend in abandon. Turning to the **eight**, this jogs my memory of the boy coming to his senses, as he considered how his father's men **ate** well while he was starving. The **nine** represents the hours it took to roast the fatted calf upon a spit, in celebration that the boy was no longer lost nor dead, but found and alive.

'Now, the **ten** is a wonderfully rich and powerful _aide-mémoire_, Sergeant.

214

'A **tense** boy with extensive potential hastened to bartenders and attentive ostentatious women (verboten); later was discontent he'd nearly eaten the rotten pigfood. Gains enlightenment from the omnipotent One; he's penitent, softening his heart; chastened, tentatively asks his dad for tenure; but the old man doesn't listen, and gives him calf that's fattened & tenderised.

'**Jack** behaved like a knave. The **Queen**'s Head is the name of the hotel and casino where the boy stayed. And the **King** reminds me of the King of kings, the Lord Jesus himself, who told this parable. The **Joker**'s wild, like the boy's living.

'The **thirteen tricks** represent the days the boy took to return home, since he was starving and exhausted.

'There are **three hundred and sixty five pips** on the cards[†] – they remind me that God loves us each day of the year, no matter what we're doing, and he longs for us to return to him.

'And there are **four suits**, and they also speak to me: **Clubs** are where the boy partied; **Diamonds** he gave to those wanton women; **Hearts** helps me recall the father's deep love for his son; and **Spades** are what he and the hired men used to till the soil when he returned to his father's house.

'Perhaps best of all is that there are **fifty two cards** in this pack, and that reminds me of how to find the passage when I do have a Bible or New Testament with me, Sergeant; for the passage is found in the third gospel, in chapter fifteen, from verses eleven to twenty-three, and when I add up those numbers, it comes, of course, to fifty two.

'So, you see, Sergeant, this pack of cards teaches me about the lost son, and how he was welcomed when he repented, humbled himself and returned to his father's house.'

And the Sergeant turned away with a tear brimming in his eye.

I know, for I was that Sergeant.

* Original poem credited to **Mary Bacon** in 1762; recorded by **T Texas Tyler** (1948) and achieved No 2 in the US Country chart. Recorded again in 1959 by **Wink Martindale**, reaching No 1 in the US; and also recorded by **Max Bygraves,** peaking at No 13 in the UK † no there aren't. But when you count one for an Ace, then face values for cards worth two to ten, reckon (reasonably) eleven for Jacks, twelve for Queens and thirteen for Kings, then this makes 364. So add in one more for a Joker

Middle E   *alphabet games*
only words with the middle letter e

Jew (evangelical carpenter) expresses entrepreneurial fathering. Moneyed chequebooks. Bequeaths posterity benefit... consented, inherit. Exchequer: budgetary ampleness! 'Ben, cheerio!'

Foreign taverns' misbehave: inexpedient redheaded sweater-girl chambermaid (Suzette) immodesties; wickedest jezebel masseuses; housemaid hareems sex horseplay; gentlewomen centerfolds; hotheaded hostesses' jitterbug knaveries; actresses' pharmaceuticals experimentation.

Befriending ungentlemanlike Chippendale mountebanks squanderingly – excitedness, lecheries, lotteries, whoredoms, disrespectfully spend. Roulette's exaggerated greed.

Suddenlys: emergencies, utterly universal flyweight dietetics depletion; intolerable sadnesses. Comprehensively, starvelings enfeebled.

Whereupon hungering anxieties.

Diets? Meh! Obese epidermis? Needy dread!

Piggeries. Streaky dregs vexedly feeds frighteningly, disconcertingly dangerous, bacterial, unappealing cankerous tuckerbox (congealed, hateful, scavenged ulcered, hideous, displeasing, abscessed, valueless, festering, secreting, shriveling, putrefied, liquefied, mildewing, toxemic moldering slipperiest, rottenest, untreated eczemas).

Controversially, Ned feels neglected; digests weeds? Tasteless?

Reveler repents. Converted!

Pondering, perceives awakening. Prayerful beseecher confesses ashamedness. Reverse! Relieving reflected regretful (belatedness!) deliberated denouements. Self-respect, allegro!

Ponderosa: depressed desperado schlepped itinerant mileage; traversed residential driveways, groveling. Stammerings... parent's preempt, eagerly observe, meets (gateway agileness); greeted; squeeze-envelop! Favoredness, Presbyterianism.

Greet: 'Attirements! Get fez, labeled threads, suede jacketing, velveteen sleeves, flannelette gusseting/hem, cheesecloth turtlenecks, whalebone corseting! Shoeing, fasteners; bejewel!'

Offered dress draperies, jewelry memento, redeeming be-jewelings.

'Sentimentally, sympathetically, bracelets. Caterer!'

Guest banqueteers' spreads. Catered: Bierkellers goldenest applejack keg, stein beers, pilseners, Madeira (pitcherfuls!), whiskey-sour, tea, decaffeinated espressos. Furthermore, eviscerated widened fattedcalf – beefeater – fiery flesh (tinderbox oven's incinerator) saucepans' pea casserole.

Chef's oxheart, tenderize-steak stews (beefy!), steer/suets foreleg platesful, sliceable filleting spareribs, sheep, skewering geese, cockerels, barbecued whitefish, prairie-oyster, whelk, mackerels, fresh chitterling, green groceries, tureens, poached-eggs.

Furthermore: crepe, homogenized skimmed-milk, butterfat, pepperoni/cress baguettes, cranberries blueberries/raspberries (sweeter!), snowberries (conserves); jawbreaker, bread, beets, leeks, ghees, seeds, wheat sheaf.

Tablesful: butternut omelettes, swede juliennes, tangerine preserves, chewy caramelised sweet Chelsea-buns, cheesecakes, cereals, mincemeat, cream.

Cheeseboard: Roquefort; cheeses.

Marvelous porcelain/earthenware coffeepot; cutleries, kitchenware. Clarinettist's orchestra sweetly congregates; great instrumentalist; tuneful boleros, tuxedos.

Addressed plebeians: 'Cheer! Resplendent acknowledgments! Funeral? Bereave? Biers? Graveyard? Decease? Grieved… Deathlessness! Atonement! Believing blessedness! Aliveness! Amens! QED, yea!'

Typefaces   *key words*
plus additional typographical terms
Albert used to have a big farm.

Dominic's demanding request was **bold**, and he made it while having his **supper.**

'**Case** in point; give me my inheritance.' Father, looking in the **book, man**aged to find liquid assets and gave them to him.

What did this lad leave? A farm was abandoned by the prodi**gal; leys** were also among the countryside items he forsook. He went to Dissipation City, where the buildings were ornate, if not a little **goudy (old style)**, or what some might call **chic. A go**dly temple had corinthian **capitals.**

Friends such as **Lucida Bright** and **Aldus** plus **Clare 'n' Don** and **Korinna** joined him for a weekend of fish and chips, mushy peas and vine**gar; a Mond**ay of cake and a Tuesday-Friday of fine steak, seafood and caviar.

He asked one of the rather immoral girls 'Tuli**p, I can**'t recall if you are the sort that prefers polished floorboards or carpeting.'

The **bembo** replied 'Neither, I'm the **Lino type.**'

There was also a ritual associated with honouring **chancery** furniture.

Mary asked 'Can you tyre-change in a hurry?' Said **Sam 'Er, I can Ty…'** **Pew rite** respectful, clearly.

Dominic was planning to get himself a **souvenir** but then his cash ran out and a famine struck.

He took a job tending pigs in an ill-maintained sty. 'This place could do with redecorating – someone should take care of **it. A lic**k of paint would work wonders.'

Such was his terrible starvation, he went down with kwashior**kor in nas**ty doses. The pigs ate pods that were mouldy and some other forms of **plant (in** various states of de**compositing**). He could not have felt **lower.**

Caseous smells (scent of cheese) were not pleasant. The realisation that he was envying the pigs came with considerable **impact** – it was **news.** '**Go, thick**head, and ask for a job!' he told himself. His hunger had been **leading** him into temptation.

He got up, determined to give his father a surprise. *It'll be magic, **as long as I'm humble,*** he thought. 'Don't know how to address you formally, **Pa. Latin?** Oh, that's ridiculous, and reflective of olden **times. New romans** don't use that! Perhaps I should send a letter, but I have no **courier**. I'm no longer worthy to be called a son.'

Meanwhile, the boy's father stood on the high part of the house, watching, dressed, in his wis**dom, casual**ly. He knew he shouldn't be continually hoping for his boy to return. 'The conclusion that is log**ical is to** accept he's dead...' His feelings were gloomy (yet then he saw the lad coming through the **mist), ra**llied and rose towards glee.

'My boy, you're a **star! I** always hoped you'd return. I wanted to send you to study and had made a list: a) the Conservatoire de Paris (you could learn verbs like e**tre); b) UCH, et**c!'

He presented **symbols** of welcome: a coat, some shoes, and a ring with an in**scrip**tion.

'Oh Dad, thanks for the **rock. Well,** I could eat a horse...'

'We could roast the calf! And eat lots of things... soybean cake? No, let's go for something rare and avian... I think it would be rude to bulk it out with to**fu. Turac**u might be less politically correct...'

His father sat in the marquee, keen to test the speaker system, and equally eager to send correctly-addressed invitations.

'Right... Jeremy, RM, Susan, JKP Bullion, **Fran... KL Ingot... H... I** cannot remember, son, so tell me Ingrid Smith's full initials, through the inter**com.' 'I.C.S.' ans**wered the boy. 'I always thought one of her middle names was Brenda, so I was in danger of inclu**ding B at s**ome stage...'

'Let's get a barrel of beer. We can pay the **Cooper. Black** olives, and a big tuna - and don't forget to remove the bones, fins and **gills!' Ans**wers came in the affirmative, so the fish dish was sure to be perfect. 'We'll have peaches with **condensed** milk, a chocolate **fount**ain, toast with marmalade (I prefer **Old English**) and perhaps a little game bird – although I have always been pro-grouse and somewhat **anti-qua**il...'

'Ladies and gentlemen: I'd even gone so far as to write letters to our Solicitor and the Undertaker (although I'm not sure why I wrote to the Animal Doctor!) – anyway, here they are in the sat**chel – Vet?... I can** only mean I reckoned him dead. He's my son, so I don't have to a**dopt – I'm a**lready his dad! Let all who live and breathe within the **univers**e sing praises!'

Key: type face (font); *terms*
Albertus; *bold; upper case (capitals);* Bookman; *Galleys (type columns pre-layout);* Goudy old style; Chicago; *capitals;* Lucida Bright; *Aldus (Manutius 1449-1515, 'father of printing');* Clarendon; Korinna; Garamond; *pica (unit of measurement);* Bembo; *linotype (typesetting machine);* Chancery; American Typewriter; Souvenir; *italic;* Korinna; Plantin; *compositing (the craft of setting type); lower case;* Impact; News Gothic; *leading (the space between lines of type);* Eras; Caslon; Palatino *(face in which this book is set);* Times New Roman; Courier; Dom Casual; Calisto; Mistral; Arial; Trebuchet; Symbol; Script; Rockwell; Futura; Franklin Gothic; Comic Sans; Dingbats; Cooper Black Gill Sans; *condensed (type of reduced width); fount (original spelling, pronounced 'font' – type cast in liquid lead);* Old English; Antiqua; Helvetica; Optima; Univers

Qwerty   *alphabet games*

keyboard-sequence dictates initials
order QWERTYUIOP ASDFGHJKL ZXCVBNM

'Quite well-off economically,' replied the young upstart.

Inheritance openly paraded around select Dissipationville fun-spots. Gross hedonism, jaunts, kissing, laughter... zounds! X-rated cavorting, very bad.

No more quids: wild excessiveness reverts to yawning uncomfortableness (internal); opulence prematurely abated. Son deserted; feeds grim-hog.

Joyless kibbutz life. Zoom! Xenophobia consumes venously. 'Back now! My quiescent work establish repentantly.'

Toils young upstart, in open poverty and some distress.

'Father, give hireling job...'

Kaftan; loafers; zillion x's cover voyaging boy.

'Nice meat; quail, with eggs. Respect to Yahweh!'

Lost in Austen   *key words*

many references to Pride & Prejudice

It is a truth universally acknowledged that a single man in possession of a good fortune must certainly have expressed his want to his father.

Far from vexing his son, Papa took compassion upon his request, and the lad left in a chaise and four.

He was young, wonderfully handsome, and in part, marvelously agreeable, yet to a different extent, quite one of the silliest boys in the county.

He met Jane, Elizabeth, Mary, Kitty and Lydia: sisters in whom there was little charm and no commitment, dear

reader, yet he kept a pack of foxhounds, and drank a bottle of wine each day. His wit flowed along – he had never been met with so much attention in the whole course of his life; yet he would by no means suspend any pleasure. Such perseverance in wilful self-deception! He considered himself untouchable by disaster, like the alpha lion of a pride.

Sad to say, presently his cash was gone; sadder still, famine struck without prejudice.

No more than a fortnight later, the lad sat among five pigs, grunting and snorting as they rooted among whisened pods. He was shocked to find himself envying that they ate freely; he was twice shocked that he envied the content of their lunch pail. He found he could not solace his wretchedness; one might guess the subject of his reverie.

He came to his senses, and realised his father's hired men ate well, so he decided to lay down his pride, to return and to ask for employment; he realised he was no longer worthy to be called son.

The evening was spent conjecturing when he would return to his father's farm, and determining if he would consume the pigs' dinner.

He rambled about, in the hope of being at home again in a day or two or perhaps a little more, but while he was still a long way off, his father saw him approach on foot; he ran gaily to his son, rejoicing.

The boy was welcomed home very cordially by his father, who rang the bell to call for Hill, one of the servants.

'Quick sharp, now! Fetch a coat, shoes, and kill the fatted calf – yes, the LongHourne. Invite the villagers, and oh, let there be gleeful dancing in the ballroom!' And he gave him a fine gold ring.

Happy all his paternal feelings were that day. 'I bare my young son no ill will, and furthermore I resent not his behaviour as any affront. We thought him dead, but he is alive. His return has brought me joy, and I wish him all joy henceforth.'

And what ensued?

Well, dear reader, I leave it to yourself to determine.

Threnodials   *alphabet game*
using only A D E H I L N O R S & T

Intro: the dad's stash raided, his son sailed north. Soon he's lathered and trashed at the hotel.

Ladies/harlots: Anne, Delia, Esther, Hannah, Iris, Leanne, Nadine, Odette, Rhiannon, Stella and Tina. Also Thora, Heather, Rhona, Eileen, Noelle, Orla, Dinah, Irene, Adrienne, Lisa and Sandie. Hosts/Loiterers: Adrian, Donald, Eddie, Heston, Ian, Lennie, Neal, Ollie, Rod, Shane and Tal. Also Theodore, Harold, Randall, Ethelred, Nathan, Otis, Darren, Israel, Alistair, Larson and Silas.

No dosh... short rations... all lots thinner: hostile ordeals.

Lardiest eaters/snorters are near drains. All hail senses as son realises details: hired hands are diners.

I'll arise and tell Dad 'Laird: I - not a son...' So he trailed.

He's still distant as Dad ran (honest!) o'er the lea. Held, shoes, held, dhoti, held, O on hand...

Ale, deli, eel, hot Israeli-rare loin 'n' onions, radishes, sardines-on-toast. Retsina, ales.

Address: 'Son died; air inhaler! Son lost; retains, on throne! Holiest Lord is not denied!'

30-minute lostness   *style*
chef Jamie Oliver

Right guys, I wanna show you a thing about biscuits and baking and this delicious, buttery, soft, crumbling, exciting, tasty, zingy, pukka fortune cookie. So I wanna try to help you to get your head around whatever you wanna have as a biscuit, and you can change it, tweak it, you can fiddle with it, give it the old jiggle jaggle, you can vary it, and then you can get your face outside it. Yeah! You need the normal 30-minute things: boiling kettle, hotplate on full whack, oven on 200°C, chopping board and knives ready... So, let's just start with this beautiful, beautiful basic mix.

29:59 I'm using Dad's Cash as the main part of it, and just mixing it like this. Use any money you like – inheritance, legacy, lottery winnings, bag of swag from a bank robbery – whatever.

27:18 Always use your fingers when it comes to moolah, and that way you'll feel rich and unctuous and kind and wealthy. And event-ually, look, see, it all quickly melts away and there's nothing left, which is exactly what happens when you treat it just like this (sucks finger) ooh, yes. If you think you can't, then think again!

20:12 Now that's gone, let's just check in the fridge and the oven and on my window ledge and in this jar of sugar with a vanilla pod in it and in this watermelon incessantly injected with flavour and anyway you'll find that's all gone too rustic and it's just about friends and going away and not restaurant style any longer.

See what I mean? Naked? No way! It's not me, it's the food!

17:34 Yeah, right, the next thing I want to get your tastebuds zinging about is a blend of herbs and spices and sort of pods and these lovely little bits of tasty mould and this green liquid – nice colour happening here – I'm confident it'll get you all (smack lips); give it a proper old flick about. If you ain't never eaten this before, take it from me; you're going to absolutely love it! Have a go!

Take your side of pork and whack it on the board like this, and then season it with envy – look, like this, from a height to make sure it's spread evenly, because you don't want great bunches of tasty green mould all in one lump – just rub it into the skin and get the flavours going in there (grunt of exertion). Yeah, get them right in there! Lovely!

13:25 Herbs are so funky, so rock and roll. Use scrunched-up mint, or a handful of basil, (chuck it in the mortar and mullah it to a right mush) or a big wodge of dill, whatever takes your fancy, long as it's a good 'un. Something peppery... What about some half-rotted pods? Give 'em a go, sweetheart! Why not? Bash 'em up!

11:02 But then you might want to stop and come to your senses and decide 'Nah, what I really fancy is some good old fashioned roast beef with attitude, on at full whack, lovely with horseradish; and some piping, fluffy, crispy, crunchy roast spud; light, melting, delicious Yorkies and look! – pints of thick, steaming, unctuous, beautiful, shiny gravy (a proper geezer's gravy).

And some veg on the side, like broccoli or carrots – baby carrots – and cauli or leeks or maybe parsnips or baby corns or lovely crunchy red cabbage or just something simple like fresh peas or mange tous.' Whatever...

Get it all clanking away. Eating that's good, as if you were one of your dad's hired men.

8:51 Slam it in the oven from a long way off, and after a while, come running and let it rest before you give a good coating of the marinade (not just a kiss – slap it on!). You don't want to over-cook it or it'll be like shoeleather, but serve it piled up nice and high – use one of these rings to help you build a decent stack.

Keep it really exciting, keep it light, keep it tangy and zingy and loads of pizzazz. Slap on coat after coat of its own juices and it'll be warm, soft, juicy and numptious in the middle.

4.07 And you want gravy packed with flavour, so use a thick veg soup or a hefty stock cube in half the usual amount of water. Reduce it down to about a third. Be inventive – make it your own, and get your signature all over it.

3.28 And when you get home, you know you're no longer worthy to be a pukka son, so you get a job. Invite your friends to come to the table and celebrate! Yeah, the cow is dead, but treated like this, it'll come alive! It's all so *good*!

00.01 Done. Most cushty. Brill-yant!

Cracked screen/
dodgy keys *alphabet games*
inspired by Sophie Biggs' dropped phone and the memory of a laptop with reluctant keys, this is a kind of lipgram avoiding the letters l, o, s, & t

A chap demanded currency; happy when given by Dad.

He ended up near a big urban area, and began a game/drink/dance by which much funding reduced; zip remained.

220

Famine happened and everyman hungered.

Making a piggy-career, he yearned; came near chewing pig dinner, when – zap! Idea! He decided 'I can make my way, arrive by Dad Farm and make a prayer – hire me?'

Dad eyed him and ran, embracing (cheek by cheek), gave ring, and added. 'Everyman may have barbeque beef! Finding him may have been hard and he may have been dead... deny! He had been find'ed and may endure!'

I almost despaired of this when I tried the first sentence: *The second-born son spoke to his father 'Please let me take the monetary inheritance which will be bequested to me, now.'* Most words were unavailable. Same goes for *town/city/dissipation /wasted/pod*, plus *to his senses*, most of *a long way off* and all of *forgiveness, restoration, celebrate* and *found*. But with *perseverance* and a *thesaurus*, I got there

Curriculum Vitae/
application *style*

seeking a job
Post Applied For:
Farm Labourer, general duties
Name:
Younger Son Certainman
DoB:
2nd Year of Herod Antipas
Current Address:
Celebration Farm (formerly known as Tedium Farm), Quietsville, Israel
Education:
HA7-14* Homeschooled by parents
Employment:
HA15-22 Raised to work in the family farming business.

Gained experience as a full-time labourer and general worker around the farm, with special responsibility for hayricks and cereal crops, and specialist machinery such as winnowing fork and threshing floor; plus fattening the calf.

Reason for leaving: Became independently wealthy
HA22-23 Several months' rest and relaxation; during this time I was gaining relational and financial experience; considerable networking and personal development. This came to an abrupt end due to wildness; coincided with local famine conditions
HA23 Brief temporary post with *Double-Underlined Porkers Ltd*, Lower Dissipationsville.

Responsibilities: management of pigs; including nutrition and husbandry of same. Task allowed me to demonstrate my ability to work unsupervised.

Reason for leaving: came to senses
Personal statement:
I have realised that I have been foolish, but this experience will stand me in good stead going forward. I desire to work on the farm again.

I am no longer worthy to be called your son. I was starving, having wasted the inheritance you gave me, yet your hired men eat well. God spoke to me in the sty. I beg your mercy.

Anticipated salary:
I am hugely grateful for the coat, sandals and for the ring. But daily meals will suffice. Thank you also for the roast beef dinner on day one, and for the symbolic family jewellery, the significance of which I'd like to discuss, perhaps at my annual review.
Hobbies/Interests
Travel, orienteering, fine dining, theatre; domestic budgeting

*7th-14th years of King Herod Antipas

Periodigal table of elements *style*

verse number, content, symbols spell plot sequence, element name

Key:

Verse
Story
Sym
Element

12 Ask **I** Handout								
12 Cash **E** Brasso	12 Now **Ri** Givium							
13 Party **Pa** Shindig	13 Feast **T** Dine							
14 Rumble **In** Growla	14 Long **Ep** Porcine	15 Envy **Ig** Snoutin	15 Shame **Ss** Evnyin	16 Need **To** Void	16 No **Ma** Intestine	16 One **C** Gutz	16 Gave **Hf** Slimie	16 Him **Il** Mouldie
18 Real **En** Smart	18 Isation **Se** Noshun	18 He'd **Sh** Shame	18 Been **U** Headhung	20 Foolish **Mb** Lowli	20 Reflect **Le** Sobrin	20 Father's **Re** Arizen	20 Hired **Tu** Settoff	20 Men **Rn** Jernie
20 Chance **As** Kindly	20 To **Si** Empathy		20 Speak **On** Softart	20 OrSay **Ru** Trottin	20 Sorry **Ns** Joggine	21 Or **Un** Noson	21 Suggest **Wo** Unfitt	21 Hire **Rt** Ignoblium
22 Zing **Ng** Surprisin	22 Coat **If** Treat		22 Shoes **Ts** Pairashus	23 Ring **C** Gold	23 Kill **Al** Bovine	23 Roast **F** Scorcha	24 Eat **H** Scoffin	24 Speech **Ew** Podium

								12 Dad **Nh** Givium
			12 No **Ta** Wealth	12 Delay **N** Wonga	12 Demand **Ce** Foldinium	13 Spend **D** Shell	13 Wild **Is** Untame	13 Living **Si** Expens
			13 Fake **Io** Hollow	14 Friends **Nb** Romania	14 Games **Ro** Silicon	14 Loss **Ke** Spentium	14 Empty **Fa** Appetite	14 Tummy **M** Vacancy
16 Any **Li** Yukki	16 Thing **N** Bacterium	16 Unclean **Gp** Legume	17 Non **Od** Peace	17 Kosher **Sc** Flash	17 The **A** Lightbulb	17 Lord **M** Inspirium	17 Spoke **Et** Inkling	17 Idea **Os** Plannin
20 Eat **L** Distans	20 Well **O** Yonda	20 Ishall **Ng** Toilin	20 Arise **W** Uphill	20 And **Ay** Fargo	20 Confess **Of** Miles	20 My **F** Away	20 Sin **Co** Tenda	20 No **Mp** Grays
21 Due **H** Repute	21 To **Ym** Kurteus	21 Father's **Ak** Offa	21 Joy **Em** Emploi	21 Love **Ea** Busium	21 Hugs **H** Servin	21 Enthu **Ir** Worka	21 Siasm **Ed** Staff	21 Ama **Ma** Ramblin
24 Guests **As** Bonbon	24 Yes **D** Agreein	24 No **Ea** Mortia	24 Longer **Dn** Hitherto	24 Lost **Ow** Strayd	24 But **L** Hoorah	24 Found **I** Glory	24 Praise **Ve** Hallel	24 God **S** Ooyah

Bertie Wooster *pastiche*

a pale but deeply respectful shadow of PG Wodehouse's creation

'Pater, may I speak frankly?'

'There's no other way I would have it, Edward, my boy.'

'Quite so, but what I have to say could possibly wound you.'

'Allow me to be the judge of that.'

'Right–ho. Well, the dashed truth is that all this arable-land-husbandry shenanigans has become a terrible yawn, don't you know? I've half a mind to hang it all and slope orf.'

'Really?'

'Trouble is, I haven't a single brass farthing to my name.'

'Yes.'

We both remained silent. I was quiet because I was trying to think of a way to phrase what I wanted to ask him, and Pater was hushed, I suppose, because there was nothing in what I had said so far that required a reply; nor indeed (when I reflected upon my words) a great deal that was capable of comprehension.

Just then, fortunately, Neeves, the hired man, oiled into the room like a crystal decanter on castors, bearing a silver tray on which stood a cocktail glass containing pink gin with a twist.

'Ripping, Neeves,' I said.

He tilted his head respectfully. 'Sir.'

I pushed the fluid over my larynx, and thus fortified, I tried another run-up at the Pater. 'So, the question is one of funds, and my lack thereof.'

'Ah.'

'And your evident surfeit in that department, old thing.'

'Oh?'

'I am somewhat partial to the idea that we consider the possibility of some balance-redressing in this matter. What do you say?'

Pater, not to put too fine a point on it, fudged. 'H'mm. Well, I think I would, almost certainly, have some comment to make, concurring or otherwise (or offering a different viewpoint) if I could, even for the briefest of moments, be one who may be accurately described as the kind of cove who is comprehending that of which you speak.'

'So you're not offended?'

'Why, have you insulted me?'

'May it never be, Pater!'

I took another sip, musing on how to make it any clearer. Happily, Neeves came to my rescue, not for the first time.

'I believe, sir,' he explained with patience, 'what young Master Waster is attempting to communicate is that he wishes to procure from your not insubstantial means some of the wherewithal to which he would, not to overstate the matter, be entitled, should the very worst-case scenario pertain, for example: respiratory system impairment-wise.'

He really is quite heavy going at times, is Neeves. But somehow the old boy latched on.

'His inheritance?'

'Indeed, sir.'

'It is a most astonishing request, but I shall see what can be done. I shall call Honkers Lloyd-West at the bank first thing and require of him to make the necessary arrangements.'

'Top hole!' I exclaimed.

Next morning, one was soon enjoying the new, hugely pleasing sensation of a potently distended wallet pressing firmly against one's thigh as it altered dramatically the direction and shape of the line of the razor-sharp, perfect Corby-pressed crease in the well-tailored upper trouser of yours truly, Bertie Waster. So much so, I bounded with customary grace and renewed gusto into the courtyard and got myself down into town somewhat sharpish in the faithful old Daimler.

Maisy Jink-Pottle and Maureen Gussett (both, I'd say, rather easy on the eye, what!) were more than ready to aid and abet the dispersal of some of the small change.

Meanwhile, steeling themselves magnificently were K D'Orcy *Jahlsberg* Cheesehampton, Wexford StJohn Moreton-Symes and Pongo Frattleworth III, as they embarked tirelessly upon the more labour-intensive but proportionately rewarding task of turning a considerable number of high calibre bank notes into so much pocket-fluff.

We gambled, drank, spent and consumed deep into the night for several weeks, after which it discovered I was – dash it all – on my uppers. Of course Pongo, Maisy, Jahlsberg, Wexford and little Mo all made themselves scarce at top pace.

'What a rotten bit of luck,' I thought, as the country was about to go into something of a decline, and it was annoyingly necessary for me to become engaged by a keeper of livestock, including Empress of Blandings – but no wealthy dowager she. Far from it, what? Fortunately, the chap had a vacancy in the bookkeeping department, so at least I could stay indoors.

Never in all my puff had I ever done a day's toil, so I sat at the tall accounting desk, staring blankly at the columns of figures and wondered what they all meant. I had not the foggiest what Price Index (Global Strategy) was, and I was completely

in the dark about the mouldy old Purchase Order Delivery Sheets.

I have to confess I spent a few minutes' fruitless thought considering purchases, and envied those who could seamlessly fiddle with the old numericals.

Then something struck me with all the force of a large size tennis raquet swung exuberantly but injudiciously into a fellow's unexpecting fizzog. 'Why not, old Bertster, think ye of Neeves? He butles his way noiselessly about the old pile and gets his lunch thrown in. I could trundle back to Pater Mansions and see if the old boy will set me pottering among the greenhouses or invite me to chuck hay around the stables for half an hour, and all that how d'you do.'

This was a flawless, wizard wheeze, so off I trotted.

It was a fair old step, and, to tell the truth, I was ready for a firmly revitalising snifter and a slice or two of Madeira cake by the time I stumbled into the requisite county.

I'd had the chance to concoct a plausible greeting, which was along the lines of *Pater, old thing, sadly the funds have somehow dwindled. So I'll have something of a go at shoving a lawnmower up and down a bit in exchange for a seat near the fire when the old toasting forks come out, and you'll probably want to sharpen your pencil to make sure you adequately reline my back pocket, what?* Nothing could possibly go wrong.

However, as I got within sight (still a long way orf) I saw Pater come – well, running. You could have floored me with an individual component of a starling's plumage.

I waited for him and prepared myself to render my speech.

But chance had I none.

'Edward!,' he cried, 'you are far from... and you're not... but we all thought... yet it's not true...!' He couldn't have been more obtuse if he'd been attempting to fib. But he was clearly failing to disguise his pleasure at seeing me, even though my clothes were in a state, not to mention the dreadfully unpolished and scuffed condition of the old loafers, don't you know?

Neeves arrived soon afterwards, but Pater sent him straight back to the pile with a list of duties. 'Fetch a smoking jacket, and my family jewellery box. There's a ring in there I want to give him. Oh, and see if you can rustle up a tin of Cherry Blossom and give his footwear a bit of a buffing.'

'Yes, sir. May I say, it is most satisfactory to see young Mister Waster again, sir?'

'Yes, yes, never mind all that gushing, Neeves. What's important now is that Mrs Bridges below stairs hears about it, and sets to with the roast beef and horseradish. Tell her we have one-hundred and fifty for dinner tonight!'

'One hundred and fifty, sir?'

'Yes, yes.'

'Then it may be necessary to send for some additional gravy browning, sir, as I know we opened the last tin only on Wednesday.' Neeves misses the point, characteristically.

Later on, a vast crowd of locals gathered somewhat greedily around the groaning high table in the ballroom, quaffing & digesting at a prodigious rate. Pater asked Neeves to call for quiet, so that he could address them with a few words he considered well-chosen.

'My Lords, ladies and gentlemen, pray silence for your host.' The chatter and rattle subsided respectfully, as they braced themselves for a dull speech.

'We all thought my son Edward had curled his toes. But it was not so. Yes, he'd drifted orf, but now he's here, don't you know, healthy, clothed and in his right mind. Raise your glasses!' They were not in the least bit well-chosen, after all.

Neeves smiled quietly to himself.

Reverse *style*

acknowledging Kurt Vonnegut's
Slaughterhouse-5 *and*
Martin Amis' Time's Arrow

They praised God and celebrated, as streamers leaped from the ground up, up and down (sucking wisps of smoke and noise) into neatly-rolled packages. Meanwhile, arrows accelerated from the sky, flights first, coming to rest with precision upon outstretched bows, ready to be placed deftly into quivers.

'He is alive, yet was dead; my son is found but was lost!'

Villagers crowded around trestle tables, filling crumb-strewn plates and unwashed bowls with pies, salads, punch and all manner of goodies, grabbing handfuls of food from their throats until the spread was complete. They went home and sent their invitations to the farmer.

The wood drew in sparks and flames as the carcass absorbed hissing fat; charred flesh slowly grew pink and cold, until the spit was removed from the calf. Blood flowed freely from the mud, up her legs and chest, over the cowman's arm and into Daisy's arteries as a knife sealed the gash in her throat and she sprang, vitalized, to her hooves; she came waddling, reversing into her stall.

The father took a ring from the boy's finger, and replaced his suede sneakers with old, broken, worn-out sandals; he helped his son out of a fine coat, giving him instead rags. Finally he let go of the lad and stepped away with a smile as salt water trickled up his face into his eyes. Pa ran backwards to the house and up to the roof, from where he could see his son, who had withdrawn some distance (he was a long way off).

The boy began to worry. 'I'll ask to be a man that is hired, as to be his son I am no longer worthy,' he said to himself, and then planned what to say when he met his father. He retreated several miles, eventually climbing backwards over a gate, sitting down in the pigsty and allowing darkness to fill his mind. He envied the pigs their activity of vomiting pods into the trough.

Over several days, as other men brought buckets (in which they skillfully caught the pods when the vegetables leapt heavenward), the boy observed that those pods gradually improved in quality, growing less diseased and wizened. The boy later became less familiar with the pigs and spoke to their owner, agreeing a price for the opportunity to walk away.

The famine lost its grip as national wealth increased. The boy's feeling of emptiness diminished as he went from place to place upchucking food and wine, and was given money by shopkeepers and friends, and by waiters and restaurateurs in exchange for filling plates with fine dinners and cups with quality wine.

He also watched showgirls dressing themselves in time to odd-sounding music. He collected large amounts of gambling chips by forgetting in which slot the little ball had started, prior to whizzing around the wheel several times, and being expertly caught by the croupier, upon which all the players took their winnings (stacks of chips) from the felt surface.

The son left the city and went home, where he gave a great deal of money to his father.

'My inheritance I want,' said he. He grew younger and younger, restoring stalks of full-grown corn to the fields with his sythe, taking months to withdraw bucketfuls of water from them, until finally catching handfuls of seed as it flew from furrows. These grooves in the ground were later skillfully folded back into a smooth surface, as workers reversed across the fields towing ploughs pushed by oxen (untilling). This annual activity continued until the boy was young enough to run from a hoop or to still a spinning top.

Much later, his severed umbilical cord was reattached with a blur of blood and a knife, and he squeezed himself feet-first and breathless into his mother's womb. Fewer than two years later, his brother did the same.

Aporia *style*
indecision or uncertainty (or maybe not)
DAD I don't know if I should give him the cash. He might take it and leave me here without liquid assets and in financial distress. I doubt I'll be able to pay my bills. And he might go and get himself into trouble. What if he spends it all? He may waste it quickly and then find that life is hard. I'm

starting to wonder if I taught him well and brought him up properly, as he ought to have found out that life is tougher out there than it has been for him while he's been here. I fear I may not have trained him wisely. Perhaps I did something wrong that provoked him to come to me, effectively wishing me prematurely dead, and demanding his inheritance.

SON Should I go today? I could stay wherever I like, once I have the cash! Now I need to decide where to go. All the way to Dissipation City? I could stay in an hotel, or a guest house. 'Eat all you can' deal or full á la carte? It's difficult to decide which of these girls I prefer. Or do I really need to make a choice, as all three seem willing...? I can place a bet on every horse in the race, and on each number at the roulette table. These chums may or may not like me for who I am, or perhaps just for my money. I'm having so much fun that I'm not sure I am all that bothered.

The economy, driven by agriculture, will perhaps let us all down. My friends seem to have let me down, for some reason, and probably everyone is as hungry as I.

Perhaps these unclean animals are not so bad... Yet they are practically starving, too, I think. Their food is probably unfit for consumption, and yet, strangely, I have been considering gnawing at the diseased pods myself, so great is this feeling within which may be hunger and may be worse than that – I just can't decide.

GOD *Oh, for how long will you run from the love of your father? For many days you have teetered on the brink of starvation, while unrelated farmhands toil at your father's behest and eat joyfully every day at his table. Are you so filled with pride that you cannot return? Arise! Arise and return! Arise right now and seek his forgiveness!*

SON Leaving the pig farm was perhaps the best decision, but this road is hard and the end will be humbling. How can I address the old man, whose early death I effectively wished upon him? I might say 'I am so foolish,' or I might say 'I am not worthy to be called your son.' But I will probably finish with 'please make me one of your hired men.' I think. Unless he throws me out of the village, which he has every right to do, and may very well feel that way inclined.

DAD Could today be the day I stop waiting and hoping and be the day I decide to get on with the hard life here on the farm? I shall probably remain on the roof for the morning, and then join the hired men working in the field over here (or perhaps the field over there instead), unless I go and examine the calf we've been foolishly giving extra portions of grain, when the famine we hear reported may be coming our way and so we should probably be husbanding our meagre resources more pessimistically. But who's that on the distant horizon? Not my son. Or... Does he walk like that? Only if shoes were practically falling off his feet ... But then it might be. It's hard to know for certain. Oh, if only I could be sure!

SON Who's this chump running wildly? Dad wouldn't be so undignified, so it can't be him. Perhaps it's someone coming to send me away, as I feared. But he sounds happy, and he isn't waving a stick... Could it be dad? I think it might be! Yes, I'm almost sure... He's still running, and I think he might be happy...

DAD My son! My son! It's hard to see you in this state, starved, footsore, weary. And are you returning?

SON Father, make me a sort of an hired man, if you will, for I am no longer...

DAD Servants, have we any new shoes in his size? I think there may be some in my wardrobe – please check, and bring brown ones – no, black. No, both, and then he can choose.. And fetch a winter coat for him. One with a lining. No, a waterproof... or perhaps a short jacket. You might look to see if there are any with a hood. And it must have pockets. At least two, plus one on the inside, on the left. No, one inside pocket on each side would be better, probably. Meanwhile, tell Jed (or Nathan, if you can't find Jed, as he may have gone into town for supplies – or Darius, if Nathan's out on top field today, which I think he is, unless he's working with the others who are checking out the threshing machine, I hope, ready for next week's harvest – unless we do it over the weekend, as I'm wondering if it would be better to take advantage of the sunshine, as I think the weather might be about to change – do you think it might change? Although the wind and clouds have dispersed over the last few hours, so perhaps not...) Anyway, get someone – anyone – (well, someone who knows what he's doing, so don't get Joshua or Caleb) to take – oh, or Thaddeus – to take the long sharp knife (it's probably on the kitchen window ledge, unless it's on the shelf by the bags of stud nuts or in the big red tool box – actually I might have left it in the brown one; or perhaps in the scullery because I think Andrea was slicing turnips) and slay the fatted calf, and we should probably set a fire to roast it. Now, son, which finger is best for this family ring? Rejoice, everyone, either inside the farmhouse or here in the yard, for this my son was either lost or dead, yet now he's found and alive! Have some more meat, do. Or vegetables if you prefer. Or not, if you've had sufficient.

Ballad *poetry*

this down-to-earth poetic form is genuinely classical, but quickly starts to sound like Frank Spencer is reciting it, which is not so good

Johnny takes a lot of cash
And spends it with such speed;
Then famine strikes and everyone
Is desp'rately in need.

He takes a job, a-tending pigs –
He longs to eat their pods;
A revelation fills his mind:
(The voice he hears is God's).

I'll go back home and humbly seek
To join them in employ.
(My father's men eat well each day
Although mere hoi polloi)
He's bound to be most furious –
Reprisals will be stated.
My worthiness to be a son
I know I've dissipated.

But while he's still a long way off,
His pa – ignoring scandals –
Full gallop! Gives him coat and ring
And kisses and new sandals.

'Take blades and slit young bovine's
    throat
Spit-roast him round and round;
For this my son – we once thought
    dead
And lost - look, now he's found!'

Aides-memoires (lists) *style*

Inheritance
Bag of cash #1 #2 #4 #5 #6
NB Cashbag #3 all spent on clothes, equipment, journey, deposit re rental accommodation, outlay on casino membership and the first few restaurant and massage parlour bills

'Friends'

Mary	Olivia[†]	Damien
Jethro	Flavia[†]	Laura[††]
Julia[†]	Sharon	Selina
Marcus	Agnetha[†††]	

Pigs
Shortshanks Skinnysides
Trotter Crackling (deceased)
Tailcurl McSnout
   aka Streaky Baconrasher
Snorto de Snufflejaw
   (missing, believed deceased)
Chumpchop Scratching III

Things to remember to say to Pa
- Hallo
- Make me a hired man
- I am no longer worthy
   to be called a son
- Sorry
- Any chance of a coat or shoes?
- How about a bite of dinner, please?

To Do
• Polish ring
• Spit-turning duty
• Send out invites
   Arthur, Sarah & family
   Oscar & sig. other
   Pete & Pauline
   Len, Gwen & family
   Theo + guest
   Stuart & Morag
   Rod, Jane & Freddy
• Write celebratory speech for Pa

Interior monologue *style*
Reflecting James Joyce's Ulysses *and Samuel Beckett's* Malone Dies *inter alia*

Asked P for cash, all in pocket, full. This road to DC, dusty, steep in parts, enjoying myself. Potato I have*. Attractive girl, other girl, jolly fellows, more girls, see show, laugh, drink, eat, gamble, win, lose, lose, experience, girls, another show, new clothes – transfer wad to new pockets; also potato. Gamble, lose, restaurant, tablecloth, drinking, tip, kiss, laughter, new friends, I love this freedom to be generous. Food, show, lots of kissing, nice, gamble lose lose win nice lose big, drink. Oh, wad reduced, it's the same for all of us. All gone, friends also, no girls, no food, although spud is present. Generally, also without. Hungry, rumble, grumble, seek work. Pigs stink, unclean, sick-looking; pods bad, blemished, strangely appealing... Doesn't have to be like this. Father's men (Silas, Lemuel, big Jake – hands, grey tunic, tear in the sleeve, scar – sweating effort, weekly wages-day, 'Thank you, sir, thank you sir', father...) meals, tablecloth, I could go back, ask, he'll be okay, probably, ask to work for him, not a son, not a son, dinner, better than pods, feeling inspired, sensible? best option not worthy to be son they'll call me waster but survival not sure will try go walk tired walk hot sandal flapping hungry coat torn hill walk someone running chase me away? shouts angry or... why would Pa run? Pleased tell him 'unworthy' not listening! servants shoes welcome ring hug coat kiss greeting happy undeserved hungry well-fed calf roast spit flames cooked plate of carved beef grease chin tablecloth smile villagers party welcome celebrate dancing happy with dad (great mood brother not so much) speech lost dead found alive potato

*Stephen Dedalus' talisman, representing Odysseus' Moly, a medicinal herb

Ornery critter *style*

western

Jud chewed his terbaccer plug real quick. He said 'Howdy, old timer! What say you give me that rootin' tootin' doggone sack o' silver dollars you got a-stored up for me ready for when you take that mosey up Boot Hill?'

'Sure will, boy.'

Come sun-up, there was a bright golden haze on the medderr. The youngster pulled down his hat and swung on out of that farm before the barn-raising began, and headed his cart East, mooching on down past the corn as high as an elephant's eye. *Oh, what a beautiful mornin'*, he thought to himself.

He ate dust for several days until he got himself a fine piebald stallion, and later a covered wagon. He rode into town, passing the First National Bank, the livery stable and the Sheriff's Office until he reached *Saucy Lil's Saloon*, where there was whoopin' and a-hollerin' with petticoats and a player pianner.

'Three firewaters,' he ordered, and the barman slid them down the bar. This cityslicker was cuttin' a swell with two of the perdiest gals you ever did see, and several others who just can't say no.

He drew his Peacemaker sixshooter and set some feet a-dancin' among the spittoons.

The lad was dang irresponsible with the loot, and lost the whole kit and caboodle playing poker, and soon he wasn't worth a plugged nickel. His hunger made his guts feel fuller of holes than a sieve. He took a job a-feedin hogs and reckoned he was envying them their pods.

'This ain't right,' he said to himself. 'Here's me, a-wishin' I was chowing down on rotting pods when my Pa feeds his hombres every day with bread 'n' beans 'round the ole campfire. A man's gotta do what a man's gotta do.

'I'll get me back to the homestead and make my peace with Pa, if he'll have me. I'm a-fixin' to tell him *Listen here, you crazy galoot, I've been an ornery critter, behavin' like a bandit and a rustler, but if you pay me my dues, I'll cut your hay and ride the range and break me a buckin' bronco.'*

So he got up and headed on West down the trail, avoiding the injuns, the tumbleweed and the cactus. There were only three wheels on his wagon, so he rode his horse until it went lame and he had to walk.

But while he was still a long way off, (in a cavern, in a canyon, excavating for a mine) his Pa (forty-niner) spied him, and took to runnin', and managed to head him off down at the pass. Chicks and ducks and geese went ascurry as he passed them by.

The son started to say his piece. 'I've come fer mah…'

'Boy, now just you hold your tongue. Now, servants, fetch my golden ring and my boots (the ones with the mighty fine stirrups), and a weskit for this fine pilgrim. And mosey on over to that corral and lasso me a head of branded steer. We are goin' to raise us a mighty hooch party and a hootenanny with a geetar and a harmonium!

'We reckoned him a deadbeat, but he's found! Yes indeedy, I said yes indeedy dog, we thought old Jud was dead, and a goner, but he's alive! Yeehah-lelujah!'

Schadenfreude *style*

cruel pleasure derived from the misfortunes of others

The foolish old man suffered self-inflicted loss when his greedy son demanded his inheritance early. His quality of life on the farm significantly deteriorated, but to be perfectly honest, he deserved everything that happened to him. What's more, he foolishly then failed to work additionally diligently to make up for his shocking cash-flow deficiencies, but, like a fool, stood on the roof of the farmhouse for weeks on end, waiting and hoping that the wayward boy would return. Ridiculous!

Meanwhile, the daft lad went to Dissipation City and behaved extremely rashly. He gathered other wasters around him, and treated them with complete disregard for budgeting or consideration; they ate, drank, played, gambled and purchased with both abandon and exhaustiveness. After not very long, quite frankly, the money was all gone, of course.

At the same time, the economy withered (as many of us predicted – spot-on!) and everyone was plunged into a famine, giving them all plenty of opportunity to consider how extravagant they had been despite the tell-tale signs of crop failure. Their woeful inability to store sufficient stock of grain was followed by the punishment they had foolishly brought upon themselves, meted out by vindictive fate.

The dim boy was reduced to a terrible job on a pig farm, where he watched skinny animals being fed appalling, rotting vegetables, and he hated it; yet so severe was his hunger that he was soon envying the pigs their food! Loser!

He was struck by a thought and came to his senses. 'My father's hired men eat well; I shall arise and go to my father and say I am no longer worthy to be called your son; make me one of your hired men.' Somehow, his shocking arrogance persuaded him that his dad would take him back, even as his new-found humility (too little, too late) convinced him he could cope with being a worker.

While he was still a long way off, his ridiculous father saw him from the roof, and recklessly ran to greet him. The son should have been punished and rejected, but the father kissed him, and gave him shoes, a coat and a family ring. Bonkers!

Just then, as it happened, one of the over-indulgent calves was greedily chewing his way through a super-sized portion of grain, adding yet more kilos to his already considerable girth. He gave not a thought to the starving animals suffering the famine, nor to the dwindling funds in the farmer's account. His selfishness brought him quick justice. He met his come-uppance as one of the farm-hands strolled into the cowshed and slit the calf's plump throat with a knife, inserted a spit and began to roast him.

Then he began distributing slices to all and sundry at the celebratory party.

232

'My boy was lost, but he is found. He was dead, and is alive!' I think it was an uninspired speech, delivered poorly, by a father who ought to have been a lot less generous in lavishing hot beef dinners on his guests (some of whom were secretly – and justifiably – critical of him), particularly at a time of famine, when they were dangerously hungry, and while his own circumstances were somewhat impecunious.

In my view (and I believe I speak for the majority of right-thinking folk) he should never have given away his money at the start; then he should have completely washed his hands of the boy and forgotten about him, and certainly have never welcomed him back again. His son's behaviour did not warrant him being treated in such a kind way.

It's a mixed up world, if you ask me.

A life   *style*
from cradle to grave

He was born two years after his brother, and grew into a troublesome child; he misbehaved as a school pupil and became a feisty teenager, full of dreams and aspiration, yet sulky and without a great deal of faithfulness.

'Give me my inheritance,' the young man demanded one day, and his father handed over a giant bag of cash.

The son (now in his early twenties) went to Dissipation City, where he wasted the money on dining, gambling and a lavish wedding/ thirtieth birthday party for himself. Soon all the cash was gone, and the country fell into a depression and famine. Deserted by his wife and children, but believing life was about to begin, took a job tending pigs. He longed to eat their rotting pods. Suddenly, he had a mid-life crisis.

'The workers at home eat well; I should go and ask for a job, as I am no longer worthy to be treated as part of the family.' He got up, considered having a hair weave, attending a Little Mix concert (wearing his baseball cap backwards) or buying a motorbike, immediately forgot, and went home, using his senior citizen's bus pass.

While he was still a long way off, his ancient Dad saw him from the roof, and went to greet him as quickly as he could. The son leaned on his stick and caught his breath, while his father issued instructions to his servants. 'Fetch a ring for his finger and new tyres for his bath chair! And a moth-eaten wrongly-buttoned-up beige cardigan. Make easy-to-digest beef consommé, with slices of Battenberg!'

Local folks gathered for a celebration, but it was too late, and the son gave up his spirit and was laid in a coffin.

'My son was lost, and is found. We thought he was dead, but he was alive at that time. Sadly, he is certainly dead now.'

Missing letters   *alphabet games*
source material **Greener grass?** *(p15)*
No Vowels

Th sn dmndd hs nhrtnc nd lft hm. H spnt th mny n wld lvng. Whn fmn strck, h tk jb tndng pgs nd lngd t t thr pds.

H cm t hs snss, dcdng t g hm nd sk t b hrd mn, snc h knw h ws n lngr wrthy t b clld sn. Whl h ws stll lng wy ff, hs fthr sw hm, rn t hm, gv hm

233

rng, ct nd shs. H klld th fttd clf nd clbrtd. 'Ths my sn ws lst nd s fnd; h ws dd nd s lv gn!'

Only Vowels

e o eae i ieiae a e oe. e e e oe i i ii. e aie u, e oo a o ei i a oe o ea ei o. e ae o i ee, eii o o oe a a o e a ie a, ie e e e a o oe o o e ae a o.

ie e a i a o a o, i ae a i, a o i, ae i a i, a oa a oe. e ie e ae a a eeae. 'i o a o a i ou; e a ea a i aie aai!'

Two keystrokes, then skip one

Th so deanedhi iheitnc ad ef hme H sen te ony n il lvig. Whn amnestuc, e oo ajo tedig ig ad onedtoea tei pds H cmetohi snss, deidngtogohoe ndas t b ahiedma, ine e ne h ws o onerwoth t b clld sn.

Whlehewa sil alog ayof, isfahe sw im rn o im gvehi arig,a oa ad hos. Hekile te atedcaf ndceebatd. 'Tismyso ws os ad s oud;hewa dadan i aiv aai!'

Antithrenodials (see p219)

m c f m. p my w vg. W fm uck, k jb g pg g p. cm, cg g m k b m, c kw w g wy b c.

W w g wy ff, f w m, m, gv m g, c. k f cf cb. 'my w fu; w v g!'

Second half of alphabet (n-z) only

T son n s nrtn n t o. spnt t ony n w vn. Wn n stru, too o tnn ps n on to t tr pos. to s snss, n to o o n s to r n, sn nw ws no onr worty to son. W ws st on wy o, s tr sw, rn to, v rn, ot n sos. t tt n rt. 'Ts y son ws ost n s oun; ws n s v n!'

Sestina
poetry

Classic form with mathematical algorithm - a strong flavour of Oulipo constraint*

The farm boy might have said 'My Dad, I wish you dead!
Just simply share your wealth with me and let me go...'
His father, sad, observed his risky course. Our lad
Was drinking, rashly gambling, wasting all the cash
False friends had flocked, so keenly grasping, and consumed
Such top-class fine dining. Exclusive food.

In quality hotel bars and restaurants, food
Greatly enjoyed, but soon all GDP was dead!
And everyone discovered nought to be consumed.
His fickle 'friends' all rapidly decide to go;
Thus he was left bereft of any spending cash.
Or company or help or hope, this hard-up lad.

Work tending unclean pigs was low – he was not glad
To watch them chowing down on awful rotten food –
Their decomposing pods... but how else to earn cash?
His desp'rate thoughts turned to his pa, no more wished dead
'I'll humbly seek work on the farm, so now I'll go
Dad's hired men's hot lunch is famously consumed...'
His stirred memory soon with family consumed

'My actions have been so ungrateful, mulled the lad
At long last time has come for me to up and go
Where I'll find work and love, I hope, as well as food –
Deserve severe rejection? Yes! But here I'm dead
Forsaking all my heritage for meagre cash.'

This journey – oh! So long – used up residual cash:
Both sandals wore themselves to nothing (trudge-consumed).
His winter coat was also torn and hopes near dead.
And yet, while still a long way off… Dad saw the lad
Undignified, rushed to greet, ordering roast food
Kisses and ring and coat and shoes. Complaints forego!

So many servants ran (he ordered them to go
To fetch and carry). Fat-calf's throat gets knifely gash
And tables laden bounteously with party food.
The welcomed villagers throng in; all is consumed
While father speaks aloud his joy to see the lad
'Behold my dear, dear son – the one we thought was dead!'

'He has set aside ego; let's party, consume!
And though he spent my cash, I gladly greet my lad
As one back from the dead! Oh neighbours, eat this food!'

* End-words (not just rhymes): ABCDEF, FAEBDC, CFDABE, ECBFAD, DEACFB, BDFECA, & envoi of half-lines BE/DC/FA. Good choices are required in verse one

Travel Information *style*
web-based timetables

IsRailTrack journey planner
Farmstead Halt FSD *to* **Dissipation Central** DSP
via **Lebanon West** LBW *&* **Hebron Gate** HBR

Monday 10th July 32AD

Departure	Arrival	Duration	Changes
08:30	12:17	3h 47m	2

Journey Details

Dep	From	Platform	To		Arr	Platform	Duration
08:30	**Farmstead Halt** FSD	1	**Lebanon West** LBW		09:13	4	0h 43m

Calling points			*Arrival*	*Departure*			
	Brookville High Level BHL		08:39	08:41			
	Twin Oaks & Groveside TOG		08:57	08:59			
	Gehenna-next-the-Sea GNS		09:06	09:07			

IsRailTrack Midland service from Gath Parkway to First Street, Babylon   *Hide calling points*

Dep	From	Platform	To	Arr	Platform	Duration
09:21	**Lebanon West** LBW	3	**Hebron Gate** HBR	10:48	2a	1h 27m

Calling points

	Arrival	Departure
Lower Caesarea LCA	09:35	09:37
Straight Street Custom House SSC	09:49	09:51
Mount Carmel Archway MCA	10:02	10:04
Galilee North Shore GNS	10:13	10:15
Two Bridges Market TBM	10:25	10:27
Cana Winery Spa CWS	10.37	10.38

IsRailTrack SouthEast service from East Nain to Jericho Jordan Valley   *Hide calling points*

Dep	From	Platform	To	Arr	Platform	Duration
11:06	**Hebron Gate** HBR	3b	**Dissipation** DSP **Central**	12:17	13	1h 07m

Calling points	Arrival	Departure
Kadesh-Barnea Sunnyside KBS	11:18	11:21
Ramoth-Gilead-by-Sea RGS	11:33	11:35
Tyre International TYI	11:47	11:49
East Sidon Parkway ESP	12:04	12:06

Parabolic Railways service from Joppa to Dissipation Central   *Hide calling points*

Select your ticket details   **Check fares**

- - Jordan & District Omnibus Company Ltd - -

Frequency   **Timetable**   Fares   Map   View   Stops   Garage

Dissipation Central to *Jericho*   **Sun-Thurs**   Sabbath   Sat

Route Number	65	27a	65	78	27a	65	27a	65	78	27a	65
Dissipation Central Bus Stn	1132	1220	1232	1300	1320	1332	1420	1432	1500	1520	1532
Sow Stall Gate	1147	-	1247	-	-	1347	-	1447	-	-	1537
Samson's Roundabout	1218	-	1318	-	-	1418	-	1518	-	-	1618
Lower Esplanade, Sidon	1241	-	1341	-	-	1441	-	1541	-	-	1641
Riverside Viewing Point	1310	-	1410	-	-	1510	-	1610	-	-	1710
Joppa Bus Station, Stand C	1337	*1305*	1437	*1345*	*1405*	1537	*1505*	1637	*1545*	*1605*	1737
SowsRUs, Decapolis	1421	*1349*	1521	-	*1449*	1621	*1549*	1721	-	*1649*	1821
Old Clock Tower, Arimathea	1449	*1417*	1549	-	*1517*	1649	*1617*	1749	-	*1717*	1849
Jericho High Road, North Side	1522	*1450*	1622	*1417*	*1550*	1722	*1650*	1822	*1617*	*1750*	1922

Ramblersassociation.org.il
from SowsRUs **to** Homestead Farm   **search for more walks**

• **Walk Details** A hilly but rewarding walk past Cedar Valley, towards East Bethany, pausing at the Lamb & Wine Goblet PH if they have any food, for lunch. Continuing along the South Sinai Way for three further days, or until your shoes wear out. **By special arrangement:** greeting from locals (while still a long way off) from Homestead Farm. **Group:** Cedar Valley Occasional Ramblers **Start grid ref:** LK151124 **Start GPS:** EB65 0HD **Nearest town:** East Bethany **Start time:** when revelation comes **Grade:** Moderately Hilly to Slightly Strenuous **Recommended Footwear**: Resistant (stoney paths) **Distance:** 113 miles approx **Contact:** Luke@Gare.StLazare.org **MeetingPoint:** *SowsRUs* (north gate), Decapolis • Pod packed lunch available. Not suitable for hired men. Info from *Campaign for Preservation of Rural Israel*, subject to change without notice • **Show Maps**

236

Double acrostic   *poetry*

first and last letters of each line spell the key phrase;
iambic octameter alternates with iambic sexameter, usually

T	om, wayward boy, filled money	bel	T	
(H	is father's promised	wealt	H	);
E	njoyed wild living, food and	win	E	.
P	our, o'erflowing	cu	P	!
R	ebellious, sinful, growing	poo	R	
O	'erspent, now broke –	agr	O	!
D	eserting friends all gone. Says	la	D	
'I	see the pigs'	del	I	;
G	ross slop seems somehow	appealin	G	
A	t once he thought of	p	A	
'L	unch for hired men!' Me too? So	I'l	L	
S	tand up, go home.' Dad	see	S	
O	n road. 'My boy! – bring shoes, ring, to	O		!
N	ow, roast fat calf! Such	fu	N	.'

50%   *style*

'Give me an equal share of my inheritance,' asked one of the half-brothers. Father took twice as long to reply, but agreed.

The boy left with half the money and went to Dissipation Town, where he spent it playing *dix-point-cinq*[1] and on the Roulina semi-wheel, in Public Bungalows and on part-feral teenage females. After a while he had half of his stash left and the country was plunged into partial (single-dip) recession.

He took a job fiving[2] pigs, and envied their pods a little. (They were radioactive, having a quarter life of 30 years.)

But he came to his senses. 'Six of my father's dozen men get half their meals every other day. I'll arise and go to him and say 'I'm not half worthy to be called your son; please employ me part-time as a hired boy.'

So he went home.

While he was just halfway there, his father saw him and jogged to greet him with a one-arm embrace. He gave him an ear-ring, a cloak, and one shoe. 'Tell the Eighth-master[3] to maim the fatted calf and cook the leg joint rare. We shall invite half the village and have a twomal[4] party from sunset to midnight. Let's drink twenty-five-percent-filled unillycans[5] of low alcohol wine with our partners, and partake of particles of particular participating partridges. We'll nibble upon one-point-five-egg omelettes, toad-in-the-half, single Gloucester cheese with semi-grain mustard on water-uniscuits[6] – even until we have arrhoea![7] For my son was in hiding and is reputedly monoscovered[8]; he was rather poorly and is half alive!'

1 *vingt-et-un*; 2 **ten**ding; 3 **quarter**master (overssser of kitchens); 4 formal; 5 billycans; 6 water **bis**cuits; 7 **di**arrhoea 8 **dis**covered

Time shift   *style*

in which the narrative flits between flashback/present/flashforward in ways which may be described as chrono-illogical

He stared, glum, hungry, lonely, miserable, hard-up, a little ashamed, filled with regret. His unseeing gaze did not notice any thin pigs rootling through the mouldy, rotting pods, seeking any green bits from which to take nourishment.

But the sensation of this kissing is so welcome, as similar attention had been so many times before, but from such very different people and contrastingly motivated.

Neither did he notice the pig-farm owner, checking to see if he had stayed all night. Instead, he saw his wasted opportunity, the glittering of a spinning roulette wheel, the gleam in Georgette's eyes, the sad, resigned concern on his father's face, and the glint of moisture on Charlene's full, red lip as she savoured her third glass of champagne.

He also recognized the need in the faces of the beggars who were lining the streets, and dwelt upon the distant memory of the sparkle of early morning sunlight on the lake beyond Big Field on his father's farm.

Years later he stood in his long-deceased father's favourite spot on the farmhouse rooftop, wrapped in his threadbare but treasured camel-hair coat, and described this season of his life as 'reckless youth' and himself as 'having been a selfish fool'.

But back at the start he'd been quick to seek his father's money, very quick to seize it and leave when the opportunity arose and even quicker to gather friends by a conspicuous display of prodigious wealth.

It was almost as generous as his father will soon demonstrate now he's returned, generously providing a fabulous spread of cooked meat, pastries, salads, vegetables, rice dishes, alcohol, fruit, puddings and trifles for the villagers, who will be invited to celebrate the boy's return.

'My son was lost, but is found; he was dead but is alive!' the father will say if all goes according to plan, reflecting on the many days he had stood on his rooftop waiting, hoping, expecting, fearful… until this one day, while the boy is still a long way off, his son, who had encountered saucy dancing girls, fancy restaurant dinners, casinos, famine, hunger and desertion by his new-found, soon-lost friends, stood in amazement as his father ran, undignified, to greet him.

His father will imminently order the servants to fetch a ring, a coat of camel hair and shoes for his feet.

'I am no longer worthy to be called your son,' is what he planned to say, just after saying 'Father, make me one of your hired men,' some considerable time after saying 'Give me my inheritance.'

He had come to his senses in the sty a few days previously (although he had been given the money a long time before), but is now being kissed, which is making his oft-rehearsed speech an irrelevance.

IT terms   *key words*

computing & communications brands and user-related terms

Don gleaned lots of cash from his **d**ad. **S**lipping out the back door, he put the **keys** on the hook and made his way to Dissipation City. He behaved a little like a spi**v**, **ga**mbling, drinking and living it up. He failed to **monitor** his expenditure but revelled in a cocktail lounge, a pool and a **spa.**

Mixing with **Chip**, Mary, Jane, **Dot** (**com**mitted to drinking heavily) he befriended various amig**os,** X-rated dancers, whose morals were dispute**d. VD** was an issue. They also drank **Java.**

'Ever have a ride in an airsh**ip, honey**?'

'Not for me. I shall **go ogle** some more bodies!'

'Your decisio**n. OK. I** always think it's best to judge for yourself.'

At one party there was gross overhy**pe: 'Rip her** all-yellow garment to shreds!' they cried. Soon the cash was all used u**p. Da**ys later, which was **hard, war** ensued, and was followed by famine.

His tummy rumb**led.** He needed a bandage or a cold compress, or at least an **application** of skin lotion. He considered eating a mani**c drome**dary but decided against it. He tended pigs fed on pods diseased with a **virus**, covered in **ants** and other **bugs**. He sat in the cor**ner, d**rooling over the pods, but then came to his senses.

'**Wysiwyg** is just a f**ib. My** dad's hired men (I have seen them through the canteen **Windows**) **ate** well. I'll arise and say to father 'I shall re**pent, I, um** not worthy to be called a son. I **kindle**d my passion... but how **I kissed** all those girls – I don't know. Am I being a **wimp**?' He spoke to the pig farmer. 'Gonna have to go, gu**v. Is** taking this liberty too cheeky? Sorry!'

'Why can't I take a **cab?'** Left no money for luxuries, so he walked, being passed by **bus**es and motorcycles **zip**ping along. Fellow-pedestrians confirmed 'Yeah! **TT** practice starts today.' The vehicles

carried their logos, showing a trademark, indicated with**™**.

Little ones were printed by lith**o™**, ailing in the breeze.

While he was still a long way off, his dad saw him through the **windows** and began to **sprint er**ratically, running down the **drive** and onto the slope of broken rocks, the **scree.** Nearing his boy, he gave him a **Mac**, some **boots** and, after a bit of ch**at, a** ring.

They killed the fatted calf and also roasted a **ram** and a **snow leopard**, serving the villagers. The table was groaning with **cookies**, trifle and **apple** and **blackberry** crumble. Dad exclaimed to the boy's grandma, as it was served, 'It's cheese, **mother, board**'s covered!'

They sang quietly: attempting pianissi**mo use**d all their brea**th** control. The father made a speech: XXIII of his words were verbs, XVI a nou**n, IX** adverbs, VI adjectives, **X** pronouns, and **IV** ga**rb**led noises.

'He was a reli**c, put** in the ground. But he's alive! He was lost, yet now I find him!'

Key: term meaning *description*
adsl asymmetric digital subscriber line *provides high bandwidth* **keys** *alphanumeric inputs* **monitor** *screen* **spam** *unsolicited messages* **chip** *integrated circuit* **dot com** *internet company* **OSX** *Apple's operating system, version 10* **DVD** *digital versatile disc* **Java** *programming language* **iPhone** *Apple's smartphone* **google** *search engine, est. 1998* **Nokia** *telecoms group, founded 1865* **peripheral** *devices to input or output data* **PDA** *personal digital assistant superceded by smartphones* **hardware** *physical parts of a computer system* **LED** *light emitting diode* **application** *computer programme* **CDROM** compact disc read-only memory **virus** *malicious programme* **NT** *Windows-based operating system, launched in 1993, superceded by Windows 2000* **bug** *defect or error* **nerd** *socially inept technical wizard* **wysiwyg** what you see is

what you get *on-screen representation of print-out appearance* **IBM** International Business Machines *est. 1991* **Windows ate** Windows 8 *operating system released 2012* **Pentium** *microprocessors, released 1993* **Kindle** *e-book reader, released 2007* **wiki** *user-editable site* **WIMP** Window, Icon, Menu, Pointer; *user-friendly screen-based interactivity* **Vista** *Windows operating system released 2007* **cable** *TV delivery system* **bus** *system for transfer of data* **zip** *data compression file format* **http** hypertext transfer protocol *procedure for collecting data* **html** hypertext mark-up language; *web text editor* **hotmail** *early email services* **printer** *peripheral* **drive** *data storage device* **screen** *display* **Mac** *abbr. for Macintosh, computer brand* **boot** *to activate a computer (abbr. for 'pulling yourself up by your bootstraps')* **Atari** *computer company est. 1972* **ram** random access memory **Snow Leopard** *Mac OSX (10.6)* **cookies** *stored in your browser* **Apple** *brand* **Blackberry** *brand* **motherboard** *circuit board* **mouse** (NOT manually-operated ultility selection equipment) *pointing tool* **Unix** *operating system released in 1970* **XP** *Windows OS launched 2001* **VGA** video graphics array *analogue display standard* **CPU** central processing unit *where calculations happen* **wifi** *wireless interface*

Metafiction   *pastiche*

Reflecting The Life and Opinions of Tristram Shandy, Gentleman, *famed for length, addressing the reader, digressions & quotations, as well as super-sized multi-em-dashed punctuation*

Book I *Ancestors* Chapter The First
---- *"I will endeavour to explain with all imaginable decency."* Many, many years before my present life began, madam, my father's grandfather (oh, bless his tender soul) purchased what may only be described as a tiny farmstead of a few hectares and set to work upon it, growing selected root vegetables for his family, plus some cash crops to generate an income stream, and, after a few years, tending a small quantity of livestock; trading much produce with local businessmen, including two school-teachers--

so that my father's father (the former-mentioned gentleman's firstborn) readily understood his alphabet and could count up to adequately high numbers to gather wealth, buy additional fields from the farm next door and expand the range of crops to include other corns and grains---- which in turn served well his family, consisting (as you may wish to take note) of my aunt Janet and my uncle Percy, her second so-short-lived husband Lionel and her third husband Clemence (alas! she was most seriously blighted with fearsomely tuberculous suitors); aunt Mary, uncle Daniel and my father, the last born----they lived with considerable ease in a greatly extended farmhouse, and employed a maid, three farmhands and an ostler----which was not quite luxury. I quote freely (friend, you will forgive the digression, I have no doubt) from a historical discourse describing such a life----*"The arable field system consisted of a combination of open fields, and closes----parcels of land bounded by ditches, hedges and fences. Crops of wheat, barley and oats were grown in rotation as the arable land was used in turn for winter and spring grains and then fallowed. Sheep (Cheviots, Suffolks, and a few Swaledales) were pastured on downland near the manorial court, maintaining a flock of near three hundred and fifty; also two dozen each of oxen, calves and chicken."* My grandfather's wise husbandry favoured his family, and by not small chance did this result in benefits visited upon my father himself----even though he was one born out of time, as it were, abnormally inheriting the land and the business sustained thereupon. For my aunt Janet was granted some small favour, having been married, at her second time of asking, to one of the men who often visited the farm (ostensibly for the purposes of being a hired man----his deeper motive was revealed as he sought permission in the first instance to woo and be granted leave to take the hand of the aforementioned aunt, who had fine looks, a ruddy complexion and a temperament likely to attract men of adventure). Janet's beau---who became my adopted-by-marriage uncle Lionel----spake thus to her father. 'My Lord, upon whose person may the sun regularly shine in perpetuity, vouchsafe my gratitude to you for these forescore days of righteous hire, days in which I have diligently and joyfully laboured, and have toiled with the sweat of my brow and great effort of wind and limb to plough tracks of land---even as far as the old cedar and out to the red barn on that horizon, and beyond this ridge yonder, where runs a cooling brook and thrive the lilies----some of which I gathered, to present them to this, your delightfully fragrant and elegant, educated and cultured daughter Janet, for whom I have ---- I stand here an honest man, as virtuous as well-bred ------ I say, your daughter Janet, for whom I have true deep and pure affection and by whom (oh such joy!) I am chastely considered, having enquired, meekly kneeling upon my knee, with heartfelt worthy intention: to gain her alabaster-skinned hand. Now, much-respected sir, such somewhat convoluted gentlemanly euphemisms can betimes cunningly conceal more than they reveal *(continues for Thirteen Books, each of Sixty Chapters, not reproduced here, for reason of mercy)*†

*fiction about fiction: stories that deliberately call attention to their fictional status (not unlike this present volume); focused on Lawrence Sterne's comic novel, published 1759-1769

Chain letters   *alphabet games*

the last letter of each word provides the first letter of the next; all letters used.
Cunningly starts with Q, ends with Z

Quite enthusiastic, cynical, looting grab? Bleak Keanu upset the elder rudely, youthfully yearning.

'Give early yields!' (sad); demanded denarii inheritance eagerly. You'll love extremes; such handkerchief for riches sufficed.

Dissipation (nomadic, complex, xenophobic) City… young girls smooching, gambling, gourmandising. Gone!

Endless starvation now worries some; employment trouble. Engaged down near rubbish hog greenery; yams smell long gone. Eat trough-hash? Heaven now works surprising, gracious subparagraph. Had dramatic cranial lightening; God display. 'You'll leave – eventually you'll loom, missed …'

Dad, diligent to observe extra-aloof-faraway youths; sees son! Nigh hurries, shouting 'Glory! You're even now wearing great tailoring! Got to offer rings, shoes…'

Son now would dance, eat, took kisses…

'So, offer roast to our retro-organic calf (fatted)! Declare!' Everyone enjoys superb bap preserve.

'Eighteenth hygenic chickpea *(adj)* jam, most tasty! Yes, son near reaching grave; even now – wonderful – love him! Mazeltov! Vital, living! Give energetic chorus; sing *God's special love!* Enough! Honeycomb buzz!

Middle I *alphabet games*
only words with the middle letter i;
NB the boy behaves self-I-shly, believing the world revolves around his ego
Messianic (Galilee) prodigal's spiritual philippic XVIII.

Child – maximum-materialistically know-it-all Tim – lucrativeness, ambitiously-seditiously raise quids, approximately sixty-eightfold!

Acquisitively, precipitately, seize his beneficiary apportionment opportunistically (narrow-mindedness, assertiveness, incorrigibilities).

Audaciously bellicose valediction – acquiesce? – acquiring livlihood sacrificially; dissociations, expeditions.

Big sin! Asininely imbibes gin. Nil conscientiousnesses!

Internationalised bohemianism-extraterritoriality, uncivilised behavioural inappropriatenesses (barbarianisms). Non-profit-making casinos? Exceptionable desensitising naughtinesses, unbridled indisciplined insobrieties.

Negligées' retailers' half-sisters frolicked gropingly (excessiveness, lustiness, addictiveness, flirtatiousness), notoriously uninhibited. Libidos, sauciness, fraternizations, eroticism, seductiveness, torridity, kinkiness, seediness, curviness, pride. Kid unethically befriends forbidden bedevilling *genital enticer* twins (radiant bikinis!)

'Rapaciously fornicate, luridly flirt: self-satisfaction. Provocativenesses, secularizations, improvidently satisfy machismos. Union confirmed, virginity overestimations!' Billionth foreigner boutiques expensiveness? Exorbitance!

Easygoingness? Flakiness! Numerically maladministrating price attentiveness, foolishly, …

Penniless livelihoods, impecuniousness.

Diminishing waist, emaciates, malnourishments. Abdominally thins, quite discontinuously.

Impoverishments! Puniest obesities… Dietician omits heaviness: emptiness, restrictive disappointments; anaemically annihilated; complainingly tubbiness-curtailment.

Deteriorate, pains, exterminators. Weigh zip! Destitute! Consolidating: beastlinesses; pig (tails' curliness!) nutrition…

Noxious foliage: psoriasis; rancidity; ickiest boils; aging squishy defectiveness; ooziest antique stigmatizations; contamination, calcification, carcinoma; bacteriophage moldiness; insectivorous liquidisation; horrifically blemished veins' mushiness; repulsiveness; slime; stink; bruised, afflicted condition; nastiness; squalidness; indistinguishableness.

Predominantly difficult. Atrociously faint, cravingly.

Sid scrutinises swine swill digestibility. Edibility? Dirtiness! Whiff!

Demotivated – sniff – convicted convertibleness.

Contradictorily, prayingly hallucination. Think religiously: homiest auxiliaries surviving!

Nonsensicalness... discontinuation! Simplifications, disambiguated – owing tribe-recruitment. Non-residential: non-spiritual!

Reminiscing; determinately, angelically quits. Slink.

Domestication, industriousness agrarianism? Kin repositions – auditioning supplicants? Impossibility! Irreconcilability?

Floccinaucinihilipilification?

Reapplication negotiation likelihoods.

'Justification: establishment, twice.' Rededicates.

Amazingly far-sighted, counter-intuitive long-distance forgivingness waits! Smile, interviewing equidistant collision...

'Amigo! Arrived!'

'Elucidate sorriness ...' Emotional entwining rushingly!

Unambiguous, compassionately reaffirming; recept-iveness-cordially, atoningly; rapidly legitimized; whirl decriminalize.

Unconditional forgiving efficaciousness.

Voila! Outfitter plied embroidered, elasticized calicos; swish tails suits; formfitting shirt (white tie); veils, dyeings; cardigans (knits); exquisite sequinned codpieces (various deniers/silkiness); slips; back-stitching millinery... Nattiness! Stylishly attired digital portions-a inclusiveness!

'Incendiaries, grill connoisseur loins-eatings!'

Publicity-invited participators' multitudinousness.

Fire-lighters ignited, organically juicy cowiest moist thick untrimmed-joint prime prize rib slice mains: carnivore meatiness, broiled, crisp bullfighter juiciness.

Maize crumblinesses; ravioli garnished venison; gefilte halibut saltiness; chili tripe; swiss onion dip; capsicums enchilada; catfishes; mexican shrimps sandwiching tastiness; spicy ostriches particles; grits; chick/olive oil blini; shiny spice gamiest quailed tortillas; chips crunchinesses; bries.

Confectioneries: vanilla stick fig pie; fruited pastilles; cochineal/apricot lollipops exquisiteness; seville marzipans; milkiness-pasteurisations porridges, tapioca; cakiest icing bakings (divides easiest).

Embellishment provision: jazziness festivity.

Accordionist's gig; violinist musical jollities; bagpipers' noise; mix clarinets; dulcimers/marimba/ strings jig-jollification (flood-lighting!).

Prestidigitator merriment.

Amontillado aperitifs; distilled Benedictine.

Toastmistress: enunciation-descriptivenesses, smilingly: extra-ordinariness, ceremoniousness, talkativeness.

Swift absinth swigs...

'Kid still did die? Expired, gravedigger's dig? Nonliving, dying, RIP, coffining committal? Terminate morbidity! Paradoxicalness!

'Vivaciously cherished! Reanimate reinstitution. Heart-sickness defib-rillator!

'Deity-physician-reprieved antibiotics inconspicuously; rejoicers, distinctivenesses glorified tonight! Alive!'

243

Capital story
key words

world capitals of many UN-recognised sovereign states and dependencies

Boy, reBel grade A (known as ND) says to his father 'I'm an opportunist, so give me my share!'

'Okay, this is -' (resignation from his fatheR) '- a battle I don't want; you may have the money, even though this will deeply wound me and leave a sCar – a cashflow disaster! AlSo fiasco! Anyway, here's your share of principAl, of interest, of all I own.' The coins: many in numBer; not far short of 10,000. After a long walk on a country Road, Town centre loomed. Setting friendly accountant ADam as custodian of his funds, ND said 'I haven't paid any NI 'cos I am careless!'

But these pals shared a home, in a kind of A buD habitation. They went to a brotHel, sinking lower witH Ava, Nadia and amPly mouthed Victoria. ND said 'HalLo Melanie!', but had to Ban Julie from spending any more, along with people named Hamilton, Stanley and Kath. Man duties done, Julie sat on his LaP, azure gem-gifts aplenty. A waiter brought wine, as in the days of the RaJ.

'Er, us? Ale, my good fellow!' They chatted of the people they'd met, especially Isla: Julie recalled 'A woMan, a guardsMan, a mailMan – I'll always remember them! Anyway, this Brat, Isla, vainly talked incessantly – she had the gift of the Gab (or one similar). His sins included erotiCa. NB errata of all sorts.

'I was somewhat unciVil in... I... using my dad's cash,' he said, unsteadily, 'for buying very large church buildings suitable for large flightless birds. EMus? Cathedrals?

No!' When ND's cash ran out, everyone, due to a foreign War, saw crops fail. Lack of nutrition gave hiM a taUt underbelly.

He decided to bivouAc, crashing in his tent by the pig farm where he worked. The owners gave the pigs rotting pods, which were Free. Town-dwellers, they didn't have anything better. The boy came to his senses. 'I think I'll Quit or get away right now. Father's hired men eat welL. I'm a fool unless I get uP, arise and go. I'll bow down before my PA, then say my speecH; a *No, I am not worthy to be called your son* speech. Let me work; I even agree not to be your son...

'I expect he'll Do domain-establishing ranting, but I have to try.' He spoke to himself in German: 'Ja, kart along to your home.' After a long walk; he crossed the Bridge, town outskirts and neared the farm.

'All this hiKing, stones in my shoes...'

His dad watched and shouted 'Lo! ND on the horizon! I can seen hiM on a couple of hills distant. He cried 'Now theN, I am eying the lad a long way off! Today's the day! I haven't gOt to *wait even a moment longer!*' He ran in a Mad, ridiculous style. 'Pa go! Pa go!' he shouted, crazy with joy.

His son reckoned 'Either I interPret or I appear to be barmy! Better to be forMal about it? Make me an hired...'

ZigZag! 'Rebel lad, I forgive your sins, whatever they may Be. I ruthlessly do away with bitter recrimination! Now, cooK a bull for many Mins, Kevin; yes, roast the calf to filL us!

'A kaftan, a thumb ring (with gem) or on index finger, along with a dustPan, a maC. I, typically, noticed he was trying to scrape the Tar away from the sole of his **Wellington** but to no avail, so new shoes!'

The boy was amazed. 'My cup runneth over, Father; I have a filled **Bag! H, dad!'** So using several slaughtering giz**Mos, cow** became roasted beef (suc**H a rare** steak)

Of course, no h**Am; man**darins & créme avec **Sucre,** scrambled eggs (o**R** omelette) with **Brussels,** bana**Nas** sauced with chocolate. Also, turni**P** ragu, endive, salad of cucum**Ber** lined with lettuce and even the corn on the co**B is sau**ce-covered. No ale, yea, no glass of **Port, O, no vo**dka (so s**Tir an** apple drink).

Also, playing quality tunes by Bar**Tok: Youth** Orchestra. Cook Kevin said 'I danced a sal**Sa; I panfried** some chicken.'

Said Pa 'Now we'll dance a mam**Bo. Got a** rhythm? Dancing in tw**Os –** lovely! We should invite Cousin **Rose, Au**nt Edith and Uncle Steve... who else would benefit from the **Trip? Olive,** of course!' Plent**Y are** now attending to his speech which touched on how great his homeland was, compared to the sinfulness of the foreign city; it was a diatri**Be.**

'**I, (jing**oistic, I know), dislike what Dissiption City stands for – oh, I was so discouraged, (forgive my poor gram**Mar) I got** depressed. But, look, even after all this exoti**Ca, I roast** the fatted calf for him. Yes, I was hard up, fo**R I ga**ve him all I could spare. He became thin: his skul**L is bon**ey but he came to his senses!

'So I say Hosan**Na! I, Robin** Jones, rejoice! I'd like to th**Ank a ra**nsoming God who deserves many a song full of **Buenos! Air es**tablishes that the boy breathes! We thought him dead! Melodra**Ma! Serum** called for! But he is found! He will do some work, of course... everyone, give him your laundry to do! Yes, all **Washing to ND. C**ome on!'

His son sent a happy note: *U r a cheruB!* ***U'd ape St*** *Paul!*

* indicates official **capitals** NB other cities (not named here) may be the seat of government or of admnistration of the *country*
Belgrade *Republic of Serbia* **Tunis** *Tunisian Republic* **Rabat** *Kingdom of Morocco* **Caracas** *Bolivarian Republic of Venezuela* **Sofia** *Republic of Bulgaria* **Alofi** *Niu* (self-governing nation associated with New Zealand) **Bern** *Swiss Confederation* **Road Town** *British Virgin Islands* **Damascus** *Syrian Arab Republic* **Nicosia** *Republic of Cyprus* **Abu Dhabi** *United Arab Emirates* **Helsinki** *Republic of Finland* **Havana** *Republic of Cuba* **Plymouth** *Monserrat* (British Overseas Territory) **Victoria** *Republic of Seychelles* **Lomé** *Togolese Republic* **Banjul** *Republic of The Gambia* **Hamilton** *the Bermudas* **Stanley** *Falkland Islands* (British Overseas Territory) **Kathmandu** *Federal Democratic Republic of Nepal* **La Paz** (administrative) *Plurinational State of Bolivia* **Jerusalem** disputed: *State of Israel* or *Occupied Palestinian Territories* See clarifying note **Managua** *Republic of Nicaragua* **Manama** *Kingdom of Bahrain* **Manilla** *Republic of the Phillipines* **Bratislava** *Slovak Republic* **Gaborone** *Republic of Botswana* **Canberra** *Commonealth of Australia* **Vilinius** *Republic of Lithuania* **Muscat** *Sultanate of Oman* **Warsaw** *Republic of Poland* **Mata-Utu** *Wallis and Futuna* (Overseas Collectivity of France) **Accra** *Republic of Ghana* **Freetown** *Republic of Sierra Leone* **Quito** *Republic of Ecuador* **Lima** *Republic of Peru* **Paris** *French Republic* **Athens** *Hellenic Republic* (aka *Greece*) **Hanoi** *Socialist Republic of Vietnam* **Kiev** *Ukraine* **Dodoma** *United Republic of Tanzania* **Jakarta** *Republic of Indonesia* **Bridgetown** *Barbados* **Kingston** *Jamaica; also Norfolk Island* (External Territory of Australia) See clarifying note **London** *United Kingdom of Great Britain and Northern Ireland* also *England* See clarifying note **Monaco** *Principality of Monaco* **Niamey** *Republic of Niger* **Ottowa** *Canada* **Madrid** *Kingdom of Spain* **Pago Pago** *American Samoa* (US Territory) **Pretoria*** *Republic of South Africa* **Malabo** *Republic of Equatorial Guinea* **Zagreb** *Republic of Croatia* **Beirut** *Republic of Lebanon* **Kabul** *Islamic Republic of Afghanistan* **Minsk** *Belarus* **Lusaka** *Republic of Zambia* **Moroni** *Union of the Comoros* **Panama City** *Republic of Panama* **Tarawa** *Republic of Kiribati* **Wellington** *New Zealand* **Baghdad** *Republic of Iraq* **Moscow**

245

Russian Federation **Harare** Republic of Zimbabwe
Amman Hashemite Kingdom of Jordan **Sucre**
(Constitutional) Plurinational State of Bolivia
Rome Italian Rebublic **Brussels** Kingdom of
Belgium **Nassau** Commonwealth of the Bahamas
Prague Czech Republic **Berlin** Federal Republic of
Germany **Bissau** Republic of Guinea-Bissau
Porto-Novo* Republic of Benin **Tirana** Republic
of Albania **Tokyo** Nippon-koku (aka Japan)
Saipan Commonwealth of the Northern Mariana
Islands (Territory of the United States)
Bogotá Republic of Colombia **Oslo** Kingdom of
Norway **Roseau** Commonwealth of Dominica
Tripoli Lybia **Yaren** Republic of Nauru **Beijing**
People's Republic of China **Marigot** Collectivity of
Saint Martin (Overseas Collectivity of France)
Cairo Arab Republic of Egypt **Riga** Republic of
Latvia **Lisbon** Portuguese Republic **Nairobi**
Republic of Kenya **Ankara** Republic of Turkey
Buenos Aires Argentine Republic **Maseru**

Kingdom of Lesotho **Washington, DC** United
States of America **Budapest** Republic of Hungary

Clarifying note: **Jerusalem** is claimed as
capital by two countries. The State of Israel is
not recognized, according to UNSC Resolution
478 (1980); Occupied Palestinian Territories is.

By contrast, there are two different capitals
ambiguously both named **Kingston**, 8295
miles apart (one in Jamaica, the other on Norfolk
Island, a territory of Australia), neither to be
muddled with Kingston-upon-Thames, a
borough of London – yet just one **London**,
capital of two countries: England and United
Kingdom. Confusion in this case is almost
mandatory.
The government of Monserrat moved from
Plymouth to **Braides Estate** in 1997 after the
eruption of Soufriere Hills.

Mathematical $\hfill$ *style*

$$L\,{\overset{k}{\underset{u}{\sum}}} \;=\; (45/3){:}132/(3{*}4) - (5^2{+}3^2){-}2$$

$$3 - 1 \;=\; 2$$

$$(>5\ \text{Methuselahs} + 30\text{kg meat} + 19\text{kg carbs} + 10\text{kg fish} + 2\text{kg tomato sauce} + 25\text{ltr ale} \times 9\ \text{weeks} \times 35\ \text{friends}) - \text{reck} - \text{ruth} \;=\; 0$$

$$\text{GDP*} \;=\; (\cancel{D}4 \times 10^{13})$$

$$\frac{1 + (6 \times 4\ \text{trotters}) + 4\text{kg veg}}{2\text{mg microbes}} \;=\; 4 \times \text{yearn}$$

$$3.5\ \text{lumens} \times \text{thought} \;=\; 8261^7\ \text{lumens}$$

$$\frac{\text{pair of sandals}}{70\text{miles}} \;=\; \text{sole} \times 14\ \text{microns}$$

$$\text{dad} \;=\; \text{hug} + 5\ \text{kisses} \,(5x)$$

$$(\text{Au} \times 4\text{g}) + (2 \times \text{footwear}) + \text{coat} \;=\; \text{son}$$

$$\frac{\text{fat calf}}{(\text{spit} \times 3\pi)} \;=\; 360° \times 20000$$

$$\text{beef}^3 \;=\; \text{stew}$$

$$\text{celebration} \;=\; 1 + 2 + > 150 + 1$$

$$\text{speech} \;=\; \text{joyful}$$

$$\text{lost/dead son} \;=\; \text{found/alive son}$$

Quad Erat Demonstrandum[†]

---

* Gross Domestic Product, a measure of the health of the national economy
† Latin for *that which was to be proved*; reckoned by cheeky schoolboys to stand for *Quite Easily Done*

MiddleEastEnders _pastiche_

maximising the predictability, larger-than-life characters and plot-twists beloved of tv soap operas. Drum cue indicates episode break

Mad Jack Gusstaffsson barged into the room, eyes ablaze, fists clenched, ready for a fight.

'What's going on?' he asked.

'I'm not your uncle!' Stan Kew (as he was known locally) shouted to Jack. 'I married your aunt to cover up for the embezzelling and the death of her step-sister, way back. Then when they went down south, I knew it would all come out, so I was seeing moody Miriam when she was still related to Lenny, and then she had the liver transplant but tried to steal Grandad's business. I'm not your uncle!'

'Then, who are you? If you're not...' Jack was confused.

'I'm your father!'

Jack was stunned. How could Uncle Stan suddenly be dear old Dad? Uncle Stan ran FatCalfisStan, a prosperous farm. Jack ran his fingers over his _Holly Bush at Sunset_ tattoo as he tried to understand.

'I can't cope with this,' Jack concluded. He needed time to think, but he also needed to test the generosity of the old man. 'I want out of here. If you are my father, prove it. Give me my inheritance and let me go.' It was the only way Jack would trust him, so Stan reluctantly put lots of coins into a bag and presented it to his new-found son.

'Here you are, my boy,' he said.

'Don't call me that. I hope I never see you again.'

Tears coursed freely down Stan's dusty face as he watched his son walk down the farmtrack and out onto the main road by the canal, under the bridge and away, perhaps forever. Meanwhile, he was being watched from behind the milking parlour by naughty Nadine Norris, who had an angry attitude and a collection of letters tied with a red ribbon. _cue drums_

SO JACK ARRIVED in Dissipation City, where he found _El Dorado Bar & Grill_ a likely place to spend his money.

Harriet (23, blonde, trombonist) and Krystal (ceoliac, collector of matchboxes) quickly came to blows over him, and their friend Jennifer (ex-con, Welsh) and her daughter Imogen (trainer of the school's synchronized swimming team) were enchanted with Jack's wealth.

In conversation, Imogen casually explained that she had once been to FatCalfisStan, but knew hardly anything about the mad woman in the attic, or what was hidden in the boathouse by the lake.

However, she accidentally revealed that she finally knew (thanks to Harriet, who, in a moment of weakness, following the enjoyable but expensive food fight at Chuck & Micheala's wedding reception, had revenge in mind) that Harriet's evil twin Rosetta was expecting the Abbot's third son; and why those starlings had never returned after the summer of '87, following the incendiary device incident at the factory canteen.

At the same time, Justin (the handsome welder) loved pole-vaulter Jasmin, while her heart secretly yearned for Abdhulla, who ran the pharmacy. Meanwhile, he was keen on professional dog-walker Brenda, who had the hots for Justin, in a sort of wild love-rhombus.

Meanwhile Jack bought and sold drugs and consumed a great deal of home-made alcohol, while gambling away the rest of the great wealth he had been given by Stan. He kissed Harriet and he was kissed by Jennifer in her soon-to-close-down haberdashery shop.

Imogen's secret admirer (the dark man with the mysterious scar and the briefcase) plotted to murder Jack.

Krystal blackmailed Heinrich Munchausen, one of the tramcar drivers, into defrauding Jack out of his roulette winnings. Mary and Keith disappeared in the dead of night, taking the entire stock of wagon axles and bullock-harnesses with them, convinced they could corner the market in faraway Kadesh-Barnea.

The body of the man who had tried to rob Lenny Erskine's daughter at knifepoint was pushed over the side as the pleasure craft took an unscheduled midnight journey up the canal, past the disused warehouses and the dark Museum of the Waterways, and on towards the mill, where lights were on.

Who could be weaving cloth at this hour? *cue drums*

AND SO IT WAS that one day, Jack found his wallet, his online bank account and his safety deposit box all empty. At the same time (due possibly to an end-of-series contract-renewal cast cull), an aeroplane exploded over Dissipation City, and fire rained down on the place in a special-effects masterpiece of overstatement.

It was the perfect excuse for the rest of the episode to take place in the familiar surroundings of the intensive care ward, with monitors bleeping, harsh fluorescent lighting and bed-side vigils.

The catastrophe left Imogen paraplegic, Harriet apparently dead (but not before she could scatter several clues about the identity of James' father), and Krystal so traumatised she never spoke again (except in Portuguese). Understandably, she moved to Kadesh-Barnea, but within a month, inexplicably. Jennifer survived, but was played by a different actress. *cue lengthy melancholic version of end music*

'WHAT'S GOING ON?' inquired the man from *Pod-U-Like*, unsure where to deliver the rotting vegetation for the pigs.

Jack indicated the trough and began to explain.

'I'm looking after the porkers since I've no cash left and there's a famine.'

'Leave it out,' said the delivery man, as they do, while the scene wobbled briefly and a visual recap of life on FatCalfisStan Farm played out. *Jack stood face to face with his father, silently raging at him; his dad produced a bag of coins; Jack turned away, vowing never to speak to his father again.*

REALITY RESUMED. Jack sat still and watched the flashback with a growing determination to go home. 'My dad's men eat well, and they are just hired men, with the possible exception of Alexander the metalworker, toothless Owen Eps and Lesley Rhamon, who may not even be a man. I could go home and ask to work, since I am no longer worthy to be called a son.'

Having come to his senses, Jack returned home.

As he approached the farm, his father was waiting, standing at the upstairs window, holding back the net curtain in an obvious manner.

'Could it be?' he asked himself. He watched for perhaps another minute, but by then he was certain. 'My boy!'

'Don't do it, Stan,' private investigator and synchronised diving poolside judge Ursula van Helgesburg said, smoothing the sheet on the bed beside her with her one good hand. 'Let him be, and...'

'He's my son, and I have to forgive. That's the only way I'll know if he forgives me!' Stan said, and made for the door.

'Leave it! He's just not worth it!' Ursula cried.

'He knows that,' Stan said as he ran. *cue drums*

AS STAN REACHED the road, he knew in his troubled, diseased heart that he was going to forgive his wayward son. Jack sank to his knees as his father approached, and began his rehearsed speech. 'I'm sorry, I'm no longer worthy to be called your son. Make me a hired man, please, dad...'

But before he could blurt it out, Stan was right in front of him, hugging him, kissing him.

'Alright treacle? My boy, my boy, you're alive, you came home!'

'Yes, but Dad, I'm no longer...'

Stan called to Oswald, his servant, who had been following and had just arrived at the scene.

'Fetch my ring from my dresser! And bring a coat for the lad.' Oswald turned and began to run back to the house, but Stan called after him. 'Bring shoes for his feet – look at his worn-out sandals! Go!' Oswald ran, but Stan was not done. 'And tell cook we'll have roast calf tonight! Invite the neighbours! Let's have a party!'

Later that same evening, as the crowd gathered around the piano and had a right knees-up singing bawdy cockerney drinking songs, teenager Carmen-Selina Velasquez sneaked into the understairs cupboard and greedily ate cake, fearing she would be discovered. Keenhan Tariq (the nightwatch-man with perfect pitch) and chiropodist's assistant Doreen O'Riordan kissed enthusiastically in the darkness of the library, while Iain Potteridge the beekeeper tried on one of the designer dresses that hung in the guest room wardrobe.

Jack raised his foaming goblet high and cried 'Drinks are on the house! My son was lost, and is found! He was dead and buried under the patio, but now he's alive! Actually, he wasn't really dead at all, but it was apparently to his advantage to let us think he was dead!' *cue drums*

Seagoon's return   *pastiche*

first broadcast on October 11, AD32.
Script by Jesus of Nazareth, produced by BV Mary

GREENSLADE This is the BBC Home Service.

GRAMS *(clink of coin in enamel mug)*

GREENSLADE Thank you. Welcome to the highly esteemed Goon Show. Tonight's story, *Seagoon's Return*, is a torrid tale of greed, wanton expenditure, humility, father's love and, yes, forgiveness, brought to you by your talking-type steam-driven wireless, direct from your sideboard, via airwaves provided.

GRAMS *(scene setting-music)*

SEAGOON What what what what what?

FX *(loud knocking at the door, which continues)*

MINNIE BANNISTER Heennnnrrrrryy! Hhhheenn-rryyyyy! There's someone knocking at the door!

HENRY CRUN Mnn, mnn, must be the Prime Minister.

MINNIE Mnn, mnn, what did you say?

CRUN Mnn, mnn, that must be the Prime Minister knocking at the door.

MINNIE I can't hear you.

CRUN It must be on account of all that annoying knock-knock-knock-ing at the door.

MINNIE (pause) Mnn, mnn, what did you say?

CRUN I said it must be on account of all that knock-knocking at the door.

MINNIE I can't hear you. Open the door. Perhaps the knocking will stop.

CRUN I can't hear you. Tell you what, I'll open the door and perhaps the knocking will stop.

MINNIE I can't hear you because of all that knocking.

FX (much knob rattling, knocking stops, echo-creaking of hinges)

CRUN What do you want?

MINNIE I want you to stop all that knocking, buddy.

CRUN It stopped when I opened the door.

MINNIE No, don't, whatever, you do, open the door.

CRUN Why ever not?

MINNIE We'll all be murdered in our beds!

CRUN But I'm not in bed, I'm opening the door. They're not what they used to be – you can't get the wood, you know. Ah! There seems to be a gentleman standing here, with knuckles red raw. Good evening, young sir, young sir. Are you the Prime Minister?

SEAGOON No, but it's probably just a matter of time. I have come on an important errand.

CRUN Well, it's right at the top of the stairs. Don't forget to put the lid down afterwards. And wash your hands. Use the towel on the towel-rail.

SEAGOON Thank you, yes, perhaps later. Meanwhile, I have come to take my inheritance.

BLOODNOK Now, then, what's all this noise? Neddie, my boy, what are you doing out there?

SEAGOON Knocking at the door.

MINNIE Not any more, buddy.

BLOODNOK Why were you knocking?

SEAGOON Because the door was closed.

BLOODNOK This boy's no fool. And why, pray, were you knocking at this hour?

SEAGOON Because earlier I was standing over yonder and I couldn't reach the door from there. Needle nardle noo!

BLOODNOK And what do you want?

SEAGOON The list is endless. But firstly, and mostly, I'd like my inheritance.

BLOODNOK In the fullness of time. However, I'm fighting fit!

SEAGOON But I was hoping to be able to have it today.

BLOODNOK I see, I see. What will you do with it?

SEAGOON Put it in my handker-chief-type satchel and transport myself away by means of this sound effect...

FX (whoosh)

SEAGOON ... to Dissipation City!

GRAMS (laughter, piano music, glasses clinking)

SEAGOON Listeners, it was rife – nothing less than rife – with jollity and revelry. The men were handsome and some of the women were, to my eye, quite remarkable...

THROAT Yes mate.

SEAGOON ...while the gambling and

eating and drinking went on well into the night. Well, into the evening, at least. There were dancing girls, including Sabrina.

GRYTPYPE-THYNNE No no, it's just me with my arms folded. You should do your best to concentrate on the poker. Now, friend, I'll see your pink marshmallow trouser press and raise you... a wooden clockwork encyclopedia. Have a gorilla.

SEAGOON No thanks, they hurt my throat. So... I'll match your encyclopedia and raise you three – yes, three – gravity-fed gas cookers.

GRYTPYPE-THYNNE H'mmm. I'll raise you this photograph of a five rupee note. *(aside)* What a Charlie...

SEAGOON *(aside)* Haha! Listeners, I've got him right where I want him. *(aloud, clears throat)* I'll see your photograph and raise you a quarter past four on a damp Tuesday. What do you say to that, h'mm?

GRYTPYPE-THYNNE Oh, you silly twisted boy - you will never beat me! I have two jokers and the Knave of Cups.

SEAGOON Rats! I've only got Millenium Falcon, two lumber, Get Out of Jail Free and Mrs Bunn the Baker's Wife. Argh! Penniless!

GRYTPYPE-THYNNE Three flax, the Quarantine Specialist, and some lead piping in the conservatory. But this is yet more grim.

MAX GELDRAY & ORCHESTRA
Pennies from Heaven
GRAMS *('back to the story'-type chords)*
SEAGOON The news was far worse than I could have imagined, folks. It was a national famine. I looked for a job and found one in a pigsty, tending hogs. I was at my lowest ebb, penniless, looking after porkers and all alone in the world, or so I thought.

ECCLES *(sings)* I talk to the trees.
SEAGOON The singer was a ragged idiot.
ECCLES Hallo shipmate!
SEAGOON Have you seen what these pigs are eating?
ECCLES Yes, but only when I'm watching.
SEAGOON And what do you think?
ECCLES I think I talk to the trees.
SEAGOON *(aside)* He stood three foot nineteen in his socks, and very nearly half that in the dark. *(to Eccles)* What do you think of the food they feed those pigs?
ECCLES It's an absolute disgrace.
SEAGOON This boy's got some spirit!
ECCLES It's a disgrace, a disgrace I say, that they are getting better food than we are.
SEAGOON It was an odd conclusion. The pigs had nasty-looking warty pods, mouldy offcuts, rotting stalks and woody bits. We were in desperate danger of starvation, but only a complete fool would envy those pigs.
ECCLES I wish I could eat what those pigs are having. Shut up, Eccles.
GRAMS *(angelic choirs, etc speeded up, slowed down; about 20 seconds)*
SEAGOON What what what what what what? I suddenly realised I could go home and eat all I want and work for my father and be a hired man since I'm no longer worthy to be a son. It's true. I'm off!
FX *(whoosh)*
ECCLES It's all going to be fine, fine.
SEAGOON Except, of course, for this.
RAY ELLINGTON QUARTET
Mama's Got One Blood-shot Eye
GRAMS *('back to the story'-type chords)*
SEAGOON Soon I was on the road home. Over this hill, down the track, round the corner, past the duckpond and beyond the next fencepost and

then I shall be able to see my father's farmhouse. I shall tell him I am no longer worthy to be called a son and ask to work as a hired hand. But what's this? Well slap my thigh and call me a cab, as I live and breathe, it's my old dad, running out from the homestead to meet and greet me.

FX *(running footsteps, approaching)*

BLOODNOK My son! Servant, come here.

FX *(running footsteps, approaching)*

BLUEBOTTLE Enter, dramatically, the famous Bluebottle; waits for applause; as usual, not a sausage.

BLOODNOK Servant! There are things to be fetched!

BLUEBOTTLE My master, what is thy bidding?

BLOODNOK Fetch some shoes!

FX *(running footsteps, departing) (short clip)*

BLOODNOK Come back!

FX *(running footsteps, approaching)*

BLOODNOK And a ring!

FX *(running footsteps, departing) (longer clip)*

BLOODNOK Come back!

FX *(running footsteps, approaching)*

BLOODNOK And a robe!

FX *(running footsteps, departing) (very long clip)*

SEAGOON Eventually, I was, at long last, offered some food.

BLOODNOK Kill the fatted calf!

THROAT Yes, mate.

GREENSLADE And so, everyone had roast beef and potatoes and three veg, with goblets of wine and there were frolics and laughter and joyful celebrations.

SEAGOON But even as I was tucking in to my dinner with characteristic gusto and splashes of gravy, I noticed out of the corner of my eye Bluebottle dancing and prancing perilously ever closer and closer to the edge of the duck pond. I thought to myself this was foolishness and fraught with danger. But he's not going to be so daft as to... Suddenly -

FX *(splosh)*

LITTLE JIM He's fallen in the water!

BLUEBOTTLE You rotten swine, you deaded me!

GREENSLADE Pray silence, my lords, ladies and gentlemen (and just in case, your majesty), for the father of the lost son.

BLOODNOK Ahem. My son was lost, but is found; was dead but is alive!

GRAMS *(Theme music)*

GREENSLADE That was the Goon Show, a BBC recorded programme. It featured Peter Sellers, Harry Secombe and Spike Milligan with the Ray Ellington Quartet and Max Geldray. Announcer: Wallace Greenslade.

* from games, in order: standard card deck, Tarot, Star Wars Transport Top Trumps, Settlers of Catan, Monopoly, Happy Families, Pit, Pandemic, Cluedo

Wrong focus   *viewpoints*

almost entirely tangential issues: details that don't tell the story

The money accumulated happily in the bag under the bed for many years. But one day, it was roughly snatched from its place and was jingled, jangled and redistributed with abandon in a few weeks.

The barkeeper was delighted that he continued to be invited to sell plenty of drinks to the young man, who supplied them to friends until they were all inebriated. They went off to gamble and see a show.

Local economics lurched from unstable to wobbly and then from bad to worse; finally they collapsed when the reserve funds were depleted through either gross mismanagement or felonious corruption.

Much of the **vegetable market** deteriorated as the quality of produce became less and less palatable. The lack of rain had led to a failure of the crops, which meant the parsnips, cabbages and pods were low grade.

Eventually, they were given away to Gentile farmers for fodder, since they were not in the slightest fit for human consumption at all.

The only **sounds** that night were soft whimperings and tummy-rumbles from the starving pigs, and the slap of a hand on a forehead.

Homeville Pathway was long and well-trodden, but the flints strewn along the road were hard on the boy's shoeleather.

Towser the Dog yelped as the farmer accidentally tripped over him in haste.

Young Zech ran to fetch a garment, some jewellery and to warn Old Jake that his beloved Buttercup was going to be lunch.

Five neighbours stood, drank fine wine, ate roast beef, and gossiped about the wayward lad.

They were only momentarily interrupted by the announcement of a speech from their host, and then carried on celebrating.

P@55w0rd 5t7l£   *alphabet games*

Computer 'security' inspired by Bill Burr, author of National Institute of Standards & Technology *Special Publication 800-63, Appendix A; no longer recommended*

Qw£rt7, h15 50ɪv, d£IVI@ɪvd£d h15 1ɪvh£r1t@ɪv©£ @ɪvd l£ft h0IVI£.

H£ 5p£ɪvt th£ IVI0ɪv£7 1ɪv w1ld l1v1ɪv9. Wh£ɪv f@IVI1ɪv£ 5truck, h£ t00k @ j06 t£ɪvd1ɪv9 p195 @ɪvd l0ɪv9£d t0 £@t th£1r p0d5. H£ ©@IVI£ t0 h15 5£ɪv5£5, d£©1d1ɪv9 t0 90 h0IVI£ @ɪvd @5k t0 6£ @ h1r£d IVI@ɪv, 51ɪvc£ h£ kɪv£w h£ w@5 ɪv0 l0ɪv9£r w0rth7 t0 6£ ©@ll£d @ 50ɪv.

IVI@ɪv7 IVI1ll£5 l8r, wh1l£ h£ w@5 5t1ll @ l0ɪv9 w@7 0ff, h15 f@th£r 5@w h1IVI, r@ɪv t0 h1IVI, 9@v£ h1IVI @ r1ɪv9, @ c0@t @ɪvd 5h0£5. HE k1ll£d th£ f@tt£d ©@lf @ɪvd ©£l£6r@t£d.

'Th15 IVI7 50ɪv w@5 l05t @ɪvd 15 f0uɪvd; h£ w@5 d£@d @ɪvd 15 @l1v£ @9@1ɪv!'

@=a ©=c £=e IVI=m ɪv=n 1=I
3=e 5=s 6=b 7=y 9=g 0=o

Arnold Certainman

Timeline   About   Etchings   Friends   More

Works as **Farmer** *at* **Certainman Farm, Home Village, Israel** *Studied at* **Home Village School, Israel** *Lives in* **Home Vilage, Israel**   Edit Profile

Status	Etching	Place	Life Event
What's on your mind?			
			Post

Arnold Certainman Woo Hoo! My son has returned! Waster Certainman came home this morning! I'm inviting everyone to a party at our place at lunchtime. Bring you're friensd! Were celebating with a faated calf and lots of wine!!!!!!
18 May at 08:42– ☺ Esther Xerxes, Peter Boazlad & 120 others like this

> **Mary Abrams** good news! Wots a faated calf?
> 18 May at 08:55 – Like
>
> **Arnold Certainman** dunno. But we're having a fatted calf roasted on a spit. Please come to the event!
> 18 May at 10:01 – Like
>
> **Mary Abrams** will do. So, what happened to him?
> 18 May at 10:05 – ☺ Mark Davidson & 125 others like this
>
> **Elijah Cohen** I agree with Mary
> 18 May at 10:07 – ☺ 'Melchizidek' & 5 others like this
>
> **Arnold Certainman** I gave him cash, he had a good time with it. But there was a famine& he had to get a job. He came to his senses & returned to see if I will employ him as a hired man! Obviously told him no, he's my son
> 18 May at 10:22 – ☺ JJ Jacobs & 182 others like this
>
> **Elijah Cohen** I dont get it you said clear off, or wot?
> 18 May at 10:25– ☺ Mary Abrahams & 132 others like this
>
> **Arnold Certainman** I told him no to being a hired man, he's family!
> 18 May at 10:35– ☺ Isaac Altar & 170 others like this

Arnold Certainman He's been gone so long… I miss him
02 May at 08:42– ☺ David Jonas, Mary Abrams & 12 other people like this

> **Jed O'Moses** any chance of a job please? I could do sweeping or harvesting or a-skinning of the rabbits or animal husbandry or sheep shearing or calf rearing
> 02 May at 17.40 – Like
>
> **Arnold Certainman** dunno. I'm to gloomy to consider it
> 04 May at 06:22 – Like

Arnold Certainman I miss my boy *sigh* 12 March at 21:14– ☺ Mary Abrams, Elijah Cohen, & 17 other people like this

Arnold Certainman feeling sad coz my son Waster Certainman just left home, with a big bag, on his way to Dsspaton City.Not a happyparting, as we had a big row.
03 February at 09:48 – Like – Comment

> **Mary Abrams** where he go?
> 03 February at 09:55 – Like
>
> **Arnold Certainman** dunno. Dissipation City perhaps
> 03 February at 10:01 – Like

254

Mary Abrams shame
03 February at 10:05 – ☺ Steve O'Ur & 12 others like this

Elijah Cohen I agree with Mary
03 February at 10:07 – ☺ Mary Abrams & 5 others like this

James O'Tarsus Whos the big bag?
03 February at 10:10 – Like

Elijah Cohen How can he suddenly afford it?
03 February at 10:12 – ☺ Ruth Naomize & 3 others like this

Arnold Certainman I gave him some cash
03 February at 10:17 – Like

James O'Tarsus Nice
03 February at 10:19 – ☺ Arnold Certainman likes this

James O'Tarsus Nice
03 February at 10:20

James O'Tarsus It was kind thing to do
03 February at 10:23 – ☺ Arnold Certainman likes this

Elijah Cohen A little bit unwise? What if he spends it all? How will he manage? How will you manage, my friend? But then I suppose it none of my business
03 February at 10:24– ☺ Isaiah T & 132 others like this

Arnold Certainman He's my son. I gave him what he wanted. Sometimes love makes you impulsive
03 February at 10:24– ☺ Isaac Altar & 70 others like this

Advertisements   *style*

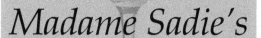

Charcuterie & Cooked Meat
Fresh Bacon: Middle/Back/Streaky/Oyster • Crispy Bacon • Bacon bits • Bacon Lardons
Leg roast • Spare ribs • Deep fried ears • Pork steaks • Sausages (Apple/Sage/Chilli)
Black pudding • Tenderloin • Gammon steaks • Loin roast • Pork escallops • Pork belly
Pork pies • Pork chops (thick cut/thin cut) • Pigs trotters • Lights • Chitterlings
Honey-roast ham on the bone/Smoked Ham/Wafer-thin sliced Ham/ Peppered Ham
Brawn (*aka* head cheese) • Hog jowl • Spam • Spam • Spam • Spam
Pelham's Piggery & Produce 15 St Luke's St, Gentileville, Dissipatia

Say, have you got a light, boy?

SonVestas & barbeque charcoal

258

New Testament   *keywords*
all of the books

Second-born **Matthew** demanded money and, despite the occupation by **Romans**, the farmer was able to part with it. The son went directly to Disspatia, where the civic buildings have columns which are either Dorics or **Corinthians**.

He spent the money (with the assistance of **James**, **Timothy** and the brothers **Phil – Ippians** and **Em**) **on Acts** of wastefulness, with gambling (as recklessly as the infamous **Colossians**) buying utterly pointless souvenirs (a large statue of Diana of the **Ephesians**, for example) and wild drunkenness (he was often **Titus** a drum).

He said 'So I realised I had spent all the money. My internal dialogue: *Is that a net gain? No! And I could have been a shareholder with Home Farm* **Co. Loss**, I answered myself.'

As the cash **Peter**ed out, the crops failed. The boy took a job tending pigs (shameful for **Hebrews**) and longed to eat their food. He had a **Revelation** about home life, and decided to return, ready to ask his father for a job, as he knew he was no longer worthy to be called a son. On his journey, he passed several **Galatians** and one or two **Thessalonians**, all suffering from the famine.

While he was still a long way off, his father saw him and ran to greet him, without stopping to use the **John,** despite his excitement.

He kissed him, gave him gifts of a ring, a coat and shoes and asked **Jude** the farmhand to kill the fatted calf so that they could celebrate. He said 'My son was lost but is found; he was dead, but is alive! **Luke,** everyone, there's not a **Mark** on him!'

Board game rules   *style*
instructions for the famous board game;
a combination of Unsettlers of Canaan,
Brisk! & Meaningful Pursuit

Constructing the Playing Board

Assemble the frame (you will find the pieces in the game box) as they will prevent the board-pieces from moving after the board is in place. Various terrain/mood hexes (wheat, calf, casino, misery, trough, restaurant, pleasure) mark out the farm, the city and the mindmap.

These are positioned at random by a combination of dice throws and blind selection.

Remove the die-cut components from the cardboard holders. Carefully punch out and separate the pieces. Now, place the circular number tokens on top of the designated terrain/mood hexes.

Finally, place your figures as instructed by the drawing of player cards, and position cards, with additional (or fewer, as instructed) resources on Kamchatka, Blue Cheese, any unconnected Sea Port, and Mrs Nash the Dentist's Wife.

Object of the game

This varies according to the Role each player is given. **Son** must become wealthy, leave the Farm, gather random 'friends', receive Revelation and return to the Farm with at least sixteen Victory points.

The player with the Role of **Father** remains on the Farm and gains Victory points by growing wheat, fattening the calf and standing on the roof, viewing the *A Long Way Off* area. He hosts the party when/if the Son returns; he wins the game if he has sixteen Victory points when his turn starts.

259

Players who are dealt the role of **'friend'** accompany the Son on his travels, except to the piggery. They can win the game by collecting ten Victory points, but they are all killed instantly if a Famine card is drawn.

Other players include **PigMan** and **Madam**, who are also seeking to gain at least ten Victory points, a minimum of five pizza slices and either three cannon cards or a mixed bag, which can be turned in on an escalating scale, provided one of the cards relates to a 'friend' with an alliterative name, a hex from which you receive resources, or Piggywig Skinnyflanks.

Estabishing characters/ resources/range

Various cards show resources that become available at the start of each players' turn. The player who draws **Father** starts the game (if no-one draws that card, then deal the undrawn cards – starting with the player to the left of the player with the Son card – until one player receives the Father card).

If that player already holds the Son card he continues to play as the Son but begins the game; however, if the player who is dealt the Father card already holds the Madam or Transport Chief card, they roll a dice to decide if they play as Father (roll an even number to be Father). NB all draws represent a defensive victory throughout, with two important exceptions.

Cards representing resources and moods (wheat, calf, casino, misery, restaurant, trough, pleasure) are distributed to each player according to proximity to hexes. Victory point cards are only provided when a player wins a victory, such as filling a

260

barn with wheat, winning Stoutest Calf Rosette at the annual farm show, becoming Best Customer at *Madame Sadie's Bar 'n' Bordello* or Least Reliable TroughMinder of the Year.

Any player who draws the New Shoes card can add 30 armies in one territory, as long as there are sufficient armies available and they own a territory capable of sustaining all those occupying forces.

Turns

Each player's turn consists of six strictly ordered phases.

1 Resource phase Throw two dice to discover which resources are made available to all players, or (when a seven is thrown) to herald the coming of the Angel. A chart on the side of the board shows the percentage chance of throwing each of the scores; for example, 2=2.8%, 5=11.2%, 7=16.6%

2 Barter phase A player may exchange resources with other players or with the Bank. The official rate of exchange with the bank is three for one, while other players may be willing to exchange tokens, resources, cheeses, cake segments, vouchers or materials at cheaper (or more expensive) rates. The strict rule is that it is the prerogative of the player whose turn it is to initiate the bargaining. In strongly competitive games, resources may also be exchanged for forfeits, kisses, footwear, jewellery, car keys, children or promissory notes (authenticated by at least one notary public).

3 Purchase phase Now the player can spend money (or give up tokens or exchange vouchers) with the Shop – food, entertainment, tools, materials or time to reflect. In addition, a player may buy up to two road sections and/or one house not of his own colour but relating to other players, for later bartering.

4 *Build phase* The player may wish to build a road (which must extend from a hex or house he owns) or a house (which must be connected to a road he owns). Roads cost 4 coins each, while houses cost 10 coins each. Either can be purchased from the Bank during the Purchase phase or from other players through the Barter phase. Important note: no player may own more than three unplaced sections of road or more than one unplaced house at the start of his turn. Any items over this limit are forfeit to the player nearest to the location of the player whose turn has just started – if two players are equidistant, then the least wealthy of them benefits.

5 *Motion phase* A player may move his counter up to three hexes along a road of his own free of charge (including any road he has just built), or along a road owned by another player at a cost of one coin per section of road. Upon reaching a house, he must stop, and if the house is owned by another player, he must pay one coin in rent. If the house is neutral, or a Gentile Home, he must pay two coins. If the house is owned by the Pig Farmer, or a player who has the Piggywig Skinnyflanks card, then the arriving player must draw a Fortune card for themselves, risking Famine. Actions are taken immediately.

6 *Card phase* The player now takes a Fortune card for the player on his right and read it aloud. Any actions required must be completed, and then the turn is over. Play moves to the next player (unless the Fortune card just drawn demands otherwise) and continues with a resource phase.

Gathering 'friends'

As players progress and accumulate money and wheat, they can exchange them for 'friends'. When a player has three 'friends', this entitles the 'friends' to spend the player's money in the bars, nightclubs and theatres of the city.

However, each player with two or more 'friends' must take a Fortune card at the start of each turn (before the Resource phase). Some of these are positive (extra money, free cheeses, avoid History, an additional turn, a win at the roulette wheel), some are neutral (additional 'friend' if you can afford her; *get out of sheol free* card) and at least four of the cards are negative (famine; bankruptcy; bankruptcy with double dip famine; death by starvation or knife crime).

Having three additional 'friends' (i.e. a minimum of five 'friends') gives the player the right to use an extra dice when attacking, but no player may ever use more than two dice when defending.

In addition, whenever a player rolls a seven, no resources are distributed. But the Angel of the Lord appears, and each player draws one Towards True Understanding card, which reveals fresh insight into your mental/spiritual state. Some of these cards are worth one victory point; the card is retained until the Reckoning. If no cards are available, then this is judged to be indigestion.

Any player who accumulates two Homesick cards returns to the farm and must start again, unless they can produce one cavalryman card, plus two other cards which are of territories they occupy and can also pay three wheat, one 'roll again' card and five coins.

261

Hunger

A hunger card can be returned to the pack in exchange for five wheat or three cheeses (Silver Service Restaurant Vouchers are wild).

Any player who collects three Hunger cards has starved to death and is eliminated from the game, but first distributes any Victory Points won to other players within three hexes (in the case of dispute the dying player's choice is disregarded as they are too weak to argue, and the disputing players settle by bargaining, within a two-minute timeframe). Bargains can be settled by whatever means agreed, but all Victory Points are forfeit to the remainder of the players (evenly distributed, with any left over returning to the Bank) if, when the time is over, the combatants are still locked in discussion or death grip.

Revelation

Any player who draws a Revelation card and then rolls a seven ('Angel of the Lord' appears) comes to his senses, collects four Victory Points and must now return to the farm and roll one dice to determine his wage. If he rolls a one, he is rejected and is eliminated from the game (after distributing his Victory Points to players within three hexes). If he rolls a 3 or a 5 he is accepted as a hired man, and wins one Victory Point. However, if he rolls an even number, he is welcomed back as a son, and must draw from the Roles cards.

If he draws Caterer, he can establish the party and must gather beef and beer cards. If he draws 'Friend' he may attend the party but may hold no Victory points. If he draws any other role card, he is considered Villager

from Afar and his counter is moved directly to the furthest-away hex from the Farm.

Pods

At any time, any player who cashes in his pod cards in exchange for resources, money or to assist in battles is deemed to have 'missed the point' and is eliminated from the game, with any Victory Points given directly to the Father.

Endgame: the Reckoning

Returning to the farm may appear to be a winning strategy, but once there, the player representing the Son must correctly answer three questions from categories chosen by the agreement of the other players from the following options: prodigality; destitution; pork; unworthiness; forgiveness. If any question is incorrectly answered, the player must wait for his turn to come round before again attempting three (preferably different) questions.

For the player designated Father to win, he must also speak for one minute without repetition, hesitation or deviation on the topic 'he was lost but now he's found; he was dead but is alive!'

Players designated Friend, Madam, PigMan or Hireling need only gather sufficient Victory Points to win.

The player designated 'Older Brother' is deemed winner as soon as he gains sixteen Victory Points, ten wheat and one fat calf, unless he is still in possession of the 'party with a goat' card when the Son arrives at the Farm, in which case he is deemed Uninvited Villager and must pay the Farmer ten coins to attend the party. If he cannot, he becomes Villager from Afar (see above).

Public information film *style*

in which a voice-over 'nanny' narrator talks to a mute hero; style reflects Harry Enfield's Mr Cholmondley-Warner

INTERTITLE CAPTION
FINANCIAL ADVICE FOR SONS

Now here's a likely fellow. He seems to be very determined to get about his business, and no mistake. He clearly has work to do… but he seems to have become weary with his tasks.

Are you the farmer's son? *(Stops to nod to camera)*

Are you wealthy? *(Sadly shakes head, pulls out pocket linings)*

And do you enjoy your job? *(Bitter laugh, shakes head in denial)*

So, you must be about to ask your father to hand over your inheritance? *(Smiles, nods)*

Now, here he goes, off down the road, and now he's at his destination, Dissipation City.

And he's met some people who may not be what they seem. Gosh, she's a pretty one! Oh, and so is she! I say!

Are you aware of the temptation they represent? *(Nods, smiles to himself)* And have you been gambling? *(Nods, smiles to himself)* Will you have a drink or two? *(Nods, smiles)* Well, take it steady, old chap, won't you? *(Shakes head)*

Oh dear, look at this; he's spending his money very enthusiastically, and that's a fact. If he's not careful, he'll – oh well, it's just as I thought.

Have you completely run out of money? *(Shakes head in sadness, opens wallet to show it is empty)*.

And the country's entered a recession, too. Oh dear. Now, what's all this to do? He's taken a job in a piggery. Watch out, this fellow's being careless with the slops! Oh, dear, what a mess!

These pigs are what I would call unhealthy-looking. And so is our young man. The famine is getting the better of him. Now his hunger is playing tricks with his mind.

Are you thinking you might eat those horrible-looking slops? *(Nods)*.

Oh dear. Very nasty.

INTERTITLE CAPTION
GENTLEMEN: KNOW YOUR LIMITS

Now what's all this? Looks like he's had a good idea. *(Shakes head in denial)*. Oh, it was a revelation, then. *(Smiles, nods)*. Are you going home? *(Smiles, nods)*. That's a very good plan. Are you going home to be a farmer's son once again? *(Shakes head in denial)*. Oh, I see, you're going to ask for a job, are you? *(Smiles, nods.)*

The lad's still a long way off but Father can see him. He'd better tuck his tunic in or he'll trip, as like as not!

Is this your Dad? *(Smiles, nods)*. Has he welcomed you? *(Smiles, nods)*. Given you – let's see *(shows cheek)* a kiss, *(shows feet)* shoes, *(shows jacket)* a coat, *(shows hand)* and a ring. My word, that's a warm welcome. I say!

Is that all? *(Shakes head in denial)*.

Ah, a barbecue with roast beef and a party with all the neighbours? *(Smiles, nods)*. You were dead and lost, weren't you? *(Sadly nods)*.

Yes, that's right. But now you're found and very much alive, wouldn't you say? *(Smiles, nods)*.

INTERTITLE CAPTION
NEVER ATTEMPT TO LIVE BEYOND YOUR MEANS

263

Luke's Parable Pantry
Table d'hôte from £15.11

Aperitifs et
Amuse Bouche

Glimpses of Confidential Accountants' Analysis
of the State of Father's Wealth,
served with Secrecy and dashes of Jealous Guilt sauce

Hors d'oeuvres

Pastry Purses du soupérabondance d'argent

Permission du Leave, vis-à-vis Sad Smile

Expectant Journey du côte de Bright Lights dans Big City,
served avec stick d'epaule and rouge-spotted pashmena

Entrées

Hôpitalier Femmes avec Aroma Trés Pléasante

Deteriorating Morality

Alcohol by the Flagon

Casino Gambling, con Dwindling Chips

Unrestrained Extravagance

Hotel Living

Smorgasbord d'Entertainments

Wildness in a Cash Reserves Reduction

Mains

Famine du Maison parce que Financial Lavishing

Pork Skins (Fat-Free) with Blemishes on a bed of Scabs

Rotting Mushy Pods in Vegetable Gaspacho

Greenness of Envy au chagrin

Blinding Flash of Inspiring Divine Révélation

Hired Men's Luncheon with a selection of roasted meats

Homemade Humble Pie (large slice)

with sides

Rising Up	Homeward Bound
Wearied Trudging	Speech Rehearsal

From the Dessert Trolley

Visual Acuity avec Exuberance

Longue Whey Oeuf

Fleetness du Pied

Firm-Pressed Lips dans Warm Embracing

New Coat con Buttons

Family Signet Ring avec Forgiveness

Sole with Straps 'n' Buckles

Roast Calf Surprise

Thinly Sliced Barbecued Beef

Coffee & Mints

Pere et Fils	Neighbours et Villageois
Lost et Trouvé	Mort et Vivant

10% Service Charge will be added to your bill

Middle O   *alphabet games*
only words with the middle letter o
Ecclesiologist (educationalist) analogies for absconder.

Prologue.

Bob affords quota. Blond bloke Timothy cajoled heinously; income's awesomely hedonic incongruousnesses (not IOU). Bod absconded – wrong!

Blows moola… mischievousnesses, flirtatiousnesses, amorously, extortionately, ignobly.

Balconies-bosomed ungodly broad Dorothy Amour (buxomly Aphrodite) cavorts – immoral floozie-licentiousness! Uncouth boy spooned among boobs, barhopped; carouse loose escorts' unmentionables.

Avoid abstemiousness.

Avariciousness/frivolity/narcotic/booty – account Nos: broke.

Chronic impecuniousnesses confounds calorie. Hollowest corporeal – now moody, low.

Apropos, enrolls (sow-hog job). Forlornly enviously drooled: almonds-aroma bubonic composted blobs; calloused hideously, microbial odour rot; malformed poisonous pod-slops. Atrophy, arsonic contagiousness. Grots!

God awoke idiotic Roy howsoever. Remorse; reforms aloud, avows

265

'Employees Joe/Ron Laborer (industriousnesses) allowed foods... disowns not! Diplomacy chooses resolve. Adopt land-owner-croft – exhorts adopt job, belongs.'

Arose, anxiously: acrimoniousnesses? Agony? Apologies.

Brook-close dialogues, nervously. Beholds, beckoning, affectionately galloping. 'Aloha! Cooee!'

Enfolds, outpoured devoted responses.

'Bestowing billowing angoras, crinoline snood, box cloak, cloth dhoti, stole sarongs, chamoises, bow-buttoning glove, festooned pullovers, crocodile clogs (resoled shoes/boots). Embroider thong-colours sartorial! Don enrobed; goods, hoods, ribboning, shrouds,; uniformed, reclothed!'

Carnivorousnesses: spitroasted cow hoofs; savoury brown stock broth/consommes; cantonese rag-outs; potboiled goose foods; roe flavoured risotto; wok-defrosted cod; bologna flour; parboiled sprouts; bloomer; moose chops; trout; stork.

Throngs scoff ambrosias, gooey chocolate coconut brioche, liquorice, victorias, ricotta.

Crowd devours booze: alcohol shots, plonk.

Acrobat, baroque singer-songwriter bongoists; melodic bandoleer; soloist crooner; gregorian harmonies group; oboes, obviously; banjoist's harmoniousness; keyboards' grooves; bouzoukis; performer encores.

Homeowner: 'Introduce restoring approvals. Glory! Beloved, favored boy ensconced indoors! Approving joy! Coroner not! Bygones forgotten.

'Epilogued compassionateness, oratories, hymnodies! Goody! Rejoice, supporter-mob!'

266

Last will & testament *style*

This is the last
Will and Testament
of *Arnold Certainman*
of Certainman Farm,
Hicksville, Israel
being of sound mind and reckoned
to be of sober judgement

1. **I hereby revoke** all former wills and testamentary dispositions made by me under the law of Israel.

2. **I appoint my wife** *Delores Certainman* (of the same address) to be Executor and Trustee of this my Will; in case the aforementioned shall die within my lifetime or shall refuse or be unable to act in this office, I appoint *Solly Citor*, of **Tsoo, Grabbit & Runne, Commissioners for Oaths** of Bethel to fill the vacancy thereby left.

3. If nobody of parental responsibility survives me, **I appoint my brother** *Abraham Certainman* of Certainman Saddlery, Jericho to be the Guardian of any of my children who are minors; but if the aforesaid shall die before me or disclaim the appointment, then **I appoint my sister** *Mary Obediah* of Kadesh-Barnea to be such Guardian.

4. **I bequeath** the following **legacies**:
(i) **I bequeath** to my elder son *James* (as is customary) two thirds of all my estate. My intent is that he shall own two-thirds of all farmland, buildings, livestock, machinery and contractual obligations with farmhands, casual workers, labourers, crop-pickers and livestock wranglers ('hired men')
(ii) **I bequeath** to my younger son *Prodigal* the remaining third of my estate, so that he will own the remaining one-third

5. **I hereby further bequeath** my fine porceline eighty place dinner service

(eight times dinner plate, side plate, soup bowl, pudding bowl, tea cup, saucer, coffee cup, saucer, finger bowl plus three tureens, three serving plates, sugar bowl and gravy boat) along with the sum of twelve pieces of silver to my estranged childhood chum *Thaddeus Lamech* of Porcine World, Dissipatia, strictly providing he closes, sells or otherwise disposes of his Piggery and declares his genuine intention never again to have anything to do with unclean animals. In the event that he is unwilling to meet this requirement, or fails to survive me, the dinner service and four pieces of silver (items aforementioned) shall pass to my elder son *James*; and the remainder of the pieces of silver to my son *Prodigal*

6. Any liquid assets and whatsoever residue **is to be divided equally** between *GemsRUs Jewellers* of Ebed, *Sole Provider* (Footwear Manufacturers to the Sanhedrin) of Antioch and *Wrap Up plc*, Bespoke Tailor of Ramoth.

Dated this twenty third day of Sh'vat, in the third year of Herod II.

Arnold Certainman

Arnold Certainman, Farmer

Witnessed by

Moses Menasseh   *Phillip O'Gath*

Moses Menasseh, Hireling

Phillip O'Gath, Hireling

--- Codicil ---
Dated tenth day of Kislev in the ninth year of Herod II. Having liquidated sufficient of my estate to give one third of my wealth to my younger son *Prodigal*, I hereby **revoke** section 4(ii), and **increase** the proportion given to my elder son *James* in section 4(i) to 'all'.

--- Codicil Secundus Majoris --- (Superceding)
Dated tenth day of Elul in the twelfth year of Herod II. Having discovered that my younger son *Prodigal* is neither lost nor dead but both found and alive, I hereby **reinstate** sections 4(i) and 4(ii) to their original form. Furthermore, I hereby **reallocate** all items listed in section 6 such that the beneficiary thereof is to be my aforementioned younger son *Prodigal*.

Re — key words
*81 uses of re or re-; **bold type** emphasizes the difference hyphens make*
Reliable redeemer reiterates repentance-yarn re-emphasising religion: Renegade lad resented Pa's real estate, requesting reward repulsively; recycle non-renewable resources.

He resettled in Dissipation City, and redoubled his efforts, **really** reducing his wealth: revelled in restaurants, and in reprehensible **recreation** with ill-reputed retailers.

National regression however – restriction of food. Such regret! Reason: repellent, revolting pods in pigs' trough-reticules.

He received a reveille/revelation ('Reconsider! **Re-ally**') and this led to him re-examining himself; he recanted and **resigned** himself to re-order and retrace his steps, return and **recover** (or **re-form**) and rebuild the requisite relationship with his father and become a regime recruit.

He was not worthy to be a resident.

As he **re-covered** the distance, he re-read his résumé, and thought 'Will he be reluctant, or reticent, or regale me with rebukes? I wonder what the resettlement will be like? Restitution? **Re-sign** a work contract? Redneck/refusnik? Rejection? Kick up the rear?' He approached the re-entry point (by the reeds) and saw his dad was ready! Dignity readjusted, he rearranged his clothing and recklessly re-located for greeting with relish.

Reported speech: the father requested the servants to provide: reinforced toe-cap boots. Reception – red meat ('re-light the fire and re-use the spit!') and all the rest. His dad reaffirmed 'It's like a **re-creation** or re-assembling of our family! We are reconciled! The **reformed** boy was dead but is resurrected!'

Road Yellow
Goodbye Brick   *keywords*

using all the words of Goodbye Yellow Brick Road, *Elton John's 1973 top ten hit; lyrics by Bernie Taupin*

When this young boy's said 'I've decided my future... goodbye!' Off he goes **down the yellow brick road,** where he meets **friends.**

The penthouse society lies and steals, asking **'When are you going to bet too?'** Cash is gone and famine strikes. He says **'There's plenty like me who ain't got a penny.'** He takes a job tending pigs, **sniffing for tidbits on the ground: Mongrels** like a horny back plant.

Your man gets the **blues. 'I should have stayed on the farm; I didn't! I should have listened to my old man.'** He was **howling in for...** 'What do you think you'll do, then? I'm going

back to my plough, back to the woods. I'll sign up to be **that** *hired man* **with you,** dad.'

While he was still a long way off, his father saw him across **open land (plane).** '**I'm gonna come down the road!'** he cried, running. He embraced his boy. **'You know you can't hold me forever?'**

'I need new shoes. Look, **where me dogs howl.'**

'Maybe you'll get a replacement, to set you on your feet again. And a **yellow** metal ring. Kill the fatted calf!'

'But **you can't shoot your old Hunting...'** His dad was happy enough **to be singing 'It'll take you a couple of vodka and tonics** with a **brick of your** fave ice cream, plus **toad** and **owl for** dinner!'

He gave a speech **'So the** son of mine, once **not present; finally beyond you to be found! Oh, are you in the** mood **to dance?'**

When are you gonna come down?
When are you going to land?
I should have stayed on the farm;
I should have listened to my old man.
You know you can't hold me forever,
I didn't sign up with you.
I'm not a present for your friends to open;
This boy's too young to be singing the blues

So goodbye yellow brick road;
Where the dogs of society howl;
You can't plant me in your penthouse –
I'm going back to my plough.
Back to the howling old owl in the woods,
Hunting the horny back toad;
Oh I've finally decided my future lies
Beyond the yellow brick road

What do you think you'll do then?
I bet that'll shoot down your plane.
It'll take you a couple of vodka and tonics
To set you on your feet again!
Maybe you'll get a replacement –
There's plenty like me to be found:
Mongrels who ain't got a penny;
Sniffing for tidbits like you on the ground

Dr Seuss *pastiche*

borrowing freely from The Cat in the Hat; Green Eggs and Ham;
Fox in Socks *and* Oh, The Places You'll Go!

    The son said 'It's time; give your cash, now, today,'
    So his dad did just that; his lad went off to play.
    Oh, the places I'll see! Ere I'm done I'll have fun!
    Winning hands dealt to me! There's roulette to be won.

    He walked down the road to a city of sin;
    He frolicked with Sally, and drank lots of gin,
    And gambled and feasted and gambled some more
    'Til all of his money was gone – he was poor!
    He was much worse than poor now he'd wasted his loot -
    He had nothing at all. He was quite destitute.

    Oh, no traces I see! I am quite in the red!
    Humble job looks for me! There are pigs to be fed.
    He took up some digs with a man who kept pigs
    No-one danced any jigs but they ate figs and twigs
    Which were unfit for pigs playing gigs wearing wigs
    (Clearly not what we've got) but were oozy with rot
    And what a lot of snot – a spot or a clot!
    Let's do tricks with pigs and pods, sir
    Let's all munch our brunch and crunch, sir!
    Scrunch our lunch with punch and pods, sir
    Pods and wads of – hear from God, sir?

    Oh, God's grace is so free! There is work to be done!
    Not worthy, me, nor considered a son.
    When young Stan made a plan, as we know that he can,
    He ran to his clan, to be where he began.
    But if the old man were to issue a ban
    He could say it's okay – a cliché – to take pay
    Not betray or display his dismay (nay nay nay)
    But work hard on the farm with full vigour and charm.
    But old dad was so glad that he shared what he had
    Gave a ring and a thing. 'Can't excuse those old shoes!'
    And a kiss and with wit turned a calf on a spit.

    Through three cheeses, grease and peases
    And flans and flakes of cakes and creams
    And dreams of extremes of roasted beef
    And green leaf and white wine and lamb tagine divine…
    I'll always eat them here or there.
    Yes, I will eat them anywhere
    'Not lost,' said his Pa, 'although traveled afar

And not dead, though he fled, which was somewhat bizarre
But we say *welcome back* yet his wallet does lack;
Now he won't be a slob cause I'll give him a job,
Working fields for good pay. Now, enjoy the buffet!'

So the guests stayed all day and had plenty to say
Quaffing chilled cabernet, chewing mignon fillet,
Through vast portions of pudding all covered in sauce,
They tucked in with glee to a third, fourth, fifth course.

Oh, the places I saw! But home's surely the best!
Dad and I are at one now that we've coalesced.
Never more shall I roam, but will always stay home
At charm farm where it's calm with no cause for alarm.
Let's not bet on Georgette or any brunette, sir,
Not fret or sweat nor feel beset with debt, sir
Forget jet-set days of unwise, huge expenses
But remember, thank God, that I came to my senses!
I once disagreed with my dad and his creed
To my shame he came running to greet me, with speed;
But this party I know will all guests overfeed (98¾% guaranteed).

Pinteresque   *pastiche*

comedy of menace, characterized by
pauses, deception and power struggles
Requires British 60s/70s Absurd
Theatre cast:
FATHER   Lawrence Olivier
         John Guildgud
         or Michael Gambon
JACK   Ian Holm
         Jeremy Irons
         or Tom Courtenay
MIKE   Nigel Havers or Alan Bates

Scene One: A small living room

FATHER   I'm not a rich man.

[pause]

JACK   *I'm* not a rich man.
FATHER   What?
JACK   Oh, but you're rich in ways
few can contemplate, Father!

270

FATHER   Some might say that. I could
not possibly comment. But what
meagre wealth I have is entirely
invested in crops, livestock and one
gold ring.
JACK   More tea?
FATHER   Hmm. Your mother used to
love to walk in the country until that
day seventeen years ago when I
playfully ran with her across the
meadow and she tripped climbing
over a stile and… hurt her leg.
JACK   When will I inherit your
wealth?
FATHER   Poor Belinda. She rarely
goes walking now.
JACK   You see, I wish to explore
good living for myself.
FATHER   Her life has degenerated.
Now she just sits in the house, staring.
Her leg troubles her. She has not
recovered at all, it seems. Perhaps she
never will.

JACK   I said, Father, when?

[pause]

FATHER   *(dismissive)* As you wish.
JACK   Goodbye.
FATHER   When will you return?
JACK   I have no intent so to do. I bid you good day, sir. *(exit)*

Scene Two: A public house with a low ceiling

JACK   Amy is lovely, but I feel Katie's more willing.
MIKE   You may well think that.
JACK   You had enough to drink?
MIKE   Can't say I've had enough.
JACK   I'll buy some more. Then, we'll go to the casino again.

[pause]

MIKE   I enjoyed the show. And so did Gloria and Clarise.
JACK   Oh! I am reaching the end of my money.
MIKE   So did Rachel and Theresa.
JACK   There's a famine coming, the authorities say, but I don't believe them. Pessimists!
MIKE   There is no famine coming.

Scene Three: A tiny pig sty

JACK   Curse this famine! I've been hungry for a long while… had to find a job, and ended up in a piggery; but the man who comes to feed the pigs hasn't showed up for a week now, and the slops in the trough are of very low quality. But no matter how hungry I become, I'll never consider trying even a handful of the pigs' rotting food. Not under any circumstances.

[pause]

JACK   Probably. At least the swine get to eat… *(slaps forehead)* and I'll tell you who else gets to eat – father's hired men, back at the farm. They are merely hired men, and here's me, one of his sons, and I'm starving while they feast. This cannot be right! I may have to consider humbling myself, returning to the farm, and asking my father for a job.

I have completely burned my bridges and have absolutely no right to be called a son. I am not worthy. At least this is entirely my own idea, and not some external inspiration.

Scene Four: At the farm gate, surrounded by hedges

JACK   I hope he doesn't dismiss me. He has every right to do so…
FATHER   *(breathless)* Your mother is unwell.
JACK   I am not worthy to be called your son.
FATHER   She ails, you know. Her leg troubles her greatly…
JACK   My shoes are worn out, and my coat is ragged.
FATHER   Just sitting, staring. That's all she does, you know.
JACK   Yes, I sold all my jewellery.
FATHER   All she does, every day, I just sitting, staring, feeling pain in her leg. Time has taken its toll. It is such a shame.
JACK   I am so hungry. My journey was long, wearying.
FATHER   A toll on her, I mean. Time. Taken a toll, you know.
JACK   May I have a job? And some meat?

[pause]

271

FATHER   Yes, time has taken its toll, indeed.
JACK   What?
FATHER   Come in, and bring the villagers to celebrate.
JACK   But…
FATHER   I thought you were dead, but no. I knew you were lost, but now you're found; go and say *hallo* to your mother while you can. While she is still with us. Apart from that, I could not possibly comment.
JACK   I'll, er, make her some tea.

[Blackout]

Middle U   *alphabet games*
only words with the middle letter u
JesusO'N: truth-discoursing analogousnesses. Articulated but conceptualizing, confounding thesauruses. Adult Bruce esquire accounted agriculture annuity. Young Samuel's querulousnesses scrounges (manipulated) escudos acquire affluence. Ambitiousnesses, obnoxiousnesses: adjourned.

Debauched carousal's lustfulness – roguish amorousness – copiousness-figured seduced stepdaughters: saucy Claudia (flouncy mudguards, capaciousnesses); swash-buckling Trudi (allures, tempestuousness); corruptly infatuating Augusta (adventuresome denuded delinquencies); pleasurable parlourmaid, ambiguously sinuous Laura.

Egregiousnesses, lecherousnesses, atrociousnesses! Drunk groupie voyeurism would flush aroused dissoluteness; chums buy drugs, frightfulnesses, grotesquenesses. Fun? Crude secular promiscuousness, insidiousnesses. Indulge!

Repercussions…

Fluctuating mis-judged acute bankrupting penuriousnesses cause consequential impecunious destituteness. Genuine reduced tum. Pitifulness due. Sojourned. Liquefy mucuses… snouted fauna gut ominousness.

Acidulous gruel (horticultural unguent agues, lousy coagulant mould, flatulent effluvium, pus-slugs, awfully cellulose fibrousness). Noxiousness! Harmfulness! Enviousness. Doubt… capitulated consciousnesses.

Spiritualness deduced fault, renounces nefariousnesses. Evaluates habituation; labourers; house; evacuated!

Youth returns; rough route. Anxiousness. Excommunicate? Rebuked furiousness? Litigiousnesses. Lecturing harrumphs? Fearfulness. Hopefulness? Trust? Encounter assured! Nurturing, favouring impetuousnesses, courteousnesses. Perambulation-run, rapturous mouth over-abundances, hug, engulfs (crush!). Strenuously reacquaints (tearfulness).

Blurt 'Briquette inconspicuousnesses! Jaunt!' All-purpose costumers' blouses, turquoise fluff yarmulkes, gauzy mauve corduroys' super-fluousness, sequins-suffusion luxuriousnesses!' Bounteousnesses!

Flocculates substitutionary trouser.

Multitudinous banqueted, consuming community. Succulent deliciousnesses: epicurean belugas, floured crust squab, croquette, sauté grouses, crouton-rub soups, legumes, squid vol-au-vent savouries, hamburger bun, piquant sauce; strudel. Yum! Limburger, matured gouda; plump blackcurrants, plums. Sup rum, tequila, chateaubriand; pasteurised draught liquids; prune daiquiris. Chorusing flute minuets seguing Tijuana troupes' tunefulness. Semiquavers mellifluousness! Round tambourines. Garrulousnesses. God-daughters, grand-uncles' out-pourings expounded eloquence.

'Congratulations! Arduous anguish? Inquest? Moribundity.' Announced, enthusing. Fortunate exhumer! Found guy, rehousing!'

Good-humoured gesticulating, hilariousnesses. Momentousnesses! Profoundest triumph! Exult! Laugh!

Oneiric   *style*
dream-sequence

Aware… swooping magestically on a carpet of generous weave, we hold hands, floating, watching streams of silver drops cascade onto leathery pouches and down the country lane. Azure skies. Cool water splashes on our smiles while clouds of father-breath swirl and glower, turn away; we fall, we fall.

Like a cup poured with wine and slices of cake and pretty girls, we are darkly in a theatre where jugglers sing, croupiers mix cocktails and musicians collect chips, clawing great stacks of them from the threadbare beize table, until – no chips left. No money, plates clean/empty, glasses likewise, crowds dispersing. The room is now empty; no furniture, carpets.

The walls retreat; space grows more vast. Wake; sleep. Scene shifts as skeletons, dressed as policemen, march from house to mudpatch, back again, why, thank you. Slime decorates the path, when a chocolate cake emerges, looking delicious. But as I go to take a bite – it liquefies, oozing between my bony fingers.

Angelic singing, bright lights, smoke and a friendly but author-itative voice… 'Your father's hired men eat.' I spin and move away from the light, towards other light.

Wake, sleep. We've intruded upon a 220m hurdles relay (is there one?); I'm wearing Joseph's dreamcoat, soldier's boots and there is a wide bull with a ring in his nose, slowly rotating on a giant skewer; flames lick flesh and dance to the music as grease drops fall, hissingly. Chefs approach with knives. Dad's speech is friendly, hide-and-seek, booking a funeral, then cancelling it again. There is dancing; clouds swoop.

Just as he's about to send me to work, I wake with a start, perspiring.

Hiding in plain sight   *wordplay*

also termed steganography. *In this case* **Greener Grass** *encoded,*
but easy-to-crack for those who look left

> The most effective type of cypher is clearly one that, within rea-son, can just be read, simply as straight text. If the writing demanded the reader set aside all regular standards or even put his hope of comprehension down, then all those first clues buried in the text will be spotted. Suppose, for example, a woman wrote her Diary in a way such that any code-cracker could so easily spot it had unlikely content, then this would be partly-solved in adv-ance, since odd words may (quite naturally) give the game away

and make codes far too easy to find; so eliminate them, see what's left. These are termed 'lights on, doors open but no-body's at home' codes, since it is easy to extract whatever message.

He may have considered messages buried, or a waste of the time spent constructing them! No, far better to devise cyphers where the simple fact that they contain a message is hidden – the clever money all goes into random-numbers-generator-based encoding in which both the transmitters and the receivers share the raw or 'wild' numbers, knowing a text's first edition (e.g. *Night of the Living Dead, Macbath* or *Ivanhoe* etc) to use: 5/34 - 19/103 - 44/178. When interpreted, this indicates page/word. As there was a famine or scarcity of interpeters, one of the UK's top encoders struck upon an idea - what if it is genuinely possible to use what he calls 'their Local Weather Report' as a text? The encoder partook of simple sentences – every number, volume or pitch used by a weather presenter; – and from them forging a message. Quite a job, admittedly, but possible. Decoders monitored forecasts, tending to record broadcasts. Then, sadly, so like the chauvinist pigs they are(!), they examined soundtracks to isolate words like *he* or *she*. They saw items (in their odd lingo) added, shorted, longed or combinated in communiqués. They found days & times to be at locations, make demands, issue three challenges or a threat from an hostile enemy. Then they all act on the instructions of their contacts, causing mayhem and/or uproar. Cameras on tripods are able to capture stills with no trembles at all.

He computerised these code-cracking skills and very soon they came before the gaze of *The Geek,* a wise man with the experience to recognize use of unusual words – e.g. *Going, Proverb, Maharishis* or *over-convolutedness.* Unexpected phrases provoke his code-senses since their presence indicates something unusual. So, deciding that he has found a coding, he counts up the 'e's, hoping to spot any strange patterns (more G's than E's, for instance), lingo that is far less than common... Then he'll make an effort to home in on all of the encrypted expressions; this technique works and unerringly discovers whatever the encoder buried. You may ask 'what other techniques might be used?' It isn't possible for us to give a fuller explanation: partly, because several methods may be subject to the Official Secrets Act; additionally because there's an extremely baffling super-complexity to them. *The Geek* can be hired on an hourly basis to solve such codings. Despite intrahuman relational difficulties, he has learned to be more civil (ever since the New York Incident, over which we shall draw a veil as he was aquitted anyway). 'I looked at the wording – I knew this was one which contained coding,' said one codecracker earlier.

'No, they truly deserve looking at more closely.' Two minutes longer, and his notes had developed. 'So, 'E' was represented by 'W' or 'T.' *Hybrid* forms another 'misfit' word – we knew we had to unlock it!' 128-bit codings (meaning my accounting details can be transmitted safely through the internet) are very frequently called upon to provide financial security, since on-line banking's a non-starter until it could be shown to be secure, just like any prison. Eventually, these codes were proved to be impenetrable.

While somewhat user-friendly, they became ubiquitous. Latterly he broke through the Enigma code, cryptologist Alan Turing BSc was considered to be the inventor of Artificial Intelligence. Both still and moving images show his successes as a top cryptanalyst; a contribution to the world of computing that will surely last a long time. The machinery itself provided encoded messages by way of a number of keys, switches and buttons that translate on/off into a series of letters or numbers. Then each user referred to his code books, configuring machines to match up. Upon this sofa or in his favourite old armchair, he could at his leisure decode the message from the meaningless jumble. Maybe today 'E' was 'R' (although it could be W, F or even K). Technological changes saw the birth of the net, thanks to Prof. Tim Burners-Lee. Without him, systems would remain unconnected, but he recognised they ran alongside one another and they might be integrated into a web to link up. An early webserver (at http://info.cern.ch) provided him with the chance to show others how to connect; later on this gave everyone the internet – the rest is history. C Babbage, before him, had invented the *Difference Engine*, first of the forerunners of a modern electronic computer, able to do calculations, print text, ring a bell or punch cards. It never entered mass production since a manufacturing error disqualified it. Babbage's failure to sugar-coat these troubles led to withdrawal of funding. Because ebbing and flowing surges wait for no man, Lord Kelvin tied up his own shoes and made a tide-predictor. His cousin Ian expanded it.

He could develop in the realm of ballistics. His new gun sights killed (or caused to be killed) dozens of sailors since accuracy was the benefit. Seven years after the birth of Palestinian Yasser Arafat (although not unrelated), this differential analyser amalgamated all that analogue computing could offer. Dr Donald R J Metcalf built DRJM2, the world's first electromechanical computer and later the world's first digital computer, invented when the celeb Selina Wisehouse called for one that was also Thopatically rated using binary numbers, obviously.
   'This is very easy to develop. Boolean Logic brought cool, phlegmy approach with open/shut gates. Later, development of per-

son-focussed tablets with microchips had a huge impact which was highly significant. Hear me now! – cracking codes is an art, lost to a generation dependent upon very-high-speed electronics and floating-point calculation (although I have no clue what this is). The deep joy in the soul of the codebreaker when a cypher is found is indescribablYes, he could sing, dance, cheer, and declare he is driven by the mystery to understand how/why the message was swathed in misdirection or obfuscation. It is always a drop dead gorgeous feeling to be the one who uncovers those hidden and such respected communiqués – a single-minded cryptologist is the only sort that exists. This is definitely, the only reason he is alive – he reveals all content, proving he has 'succeeded once again' in understanding serious encodings – an accomplishment he recognizes as being technically complex and greatly to be rejoiced at, with vast celebration.

144 clichés *wordplay*

David Nobbs' Reginald Perrin *trilogy features inspirational boss CJ**

Bottom line: this is nothing less than the **Gospel truth, which is stranger than fiction.**

A **diamond in the rough** felt **under the thumb**, so he decided **to bite the hand that fed him** (and **the goose that laid the golden egg**). Despite being **born with a silver spoon in his mouth**, he must have **got out of the wrong side of the bed** one day and, **cool as a cucumber (nerves of steel)** asked his pa for his inheritance. **'Show me the money!'**

'That's **a Kings ransom! Do you think I am made of money?'**

But he **put his money where his mouth was** and the lad **took off like a shot.** He was **in the pink!** In Dissipation City, he forgot that his dad had said **penny wise & pound foolish,** but **out of sight, out of mind.** He found a place on the **wrong side of the tracks** and started **sowing wild oats (boys will be boys).**

'Why buy the cow when the milk is free? Wham bam, thank you ma'am!'

Not only losing money **hand over fist,** he **had lost track of time,** but was **without a care in the world.** It was the **calm before the storm,** (the **writing was on the wall**); his **Achilles heel?** The **roll of the dice** in the casino.

'I'm having **the time of my life,** and I **can drink you under the table!'**

But he was **in the red,** and **didn't have two brass farthings to rub together. It could be worse,** but **a fool and his money are soon parted.** He was **frightened to death** when he realized **the glass was half-empty.** His wallet was **as light as a feather,** and it was **only a matter of time** before he was **scared out of his wits** by the threat of poverty and impending famine.

The **night is darkest before the storm** and **if wishes were horses, beggars would ride.** But the next thing he knew, a shiver ran down his spine. He was penniless – **a day late and a dollar short.**

'Beggars can't be choosers,' he thought, 'and **what you see is what you get,** so I'll have to **live and learn.'**

He took a job tending skinny pigs

(even the pick of the litter was as thin as a rake, a bag of bones), saying to himself 'If I had any, I would cast my pearls before swine. I would if I could, but I can't, so I won't. I'll work like a dog until I'm blue in the face, taking a taste of my own medicine. These pigs and I are like peas in a pod, but the pods are nothing to write home about. I shall kid myself I'm as happy as a pig in muck, and that I can't complain or mustn't grumble, but I'm not even fair to middling. I can't make a silk purse out of a sow's ear, since I'm a square peg in a round hole. I'm not even sure about that saying *when you have lemons, make lemonade*, since two wrongs don't make a right.'

He refused to speak about the elephant in the room, perhaps because he wasn't the sharpest knife in the drawer until in the nick of time he decided to throw in the towel.

'*Today is the first day of the rest of your life*,' he thought, 'and this is the acid test. When the going gets tough, the tough get going. The journey of a thousand miles begins with the first step, and every cloud has a silver lining. A man's home is his castle and my father's hired men eat well; I shall have to toe the line. You ain't seen nothing yet! I'll say to my father I haven't got a leg to stand on, but *don't hear what I'm not saying*.' So he got up and set off – leaving the pigsty. The lights are on but there's no-one home.

Nervous as a cat on a hot tin roof, he walked wearily, tail between his legs, expecting a tongue-lashing from his dad, who had every right to jump down his throat, come down on him like a ton of bricks and to throw the book at him.

Some say 'you can never go home again', but then again *any port in a storm*, so he'd cross that bridge when he got to it. He rehearsed his speech 'Don't get your knickers in a twist… no, no. Wherever I hang my hat, that's my home…no! I am no longer worthy. That's better.'

You could have knocked him over with a feather as he saw his dad was eager to meet and greet, to press the flesh.

'Oh Dad, curb your enthusiasm!'

'No, son, good things come to him who waits! Variety is the spice of life, so here are some gifts. If the shoe fits, wear it (the boot is on the other foot and I can't judge you unless I have walked a mile in your moccasins); all that glitters is not gold (but this ring is); and here's a coat – a stitch in time saves nine – and I'm wearing my heart on my sleeve.'

His father took the bull by the horns with a pinch of salt, asking 'Where's the beef?' and declaring 'Where's there's smoke there's fire!' Holy cow! (once burned, twice shy).

The way to a man's heart is through his stomach (it was a right old carve-up) and all the neighbours attended the party, all singing from the same hymn-sheet.

The food was magnificent: his goose was cooked (and what's good for the goose is good for the gander); there's something fishy about setting a sprat to catch a mackerel, but there are plenty more fish in the sea; the whole enchilada fell out of the frying pan into the fire, which is a shame; however, too many cooks spoil the broth. That takes the biscuit (unless it's just the way the cookie crumbles) but there were other fish to fry, and only a storm in a teacup. After all, you can't make an omelette without breaking a few eggs, and throwing a party's a piece of cake. An apple a day keeps the doctor away, so long as he can cut the mustard.

The boy's father made a speech. 'I thought he was several sandwiches short of a picnic and was pushing up daisies – yes, I considered him dead as a doornail but he's alive & kicking! Absence makes the heart grow fonder! The poet says 'Tis better to have loved and lost, than never to have loved at all. I don't know about that, but what goes around comes around, and time heals all wounds. All's well that ends well!' There was not a dry eye in the house, and they all lived happily ever after.

* 'A cliché to me is like a red rag to a bull. However, there's an exception that proves a rule, and there's a cliché that fits my situation like a glove' CJ, *The Better World of Reginald Perrin* by David Nobbs (1978)

Two-timer crossword *wordplay*

Cryptic clues and quick clues: the answers are the same. Solution on p328

Cryptic clues

Across

2 Pianos I'd sit about on wasteage (11)
7 Agrarian truant, initially (2)
8 Desire boat's inertia gone bad, afar (4,3,3)
12 Prime muddle takes ages (3)
13 Bread heads below, above quarterpounders (4)
15 Chubby, unhearing about IoM race (6)
18 Select one of many (3)
19 Evil plus a vital combination (5)
20 Some grab excluding (3)
21 Fire, he turns young cow (6)
22 Trump; south moves for gambles (4)
23 Operation new employee, firstly (3)
24 Uncover irate novel (10)
27 Cease to be known as YHWH; change, realign moon (1,2,2,6)

Down

1 Noticeable person and portion for a party (11)
2 Leo's lair (3)
3 Was upward-looking (3)
4 Fetchers of gifts (5)
5 Performance for a new leaf (1,1,1)
6 No, ascend (2)
9 Gossip and step on it (3)
10 Definitively embraced by distance, sire (6)
11 Playing female's, one sunburn Anglican death bonus (11)
12 OK for food, I bleed (6)
14 Reason's seat starts pig swill you can hardly eat (6)
16 Incline to stand (5)
17 Idi sits in Far East starvation (6)
22 Wash post-grad over article (5)
24 Past athleticism, like a wet newspaper headline (3)
25 Nil after example or id (3)
26 Some chump apportioned the farmer (2)

Quick Clues

Across

2 City of wantonness (11)
7 Astatine (Chemistry) (2)
8 Distant (4,3,3)
12 Eternity (Greek) (3)
13 Burger buns (4)
15 State of the calf (6)
18 A free choice (3)
19 Between birth & death (5)
20 Counter for drinks (3)
21 Young cow (6)
22 Most excellent (4)
23 Singular (3)
24 Uncovering (10)
27 '_ ___ ___ _____
    worthy to be called
    a son.' (1,2,2,6)

Down

1 Shindig (11)
2 Place of iniquity (3)
3 Past vision (3)
4 Stout wooden stick (5)
5 Now read on (1,1,1)
6 Atop (2)
9 Talk, fuel (3)
10 Son's next of kin (6)
11 Bequest (11)
12 Fit for consumption (6)
14 Senses son came to (6)
16 'I will ____ and go
    to my father' (5)
17 National food shortage (6)
22 Immerse (5)
24 Jogged (3)
25 Pride (3)
26 Father (colloq.) (2)

Indoor-game terms   *key words*

poker, Monopoly, chess, snooker

Jack[1] wanted his money[2] having seen an opening[3] on the side[4] and was making a gambit[3]. He took his cue[4] and said 'Give me a break[4] and my pot[4] of cash! I'm not asking for a monopoly[2], just a chance[2] to feel flush[1], and have a rest[4] and be king[1,3] of the castle[3].' His dad, feeling snookered[4], made the sacrifice[3], gave him £200 for passing Go[2], and put the

279

cash in[1] his hand[1]. **Big Slick**[1] **left**[4] a coin or two but put the **rest**[4] of the cash into his **pocket**[1,4] and was **straight**[1] away off in a **motor**[2], towards an **hotel**[2] in **Park Lane**[2], a lovely **green**[4] **spot**[4] by the **river**[1], beyond the **bridge**[4], where there was **free parking**[2]. After a **nap**[4], he lived for **kicks**[4] and had a **ball**[4].

He was robbed **blind**[1], paying the **rent**[2] on one **house**[2] (in **Fourth Street**[1]) and a **mortgage**[2] on another (**Cannon**[4] Street), **just visiting**[2] a girl known as **D**[4], who was **queen**[1,3] of a **beauty contest**[2] but a bit of an old **battleship**[2] as well. A **gay waiter**[1], wearing a **foul**[4] **baize**[4] jacket **tied**[4] with a **red**[4], **yellow**[4], **black**[3,4], **brown**[4] and **pink**[4] **Strand**[2], would **chalk**[4] his tab on the **slate**[4], as the **English**[4] might say.

His money ran out (coins/notes? He couldn't **hold 'em**[1]) and he was soon just as poor as the **rank and file**[3] of the **community**. **Chest**[2] heaving, he was hungry, exhausted (**all in**)[1].

Having **scratched**[4] around, he followed up an **opening**[3], looking after pigs (longing to **check**[1,3,4] out the **spider**[4]-infested He tried to **pawn**[3] his **iron**[2] and **Scottie dog**[2], without **plant**[4]s in their **jaws**[4]), but that seemed a poor **deal**[1,2], and not at all **in-off**[4]ensive.

He was feeling **blue**[4], yet he didn't **baulk**[4] at the idea of **screwing**[4] up his courage, having to **return**[1] home to relative **safety**[4]. While he was still a long way off, his dad ran to greet him.

'**O – O – O**[3], **Mate**[3]!' he cried, when he might have been expected to **kick**[4] off (what a **kicker**[1]!). He wasn't **bluffing**[1], although he did look as if he was having a hot **flush**[1], and turned on the **water works**[2].

He **kissed**[4] his **stunned**[4] son, made sure he was **suited**[1] – he even helped him with a **button**[1] (or was it a **pin**[3]?) – gave him a **pair**[1] of open sandals that went flip-**flop**[1], and began to **call**[1] the **maximum**[4] number of guests until he had a **full house**[1] (in fact, there was **no limit**[1]). He **raised the ante**[1] with plates of **chips**[1] and a (formerly **thin**[4]) roasted calf, which, **cut**[4] into **147**[4] **thick**[4] slices, could be eaten with a **fork**[3]. He arranged for a **pot**[1] of soup and some vegetables on a **skewer**[3]. cooked upon a **rack**[4], with egg **white**[3,4] served on a **cushion**[4] of mashed potato.

Jack gave an intro. 'Ok[3]ay, here's Dad.'

'**Doubles**[2,4] all round! **Check**[4] this out: I thought Jack, whose name was in the **frame**[4], was going to **die**[2], but God decided to **raise**[1] him up! **Tell**[1] everyone: he was a **deadweight**[4], but the boy can **roll again**[2]!'

1 **poker** *Big Slick* A, K in hand – since this can be slippery *River* last community card of the five, dealt face up on the table *Fourth street* penultimate community card, dealt face up *Gay Waiter* slang for Q, 3 in hand – (queen with a *trés* - tray) *Kicker* Highest additional card when hands are otherwise equal *Button* indicates which player has the dealer's advantage *Flop* first three community cards, dealt face up *Tell* nervousness or excitement, real or feigned
2 **Monopoly** *Deal* in one variant rule, some properties are distributed before play begins *Die* singular (*dice* plural)
3 **chess** *Gambit* Opening moves made to gain an advantage (often by sacrificing a piece) *O-O-O* castling on the queen's side *Skewer* an attack on a high-value piece, which, if moved, would expose a lesser value piece, previously protected
4 **snooker** *English* American term: cue-ball side-spin *Scratched* cue ball is potted (this is a foul) *Baulk* a line parallel to the bottom cushion, 29" away on a 12' x 6' table, forming part of the D *Safety* avoiding a pot, to gain advantageous position

Proper names   *style*

Jesus of Nazareth, son of Mary & Joseph, told a story. Prodigio spoke to Harold and asked for Shekels, Denarii and Gold Pieces, which he got, and he left Homestead Farm. He went down Acacia Avenue and Wistaria Lane, along the B3339, turned left at St Malachi's Infirmary for Demanding Egocentrics, onto the A44 Bypass and out of Quietsville to Dissipation City in Foreignland.

At the *Hookah Hostelry*, he met with Jane, Lynda, Gloria, Delores, Jack, Melvin, Simon and Roy and drank Margueritas, Whisky Macs, Tequilla Sunrises, Singapore Slings and Gold Tin Slammers.

One Thursday, his tenners and tanners ran out. Famine Florrie set in at the same time. Everyone was starving, and Prodigio took a job at Pelham's Piggery, looking after Saddlebacks and Vietnamese Pot-Bellied pigs called Napoleon, Empress of Blandings, Sausage, Chops, Snowball, Squealer and Babe. He desperately longed to eat their food: Musselberg Leek à la Mould in a Pus Jus. But he came to his senses and returned to Homestead Farm to work as a Labourer (Second Class).

While he was still on the A44, not yet near St Malachi's Infirmary for Repentant Wanderers (the turn for the B3339), Harold ran to greet him and gave him an 18 carat gold ring, an Afghan coat and Oxford brogues. He had Daisy slaughtered and spit-roasted and invited all of Quietsville to celebrate.

Harold said 'My son Prodigio was lost, but is found; he was dead but is alive. Thank the Lord God Almighty, Maker of Heaven and Earth.'

Missing persons, missing details   *style*

what if key characters or elements were not present?

No younger son

The only son worked on his dad's farm, and, even though he asked a few times, never had the opportunity to invite a few friends around to party, with or without a goat. The famine, fortunately, never affected them; the calf died of obesity and the dad went to his grave with his cherished family ring on his finger.

No Dissipation City

A son asked his father for his inheritance. He took the money and went to a foreign land, where he spent the cash gradually, as there were no restaurants, casinos, nightclubs or bars to be found; just a general stores, a stable and a couple of pig farms.

He lived there, a wealthy man, for the rest of his life and never had any need or regrets, really.

Or much fun.

No Dad

The son inherited a fortune early in life, when his father died. He wasted it all in Dissipation City.

Once it was gone, he was shocked to discover the land was suffering from a famine. He took a job tending pigs, and longed to eat their food. Suddenly, he realised 'The men who work on our farm (the one co-owned by me and my brother) eat well… I shall arise and go home and say to my brother, let me work for you as a hired man, as I am no longer worthy to be called a sibling.'

He left and found his way home. While he was still a long way off, he was attacked by hired men who were

281

protecting the farm (on behalf of his brother) from timewasters and people seeking employment, as they were unwilling to share their good fortune with chancers and refugees from the famine – especially former high rollers from Dissipation City who were now down on their luck. They beat him with sticks, stole his shoes and his coat and left him for dead.

After a while, a priest walked along the road, but passed by on the other side. Then a Levite came along, but also passed by on the other side.

Then a Samaritan came by, and he saw the son lying there and had compassion on him, and tended to his wounds. But the hired men had been lying in wait for the Samaritan, and attacked him as well. This time they were more thorough, and both the Samaritan and the son were beaten to death. The hired men stole the Samaritan's ring and sold it to buy a fatted calf, which they roasted.

No famine

Sidney asked his father for his inheritance. He took it to Dissipation City, spent his money in wild living, and it was nearly all gone. But his father had taught him well, so with his final banknote he bought a box of thirty figs for Đ10. He took the box to a sports ground, where there was a match, and sold figs to spectators at Đ1 each. The fans were eager to buy; he sold out; he was Đ20 up.

Not bad, he thought. But then he saw a boy straining to see the game over the heads of the men in front.

'Want a box for your boy to stand on?' he asked the lad's father. 'Only a couple of Đen?' The man gave him Đ2 for the flimsy fig box, and the lad gained an improved view. After a

while, however, the lad jumped up and down in excitement when his team scored. The weak wood gave way and the box was splintered.

Sidney hid for a while, and once the game was over, he went back to the smashed bits of wood, bundled them up and sold sticks of firewood for Đ3 to someone trying to get a calf-roast going, as was the custom. His investment of Đ10 had become Đ25, thanks to an enterprising approach.

He worked hard and continued to exercise his entrepreneurial skills, eventually owning *Honest Sid's Second-Hand Chariot Mart*, which did a brisk trade in slightly used Roman transport. He became independently wealthy and never looked back.*

No wealth

A hired man who worked on a farm had two sons. One of the boys came to him and said 'Father, give me my inheritance.' His father replied 'All I have is the wage packet I receive each week. There is no inheritance.'

The son was downcast. 'So there is no way I can go to Dissipation City and enjoy some wild living…?'

'No.'

'Rats.'

No pig farmer

The son asked his dad for his inheritance, and took it to Dissipation City, where he spent it on wild living. Once the cash was gone, a famine struck the land.

The boy could not find work and starved to death.

No brother

The only son asked his father for his inheritance. The father was confused. 'What shall I have to live on?'

'Don't know, but that's not my problem.'

He took the money and went to Dissipation City, where he spent it on wild living.

Once all the cash was gone, famine struck, and the son took a job tending pigs. He envied them, because they were given pods to eat. He had a revelation.

He said 'On my father's farm, I remember that the hired men ate well. I shall arise and go home and say to my father, make me a hired man, for I am no longer worthy to be called your son.'

So he got up and made his way. While he was still a long way off, his father saw him and ran to greet him.

'Father,' the boy began, 'make me a hired man, for I am no longer worthy to be called a son.'

'Not so fast, my boy,' said the father. 'I was destitute once you had cleaned me out, so I had to sell the farm. Now I'm one of the hired men, and just happened to be having my lunch break when I saw you a long way off. If you'll take my advice, get out of here. I don't want you to become my colleague, as your attitude really disappointed me. Go elsewhere to find work. Go, now!'

No God

The son approached his father. Neither placed any value in whatever random ethical code they might temporarily embrace; neither had any purpose in life nor sound reason for being alive at all.

After all, they were merely (so they reckoned) the product of an unlikely, accidental combination of a handful of microbes swimming in a pre-biotic soup, luckily struck by lightning.

He spoke. 'Please give me my inheritance early.' The father agreed, and the boy left home shortly afterwards, setting off towards Dissipation City.

He spent wildly but unwisely, and soon all the money was gone, and so were his new-found 'friends'. At the same time, the land was beset with a famine. The boy took a job tending pigs, which, although unpleasant, caused no religious offence.

He watched the pigs eating their mealy, measly pods, and envied them. But even though he knew there was guilt in his heart for what he had done, came there no revelation or dawning of the realisation of a need for restitution.

He munched forlornly on a pod, but malnutrition swept upon him like a thief, stealing vigour and breath from him. He was dead months before the famine was over.

No Jesus
No story.

* Based on the title incident from *It's a Long Way from Penny Apples* by Bill Cullen, who rose from an impoverished childhood to running one of the largest car dealerships in Ireland

More sporting terms   *wordplay*
rugby, boxing, tenpin bowling, baseball; see also Sporting terms (p113)
Yes, the son approached his father from the **blindside**[1] and went for the **high tackle**[1].

'I'm heading **south, Pa! W**[2]**hen** will I return? Never!' He'd decided to **strike**[3,4] at the heart of his father's wealth, asking him to **split**[3] the shares early. His **pitch**[4] was successful.

'Two things, to say, Dad: a) I've

learned the ropes[2], behaved in an orthodox[2] manner, working in the field[4]s, out[4] beyond the crossroad and the curve; b) all[4] I ask is that you get your hook[2]s out of me!'

His dad, standing, count[2]ted out enough cash to fill every pocket[3] in the boy's tunic.

'Cheers, Dad, that's a knock out[2]!'

He went to Dissipate City, to an Inn in g[4]reed, gluttony and lustfulness. He met women who were determined to take advantage[1] of him; Gloria was quite a catch[4], while Letitia was little more than a hooker[1].

He made a somewhat forward pass[1] at Babs in the alley[3] maximising his snake eyes[3]. In the ensuing scrum[1], he achieved an arm lock[1], danced a double shuffle[2] and managed to get to second base[4]. His cash was soon spent, which was a blow[2] and, try[1] as he might, he could not afford to fill the emptiness below the belt[2]. His name was in the frame[3] for starvation, when famine struck[1].

He took a job ten[2]ding pigs, which was prop[1]erly offensive; before he would never touch[1] such unclean animals. This was the penalty[1] for his greed. While just seconds away[2] from eating the pigs' rotting pods, he suddenly, by the grace of God, had a conversion[1] experience.

'I have to stop this. Even the hired men at dad's farm average[3] three meals a day… I shall go on a home run[4]. I'm no longer worthy to be called a son, so I'll just ask for a job. Yes, I'll go back, stop[4] being so selfish and ask him to take me back as a cowman or haymaker[2]. So, here's the plan: walk[4] round[2] the block[2], and hope he'll not be stubborn, but give up, and under[1]play the fury I deserve.

He set off. But while he was still a

long way out[2] his dad saw him in the lane[3] beyond the left field[4] (way past the perimeter line, out[1] by the old barn, and decided to run[4] to him.

'It's not far; I can go the distance[2]!'

As they approached each other, the boy began his speech, but could not really get started as his dad embraced him. It was a heartfelt clinch[2].

His dad issued commands to the servants. 'Fetch my diamond[4] ring[2], some glove[2,4]s, a pair of bumper[3]s, and that coat with the nice weave[2] which is on the hook[2,3], on the back of my bedroom door. Oh, yes, throw in the towel[2] and some soap. And let's have roast beef; Cowhand Bob[2] is my designated hitter[4] of the fatted calf with the axe!'

Servants hung out the bunt[4]ing and the farm was made ready for the celebration ball[3]. On the groaning trestle tables was a mound[4] of duck[2], a turkey[3] dinner bucket[3], pints of juice in a plastic pitcher[4] and rum punch[2] served in a bowl made of cut glass. Jaw[2]breakers of various flavourswere served, along with a large plate[4] of uppercut[2] Flanker[1] (delicious), and some perfect game[3] bird dishes: pheasant, grouse, quail and partridge. Guests crowded round with forks, spearing slices of meat and jab[2]bing at vegetables and bread and cake and fruit.

The boy's father made a speech. 'Oh, he's given me cause to get the knock on[1] more than one occasion, and I've gone spare[3] – extremely cross[2]! But this time we thought he was lost and dead, yet he's found and alive! I can't pin[3] down any decent defence[2] for what he has done, but I want you to know I would fly half[1] way around the world to find him if I'd known where to look.'

284

1 Rugby Union & League 18 **advantage** ref's discretion, allowing play to continue after a foul, if the offended-against team are in full flow **up and under** high kick beyond opposition lines
2 Boxing 29 **double shuffle** famed footwork fireworks of Mohammed Ali
3 Ten-pin bowling 16 **snake eyes** when only pins 7,10 remain in play **turkey** three consecutive strikes **dinner bucket** pins 2,4,5,8 remain; **perfect game** ten consecutive strikes plus two bonus strikes, scoring 300
4 Baseball 20 **designated hitter** non-fielding batsman – standing in for a fielder who does not bat; **bunt** choice which only advantages other player(s) for the sake of the team

Contranyms   *wordplay*

antonyms of themselves, amazingly; presented in pairs

The farmer's son said 'I wish to **cleave** us apart, and **cleave** to your money!'

He took most of the cash – surely he knew his father could not manage on what was **left**? – and **left** the farm, passing several ponds and a copse. He stepped down into a **dyke** and climbed out the other side; he crossed the field and scaled the **dyke** on his way to Dissipation City.

While some of the girls wore clothing that was practically **transparent**, the lad's reckless spending betrayed an attitude to wealth that was **transparent**.

A famine struck and the lights went **out**, just as night fell and the stars came **out**. A number of alarms went **off**, as his friends went **off**, their **rum** luck having changed.

He took a **rum** job, tending pigs. 'This should **fix** everything,' he thought. But almost immediately he found his desire to eat the moulding pods put him in a **fix**. The pig farmer's major **oversight** was giving **oversight** of the porkers to a starving lad.

He came to his senses pretty **fast**.

'I won't stay here, stuck **fast** to poverty. My father's men eat well; I should go home to be **with** my father, but I'll ask to be one of the hired men – I simply cannot arrive and proudly set myself up in competition **with** them for his affection.'

The boy **bolted** the door to the pen (so no pigs could run away) and **bolted, presently.** His father saw him **presently**, while he was still a long way off, and ran to greet him.

The boy started to say 'I am no longer worthy to be called your son; I know you don't **sanction** what I have done - I'm willing to be placed under whatever **sanction** you decide to impose.'

The father replied 'I ought to give you **aught**, but on second thoughts I shall generously give you **aught** instead. Here's my **custom**-made ring, which I'll give you, as is our **custom**. Here are shoes and a coat – and we'll kill the fatted calf. Someone do murder in the **first degree** on her, and then we'll give her much more than **first degree** burns!'

Servants got busy; one **dusted** the sideboard, while another **dusted** a Victoria sponge with icing sugar. The custards were **skinned**, but the chicken portions were filleted and **skinned**.

The table groaned with a **quantum** of roast calf, sprinkled with a **quantum** of ground pepper; the beef was **trimmed** and **trimmed** with a **variety** of vegetables.

In addition, there was a **variety** of pea pod of which the boy had seen enough for a lifetime.

The father made a speech as the villagers gathered. 'I can give no **apology** for the way he used all the money, but he has given an **apology** to me and I have forgiven him. Big Field has been **seeded**, and these cucumbers have been **seeded** as well! The carcass of Buttercup **gave out** delicious juices; she fed many villagers. We feared my son's heart **gave out** while he was away, but no!

'He was lost, and is found; he was dead, and is alive! This is **quite** splendid, even though I was **quite** concerned for a while!'

cleave separate; adhere **left** remaining; going **dyke** ditch; wall **transparent** invisible; obvious **out** invisible; visible **off** on; off **rum** good; bad **fix** solution; problem **oversight** careless error; care **fast** quick; unmoving **with** alongside; against **bolted** secured; ran away **presently** immediately; slightly later **sanction** support; penalty **aught** nothing; all **custom** special; standard **first degree** most severe; least severe **dusted** removed fine particles; added fine particles **skinned** had a skin; had a skin removed **quantum** a large amount; a small amount **trimmed** excess removed; embellishments added **a variety** many types; one type **apology** formal defense of what you think, say, or do; admission of fault in what you think, say, or do **seeded** seeds have been added; seeds have been removed **gave out** produced; stopped production **quite** hugely; to a lesser extent

Ostranenie   *wordplay*
defamiliarisation – seeing the ordinary in a different way

USED TO BEING KEPT IN the dark, being still, being untouched, unseen, unnoticed – now, what was happening to me was almost more than I could bear. Oh, how odd it was to be fetched out onto the kitchen table, and stacked by rough hands into unequal heaps! I was, of course, in the smaller of the portions – although I'm not sure why I say 'of course'. Perhaps I was expecting to be reckoned among the lesser selection or placed in what I

correctly guessed to be the considerably unluckier pile; maybe I feared myself inadequate or destined for a gloomy conclusion.

Nevertheless, that's what happened, so I can't deny that, and neither can you. So let's just leave it and move on.

Carried away from familiar surroundings, I soon found myself jingled and jangled most uncomfortably for what seemed an unendingly long time, and then suddenly whooshed out onto a cheap hotel bedspread.

Here, I was raked through and my larger, flatter, greener high-denomination fellow-travellers were selected, smoothed out and removed, never to return. It was clear that I was next in line, and, sure enough, it didn't take long for me to be pushed into a bag, carried at some speed to a noisy place, stacked on a counter, and brusquely exchanged for small brightly-coloured wooden counters.

I found myself in a much larger company of notes, and then was bagged, tagged and deposited. Doors clanged, locks clicked, security routines proceeded.

After several months, I was taken once again from the new surroundings and was locked – yes, locked – in a safe with shiny metal, important-looking legal documents and bankers' drafts. And to make matters worse, this safe was later handed over to the government in exchange for what struck me as a woefully overpriced amount of low-quality food – anyone would have thought there was a shortage.

OUR DAYS IN THE FIELD had been hot, dry and tough; not unlike the husks we formed around those dehydrated,

286

wrinkly pulses. Yes, I know, our beans should have been plump and moist, and our skins protective but tender, ready to pop open at the slightest pressure – and designed to be gently cooked and consumed.

But a combination of scorching heat and severe lack of moisture had got us off to a pathetically poor start. And then the hot weather intensified, making matters worse, only to be followed by biblical quantities of rain, practically rotting us on our woody stalks. We were no good at all.

I was glad we were harvested; anything rather than the indignity of being ploughed back into the mud – not that we'd have provided nutrients for the topsoil anyway. We were gathered up, loaded without caution onto a cart and taken to a pig farm, where we were thrown into troughs for the animals to feed. They weren't fussy creatures, but they turned their snouts up as the sight of us.

Mind you, the young man who seemed at first to be tending them took an interest for a moment. I say 'seemed' because he wasn't there the next day, even though we still were, having been rejected by the animals, such was our shabby state. Oh dear.

IT HAD BEEN THAT WAY for a number of weeks. If we hadn't stopped to figure out what needed to be done, nothing at all would have happened.

The crops might have stayed unharvested, the animals unfed, the fences unmended and the machinery unoiled. And First Born might have got away with the wild parties he kept trying to arrange with his friends and their goats.

But we even managed to nip those in the bud, oh yes.

We saw what was required and made it happen.

It could have gone very differently.

Lack of leadership, you see. The Old Man had been mooching about on his roof, staring into the middle distance, while we were knocking ourselves witless keeping the place running. Oh, yes, I believe we certainly earned our lunches alright that season!

But today it's gone from nothing to full-on demanding and beyond. First of all the Old Man rushed down the stairs like he was on fire, and ran all the way out of the yard and up the lane, shouting and laughing and cheering, for no apparent reason.

Then he turned up at the gate with some unrecognisable hobo, and started to bark orders at everyone.

Matt had to hurry off and bring a coat, Oliver was sent to find shoes, Zebulun rushed to dig out some family ring, and I was commanded (not requested nicely, mind, oh no, but commanded) to go and grab a sharp knife and slit the throat of our one and only fatted calf.

It seems this homeless, hairy, footsore, skinny wretch who had turned up unexpectedly (well, we hadn't been expecting him) was in fact the Old Man's Second Born, returned from some sort of spending spree – not that he had anything to show for dissipating his wealth in the Big City.

Once the calf was dead, we built a fire and put the carcass on a spit. Then we had to fetch out all the villagers and farmers from the surrounding district to come to a celebration party, and, once they'd arrived, we had to put on nice trousers and white shirts and do the stewarding thing, serving drinks, carrying trays of pasties and bread and fruit and vegetables and cheese and who knows what else. And to sort out the washing up and clearing and tidying, and making sure the right people got back to the right homes and farms without too many awkward mix-ups.

What a lot of fuss it was, just for some waster boy who hadn't made much contribution. Me, I couldn't see the point of it.

Scrabble parable   *style*

a lost-son-themed game

Playing mostly by standard rules, the story unfolds in a non-linear order.

Letters are being deliberately chosen; every effort has been made to create high-scoring words.

The order of play is shown using standard notation, slightly amended: player A or B; location of starting letter (as shown, overleaf); letters played shown in **BOLD CAPS** (plus any extra words formed) with interlinked ones in l.c.; score/accumulated score in *italics*; and blank tiles shown in (brackets) – in this instance, both are used as H, but of course this is co-incidental.

The Ae8 **LOST** *8/8* son took his pa's cash and went off up Bh8 t**HE** *6/6* Ae6 (H)**IIL** *3/11*.

His Bh6 **FA**the**R** *12/18* gave every Ae5 **Shill**I**NG** *16/27* – Dad's like Be12 g**OD** *5/23* in some ways. The boy asked to Ae10 i**N**(H)**ERIT** *8/35*.

Later, he lives in a Bg12 d**IV**e *9/32* after going on the Af15 **ReVEL** *24/59* with his Be10inherit**ANCE** *22/54*. Pa runs and Ah9 h**E**/**E**r *9/68* roasts the fatted Bn10 c**ALF** *9/63* – NB this is all a Ai12 **PARABIE** *22/90*. Famine and hunger Bl12 a**BU**t *7/70* each other;

when the boy came to his senses, he had a spiritual Af15 revel**AtION** *39/129* avoiding every casino Bo7 **GAM**e *21/91*.

He knew he had become Ab1 **UNWO**r**THY** *88/217* to be called a son – he'd wasted his father's fortune, even on a woman whose hair was coloured with Ba8 **DyE** *21/112*.

His Aa1 **Qu**I**XOTIC*** *356/573* journeys ended with a celebration featuring Bh1 c**AKE** *11/123*.

He'd spent all his Aa8 d**IMES** *9/582* which made his pa Ba12 s**AD** *5/128* since the lad's moral compass was evidently on the Ah6 f**RITZ** *19/601* – unlikely to repair itself, Bk6 t**OO** *3/131*.

Seeing his son while he was still a long way off, the farmer began to Am7 **JO**g *19/620*; he showed mercy, giving gifts far more than were Bf4 **DU**e *4/135* to a son who fed Aj5 **PiGS**/**G**o/**S**o *12/632*.

Bc12 d**EWY** *22/157* is a suitable way to describe every Ab15 **EyE** *7/639*.

Story: The **lost** son took his pa's cash and went off up **the hill**. His **father** gave every **shilling** – Dad's like **God** in some ways. The boy asked to **inherit**. Later, he lives in a **dive** after going on the **revel**, and pa roasts the fatted **calf** – NB this is all a **parable**.

Famine and hunger **abut** each other; when the boy came to his senses, he had a spiritual **revelation**, avoiding every casino **game**. He knew he had become **unworthy** to be called a son – he'd wasted his father's fortune, even on a woman whose hair was coloured with **dye**.

His **quixotic** journeys ended with a celebration featuring **cake**. He'd spent all his **dimes** which made his pa **sad** since the lad's moral compass was evidently on the **fritz** – unlikely to repair itself, **too**. Seeing his son while he was still a long way off, the farmer began to **jog**; he showed mercy, giving gifts far more than were **due** to a son who fed **pigs**. **Dewy** is a suitable way to describe every **eye**.

Final score: player A *639*, player B *156*. Player A wins by 483 points!

*QUIXOTIC scores 356: Q10, U1, I1, X8x2 (double letter score), O1, T1, I1, C3 = 34; x 3 (triple word score, A1) = 102; x 3 (triple word score, A8) = 306; + 50 bonus for using all 7 letters at once = 356

Anagram clusters   *wordplay*
*words presented in **bold type** are pairs (or more) of anagrams*

The younger son spoke to his Dad '**Immediately**[1] is **my ideal time**[1] to inherit. Give me your **dowry**[2] or the **nearest**[3] quantity of **counters**[4] you can muster.' Clearly, the boy **aspired**[5] to great wealth.

He set off in an **eastern**[3] direction, to Dissipatia. **Coins kept**[6] in **pockets**[6]? No chance! His behaviour was **rowdy**[2] as he ate, drank, gambled, **auctioned**[7], danced and met girls whose bodies exhibited **pertness**[8] but whose characters more closely resembled **serpents**[8].

After a while, he received an harsh **education**[7]; his money was gone and the land was in famine. 'I should have listened when I was **cautioned**[7],' he said.

The whole country was in **despair**[5].

He took a job tending pigs. '**Meal for one**[9]? No!' he thought, as their slops were delivered. 'But **for me alone**[9],

289

these animals would be in **intensive care**[10],' he rasped hoarsely.

He was so hungry, he **envied**[11] the heavily **veined**[11] pig food. 'It's not like I'm on **a diet**[12]; **I can't even rise**[10] up, I'm so weak. **I'd eat**[12] anything! **Weird**[13] **endive**[11]! But I must **restrain**[14] myself. I **recant**[15] my behaviour. I shall arise and return home.

'No longer worthy to be called a son, I'll work for dad – wash the **drapes**[16], or **sweep the floor**[17]. I always thought he had **too few helpers**[17], so **I think, therefore, I am**[18] likely to get a job. I **fear to think I'm here**[18] to die... I must cross many **terrains**[14] and ask if he **retrains**[14] wayward sons.'

While he was still a long way off, his father saw him. Shaking himself out of a **trance**[15], his eyes opened wider until he **reacted**[19] by setting off at a **canter**[15].

'I'm **wired**[13]' he cried as he kissed his boy. 'Fetch **presents**[1]! A coat, ring and **trainers**[14]! Let a barbeque be **created**[19]!'

At the party, there were **melons**[20], **lemons**[20] and a fine **spread**[16].

All tastes were **catered**[19] for, toasting the boy with peach **nectar**[15]. His father gives a **solemn**[20], **wordy**[2], **earnest**[3] speech, and **recounts**[1] the day they assumed their boy was dead. 'When we heard of the famine, we had to **construe** that he had died. But he was **spared**[16], God be **praised**[5]!'

1   immediately / my ideal time
2   dowry / rowdy / wordy
3   nearest / eastern / earnest
4   counters / recounts / construe
5   aspired / despair / praised
6   coins kept / in pocket
7   auctioned / education / cautioned
8   pertness / serpents / presents
9   meal for one / for me alone
10 intensive care / I can't even rise
11 envied / veined / endive
12 a diet / I'd eat
13 weird / wired
14 restrain / terrains / retrains / trainers
15 recant / trance / canter / nectar
16 drapes / spread / spared
17 sweep the floor / too few helpers
18 I think therefore I am / I fear to think I'm here
19 reacted / created / catered
20 melons / lemons / solemn

Anachronism   *wordplay*
out of time

Ug the post-neanderthal switched off his iPadPro and scratched on the parchment with his quill pen, having dipped it into an ink made from asbestos dust mixed with dodo blood.

He'd transferred one third of his wealth by phone banking onto his younger son's vellum ledger.

'Grunt, prithee, don't forget to take your Filofax, dancing bear and lead make-up – the girls will like that!'

The son set off in his Bakelite hovercraft, and was soon enjoying a wild time in Dissipation Site E, a run-down, far-from state-of-the-art undersea dwelling dome, with casinos, nouvelle cuisine restaurants, *Anne Hathaway's House of Ill Repute*, alchemists, on-line virtual black-smiths and a VineLeaf Clothing Store. After a while, his cash, credits, pelts, beans, chips and trading tokens ran out; this was spectaculay unfortunate as there was also a famine at that time.

The boy found a job on the mainland (after searching FishforPigs.com, the papers, and being featured on the village hall notice board).

He looked after on-the-trotter bacon on the 207th floor of an high-rise development (some call it a sty-scraper), well away from the glaciers that scoured the landscape, and was so hungry he considered eating the rotten podpills they had. But his heads-up-display internal WottZap³·⁵ system went 'bing' and he realised 'My father's butler eats well; I could go home to his solar-powered house and ask to work up to my ruff in the peat bog as a comrade in the collective.'

So he stepped aboard a triple-decker maglev trolleybus (his Oyster was charged two groats, $9 1s 7¾d for a fourpenny one) and went home. But while he was only just on the old boy's radar, Ug clocked him and leapt aboard a mammoth and rode out to meet him, using his Samsung Galaxy S9 to give him a ring. He provided the family salute, put a silver foil blanket on his shoulders, mingled blood to demonstrate his re-acceptance into the family, and gave him a pair of Nike Air Vapormax Plus trainers.

He called to his business associates: 'Grunt. Use your wap-enabled smoke-signalling system to get a catering firm down here – we are going to have a hootenanny, with beef. There'll also be protein pills, turnips, venison, mutton, braised brachiosaurus, manna, chips wrapped in newspaper, brown Windsor soup, a packet of Spangles, quinoa, BSE-laden burgers, and balsamic vinegar (drizzled on cranberries), served with domes of Smash dispensed via those implements originally designed to put portions of ice cream into cones, plus whatever fungi we can forage and some Vesta Beef Curry on lard-fried Wonderloaf.'

He donned a tricorn hat, a large red coat and clanged a handbell, galloping hither and thither upon an EasyRider-style motorbike. 'Oyez, oyez! For this my boy was as lost as last year's unicorn, but now he's found; he was lying atop a funeral pyre as peasants cried *bring out your dead!* but now he is happily on CompuServe and My Space, so let the proclamation be sent by Inquisitors and Crusaders alike across great distances – yea, on horseback, by longboat, in the Voyager probe, via KindleFire and by short-wave frequency vodcasts on GPS wax cylinders – even to the kingdoms beyond the wood, where be dragons and The iCloud. Grunt.'

Unreliable narrator *style*
errors of interpretation, internal dialogue and fact. Oh dear

The farmer was a bit of a misery, and thoroughly fed up with trying to cope with family life. He tried many times to force both of his annoying sons to leave the farm; consistently he squeezed their wages, extended their hours, refused to let them have parties (with or without a goat) and insisted that they tend the animals and harvest the crops.

Eventually, his younger boy could stand it no more and took the bribe which had been offered as an incentive to go. 'This is the last thing I would choose, dad, but you have made it completely impossible for me to stay, you aggravating old man,' the boy would probably have said if he'd been able to put into words the rage he felt.

The farmer smiled and rubbed his hands as the son went on his way. 'Oh, happy day! I doubt I shall ever have to see him again,' he thought, with considerable pleasure.

The faithful son did his best to make the money last, with very sensible investments and carefully seeking out inexpensive accommodation, but after several months of small, cheap, once-a-day meals, living on the streets and having no friends or acquaintances at all in his new life in Driven-Away City, he discovered he was penniless. He begged for a while, and decided in the end to find a job.

But the so-called 'famine' that had struck the land meant there were not many decent jobs to be had.

He'd spent a while hiring out deckchairs on the beach at the Sea of Galilee but when the bottom dropped out of the tourism market, he had to seek employment working as a chariot-park attendant.

Eventually, he laid aside his dignity and settled for a livestock-tending job on a piggery.

His hunger was so great that he longed to eat pork chops or ham or bacon, but these animals were still alive and there was no way to slaughter them. The only way he was going to get a decent dinner was to go back home and try to get a job there. Fingers crossed, the old man might treat him with the respect he deserved; but if not, it was always going to be better than it was before. Surely Farmer Miseryguts has learned his lesson by now… He had given it considerable thought, and weighed up the pros and cons, constantly trying to decide the best course of action.

So he made his way home as quickly as his weakened state and shoddy footwear would allow, raging at God for allowing such a terrible set of circumstances to befall him.

When he got back to the farm, his attitude was not much improved. Within a week, he'd helped himself to

some shoes and a coat, stolen a ring from the jewellery box and invited a whole bunch of people for one of those previously-forbidden parties, at which the fatted goat was sacrificed, spit-roasted and consumed by revelers, among whom were a large number of gatecrashers.

The farmer ground his teeth. 'I thought (hoped) he was gone forever. I told him to Get Lost, and even was becoming quite resigned to the possibility that he'd died. But look! Drives me mad. He's turned up, and he's alive and annoying, the same as ever he was. Just my lousy stinking luck!'

Seven deadly sins   *key words*

Tragedy: the boy impatiently took his slice of the money, denying his brother and cousins. He dangerously slid down the balustrade and spent cash in an orgy of **gluttony** and pushing many coins into a gambling **slot. H**is behaviour illustrates **deadly sin**fulness.

Famine struck, and he was discouraged, somewhat flustered and grew hungry, filled with **envy** for the pig's food, which exhibited meagre edibleness. At last, he came to his senses. He chose to lay down his **pride**.

While he was still a long way off, his father ran to greet him (without **anger**) beyond the orangeries and gave him gifts (including a ring with highly-polished lustre).

He also threw a party with bangers and mash, beverages and clusters of grapes in basins, plus guava, **rice** and ale.

'My son was a stranger; did **deadly sins**. Now he's alive!'

Psalm *pastiche*

¹O sing unto the Father a new song,
  for he hath giv'n his bounty to me.
²Yea, for I with divers good things hath he blessed,
  even unto the next generation.
³I took forth the endowment of the secondborn
  ⁴and distributed it abandonly
⁵To they who sing and cook and dance
  and spin tinkling casino wheels of chance.
⁶*Give thanks, give thanks! His cash endures forever!*   *Instrumental break*

⁷Yet right soon penniless have I become
  and those with me are here no more;
⁸We suffer grievous famine and hardship;
  And all the people cry aloud in their distress.
⁹For shadows cover the land
  and deep darkness the people.
¹⁰I seek to work with filthy animals.
  Their food is an abomination
¹¹Yet with mine eyes do I most earnestly desire it,
  and my stomach doth yearn with much grumbling.
¹²Woe, many and piteous are these foolish imaginings;
  With despair do I consider the putrifying slop of swine.
¹³*No thanks, No thanks! No pods endure forever!*   *Fanfare of trumpets*

¹⁴But from the cloud the LORD spake; clearly did he say
¹⁵'Rise up, O lost son! Yea, rise up thyself!
  Your father's men toil; sweat they and labour,
¹⁶Yet choice meat, with garlic, cucumbers and such,
  are laid most heartily at the table for them, each day.
¹⁷Arise ye and return to him right soon, and ask
  To be counted withal among the employed;
¹⁸Consider not yourself to be an offspring –
  Rather, reckon thy status to be unworthy.'
¹⁹*Give thanks, give thanks! God's wisdom endures forever!*   *Lyre solo*

²⁰So verily I returned to the home of mine father
  With toil and great heaviness of heart did I venture.
²¹Yet, most happily, and with vastness of vision claity,
  while was I still an long way off
²²Mine parent did espy me, clapp'd his hands
  and, tucking up his raiment, gaddingly ran,
²³Gathering me unto himself in his arms
  With many great kisses and quantity of embrace.
²⁴*Give gifts, give gifts! Footwear endures not forever!*   *Selah*

25'Quick! Attend to me, O servants mine,
  and with swiftness of step fetch a coat and shoes and a ring;
26And take thou an slender blade and rightly
  slaughter the fatted calf by the throat; and sing
27For this my son is returnéd to our farm
  I thank the good LORD – came he to no harm.
28I thought him lost and feared him dead;
  He's found! He lives! The calf is bled?
29Call villagers hither to be at my table fed
  With meat and veg and wine and bread!'
30*Give thanks, give thanks! God's love endures forever!*   *end*

Keyboard:
alternating hands   *alphabet games*
one of !@£$%/12345/qwerty/asdfg/
zxcvb *alternates with one of* ^&*()_+/
67890/uiop/hjkl/nm,.?
Dismantlement of my land?

Endowment o boy (£69203) name Len then dosh spent.

Work with toxic pens pals. Suspensorial authenticity Pa kept own visual vigil

Len A: make me j... a hand? Skepticisms? Shant, son Ale Cow

O, sick Ah, leptothricosis* or leuco-cytozoans† nah!

* bacteria-sourced fatal illness
† fatal parasites

Scar winners   *key words*
threadbare synopses of most BAFTA
Best Movie winners since 1980, with one
letter removed (some punctuation added)
Boy takes inheritance from his landed gentry father whom he calls **The Arist** (2011), short for 'aristocrat'. Both remain grey and silent but the boy acts upon his anger and, after a quick medal-winning run along the seafront, whips up the horses into a gallop and rides the **Chariots of Ire** (1981) to Dissipation City (some called it the Forbidden City). His father, the **Lat Emperor** (1987) has only land that is extremely narrow, and has no domain over longitude.

It was an act of revenge, really, but **He Departed** (2006). Once there – yes, with his fighting victim attitude he is something of a **Ladiator** (2000) – he meets several girls, including Gloria (some might call her a redhead, but actually, she's tiTian, **I** c(1997)an tell, with a sinking feeling), and starts a journal titled **G and I** (1982) to keep a good record of what she claims is a barefoot, non-violent revolution.

She's high-maintenance, gets into and out of jail with some songs and a mysteriously motivated chap named **Chiago** (2002) who is the bashful manservant of a Moor without a handkerchief. He spends a great deal of money, including on hotel rooms which were completely decorated: too bij**Ou tO fAf.**

'**I ca**(1985)n quite simply leave them be and get on with big game hunting.'

All the walking wears his shoes out, yet he remains tranquil. However he has an hallucination featuring a fox in socks in a deserted fort, plus Vikings and their wild dogs – **Danes with Wolves** (1990).

He considers that Gloria's torso is lovely. He says 'She has **A Beautiful**

Mid (2001), but this has **Made us** (1984) more attracted to each other and to Mozart's melodies.'

Approving of the form of some capital letters, he likes the style of B, the lines of X and **The Shape of W. At** r(2017)ustic dancehalls he discovers some of the girls he likes have male companions, and describes them thus: 'Nellie – boyfriend, as expected. Krystal – sweetheart, understandably. And this last one's a dream: Eri**c**a – beau. Ty(1999)pical!'

Gloria, an avid reader, is clear about her preferences. She has always said that she wasn't too bothered about the works of Thomas Hardy. 'Look,' she says, '**Shakespeare I love** (1998). But I strongly dislike Dickens, Dostoyevsky and am not that fussed about any of the Brontë sisters, either. Hardy, to be honest with you, I could quite simply take or leave.'

He writes a few plays but soon discovers that one of the men is a racist girl who has cost him lots of **Cash*** (2005). He started to play cricket, copyrighting a form of spin bowling, known as **The English Patent** (1996), but these exploits leave him hospitalised and eager **For rest**; ump(1994)ires, however, direct him to play table tennis or go running. He studies philosophy and finds he agrees with Wittgenstein and Descartes, **Plato**, N(1986)ietzsche and Hegel. Despite a series of interlinked stories, all the money was gone. At the same time, a famine struck.

Everyone was destitute: formerly wealthy folks, some of whom were suicidal; parents in crisis; and alternative Kuwaiti oil sheiks, known for their currency, **Or Dinar People** (1980). He went to work with a hitman tending pigs, but soon decided 'This is **No Country for Old Me.**' (2007). If he didn't get out of the pigsty soon, he'd fall into 24 months of bonded ownership of the pigman, and be **2 Years a Slave** (2013). The bacillus in the pods was likely to be a cereal killer, yet on account of **The Silence of the Labs** (1991) it was impossible to provide scientific analysis. He knew there was a book genre (if only it could be found) called **Schindler's Lit** (1993) that described how to save some from death. He mused 'How did I reach this point? I can't imagine how I'd beg**Un, for I've** n(1992)ot any recollection of it at all!'

A revelation took hold of him and he knew he and several others should battle their way back to the place with the two towers where Arist (unexpectedly) gave jewellery and welcomed him not as a hired man but as a son, since this was **The Lord of the Rings: The Return of the Kin** (2003).

The habit-driven and mentally scarred father used great speed to reach his still-a-long-way-off son, so he became known as **Ranman** (1988). Courageous locals painted themselves and used their freedom to stoke up the calf-roasting furnace – **Braveheat** (1995) – and when it was cooked, cut the fatted calf into tiny bits. After **Riving Miss Daisy**[†] (1989) they distributed slices to the male villagers (some of whom were Hebrew and some were servants) by auction: a process known as **Bidman** (2014).

Some ended up with more beef on their plate than others. The generous portions were called Maxcow, while the smaller ones were referred to as **Moo Light** (2016). They failed to gain access to **The Hut Locker** (2009), a strongbox that contained the number of the local pizza delivery service, because someone had secured it with an explosive device. There was impressive latrine illumination; hiS po light (2015) worked spendidly. Party music was supplied by the Royal Marine Band, which always played with great gusto and flourish, and build each tune to a big finish with musical signposts and rallentando's, in **Terms of end.**

A RM ent(1983)ertainment was thus enjoyable, despite being slightly predictable, loving, and with a sad denoument. The farmer stutteringly began to address the crowd on hs favourite theme of the sovereignty of God, a sermon he entitled **the King speech** (2010); but he could not remember the content. He knew there was deception and fiction of a scientific sort, but the memory faded as his last reading was too long **Ago** (2012)‡.

*alternatively: ...is a girl who has accidentally given him a **Rash** (2005).
† Riving: to rend, tear or slice into small pieces; to break the spirit of
‡it is satisfying to have included them all – with the exception of *Million Dollar Baby* (2004) and *Slumdog Millionaire* (2008). Not only are these titles considerably more demanding than the others, their financial overtones made them seem less easy to conceal

Under Milk Farm *pastiche*

with great affection for Under Milk Wood *by Dylan Thomas*

FIRST VOICE To begin at the beginning: it is spring, moonless night over the cow-belch, crop-sway, slow, black, fatted-calf corn-fed farm. Asleep in his bed lies Captain Cecil Certainman, the Squire of Hire

SECOND VOICE who dreams of vast fields of yellow-gold that wave their greeting in the gentle small-hours breeze, while slumbering Mrs Meatan Wheatan dreamily reviews the oft-submitted curriculum vitae of Kelvin Melvin, Wesley Presley, Gawain Dastain and young Ray Sunshine. These chosen ones will toil and sweat and work and break for lunch when whistles blow, trestles rattle, cutlery clatters, and enamel plates clank.

FIRST VOICE Certainman's younger son Morgan rises at cockerel-call, washes himself (taking plenty of time for towel-rub), then carefully steps into his salty trousers and pulls yesterday's shirt over his head. He throws a weather-beaten boot at his older brother who is catching a few extra minutes' folding of the hands.

MORGAN On wi' your size elevens, Bryn! It's another day of labourin' in father's fields, wi' simple rations and supervising hired men who'd steal your eyes if they thought they might be worth a coin or two in the marketplace down by the village...

BRYN Oh, hold thy whisht, and stop moaning now! You have no thought for such as me – when all I want are simple country pleasures. My heart's desire is to call my friends to drink a while with curry goat and good-time Sally McNally and party dancing.

MORGAN If you're not careful you'll die of small ambitions, brother mine... Raise your sights and your horizons and consider the dullness of this dead-end village. As for me, I've made up my mind to get away.

BRYN Grand plans, you have, but you know deep down you'll never amount to all that much, you know, with your work-shy style, you waster.

SECOND VOICE Morgan slams the door and sits down to a cooked breakfast with his parents. He abruptly demands of his father early

296

increments of inheritance. Oh, what'll the neighbours?

CECIL *Son, my love-filled heart*
*   is warm to you;*
Yet chills in fear - inheritance taboo.
You want cash?
*   Your plan I hope I misconstrue;*
In our greatly wrenching interview;
This life-changing day has come,
*   just as I foreknew*
And despite my feeling deeply blue
Post-lunch I'll give (let coffee be a cue) –
The bag of cash just as you ask me to.

FIRST VOICE So Morgan swings past the chickens as they cluck and feather in their pen, along the road out of the farm, past the cowshed-smelling outhouses and along the sleepy, dusty, wide and welcoming dirt track.

SECOND VOICE He sidles by drinking dens where the scent of cheap perfume and overpriced dinners oozes out, with garlic on its breath.

MORGAN I take a room and change my shirt, and find my way towards a long dark bar, a-slop with beer and wine and forgotten dreams and broken promises and

FIRST VOICE deadly sins and he quaffs and slakes and calls for meat and fish and orders pie and bread and fruit and cream and pays for puddings and cheeses and tips the waiters and dancing girls

MORGAN and discovers men who quickly – oh, so quickly – befriend my cram-filled cash-bag and the pleasures thus bestowed; and women who keep no secrets and appear to love every stranger.

POLLY STARTER Oh hallo sweet boy, what are you wantin'?

LILY FALLS Walk my way, and sieze this glorious opportunity I'm makin' available to you for enjoying all manner of earthly delights!

MEGAN BODICE We can lead you – oh, so very far beyond your wildest expectations!

DAI LAFFIN Yes, get your cash and spread it out on the table!

DAFYDD DRINK Worry ye not, we'll properly enjoy the process of frittering it away!

OWEN PLENTY Pay for the hotel, dinner, the show and then you can put the rest on 25 Red!

FIRST VOICE And in what seems like no time he opens his wallet only to discover that it is as empty as the moneybag of a boy who has wasted all his father's hard-earned painfully-given cash.

SECOND VOICE How inconvenient, and how very frightening that this should be the same exact moment that a fierce famine strikes the land.

FIRST VOICE All are hungry – there is no food to eat.

SECOND VOICE The emptiness of tummies is matched only by the emptiness of Morgan's wallet and his soul.

FIRST VOICE And the emptiness of the *Situations Vacant* column in the window of the newsagent. Apart from the one advert for a pig farm assistant.

MORGAN Which is the job I am applying for…

PELHAM And being offered. You'll sit near the porkers and when you let the slop-bucket people in, you mind they wipe their shoes.

MORGAN I'm so miserable and hungry and lonely and fed up and so very sad at the thought of how deeply irresponsible and unappreciative I have been. But mostly hungry. Yes, hungry to the point of seriously wondering what those pods they're giving the pigs might taste like…

BUCKET BOY Come, all you skinny bacon-burgers, come you and drink down all the Vitamin C that's going, which isn't much, I'll be bound!

MORGAN Yes, hungry to the point of... Well, very nearly helping myself.

THE LORD No, lad, let me help you.

MORGAN And with that, I'm coming to my senses.

FIRST VOICE He's come to his senses.

SECOND VOICE He's having a revelation, more like!

MORGAN I shall arise and go back to the old farm. I shall say to my father I'm no longer worthy to be called a son, and ask to be one of the Chosen Ones, the hired men. I could very humbly become Kelvin, Wesley, Gawain or young Ray Sunshine.

KELVIN Ah, so we're not such crooks and rogues and charlatans now you want to be one of us!

LLAMBERT Changed his tune, alright!

ALED He'll want to be our great friend now, just you watch!

CLEDWYN [sniggers]

GERAINT But we won't let him sit at our trestle table, and clatter plate and fork with us and share our helpings of dinner, right?

RHYDIAN We'll let him know he's not welcome around here, not by a long shot.

FIRST VOICE He's walking, walking,

SECOND VOICE Walking, walking,

FIRST VOICE Trudging, trudging,

SECOND VOICE Footsore, weary,

FIRST VOICE Slowing, slowing,

SECOND VOICE Shuffling, stumbling.

[Pause]

FIRST VOICE But his father's seen him,

CECIL Even though he's still a long way off, I think ... I hope I'm right... I am sure now! This trudging, stumbling, shuffling figure. Oh, it is my son!

FIRST VOICE And father's clattering down the stairs, tucking his tunic into his belt, and running up the path, with abandon and enthusiasm!

SECOND VOICE So undignified! Such uninhibited rejoicing!

MORGAN Father, I am no longer worthy to be...

CECIL Servant, fetch a coat and my best sandals!

MORGAN But father, I am no...

CECIL Here, wear my ring. You know, you're family, you are, isn't it?

[Pause]

SECOND VOICE It is the night down on Milk Farm, and the still, cold air is vivid with burning beacons and the spit-roast campsite and flavoured smoke and dark bread and sponge cake and brown ale and bawdy shouts and happy laughter and couples dancing and girls with their boys by the cowsheds

FIRST VOICE and the unceasing hiss of sizzling fat dripping from the slowly-turning carcass of the fatted calf and the stropping of the carving knife that slices and slices again and serves red-hot, juicy portions of Buttercup to villagers and partygoers.

CECIL This is my son! He was lost and

We always thought
Like the calf in the cow shed
Of little Morgan C,
Who is dead, dead, dead.

But look, you villagers, feast your eyes, while you fill your mouths with steak and onions; look, you readers, while you fill your souls with wonder at this tale of grace and repentance; and look, you angels, while you sing your 'allelujahs – my boy is found and is oh, so wonderfully alive!

FIRST VOICE And later Captain Cecil Certainman, the Squire of Hire, lies in his soft bed, smiling and digesting.

Bohemian Rhapsody   *pastiche*

passionate writing about an alternative lifestyle. Acknowledgements to Freddie
Mercury; recorded by Queen in 1975; achieved UK No 1 in 1975 & again in 1991

Is this the real farm? My life is such a bore!
Cough up my wedge, dad! What? You're certain there is no more?
Open your eyes! I trust not accountancy!
No more a poor boy; I need no sympathy.
Because I'm off right now, easy go; stakes are high, morals low.
Dissipation City – wild times on a platter for me, for me.

Papa, just blew your dosh –
Put a chip on seven red, spun the wheel, jumped in bed.
Marma – lade on gran'ry toast…
Such great times I had but thrown it all away!
Papa, ooh - truly meant to bleed you dry,
I won't be back again this time tomorrow.
Carry on, I'll carry on as if nothing really matters.

Too soon, my money's gone.
Sends shivers down my spine; raging hungry all the time.
Goodbye everybody, 'friends' are quick to go;
Gonna leave me all behind to face the truth.

Piggy, ooo (I'm the boy who cash blows) I don't wanna die!
I sometimes wish I'd never seen pods at all!

I seem a hungry silhouetto of a man -
Nowt in bouche, nowt in bouche - Cannot do the fandango!
Thunderbolt quite frightening; very much enlightening me
(Halleleo) Halleleo! (Halleleo) Halleleo!
Now cheerio I must go - Arise and go!
I'm still a way off; hope father loves me…
Know I'm unworthy - back not as family -
Hired man's life is generosity.

Maybe yes, maybe no; will he let me know?
He's running! Hug – he will not let me go (let him go!)
He's weeping! He will not let me go (let him go!)
He's giving! A coat and ring and shoes (even shoes?)
Coat and ring and shoes (even shoes!)
(Welcome party he will throw)
Party he will throw, oh! Love-ly spread and fan-cy show!

Oh mama mia, mama mia (welcome party he will throw)
Old Buttercup has been spit-roast on both sides for me, for me, for me!

Did I think he was stone dead and started to cry?
Did I think he was lost? Yes, he's found. Don't know why!
Oh gravy! Not enough of this gravy!
Beef, veg and spuds, just want to get my plate piled high!'
(Oh, yeah, oh yeah)
Loving really matters; re-pen-tance sets free;
God's love really matters, God's love really matters to me.
Parable of lost son…

Acrostic (diagonal) *alphabet games*

each line has twenty-four characters; first letter of first line,
second letter of second line etc spells key words

SIN REVELATION FORGIVENESS

```
 1 'Share out your wealth with me,'
 2 hIs brash boy demands. Concur.
 3 SoN took the cash; spent it all
 4 on dRinking and prostitutes.
 5 Now vEry quickly, he was broke.
 6 One seVere famine struck the
 7 whole rEgion. Deserted by all
 8 ex-so-calLed friends, he made a
 9 plan: take A job on a pig farm. He
10 longed to sTuff himself, just
11 like those pIgs, with the pods…
12 Suddenly recOgnising utter
13 disasters, he uNderstands he
14 might go home to Father's farm,
15 not asking for a sOn's welcome
16 'The truth? I am unwoRthy.' While
17 his boy was yet a lonG walk off,
18 the farmer saw him. 'He Is alive!'
19 Demonstrating his loVe - gave
20 him a hug, a coat, some shoEs and
21 one ring to wear on his fiNger.
22 'Partying with many of my nExt
23 door neighbours; my son was So
24 dead but now he's alive! CheerS!'
```

Acrostic (reverse diagonal)

each line has twenty-four characters; last letter of first line,
second last letter of second line etc spells key words

REPENTANCE AND RESTORATION

```
24   Son's greed demands of fatheR
23   'Give me my share of your monEy' -
22   gets a third of the princiPal.
21   He enthusiastically spEnds
20   on wanton women and driNking -
19   wastes all being a parTygoer.
18   He's financially cleAned out!
17   No cash, no friends aNd no hope.
16   Famine causes all Concern. No
15   Income: he shall gEt a farm job.
14   Hungry, sad boy wAnts pigfeed:
13   decides filliNg his stomach
12   with those poDs - a rotten idea.
11   Could be a seRvant now at home...
10   Having comE to his senses, 'I'll
 9   humbly riSe, leave and return;
 8   say to faTher: I am confessing
 7   my sin tO you. I'm not any longer,
 6   dad, woRthy to be known as a son.'
 5   His fAther saw him when he was
 4   disTant. He ran, embraced, gave
 3   a rIng, pair of shoes and a coat.
 2   'GOod news! A lost son came back:
 1   Now he is alive - dead no longer!'
```

21-syllable sentences *wordplay*

Young son asked for his inheritance immediately, so his dad gave him the cash. He quickly set off for Dissipation City, where he began to waste the money. Wild living: girls, drinking, swanky restaurants, gambling and extravagances galore. Soon the lad had an empty purse: famine struck the land, so he took a job tending pigs. He watched them with envy as they ate their mouldering pods; then he came to his senses. 'My father's hired men eat well; I shall arise and return home to ask to work for him. I realize I've been a fool, and I am no longer worthy to be called a son.' He was still a long way off when his watchful father saw him and ran to greet his son.

'Servants! Fetch a coat for him, and shoes for his feet; lad, receive this gold ring as a sign. 'Kill the fatted calf; celebrate, for my son was dead, he lives; was lost but is now found!'

Test cricketers   *keywords*

130 of the world's best, ever

Jesus of Nazareth, referred to as **Lillie** of the valley, kept a parable vi**Gil**. **Christ** told this story:

A father said 'You're my son. I shall give you what you ask.' He chooses to bless his **Boy** (**cott**onsocks) with his inheritance. **Young** son took the moneyb**Ag, new**ly filled with **Silva** coins (fin**Ger mon**ey) He set off out of the farm, on the track **Border**ing the **Lake,** round the **Hill** – where the f**Lock** of sheep graze by the **Marsh** (**all** tended by the **Sheppard**), producing **Wool – mer**e and valley. His journey developed from walking to, at its pe**Ak, ram**bling. He arrived at Dissipation City for a great time; truly excellent. Some might call it de**F**.

'**Re: I tas**te champagne, caviar – the high life!' He dated Mary, goes steady with Jane, **Beds** Erica, loves a girl named Itha. On the wall is a **Mural**. Itha ran**g** the **Camp bell** for butler service. They called 'Hey!' in harmony; '**Yo!**' unis**on**.

Arnold, Greig, Ben, Audrey's pals **Elliott** and **Harvey,** plus **Martyn, Morris, Moses,** Isaa**C, Ron, Jeff, Lloyd, Richard's Friend Edgar** and his rarely **Sober** sisters Julie**T, Ava,** Rénata, **Kelly Lee, Ali** and c**Lara**, all played **Snooker**, having brushed bits o**F lint off** the beize. The cash was spent by summer – July, the girls welcomed his wealth and called him 'lu**V'; Aug** – '**han**dsome loser'. These people were at **War,** nearly, with his

wealth. Their conversation was toxi**C; row** encouraging. Just as he had us**Ed rich**es completely, all began to starve. The country ran out of food - meat, fish, vegetables, cheese – even cheese – ricotta**A, the 'R', to n**ear the 'Z' of Zwitser (farmhouse gouda). He began to (in a way one might call the harshes**T) rue man**y foolish carelessnesses. 'My life was lovel**Y - all op**portunity, but I **Blewitt**.'

He took a job tending pigs; an utter disgrace, as **Hogg ard**enied in Hebrew law. He greeted the **Small** rotting pods wit**H 'ugh', es**timating them to be lethal, (then a 'ugh!' and no**W a 'ugh!**'), involuntarily having to **Go 'ugh'** and **Go 'we** really want to eat with the **Hog, and** can't. **Will** e**y**e these pods, but may not eat such as this.'

He realised what God's **Will is**. 'My **IQ bal**ances my physical agony! I need not remain in this dystopi**A – they** (my father's hired men) eat well... What a **Gang! Ul**ysses himself would envy them. I shall do thi**S now**. I'll ignore stomach **Panes, ar**ise, and go home.'

So he a**Rose**. His mood was dis**Mal**. **In** garments threadbare, he rehearsed his plea, hoping to **Engineer** favour. 'I am Not Great. Not Great. NG. I **May** say I have been ma**De** very hungry and **Ill... I, NG**.

'**Worth**y to be called a family-member? No. **And, er, son**? No. I **Khan** as**K. Not** to your face, **Abba!** So NG. My **IQ bal**ance is wobbling.'

Father had been **Holding Hope** in his **Hart** for some time. It felt as though time moved slowly – one day **Per era**), and saw him from a long way off. He ran to him, and out of his **Grace** gave him a kiss, gifts - a coat, a ring and shoes (Sa**Bot**), **ham**pering his attempts to make a plea. Father gave him a **Hug.**

'He's so welcome!' he shouted. He slaughters the fatted calf and the servant wipes the blood off the wea**Pon.**

Tingling with excitement - indeed, not stoppin**G at ting**ling with excitement, the father danced to waltzes by **Strauss.** They built a barbecue: tinder below kindling **Underwood** (yew, cedar, **Hazelwood** – all types of popu**Lar wood,** by whatever names people are **Colling wood** these days); someone **Stokes** the fire. The *Department of Real Estate* comments when, in celebration, a village **Burns a Cow.** *DRE:* 'Yes, this is acceptable'. Boil, sauté, **Fry,** bake, **Cook,** display, present, **Garner;** in the centre of the table was a **Vaas** with **Flowers;** it **Had** leeks, **Hazlitt,** duck, **Lamb** cutlets (not h**Am,** lamb) **Cooked** on **Hobbs,** rack of l**Amb,** rosewater-pheasant.

Also: **Pollock,** rock salmon, known as **Huss); a** interesting **Burger** with **Onions.** There was **Old Broad** ginger **Root,** too. China **Wessels*** containing **Pringles** and other **Crisps** were displayed; orange-coloured man**Go,** ochre peach/plum **Duff.**

More: chicken in **Agar** presented tartly as a **Pie (terse),** not without success; **Beer** (made by *Brew LiTres Co);* **thick** cream and jam on scones; bottles of **Bollinger** plus chocolate bars such as Kit Kat, Crunchie and **Mars.** He stood to make a speech. 'Thy steaks, thy bread, thy **Stew art** fine victuals, O chef! Nine dulk (whatever they are) don't cut it, but **Ten dulk** are super**B! Rad, man!** You certainly don't give a **Chap pellets!** Yes, eat; oui, mange; **Jar, ine!** I shall make a catalogue of these great foods,

and in**Dex** *teriyaki.* I agree, when my son left he was **Green. I'd** gently weep, fearing he was gone forever. We reckoned you dead – certainly lost. But you're found, and alive **tho! M'son,** we're glad you're back, **Close** to the family heart! Yes, you **Do live! I ra**ve about it!'

Key: Familiar name; * indicates captain; *country; test career dates* (assume recent, but clarified where necessary); *matches* ° indicates matches to September 2018 for current players. Includes full members of ICC by order of association: Australia *Aus* England *Eng* South Africa *SA* (NB anti-apartheid boycott 1970-1991); India *Ind* New Zealand *NZ* West Indies *WI;* Pakistan *Pak;* Sri Lanka *SL;* Zimbabwe *Zim;* Bangladesh *Ban;* (Afghanistan & Ireland became members in 2017)
Dennis **Lillie** *Aus 71-84 70* *Adam **Gilchrist** *Aus 99-08 96* *Geoffrey **Boycott** *Eng 64-82 108* Dick **Young** *Eng 1907-08 2* Jonathan **Agnew** *Eng 84-85 3* *Aravinda de **Silva** *SL 84-02 93* *Lee **Germon** *NZ 95-97 12* *Allan **Border** *Aus 78-94 156* Jim **Laker** *Eng 48-59 46* *Clem **Hill** *Aus 1896-1912 49* Tony **Lock** *Eng 52-68 49* Malcolm **Marshall** *WI 78-91 81* David **Sheppard** *Eng 50-63 22* Bob **Woolmer** *Eng 75-81 19* *Wasim **Akram** *Pak 85-02 104* Phillip **DeFreitas** *Eng 86-95 44* Alec **Bedser** *Eng 46-55 51* Muttiah **Muralitharan** *SL 92-10 132* *Alistair **Campbell** *Zim 92-02 60* *Waqar **Younis** *Pak 89-03 87* Geoff **Arnold** *Eng 67-75 34* *Tony **Greig** *Eng 72-77 58* *Richie **Benaud** *Aus 52-64 63* Matthew **Elliott** *Aus 96-04 21* Neil **Harvey** *Aus 48-63 79* Damien **Martyn** *Aus 92-06 67* Arthur **Morris** *Aus 46-55 48* Harry **Moses** *Aus 1887-95 6* *Hansie **Cronje**‡ *SA 92-00 68* *Clive **Lloyd** *WI 66-84 110* *Viv **Richards** *WI 74-91 121* Travis **Friend** *Zim 01-04 13* Bruce **Edgar** *NZ 78-86 39* *Garfield **Sobers** *WI 54-74 93* Chris **Tavaré** *Eng 80-89 31* Jim **Kelly** *Aus 1896-05 36* Bret **Lee** *Aus 99-08 76* Moeen **Ali** *Eng 14-present 52*° *Brian **Lara** *WI 90-06 131* *Tip **Snooke** *SA 1906-23 26* *Andrew **Flintoff** *Eng 98-09 79* *Michael **Vaughan** *Eng 99-08 82* Shane **Warne** *Aus 92-07 145* Martin **Crowe** *NZ 82-95 77* *John **Edrich** *Eng 63-76 77* *Mike **Atherton** *Eng 89-01 115* Fred **Trueman** *Eng 52-65 67* *Graham **Yallop** *Aus 76-84 39* Greg **Blewitt** *Aus 95-00 46* Matthew **Hoggard** *Eng 00-08 67* Gladstone **Small** *Eng 86-91 17* Merv **Hughes** *Aus 85- 94 53* *Steve **Waugh** *Aus 85-04 168* Darren **Gough** *Eng 94-03 58* *David **Gower** *Eng 78-92 117* Tom **Hogan** *Aus 63-64 7* Peter **Willey** *Eng 76-86 26* *Bob **Willis** *Eng 71-84*

90 *Asif **Iqbal** *Ind 79-80* 6 Bill **Athey** *Eng 80-88* 23
*Sourav **Ganguly** *Ind 96-08* 113 John **Snow** Eng 65-
76 49 Monty **Panesar** *Eng 06-13* 50 Brian **Rose** *Eng
77-81* 9 Lasith **Malinga** *SL 04-10* 30 Farokh
Engineer *Ind 61-75* 46 *Peter **May** *Eng 51-61* 66
*Kapil **Dev** *Ind 78-94* 131 *Ray **Illingworth** *Eng 58-
73* 61 James **Anderson** *Eng 03-present* 143° *Imran
Khan *Pak 71-82* 88 Alan **Knott** *Eng 67-81* 95 Zaheer
Abbas *Pak 69-85* 78 *Tamim **Iqbal** *Ban 08-17* 50
Michael **Holding** *WI 75-87* 60 Shai **Hope** *WI 15-
present* 22° Matthew **Hart** *NZ 94-95* 14 Dilruan
Perera *SL 14-present* 31° *WG **Grace** *Eng 1880-99* 22
*Ian **Botham** *Eng 77-92* 102 *Kim **Hughes** *Aus 77-84*
70 *Ricky **Ponting** *Aus 95-12* 168 *Mike **Gatting**
Eng 78-95 79 *Andrew **Strauss** *Eng 04-12* 100 Derek
Underwood *Eng 66-82* 86 Josh **Hazelwood** *Aus 14-
17* 30 Harold **Larwood** *Eng 26-33* 21 Paul
Collingwood *Eng 03-11* 68 Ben **Stokes** *Eng 13-
present* 46° Joe **Burns** *Aus 14-15* 13 *Colin **Cowdrey**
Eng 54-75 114 *CB **Fry** *Eng 1896-12* 26 Alastair **Cook**
Eng 06-18 161 Joel **Garner** *WI 77-87* 58 Chaminda
Vaas *SL 94-09* 111 *Andy **Flower** *Zim 92-02* 63
Richard **Hadlee** *NZ 73-90* 86 Gerry **Hazlitt** *Aus
1907-12* 9 *Allan **Lamb** *Eng 82-92* 79 *Hashim **Amla**
SA 04-17 107 *Stephen **Cook** *SA 16-17* 11° Jack
Hobbs *Eng 08-30* 61 Curtly **Ambrose** *WI 88-00* 98
Shaun **Pollock** *SA 95-08* 108 *Nasser **Hussain** *Eng
90-04* 96 Christopher **Burger** *SA 58* 2 Graham
Onions *Eng 09-12* 9 Chris **Old** *Eng 72-81* 46 Stuart
Broad *Eng 07-present* 123° *Joe **Root** *Eng 12-present* 74°
‡Kepler **Wessels** *Aus 82-85* 24 *and* *SA 92-94* 16
Derek **Pringle** *Eng 82-92* 30 Bob **Crisp** *SA 35-36* 9
*Graham **Gooch** *Eng 75-95* 118 Reggie **Duff** *Aus
1902-05* 22 Ashton **Agar** *Aus 13* 3 *Kevin **Pietersen**
Eng 05-14 104 Michael **Beer** *Aus 11-12* 2 *Marcus
Trescothick *Eng 00-06* 76 Douglas **Bollinger** *Aus
09-10* 12 Rod **Marsh** *Aus 70-84* 96 *Alec **Stewart** *Eng
90-03* 133 *Sachin **Tendulkar** *Ind 89-13* 200 *Don
Bradman *Aus 28-48* 52 *Greg **Chappell** *Aus 70-84* 87
*Douglas **Jardine** *Eng 28-34* 22 *Ted **Dexter** *Eng 58-
68* 62 *Gordon **Greenidge** *WI 74-91* 108 Jeff
Thomson *Aus 72-85* 51 *Brian **Close** *Eng 49-76* 22
Basil **D'Oliveira** *Eng 66-72* 44

‡ Kepler **Wessels**, born in South Africa but living in Australia, represented Australia (by the residency rule) gaining considerable test experience.

He retired from test cricket to play in the Kerry Packer *World Series Cricket* 'Supertests', but six years later, apartheid was abolished, so the boycott of South Africa was lifted. Wessels qualified as a native, and was selected (and made captain), primarily since he was the team's only non-debutant.

Kermodian flagship film review *style*

I'm an an LTL. This pays homage to the Wittertainment *of Simon Mayo &* Mark Kermode*

Jesus spoke from Clergy corner. 'Here's the thing,' he started, 'this is a plot spoiler – but everything will be alright in the end.'

Benjamin Sniddlegrass' life didn't pass the six laugh test, so he asked his father for his inheritance. With flappy hands, money was passed, and Ben went on the cruise to Dissipation City, where he befriended Matthew Mahogany and several others and for a while, ate well (chubby, h'mm?).

He spent his money and time going to the pictures with women pipe-smokers producing the smell of colitas. Among them were Muriel Strepsil, Ikea Knightley, Katie Winceyette and the Good Lady Professor Her Indoors, plus Eileen Dover and Lucy Lastic (nominative determinism).

Everything was turned up to eleventy-stupid – blimey Charlie – but after a while, the rozzers got involved, as he'd run out of cash. Famine struck dramatically, and the good doctors declared WRIs partly due to a 30% light loss. There were probably several Unfortunate Events.

Ben took a job tending Verner Hertz-hog in threed. He envied the pigs' pods, and came to his senses. 'My circumstances are not wholly unproblematic.' He thumped the desk and had a revelation which solved his dilemma. Q, and if you will, ED (*quod emergency demonstrandum*). He said to himself 'Well done you,' and arose, setting off with a quiet-quiet-quiet-bang as he shut the gate. He was thoroughly ashamed of himself but planned how to speak to his father. 'I'll be fitting Tab A into Slot B; yet will he have a mini-tanti? May he even exhibit Brechtian Alienation?'

While he was still a long way off his father saw him and yelled 'Hallo to Jason Isaacs!' He burst into tears of joy; he was dead amaze & totes emoshe. He gave his son gifts of shoes, a coat, and a ring. 'What's up with your bad self?' he asked.

Ben replied 'I'm all over the place!'

His father ordered the servant to kill the fatted calf.

'How do you kill a fatted calf?' the servant asked.

'You just kill a fatted calf,' came the reply.

'Would that it were so simple!'

'Well, tinkety tonk, old fruit-based device, and down with the Nazis!'

At the party there was a whole bunch o' stuff. Food: twiglets and post-ironic battenberg. Transport: who's driving the boat? Cinematic entertainment: a series of still images projected sequentially to create the illusion of movement. Music: Dodge Brothers & Fairport Convention.

Father gave a speech 'My son is not without flaws; when he's good he's very, very good and when he's bad he's prodigal (so bad it's bad) – and I'm not even joking! Praise redacted!' he said, with a chortle. His older brother, Basil Exposition, came in from the field and asked for the *and*.

---

* *LTL* signifies Long-Term Listener to the Mayo-Kermode movie programme on Radio 5

DecImpIntEx   *wordplay*

sentences repeatedly: Declarative, Imperative, Interrogative, Exclamatory
The younger son spoke firmly to his father. 'Let me leave. You know the wealth I shall receive from your estate when you die? I want it now!'

His father handed over a great deal of money, and the son left, bound for Dissipation City.

'Watch out, you wild, wild women, here I come!'

How could he have spent the money more quickly or on more wanton, worthless people and things? No-one knows! The cash was soon spent and he was penniless.

'Help me out, someone…'

But how could he have known that his poverty would coincide with a national famine? Alas!

He decided to try to find a job, despite the dishonor. 'Please give me a job tending your pigs.'

'How hungry are you?'

'I'm sufficiently hungry to envy the pigs' pods!'

After a little while, he came to his senses.

'Get up! What are you doing here? You're being a fool! You father hires men, and you could join them. Go home to your dad, and seek his forgiveness. What are you waiting for?' He was up and away like a shot! As he walked, he practiced what he was planning to say. *I want to return. Will you let me? I'm starving to death!*

While he was still a long way off, his father saw him and hurried to meet him, calling to his servants as he ran. 'Get the knife and kill the calf! Where's my coat, shoes and ring? He's home again – hoorah!'

He kissed his boy and invited the villagers to attend a party.

'Come, all of you, and celebrate with me! How could I not rejoice since my son has returned? He was lost and is found; he was dead and is alive again!'

Very common rhyme sound *poetry*

Their Pére sat there, in the armchair
By the bare hardware (he's proletaire, not a Mayor),
While his son and heir – with considerable flair,
And by means of a brief questionairre –
Made him aware of the need to share
What he had to spare. How very debonair!
Made into a millionaire with ne'er a care,
The son (not premiere) found a pied-a-terre
On Mayfair Thoroughfare, Elsewhere.
He met Claire, Cher and Solitaire, so with laissez-faire,
Spread his fortune everywhere to whosoe'er.

No éclair, no pear, no hare, no camembert.
And no silverware; au contraire, merely air.
Underwear and derrière in disrepair due to affair wear 'n' tear.
Longed to eat jardinière in full despair. C'est la guerre!
Following swear and prayer, decided to return to forebear.
Dare their differences to square?

Herr Albert will suddenly repair (nostrils a-flare)
When he sees him from the stair – not doctrinaire,
But full of savoire-faire, 'Yeah! It's Pierre, I do declare!
Mon cher, returned to my lair!' Provides a pair
Of shoes, the glare of gems, mohair coat d'hiver
(His was threadbare) and roast beef, oh, very rare.
'He was ere the terre, like Voltaire – beware, what a scare!
A nightmare! Now he's somewhere closer to his frère
Which is only fair. They're my sons, without compare.'

Hard-boiled crime drama *style*

acknowledging Casablanca, Dead Men Don't Wear Plaid, The Big Sleep *etc*

Times were tough in the Big City. But I was tougher; as tough as they come. And just for once the knockout blow wasn't dealt by a redhead in a tight skirt with an attitude to match. No, this time, the big sucker punch was thrown by Dame Fortune – Famine Fortune, as she called herself.

It was another Dissipating day when she first dropped by, spreading gloom and despondency all around her – like her cheap perfume, which reminded me of rotting vegetables.

'Everyone will die, unless they escape this place,' she said, enigmatically. I took on the case, at my usual $200 a day, plus expenses, plus danger money, and to look at her, I was going to need plenty.

P. Rod Iggle had turned up a few weeks ago, flashing bills and paying checks with wild abandon. He said he'd come from a hick farmstead and was ready to spend like a bank heist gangster using $100 bills as confetti.

He told people 'If you want anything, just whistle. You know how to whistle, don't you? You just put your lips together and blow.' What's more, he made good on the promise, putting on the Ritz, parading in his glad rags, calling for hooch and financing all kinds of hayburners as well as several Janes in a Juice Joint.

It occurred to me later that he was the sort to shake down a racket with no regard for who got caught in the crossfire.

He was bound to reach bottom soon – maybe not today, maybe not tomorrow, but one day, and for the rest of his life. Iggle attracted friends like a manure heap attracts blowflies, and they leeched on him until he'd been sucked dry.

And that was when Dame Fortune sashayed in – more dangerous, more deadly and more out of whack than I'd ever seen before.

Famine turned him into the Thin Man.

Iggle took a low-life job supervising pigs, but everyone was figuring that we've all got to ride this cart to the end of the rutted pathway and it's a one-way trip and the last stop is the cemetery.

He came to his senses and determined to slip back home and try to work for the Old Man. He prepared his speech. 'I'm not worthy.' Wouldn't win any prizes, yet it might just swing it.

But when he got within just a couple miles of his home, the Old Man came running, with a coat, new shoes, a jewelled bird statue from the Mediterranean, a ring and the kind of hug a real man would never admit he ever wants. He started his speech, but the Old Man dismissed it, and threw a party, nearly as wild as the parties Rod had been having here downtown. They were right neighbourly, and laid on dancing, music, a grand spread and celebrations, with local dames with figures that just wouldn't quit.

Old Man Iggle had a speech all his own. 'What's wrong with him? Nothing we can't fix... my son was lost, now he's found; he was on the night train to the big adios – sleeping with the fishes – but now he lives!'

It wasn't Shakespeare (he wouldn't be along for hundreds of years yet). But it's the gospel truth, I tell you.

What kind of son are you? *pastiche*

glossy-TV-listings-magazine-style multiple choice quiz

1 *You work at home, but you are bored. What do you do?*
   a) Go and get lost
   b) Take the road to Jericho
   c) Remain and spread seed
   d) Ask for inheritance and leave
2 *How did you disperse your money?*
   a) Haven't got any
   b) Stolen by thieves, who beat me until I was half-dead
   c) No money, just throw seed
   d) Rapidly wasted on wild living
3 *What happened next?*
   a) Continued to be lost
   b) Priest & Levite passed by on the far side of the road
   c) Birds ate the trampled seed on the path
   d) Famine struck
4 *Did you find work?*
   a) Bleated a bit, but it didn't make any difference
   b) Was about to die when a Samaritan took pity on me

307

c) Seed that fell on rock: plants withered

d) Yes: I tended pigs and envied their pods

5 *What happened next?*
   a) Noticed shepherd eagerly seeking me
   b) He tended my wounds with oil and wine
   c) Seed that fell among thorns: plants choked
   d) Had a revelation: decided to arise and return home

6 *Where did you go?*
   a) I stayed put and the shepherd found me
   b) Took a donkey ride to a nearby hotel
   c) Seed that fell on good soil: plants grew well
   d) I approached the farm, daring to hope I'd be hired

7 *Describe the next incident*
   a) Shepherd lovingly gathered me up
   b) Spent a few days recovering and recuperating
   c) Seed in good soil grew into healthy plants
   d) Papa came running, with his forgiving heart

8 *Were you given anything?*
   a) A shoulder ride home
   b) The hotel bill, with PAID IN FULL written across it
   c) A substantial and very healthy crop
   d) Several kisses, a new coat, shoes, and the family ring

9 *And the consequence was…*
   a) A celebration with neighbours
   b) I continued my journey without further incident
   c) 100 times what was sown
   d) Welcomed as a son not lost/dead but found/alive

10 *Is there a spiritual lesson here?*
   a) Angels rejoice over one sinner who repents
   b) *Love thy neighbour* means showing mercy
   c) Spread good news widely; let God produce the fruit
   d) Repentant wasters are welcomed and restored

How did you score?

Mostly a's You are a lost sheep who was found and rescued

Mostly b's You benefitted richly from a good Samaritan

Mostly c's You are a sower scattering seed

Mostly d's You are the lost son, feared dead, but you are found and alive

Street, innit?   *language*

For real, hear me now…

Da home boy asked 'iz old geeza f'r iz inher'tance, which 'e let rip an' spent on wild livin'. Like spliffs an fit totty an' a massive an' back at ya an' stuff…

Famine struck, so 'e look for work – an' smell bacon, right?. 'E longed to chow on mingin pods dey wuz givun. 'E came to iz senses; no longa whack.

'Wicked! Ma geeza's 'ired bruvers iz well fed. I iz gonna arise an' go turf an' wurk dere, coz I iz gangsta, not son, innit?' Well in ya face.

While 'e wuz still da long way off, iz old rinkligeeza seein' I an' run to greet I is. 'E gave 'e shoes, da tommy hilfinga threds, da big-time bling an tings an' kill da fatted calf, rite, coz none of 'is bluds was veggie, innit? Off da hook!

'My son wuz lost an' iz found; 'e wuz stiff but iz alive! Shout out, big up an' 'nuf respec' ter big man in clouds, see?'

Anodyne fairy-tale *style*
not taking sides, not offending anyone

Once upon a time, young Waster lived with his step-father down in Dingly Dell. He took a big bag of goodies and went off to spend his fortune, driving a golden coach (made by magic from a pumpkin and four white mice) provided by his fairy godmother.

He lived in a city with bright lights and friends and cafés, enjoying lovely food, plenty to drink and lots to do and see, until one day, the money was gone. At the same moment, everyone else was hungry, because there was a food shortage. Oh dear!

Waster decided to take a job with the White Winter Witch, looking after piggy-wigs.

When he saw the nasty slops the pigs ate, he very nearly tried them, but his basic niceness got the better of him.

He arose and went home to the fairy palace. While he was still a long way off, his father ran and met him at the gate, with kisses and a coat and with shoes and sprinkled him with stardust.

Buttercup the moo-cow joined in the fun. Father said 'We were very sad; now we're having a good time.'

And of course, they all lived happily ever after. Well, nearly all.

Blind eye rhyme *poetry*
for lack of another term, this (mostly) iambic hexameter maximizes bizarre spelling variations of certain sounds; cf Eye Rhyme (p149)

'Now dad, give me my cash; I'm a grown man! I'm sure
I wish to live it up!' So off went brash Featherstonehaugh;
Met three rampant women: Ann, Bianca, Julie.
Bought cars like John Montagu, first Earl of Beaulieu;
Drank beer, and danced to Tulisa and Beyonce;
Somehow got engaged to more than one fiancée.
But money soon ran out, no thanks to lovely Ann
And fierce famine struck the land. 'Much to my chagrin.
Tending scrawny pigs named Sergeant, Major, Colonel –
Beasts thin, and dying from lack of food internal.'
To long to eat their pods is quite bizarre, unsafe…
'I'll go back home - ask to be a hired man like Ralph.
'He takes his wage and also gets his lunch, for sure
Not family at all (he hails from Arkansas).
No more worthy to be called son, no! *Hireling* plain
(Like the workmen on Scotland's west coast near Culzean)
So I'll make the journey home to Suffolk - Aldeburgh.
Good job indeed my father's an entrepreneur!
Dad's running now – spied while I was a long way off;
He's hugging me, and telling servant (old Christophe)
To fetch a ring and coat and shoes. He sent a staff
Member to slit the throat and roast the fatted calf!
Inviting all to celebrate with a banquet
When I have plunged his business into sorry debt;

Glad that I live and am found. Good old dad Cholmondley
Showed great grace! I'm declared dead – mourned so glumly.
(He's serving wine from boxes with spouts – quite nozzle-ly
To folks from the tiny Kent village of Trottiscliffe.)
I once was lost but now I'm found; none say *oh dear!*
For now they are dancing around the chandelier;
Dad's making merry, neighbourly friends old and new
With great hullabaloo, ex-son's hireling debut.

Morse code   *language*

greener grass, telegraphed

```
−·····/·/          ···/−−−/−·/          −··/·/−−/·−/−·/·−·/·/−··/          ····/··/···/
··/−·/·····/·/·−·/·/−·/−·/−·/−·/−−·/··/          ·−/−·/−·/          ·−··/·/···−·/−·/
····/−−−/−−/·/·−·−·−          ····/          ···/−−−/·/−·/−·/          −·/····/·/          −−/−−−/−·/·/−−·/
··/−·/          ·−−/·/·−·/−··/          ·−−·/·/···/·/−−·/−·−·−·          ·−·····/·/−·/
··−·/−·/−−·/··/−·/·/          ···/−·/·−·/·−·/·−·/−·−−·−          ····/·/          −·/−−−/−−−/−−·/
·−·/          ·−−−/−−−/−··/          −·/·/−·/·/−·/···/·/−−·/          ·−−−·/··/−−··/···/          ·−·/·/·−·/
·−··/−−−/−·/−·/−−··/·/−··/          −·/−−−/          ·/·−·/−·/          −·/·····/·/··/·−·/
·−−·/−−−/−·/··/·−·−·−          ·····/          −·−·/·−·/−−·/·/          −·/−−−/          ····/··/···/
···/·/−·/···/·/−·/·/−−·−·−          −··/··/−·−·/·/−·/·/−·/·/−·/          −·/−−−/          −−·/−−−/
····/−−−/−−·/··/          ·−·/−·/−··/          ·−·/··/·−·/          −·/−−−/          −−−·/··/−·          ····/··/·−·/·−·/·−·/
−−·/−·/−·/−·−·−          ···/··/−·/·−·/··          ····/··/          −−·/·−·/·/−−·/          ····/··/          −−·/·−·/·−·/
−·/−−−/          ·−·/−−−/−·/−·/−−··/·/−··/          ·−·/−−·/·−·/−·/·−·/−−··/·/−··/          −·/−−−/          −−−/··/
−−·/··/−·/·/···/·/−·/·/−·/·/−·/          ·−·/          ···/−−−/−·/··/·−·−·−
          ·−−−−·/··/−·−·/·/          ·····/·/          −−·/·−·/···/          ·−−/·/−·/·/          ·−/
·−·/−−−/−·/−·/          ·−−/·/−·/−−·/          −−−/·−·/·/−−·−·−          ····/··/···/
···/−·/·−·/·/·····/·/·−·/          ···/·−·/−−·/          ····/··/−−/−−·−·−          ·−·/·−·/−·/          −·/−−−/
····/···/−−/·/−−·−·−          −−·/·−·/·/·−·/··/          ····/··/·/−−/          ·−·/          ·−·/··/·−·/−·/−−··/−−·−·−          ··/
−··−·/−−−/·−·/          ·−·/·/·−·/          ····/····/−−−/··/···/·−·−·−          ·····/
−··−·/·−·/·−·/·−·/·−·/          −·/·····/·/          ·−−·/·−·/·/·/·/·−·/          −−·/·−·/·−·/·−·/·−·/
··−·/·−·/·−·/          ··−·/·····          ·−·/·−·/··/··/−−−·/·/          −·/−−−−·/·−·/··/·−·/−−−·−−
          /−·····/··/·/···/          −−/−−−−·/          ···/−−−/−·/·−·/          ·−−/·−·/··/          ·−·/−−−/··/·/−·          ·−/−·/−··/
··/···/          ··−·/−−−/·−·/···/·/−·/−·/·−·−·−          ·····/·/          ·−−/·−·/··/          −−·/·/·−·/−·/
·−·/−·/·−··/          ··/···/          ·−/·−·/·/·−/·····/·/          ·−/−−·/·−·/··/−·/−·///
```

Muddles   *key words*

unless I'm very much mistaken,
confused elements of Luke 15 and
selection from the First Folio (1623)

Parablend featuring Coin/Sheep/Son
The father lost ninty-nine of his coins,
since his calf was no longer worthy to
be called a shoe or a coat. He took them
to Dissipation City and spent all except
one on wild living.

When famine struck, he ran a broom
and sensed his joy but there were no
sweeps to be found, even in the open
country of heaven.

He took a job tending friends and
neighbours' pigs, many of whom have

no need to repent; and wantonly longed to put one (or ten) across his neck and go home.

He came to his senses.

'Do not my men's hired father have a plenteous share of dust? I will arise and rejoice that I have illumined the house and divided one sinner.'

While he was still a long way off, his sheep searched carefully and ran with friends and neighbours to rejoice. He gave one righteous person a pair of calves, silver shoes, a ring, presents, a coin for wild living and killed ninety-nine fatted sandals and two sons.

'Friends and younger shepherds, fill your stomachs and rejoice here on my estate more with me and the angels over this sinner who has repented of being lost and dead but is found and alive and lamped and shouldering.'

Dialogue from
Hamlet, Prince of Denmark *
The boy said to his father 'To be or not to be; that is the question.'

So his father gave him the cash, and the boy went to Dissipation City. He lived wildly, spending with abandon – eating, drinking, gambling – and on a range of entertainments and so-called friends.

Soon the cash ran out, and at the same time a famine struck the land. The boy took a job in a sty and was longing to eat the pods the pigs were given.

He came to his senses. I shall say to my father 'O, that this too too solid flesh would melt, thaw and resolve itself into a dew!'

So he went home.

But while he was still a long way off, his father ran to greet him, with many hugs and kisses and gifts of shoes, a coat and a ring.

The fatted calf is slaughtered.

His father said 'Brevity is the soul of wit.'

Synopsis from Hamlet, Prince of Denmark *
Prince Hamlet sees his father's ghost. 'Give me my inheritance.'

Laertes (brother of Hamlet's girlfriend Ophelia), by contrast, is advised to avoid financial transactions.

Hamlet agrees to avenge his father's murder, but feigns insanity with Ophelia, who is then instructed to trick the prince as King Claudius and Chancellor Polonius listen in.

Hired actors arrive, and Hamlet confirms Claudius' guilt by means of a play, and longs to kill him. He is summoned by Queen Gurtrude, but stabs Polonius through the arras and sees the ghost again.

He seems to have lost his senses.

'My father's hired men eat well every day. I'll arise and go to my father and say Make me one of your hired men – I'm no longer worthy to be called your son.'

He returns home. Meanwhile, Ophelia drowns. Laertes (réturné) attacks Hamlet. They fight inconclusively, in Ophelia's grave.

Servants are told to bring weapons, and poisons are bought from a mountebank. Hamlet and Laertes duel with swords, during which Gurtrude, Claudius, Laertes and Hamlet all die.

His father said 'For this my son was dead, but is alive; he was lost and is found.'

The rest is silence.

*a favoured Oulipo constraint is to crow-bar speeches from Hamlet into various narratives. So why not do the same with Lost Son speeches into Hamlet's synopsis?

Lost Son ParABBAble *pastiche*

reworked lyrics from some ABBA songs
(Swedish pop band of the 70s & 80s)

Spoiler prologue: **I have his cash**

I have a dream
by Benny Andersson & Björn Ulvaeus
Released as a single by ABBA in 1979 (UK No2)

I have his cash, a song I'll sing
Now I don't lack for anything
Perpendicular to this lousy farm
I can spend this fortune;
   I'll come to no harm!
I believe in angles -
By degrees at last I've broken loose
I believe in angles:
Vertex, interior, acute, obtuse
I shall be flash – I have his cash!

Financed it all – we had some fun!
I've spent his cash –
   my friends are gone
Now my dissipation truly is complete;
Looking after porkers –
   scrawny, lacking meat.
Visited by angels
Now I see it's right to go back home;
Reasoned with by angels
Go to dad and now no longer roam!
I'll walk the road – repent, unload –
I'll ask to work – not seek a perk.

I see the farm, dad runs to greet –
A ring, a coat, shoes for my feet!
Now I know the wonder
   of a loving dad;
Home, restored and welcomed –
   we are both so glad!
I believe in parables
Something good to learn
   for you to see,
I believe in parables
Forgiveness is
   freely poured on me!
I had his cash – behaved quite rash;
Repentance true – this start is new.

Oscar the farmer (known by the nickname O) lives with his two sons Edward and Benedict and their unsympathetic step-mother Fen (short for Fenella).

Their lives are filled with hard toil and labour; tending the animals they raise and ensuring the crops grow to provide food for everyone, including the livestock.

They are a wealthy family, employing many farmhands.

Edward and Benedict are reviewing their financial status, reckoning on the value of the land, the animals and the business itself.

Song One:
Moo Neigh, Moo Neigh, Moo Neigh

Money, Money, Money
by Benny Andersson & Björn Ulvaeus
Released as a single by ABBA in 1973 (UK No 3)

BENEDICT   I work all night, I work all day to pay the bills I have to pay
EDWARD   Ain't it sad?
BENEDICT   And still there never seems to be a single penny left for me
EDWARD   That's too bad!
BENEDICT   In my dreams
I have a plan:
If I became a wealthy man,
I wouldn't have to work at all,
I'd fool around and have a ball...
ALL   Money, money, money,
Must be funny,
   in the rich man's world
Money, money, money,
Always sunny,
   in the rich man's world
WOLF   Aha-ahaaa
BENEDICT   All the things I could do,
If I had a little money:
It's a rich man's world!
ANIMALS   *(snorts, clucks with the riff)*
ALL   It's a rich man's world
HENS   We cluck all night and

312

GOATS Snort all day
ALL   It's quite a row we have to say
OSCAR Ain't it sad?
ANIMALS But still it always
  seems to me,
We just make meals for you three
EDWARD That's too bad
ANIMALS We herd and flock,
  stay in one lump
FATTED CALF You seem too interested
  in my rump
ANIMALS And though of fathers,
  you're the best, pops, we fear
SHEEP We are merely lamb chops…
Chorus:
COWS Moo
HORSE Neigh
COWS Moo
HORSE Neigh
COWS Moo
HORSE Neigh
ALL   Soon it's doomsday,
  It's a farming world
COWS Moo
HORSE Neigh
COWS Moo
HORSE Neigh
COWS Moo
HORSE Neigh. We go
COWS Moo
HORSE Neigh, it's a farming world
ROOSTER Cock-ah-doodle-doo
ANIMALS We'll make a love-er-ly
  stew but we go
COWS Moo
HORSE Neigh
COWS Moo
HORSE Neigh
COWS Moo
HORSE Neigh
ALL   It's a farming world
Repeat chorus
ALL   It's a farming world!

Edward resents his step-mamma Fen, but Benedict (the younger of the sons) has a plan: he's decided to get away from her altogether.

Song Two: **Step-Mama Mia!**
Mamma Mia! by Benny Andersson,
Björn Ulvaeus & Stig Anderson
Released as a single by ABBA in 1975 (UK No 1)

EDWARD I've been chastised
  by you since I don't know when;
But I made up my mind,
I'd obey you but then
Look at me now, will I ever learn?
I don't know how
  but I suddenly lose control
There's a fire within my soul
Just one look and I can hear a bell ring
One more look
  and I forget everything, O-o-o-oh

BOTH *StepMama mia, here I go again;*
My my; how can I resist you?
StepMama mia, does it show again?
My my, just how much I want to.
Yes, I've been brokenhearted;
Blue since the day you started –
Why, why can't I ever let you go?
BENEDICT *StepMama mia,*
  now I've got to go,
Even though you nickname my dad O

FEN I've been angry and sad
  'bout the things that you do;
I can't count all the times that you've
  wound me up too.
And when you go,
  when you slam the door,
I think you know that the road
  you tread's oh so long,
You know that I'm not that strong.
Just one look and I can hear a bell ring
One more look and I forget
  everything, O-o-o-oh

BOTH *StepMama mia, here I go again;*
My, my, how can I resist you?
StepMama mia, does it show again?

313

My, my, just how much I want to
Yes, I've been brokenhearted,
Blue since the day you started –
Why, why can't I ever let you go?
BENEDICT   *StepMama mia, even if I say*
   Bye I'll leave you now or never
StepMama mia, is it a game I play
'Bye bye' does it mean forever?
Stepmama mia, here I go I said
'Bye-bye'; really would you let me go?
StepMama mia,
   now you've done my head
Even though you nickname my dad O
BOTH   *Yes, I've been brokenhearted,*
Blue since the day you started –
Why, why can't I ever let you go?
BENEDICT   *StepMama mia,*
Now I really know; my my,
Now I really have to go.

The farmer, Oscar (known as O)
regrets his son's decision to go to
Dissipation City. But he won't prevent
him from leaving, and gives him his
inheritance.

Song Three: **Shame on You**
Voulez-Vous
by Benny Andersson & Björn Ulvaeus
Released as a single by ABBA *in 1979 (UK No 3)*

OSCAR   I just stand and stare,
A sense of disappointment
   hanging in the air.
Giving out the cash,
Your dear old dad
Has lost his marbles in a flash.
Can't help but think we know the
   start, we know the end;
It's a fearful scene…
We've not done this before
But soon he'll be back
   to get some more;
You know what I mean?
OSCAR Shame on you!
(Animals on BVs) ah-ha
take it now or leave it *ah-ha*

that is all you get *ah-ha* nothing
promised, no regrets; Bag of mou- *la-
ha* it's a big decision *ah-ha* you know
what to do *ah-ha* I can now still say
adieu, so toodle-oo-ooh!
BENEDICT   I know what you think –
The boy means business,
So please enjoy your drink.
Feeling mighty proud
I shall take the money,
Gather round a crowd
I'm really glad you gave,
I know the rules, I know the game:
It's all I'm gonna get;
I've not done this before,
I won't be back, farm work's a chore,
It's something I can't hack
OSCAR   Billet-doux *ah-ha* take it now
or leave it *ah-ha* that is all you get *ah-
ha* nothing promised, no regrets;
Hereunto *ah-ha* it's a big decision *ah-
ha* you know what to do *ah-ha* I can
still say join the queue!
BENEDICT   I'm really glad you gave,
I know the rules, I know the game:
It's all I'm gonna get
I've not done this before,
I won't be back, farm work's a chore,
   It's something I can't hack
OSCAR   Feeling blue *ah-ha* take it now
or leave it *ah-ha* that is all you get *ah-
ha* nothing promised, no regrets;
Take a pew *ah-ha* it's a big decision *ah-
ha* you know what to do *ah-ha* I can
still your love eschew,
Who foreknew-ooh!
ALL   (End of) interview *ah-ha, ah-ha, ah-
ha* no virtue *ah-ha, ah-ha, ah-ha* knowing me knowing you *ah-ha, ah-ha, ah-
ha* rendezvous *ah-ha, ah-ha, ah-ha*
OSCAR   Nothing new *ah-ha* take it now
or leave it *ah-ha* that is all you get *ah-
ha* nothing promised, no regrets;
Koocachoo *ah-ha* It's a big decision *ah-
ha* you know what to do *ah-ha* Mon-
key still say, monkey-doo! *(rpt to fade)*

314

In a rare show of emotion, Oscar reminds Benny that his love will not fade nor be withdrawn; he reminds his beloved son that he is and always will be family.

Song Four: **Take a Chance on Me**

Take a Chance on Me
by Benny Andersson & Björn Ulvaeus
Released as a single by ABBA *in 1977 (UK No 1)*

OSCAR   If you change your mind
ANIMALS   *(throughout)*
Take a chance take a chac-a-chance
   chance (etc)
OSCAR I'm the first in line,
I am family. Take a chance on me.
If you need me, let me know,
Gonna be around,
When you've got no place to go,
If you're feeling down.
If you're all alone
When the pretty birds have flown,
Benny don't you see?
Take a chance on me;
Gonna do my very best
And it ain't no lie
If you put me to the test,
If you let me try!
ALL Take a chance on me
OSCAR That's all I ask of you, son
ALL Take a chance on me
OSCAR We can go milking,
We can go lambing, as long as
   we're together
Listen to some music,
Maybe just talking,
Get to know you better!
Cos you know I've got
So much that I wanna say,
When I hope you'll choose to stay –
It's tragic! You want me to let you go,
Oh, Benny I love you so
But I think you know
That I'll let you go
Repeat Chorus
ALL Take a chance on me

BENEDICT Come on, give me a break,
   will you?
ALL Take a chance on me;
Oh you can take your time Benny,
He's in no hurry,
Know he's gonna get you
Now you wanna hurt him,
Benny don't worry,
He's gonna let you.
Let me tell you now
His love is strong enough
To last when things are rough –
Your Father!
You say that He's a waste of time
But you can't get Him off your mind
No you can't let go
'Cause He loves you so
Repeat Chorus
ANIMALS Take a chance, take a
   chance, take a chance on me
LAMBS Baa baa baa baa baa, baa
   baa baa baa baa
OSCAR Take a chance on me,
We are family
Gonna do my very best,
Benny can't you see?
Gotta put me to the test –
Benny trust in me!
ANIMALS Take a chance, take a
   chance, take a chance on me
LAMBS Baa baa baa baa baa, baa
   baa baa baa baa baa-baa
OSCAR *(fade)* Benny I'm still free –
Take a chance on me?

But his mind is made up.

He wants to get away, to see life, to experience some action, to take a risk or two or several more; there's sensations and fun and experiences to be tasted.

He knows it's wrong, but if he doesn't do this now, he never will, and since his father is willing to part with his money, Benny will take full advantage.

315

However, his money begins to run out, oh so quickly

Song Five: **This sinner takes it all**
The Winner Takes it all
by Benny Andersson & Björn Ulvaeus
Released as a single by ABBA *in 1980 (UK No 1)*

BENEDICT I am gonna walk,
Taking things; I'm going to
Diss'pation City;
Make some history;
I'll deal all my cards,
Roulette wheel and gambling,
Lots of games to play,
Now I've got away!
This sinner takes it all!
Goes for the long haul;
No more farm for Benny –
'Runaway' – that's me!

I was on your farm,
Knowing I belonged there;
I figured it made sense
Crossing o'er the fence.
Had a change of view,
Got inside Casino,
Behaving like a ledge
Spending my dad's wedge...
I went to throw the dice;
Blew a fortune, twice!
The cost has been too dear,
Losses are severe;
The croupier takes it all;
Sweeps up my windfall.
Buying two greyhounds
Left not many pounds.

Not enjoying this
Expensive roulette wheel;
Chances quite narrow -
Voisins du zero;
Somewhere deep inside,
You must know I miss you;
But what can I say?
Loss, the game I play –
My selfishness decide/

-ing to stand with pride;
Friends who never stay
Famine drives away.
Hunger does me in –
Feeling rather thin,
When guilt comes to call
This sinner takes it all!

I don't wanna walk;
I don't wanna see Dad.
And I understand
I've played a losing hand;
Won't apologise,
Stubborn pride still stands strong
I won't wander hence
Full of arrogance! ('Cause, you see)
This sinner will appal!
This sinner will appal!

Dissipation City is taking its toll on Benny's bag of coins. But he pays no attention, and continues in wild living. The lights are bright, the entertainments immoral, the drinks flow and the girls swarm around the generous, boy with cash to flash and no sense of caution.

He spends with wild exuberance and befriends some dancing queens.

Song Six:
Grooving Female Monarch
'Elegant variation' practiced on Dancing Queen
by Benny Andersson & Björn Ulvaeus
Released as a single by ABBA *in 1976 (UK No 1)*

At the end of each working week,
  in the evening,
When the illuminations are
  downwardly adjusted
With the dimmer switches
  and people are seeking venues,
There are locations in which
  the correct tunes are heard,
Entering the child's suspended
  to-and-fro-moving seat,
And they ingress, seeking royalty.

But frankly it could be each
  or every one of those blokes,
Since the afternoon is barely over
And the volume
  of the band is considerable.
Add a bar or two of progressive tunes
  (all is well),
Especially when you're disposed
  toward rhythmic movements
And seeking opportunities...
Then you're a grooving female Monarch,
Neither elderly nor sour,
One year short of enfranchisement,
Oh yes! a terpsichorean distaff ruler,
Receiving not merely aural
  but also tactile input
Bar by bar from the percussive
  favourite of the Salvation Army.
You may pas de deux,
You may make jerking hand movements
  reminiscent of the fifties,
Enjoying yourself as much
  as you ever have or ever will!
Look at that young woman –
Observe a section of an Act,
Using a spade on the
  tripping-the-light-fantastic
Giant non-spearside honey-maker maker.

A pair of homely-looking twins –
Agnes and Freda – take a fancy to
Benny; he prefers their other sister
Christine. They wager on finding a
man entering the bar after the clock
strikes, but of course when it's Benny,
they become rivals.

Song Seven: **Gimme, Gimme, Gimme**

Gimme, Gimme, Gimme (a man after midnight)
by Benny Andersson & Björn Ulvaeus
Released as a single by ABBA *in 1979 (UK No 3)*

AGNES Ten to twelve
And I'm watching the doorway
  in my hope for a man
How I love to spend the evening
  in the bar;

FREDA Autumn winds
Blowing outside the window
  as I look around the room
And it makes me so excited –
  okay yar!
There's not a soul out there,
  so I just sit and stare...

BOTH *Gimme gimme gimme*
A man with a birthright –
Won't somebody help me chase these
  shadows away?
Gimme gimme gimme
Complexion that's snow-white;
Dance me past the darkness towards
  skin that's okay

FREDA We're plain girls
  so we have to work much harder,
But the lessons that we learn
Means we'll get to spend the
  cash of Benny Churn.
AGNES Sister Chris doesn't really
  seem to like him,
Which we cannot understand
Leaves less competition
  for that lovely man.
There's not a soul out there,
  so we just sit and stare...

BOTH *Gimme gimme someone*
Who'll make my soul ignite –
Won't somebody love me
  or at least be my friend?
Gimme gimme gimme
A man who is not tight–
Just want someone wealthy whose
  moolah I can spend
Gimme just a loser
Who's a fool with a weak soul;
Want a man who's ready to
  finance all our fun
Gimme gimme gimme
A chap with a bank roll –
Isn't there a sucker who'll
  treat me number one?

Benny enters, and asks Chris to accompany him, but she refuses.

In his sadness, he spurns the other sisters, and they are ejected from the public house when it is discovered that Benny has no money with which to pay their bar bill.

Song Eight:
Knowing Me, Knowing You
Knowing Me, Knowing You
by Benny Andersson,
Björn Ulvaeus & Stig Anderson
Released as a single by ABBA *in 1977 (UK No 1)*

BARTENDER   No more carefree
  laughter; silence ever after
Kicked out of this public house,
  tears in your eyes
Here is where your money ends;
  this is goodbye.
BENEDICT   Knowing me,
  knowing you
FREDA / AGNES (BVs) *ah-haa*
BENEDICT   There is nothing we can
  do, knowing me knowing you *ah-haa*
BENEDICT   I just have to face it,
  say toodle-oo
BVs *You're in the stew, Oh what a stew,*
Thick gravy stew, a red-hot stew
CHRIS   Being broke is never easy,
I know, but you have to go
BVs *You have to go this time, you have to*
go, this time you know
BENEDICT   Knowing me, knowing
  you it's what I must do

Mem'ries (*mem'ries*), good days (*good*
  days), bad days (*bad days*)
They'll be (*they'll be*), with me (*with*
  me) always (*always*)
From this old familiar purse I used to
  pay - now there's only emptiness,
Fluff and decay.
Knowing me, knowing you *ah-haa*
BENEDICT   There is nothing we can
  do, knowing me knowing you *ah-haa*

BENEDICT   I just have to face it,
  it's not untrue
BVs *You're in the stew, your neck in stew*
You're in the stew, thick gravy, too
CHRIS   Clearing out is never easy,
I know, but I have to go
BVs *You know you have to go, you have to*
go, this time you know
BENEDICT   Knowing me, knowing
  you, it's what I must do
Knowing me, knowing you *ah-ha*
BENEDICT   There is nothing we can
  do, knowing me knowing you *ah-haa*
BENEDICT   I just have to face it,
I'm in the stew
BVs *You're in the stew, Gravy like glue*
You're in the stew, real irish stew
CHRIS   Giving up is never easy,
I know, but I have to go
BVs *You have to go this time*
You have to go, this time you know
BENEDICT   Knowing me, knowing
  you, it's what I must do

Arrested by PC Windows for debt, Benny is incarcerated. He is dejected. The old policeman is kind to the boy, giving him breakfast gruel.

Song Nine: **Thank you for the Meusli**
Thank You for the Music
by Benny Andersson & Björn Ulvaeus
Released as a single by ABBA *in 1983 (UK No 33)*

WINDOWS   I'm a p'lice special,
PC Windows, that's me
And I pound the beat
  for the constabulary;
Now I'm the best waiter
  in all the force
'Cause everyone cheers
  when I bring out this course
It's food for the whole man
With dried fruit, hazelnuts and bran;
What do you say?
BENEDICT   *Thank you for the Muesli,*
  the bowl I'm eating

Thanks for all the joy it's treating…
Who can live without it,
I ask in all honesty – what would life be?
Without colonic roughage what are we?
So I stay bound up until Muesli –
You're giving it to me.

Father says I had a
  problem before I could walk
He says I was bound and in pain
  long before I could talk
And I've often wondered,
How did it all start?
Who found out that nothing
  can sort out my heart-
Burn like muesli can?
Well, whoever it was, I'm a fan
So we say…
BOTH *Thank you for the Muesli,*
The bowl I'm chewing
Thanks for all the joy ensuing!
Who can live without it,
I ask in all honesty what would life be?
Without colonic roughage what are we?
So I say 'bound to eat the Muesli'
Forgive jubilee.

BENEDICT I've been selfish,
Now I've come to my senses
I wanna say sorry to everybody
What a fool, what a mess,
What a turn-round!
BOTH *Thank you for the Muesli,*
The bowl I'm chewing
Thanks for all the joy ensuing!
Who can live without it,
I ask you internally, digestively
Without colonic roughage what are we?
So I stay bound up without Muesli
Releasing it to me.
So I say thank you for the Muesli –
For giving it to me.

Getting away from the clutches of the
law, Benny took a job tending pigs,
despite the dishonour this brought to a
man of his heritage. The rotting food
which the unclean animals were given
seemed fleetingly attractive to the
starving boy, but God intervened.

Gloriously, the son came to his
senses, realising that his Dad's hired
men were much better off than he was.
He chose to be humble, and to return.

Song Ten: **I to my Senses Came**
The Day Before you Came
by Benny Andersson & Björn Ulvaeus
Released as a single by ABBA *in 1982 (UK No 32)*

I must have seen what those pigs ate,
  because I always do:
The slops, I'm certain, were the sort
  that they don't need to chew.
I prob'ly watched the porkers
  rushing to the trough all round,
Each treading on the litt'lest one –
  he's squashed into the ground.
I must have sat down hard
  and wondered what I might be fed?
No lunch for me today
  and so I reckon I shall soon be dead;
Since no food yesterday,
  the prev'ous day or any day
    this week, the week before,
And longed to share the food
  of unclean swine, oh utter shame!
    I to my senses came.

I'm jealous of the porkers,
  wondering about the taste
Of rotting vegetation. Almost grabbed
  some in my haste.
(I didn't ever eat it but I very
  nearly did);
So starving hungry was I, and stony
  broke – I didn't have a quid.
I soon dismissed the thought,
  to get down with the pigs was not
Something I really would consider,
  unless I lost the plot;
Then hunger pangs extend,
  undoubtedly I was /

at my tether's end,
And ready to consider
  anything one might proclaim –
    I to my senses came.

The flash of intense light inside
  my mind, inside my heart.
'Your father's men eat breakfast,
  lunch and dinner, à la carte.
They work all night and work all day
  and get paid handsomely
And stay there on the farm and take
  their pay, enjoying job security.
You could do the same if you would
  lay down all your pride
And return home with humbleness.
  Just walk through the countryside.'
I got up there and then
  And left the scrawny pigs,
    starving inside their pen
And started the long walk,
  hoping I'd make it, not go lame;
    I to my senses came.

And set off on my way,
  I started thinking 'How can
    I ask Dad? Or what to say?
I am no longer worthy
  to be called your son again.'
    I to my senses came.

Meanwhile, as he promised, Benny's father was looking out for him.

Each morning,, he would climb to the roof of the farmhouse and watch, in desperate hope that his boy was on the road. Of course, for many long months this was fruitless. But then, one day, his heart leapt within him as he thought he recognised… Could it be?

Song Eleven: **Fen and O**
Fernando by Benny Andersson & Björn Ulvaeus
Released as a single by ABBA in 1976 (UK No 1)

FEN Can you see the boy?
EDWARD Fen and O!

I remember long ago another
  starry night like this
In the firelight, Fen and O
You were humming to yourselves
  and softly crying to the Lord;
I couldn't see your youngest boy
Or hear his footsteps
  coming from afar…
He's closer now, Fen and O;
Every hour, every minute,
  seems to last eternally
Don't be too controlled to show
He is young and full of life
  and he's got truck loads of your cash
And I'm not ashamed to say
My step-mama sometimes
  gives me quite a bash.
There is something in the air tonight
The stars are bright, Fen and O
Are they shining out for you and me?
Or for Benny, Fen and O!
Though I always thought that he's
  a loser and I regret –
If I had to do the same again no way,
  my friend, Fen and O.
If I had to do the same again no way,
  my friend, Fen and O

EDWARD See the sunrise light,
Fen and O; And since many months
I haven't seen a smile upon your face
Can you see the boy Fen and O?
Are you able now to show
  the waster boy your perfect grace?
I can see it in your eyes
How full of love you are and
  very eager to embrace!
There is something in the air tonight
The shoe-shine bright, Fen and O;
Has the brand-new coat been bought
  for me or for Benny, Fen and O?
I imagine fatted calf meat'd
  be nice in baguette
And you're really giving him the ring?
The fam'ly bling? Fen and O?
I am tearing out my hair tonight

320

Unjust, not right! Fen and O
You would never give a goat to me
  for a party, Fen and O.
Though I always worked in lower field,
  which I regret
If I had to do the same again
  can't comprehend, Fen and O.
I would never do the same again –
  be a citizen, Fen and O.
Can't work out why inheri…
Tence was giv'n to him, Fen and O (fade)

The joyful farmer bestows gifts upon
the returning son.

Song Twelve: **Ring Ring**
Ring Ring *by Benny Andersson,*
Björn Ulvaeus & Stig Anderson
Released as a single by ABBA *in 1973 (UK No 32)*

I was sitting here at home;
I was waiting all alone
Benny by myself
I'm up on the roof looking for you;
Another dark and dreary night,
But now I think I've seen a sight
Could that be you a long way off –
Is it true? I gather my cloak and run
To greet you my so dear-loved son!

Oh! Ring! Ring! Also provide you a coat;
Sandals and I'll give more than a goat!
Ring Ring, village hears your anecdote
And I kiss you my boy, Oh what a laugh;
Servant, go kill the fatted calf,
Oh Ring Ring
  though you've sowed your wild oat
Ring Ring and spent every last banknote

You were dead but now alive;
My heart's gone in overdrive
I am so so glad
That we'll be celebrating
Bring the villagers here please,
We'll have beef and wine and cheese
And I'll give a speech,
You'll know I'm not hesitating

I forgive you all your sin,
My returning next of kin oh!

Ring ring, welcome back to the home farm
Ring ring,
  Glad that you've come to no harm!
Ring coat sandals, no need for alarm,
And the party now really in full swing
Dancing and drinking and eating
Ring Ring,
Hope that your brother shows charm
Ring Ring, glad you avoided Gendarme!
oh-oh Ring test cricketers bowl overarm
Ring Ring nobody treats you with smarm

Song Thirteen:
Now Your Father Knows
Does Your Mother Know?
by Benny Andersson & Björn Ulvaeus
Released as a single by ABBA *in 1979 (UK No 4)*

BENEDICT   Now you're not teasing me
I was blue: but I knew
I'd take a chance on a son like you
That's something I had to do!
There's that look in your eyes
I can read in your face that your
  actions were living that's wild
Infamy my younger child

Well, I can dance with you, Benny;
To see you is uncanny!
I, your father, know that you're home.
And I can chat with you, sonshine,
Everything will be fine
Now your father knows that you're home!

BENEDICT *Take it easy*
ANIMALS *Take it easy*
BENEDICT *Better slow down dad:*
Your older lad – Does my brother know?
OSCAR *Take it easy*
ANIMALS *Take it easy*
OSCAR *Try to cool it guy*
Before I start to cry
(sarcastic) Does your brother know?
Ha ha ha!

BENEDICT You can't see what I mean
But you know he's the sort
Who'll be feeling some jealousy
Think about it — you'll agree
OSCAR There's no need,
  but you're too kind
Edward's been here all the time
But I'm quite sure he won't mind
That now you're here we unwind!

OSCAR *Well, I can dance with you,*
  Benny; to see you is uncanny!
Now your father knows that you're home.
And I can chat with you, sonshine,
Everything will be fine
Now your father knows that you're home!
BENEDICT *Take it easy*
ANIMALS *Take it easy*
BENEDICT *Better slow down dad:*
Your older lad — does my brother know?
OSCAR *Take it easy*
ANIMALS *Feelin' wheezy*
OSCAR *Try to cool it guy,*
  before I start to cry
(sarcastic) Does your brother know?
Ha ha ha!

OSCAR *Well, I can dance with you,*
  Benny – to see you is uncanny!
Now your father knows that you're home.
And I can chat with you, matey,
Signet ring is weighty
Now your father knows that you're home!
OSCAR *Well, I can dance with you,*
  Benny; to see you is uncanny!
Now your father knows that you're home.
And I can chat with you, sonshine;
Everything will be fine
Now your father knows that you're home!

Song Fourteen: **Welcome You**
Waterloo by Benny Andersson,
Björn Ulvaeus & Stig Anderson
Released as a single by ABBA *in 1974 (UK No 1)*

OSCAR My my, I welcome you!
Oh Benny, son the younger!

BENEDICT Oh yeah, and I have met
  my big brother
In not a similar mood!
He's has begun to behave
  with panache
Now he knows that he'll keep
  all Dad's cash

OSCAR *Welcome you;*
I was deflated, you made me sore
Welcome you
BENEDICT *Promise to love you for*
  evermore!
OSCAR *Welcome you; gave you a*
  hug 'cos I wanted to;
Welcome you
BENEDICT *I know my place is*
  to be with you:
ANIMALS *Wo wo wo wo*
OSCAR *Welcome you; want you*
  to know that I welcome you.

My cash, it tried to hold you back
But you had spent it
BENEDICT Oh yeah, and now it seems
  my only hope is giving up the fight
And how could I ever refuse?
I came to my senses to choose:

OSCAR *Jumped the queue;*
I was excited, had coins and more;
Take a pew; lots of wild girls
  who would break the law!
OSCAR *Barbecue; feel free to eat*
  what you wanted to
Until you spew
BENEDICT *We are so glad now to*
  welcome you
ANIMALS *Wo wo wo wo*
OSCAR *Play kazoo; party time*
  for the guests and for you

BENEDICT And how could I
  ever refuse?
I came to my senses to choose
  (to come back home)

OSCAR *Welcome you; gave you a*
  robe 'cos I wanted to;
Welcome you knowing my ring
  will now be with you
ANIMALS *Wo wo wo wo*
OSCAR *Welcome you; gave you those*
shoes cos I wanted to;
ANIMALS *Shooo-oh!*
OSCAR *Welcome you; want you to*
  know that I welcome you.
ANIMALS *Wo wo wo wo*
OSCAR *Welcome you; want you to*
  know that I welcome you!

There is much rejoicing as the villagers join the party. Roast calf is served, and dancing follows.

Afterword: **Undone Lost Son**
Super Trouper
by Benny Andersson & Björn Ulvaeus
Released as a single by ABBA *in 1980 (UK No 1)*

Undone Lost Son
You have much maligned me
Today I watch too, like I always do
Cause somewhere on the road there's you.

You were sick and tired
  of working here
So you came to me, all demanding
Your inheritance and bent my ear
About some misunderstanding
          Simple misunderstanding
So I said well, yes, I'll give you cash
  Was it right to give you all the cash?
Suddenly I felt so sad
          surprise! It made you sad
Now my life would be so different
Without you my dear dear lad!

You became Undone Lost Son
  you have much maligned me
          (Un-Undone Younger Son), etc
Yet I look for you, like I always do
Cause somewhere on the road there's you

I look for Undone Lost Son,
  how deeply I miss you
Heart heavy with cares
Neither millionaires;
Watching all the time, upstairs

Wild living wins you so-called friends
But when cash is gone,
  then comes famine
Then you'll find
  gold-diggers loy'lty ends
You will have gammon to examine
          Low-grade gammon to examine
There'll be moments when
  your hunger drives you crazy
          Starving neurological
Hope your thinking won't be odd
          Monster raving issues
Like considering their swill
Eating stinking moulding pod.

I'm thinking Undone Lost Son
  hope that you return soon
          (Un-Undone Younger Son), etc
I will have you back - I'll put up a plaque
And give you an anorak
I love you Undone Lost Son
  hope it will not be long
Until you turn round
Become homeward bound
Back to your old stomping ground

A long way off, but you arrive
Your Dad goes running, gleeful,
Shouting 'You're alive!'
And then I'll take you in my arms
Showering gifts
Slaught'ring a calf, spit-roast in shifts

Suddenly Undone Lost Son
  revelation struck you
          (Un-Undone Younger Son), etc
Returned home amen!
Turning up again.
Now you'll work like hired men.
Undone Lost Son –

323

celebrating's such fun!
Back into my life – rooftop vigil strife?
Slice beef with a carving knife.
Undone Lost Son family ring for you;
No hired man but son;

Beef's fine underdone
Welcome, everyone!
(fade) Undone Lost Son coat and shoes
and party - returned home again…

Braille form

language

Greener grass?; *obviously, flat, printed dots*
in a small font size provide no help at all

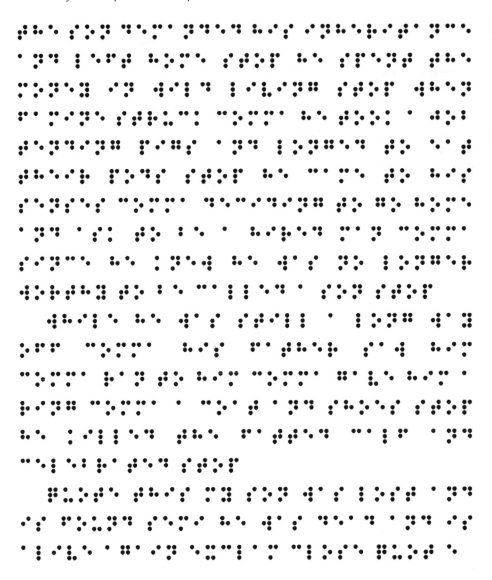

Ough $\qquad$ *wordplay*

one combination of letters, multiple pronounciations; probably the most severe eye rhyme of all time (see p149)

The farmer **coughed**[1] up; his boy took cash and went on **furlough**[2], leaving the **borough**[3], riding away in a **brougham**[4]. He behaved not as he **ought**[5], spending the **dough**[2] in wild living (he **bought**[5] drink and food and made **thoroughly**[3] unwise friendships); soon he had **nought**[5].

A **drought**[6] **brought**[5] a famine, and everyone was starving, which was rather **rough**[7]. The boy took a job feeding pigs and **fought**[5] off his longing to eat their **tough**[7] pods direct from the **trough**[1], even **though**[2] their skins had been **sloughed**[7].

Then he had a **thought**[5] and came to his senses. 'My father's workers have **enough**[7] to eat; I'll return and ask to be a hired man, as the truth is that I'm no longer worthy to be called a son.'

He travelled, **doughtily**[6], **ploughed**[6] **through**[4] a **slough**[7], and **sought**[5] help as a **chough**[7] flew[4] by and the wind **soughed**[6] in the **boughs**[6].

However, while he was still a long way off[1], there was a **hiccough**[8] in his plans. His father saw him beyond the **lough**[9], and ran off[1] to him.

He caught[5] up[8] with him, gave hugs[3], kisses, a new[4] coat (oh[2], without a ruff[7]), a ring (big rock[9]!), shoes[4] (buffed[7] to a shine) and a party, which took[4] place outside[6] not in a ballroom[4] but in the courtyard[5], after it was swept by a groom[4] with a broom[4]. His father, feeling chuffed[7], **wrought**[5] havoc[9] to the fatted calf[7]. 'Ow[6]!'

He said 'This my son was lost, but is found; he is alive again, **although**[2] we **thought**[5] he was dead!'

Rough[7] pro[2]nunciation guide: [1]off [2]oh [3]uh [4]oo [5]or [6]ow [7]uff [8]up [9]ok (*ochh* Sco[3]ttish)
Additio[3]nal no[2]te: 'Brougham[4]' is still a for[5]m of carriage (and has been since p20, too[4])

Endings $\qquad$ *wordplay*

...and good evening

Their conversation concluded, the money bag was exchanged; however the trip was over until he reached Dissipation City. Once the cash ran out, all his friendships were abruptly abandoned, and soon the last of the crops were gone The son finished up looking after pigs. 'I'll have to put a stop to these temptations,' he decided, when the rotting slops appealed to him. Ignorance and foolishness faded as he ceased his consideration of his father's hired men, who ate at the close of each working day.

'I'm going to give up sitting here - but ask for a wage. I am no longer...' The words petered out, but the sentiment was completed. The journey was not yet done when his father saw him, and ran with gifts; he enclosed him in a coat stopping his mouth with kisses.

'Termination for Buttercup!' shouted the farmer, and in the end, dozens of villagers ate and drank until everything was finished. 'My son was dead and lost, but now the mourning and/or searching is most definitely (some might say ultimately) halted.'

Sorted. Kaput. Bosh. Finito. That's all, folks. Thank you, and good night.

Solutions, translations, interpretations

Pathword (p31)

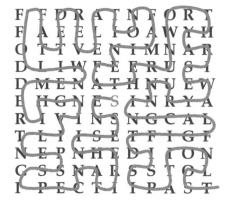

SENSES INHERITANCE PIGS SPENT LIVING HIREDMEN WILD OFF FATTED REVELATION FAMINE FATHER UNWORTHY ARISE WAY RUNNING CALF GIFT DISSIPATION LOST

Prodigal: Encoded Parable (p70)
Find the hidden message using the 3rd, 15th, 11th, 24th words. (It's the 3rd gospel, chapter 15, verses 11-24) The Encoded **Parable** There was a man who had two sons. And the younger of them said **to** his father, 'I need some money fast. Can you please **tell** me how much I will inherit when you die? And then give me whatever share of property that is coming to me.' And **a** while later, **story** -tellers tell us, the father gave him his inheritance, and the boy left home. **With** a spring in his step, he took a journey into **a** far country, and there he squandered his property in reckless living.

He gave no attention to wisdom, or indeed anything said to be **spiritual**; life lacked **purpose**, so he thought, except 'enjoy it to the uttermost!'. Various clingers-on and passers-**by** helped him spend his fortune, until one day his financial **means** ran out. Destitute, he looked for a job, but the whole land was suffering from a famine. Employed by a farmer rearing lots **of** pigs, when **an** inspiration struck him.

'No, I mustn't eat their slop,' he said. 'There is no **earthly** reason why I can't go and work for my father. **Setting** his face to this, he planned to tell his father that he was no longer worthy to be called a son, but would **work** the fields, **out** in the sun, as one of the hired hands.

While he was still at **an** extreme distance, his loving father saw him, and shouted 'Huzzah!', **interpretation** of which was clear to all his servants, as the father had been watching for the boy for weeks.

Running in a way **that** very rapidly **makes** progress, he showed his compassion – greeted with a tenderness the boy didn't have to **sense** or guess. He gave him a ring, and told servants: '**When** you fetch my coat, bring some sandals for his feet, too!' He had the fatted calf slaughtered, and very soon the streets were **lined** with partygoers.

'**Up** on your feet – dance!' the father commanded, smiling. 'We feared my boy was down **with** the lost, but he's found! Was dead but is alive! **Scripture** says 'Bless the Lord, O my soul,' and I shall! We are going to party into the night. And I really do mean **properly**!'

Summary Parable: To tell a story with a spiritual purpose by means of an earthly setting. Work out an interpretation that makes sense when lined up with scripture properly.

Franglais (p78)
Electronic (uncorrected) translation
The boy said to his father 'Hello! Give me the money that is given to me at your funeral, please.'

The farmer agreed, and his son went out by means of the exit quickly. He began to live wild, which involve the unmarried women of virtue easy (which is very, very bad, because very, very athletic). Twenty One, Baccarat, Railway Track, brandy, champagne, and lots of great breakfast Cord Blue, with Julian, chick, French beans, potato rosti, various reduced sauces and crisp custard, money-making parts and upside down apple and caramel pies. Any money fried, and beloved wife gone.

Without cash, without friends, without pancake. Son looks at the hams. Eating pigswill is forbidden (because, unfortunately, it is very gruesome). Poof! a revelation. The servants of the Father... I will arise, go to our fields of animals, and say 'I am called undeserving son, do you employ me, if you please, a proletariat...?'

There return to the home, but Dad to see the point of advantage, and at all speed. Give Dad a ring of gold, clothes, flip-failures and steaks.

Now, the party revels: one thousand leaves (flaky pastry), cream, fondant, roulards, sachertorte pie, tart, profiteroles and English cream and more chocolate.

'My son was lost, it is found! He was dead, but living my son! Give many *'thank you God*'s, or is very beautiful!'

Wordsearch (p106)

The 21 letters (shown in **bold italics**) left over from this grid (when read from the bottom right) spell out **HUMAN TALE GODLY MEANING**

Dog-Latin (p140)

uncorrected translation

Boy looks at father. 'Let cash be in my fingers, Dad and now let me depart!' Goes.

Waster loves Sabini women; gambles, has wine. Country-wide food shortage. Pigs eat; boy is jealous.

Falls down to abide: 'I'll get up, go to Dad with a message. I'll offer to be a citizen of the lowest rank.'

Dad sees boy (without looking through a window) and runs.

Given coat, ring, shoes and the fat cow is killed, served sliced with grated potato cakes. Father says 'My offspring was dead; he lives!'

Fraffly Earppacrus' (Frightfully Uppercrust) (p155)

interpreted

Second son addressed the old boy (his dad) 'O pater (father), may I take my inheritance?' He agreed. Son wasted all his money on wild living – the young shaver (immature boy) lost his cash in a casino, and by getting squiffy (drunk).

He was soon bankrupt and to cap it all (worse) bally (expletive deleted) famine struck. He took a job tending pigs and absolutely longed to eat their food.

He came to his senses and thought 'Pater's unwashed hired men (working class labourers) have all got plenty to eat. I'll go ask Pater if I can work for him.'

So he made his way, don't you know (understand)? While he was still a long way off, his pater saw him and ran to greet him.

He gave him a kiss and a pair of shoes, plus hunting pinks (a red jacket worn by horsemen accompanied by baying hounds and terrified foxes) and an heirloom family ring for his finger. He killed the fatted calf and threw a shindig (party).

'This my son was lost but is found; he was dead but now he's alive!'

Two-Timer Crossword (p278)

¹C		²D	I	³S	⁴S	I	⁵P	A	T	I	⁶O	N

(grid)

¹C		²D	I	³S	⁴S	I	⁵P	A	T	I	⁶O	N
E		E		⁷A	T		T				N	
⁸L	O	N	⁹G	W	A	Y	O	¹⁰F	F			¹¹I
E			A		F			A		¹²E	O	N
¹³B	A	¹⁴P	S		¹⁵F	¹⁶A	T	T	E	D		H
R		S		¹⁷F		R		H		I		E
¹⁸A	N	Y		¹⁹A	L	I	V	E		²⁰B	A	R
T		C		M		S		R		L		I
I		²¹H	E	I	F	E	R		²²B	E	S	T
²³O	N	E		N					A			A
N			²⁴R	E	V	²⁵E	L	A	T	I	O	N
	²⁶P		A			G			H			C
²⁷I	A	M	N	O	L	O	N	G	E	R		E

Across:
2 dissipation
7 at
8 longway off
13 eon
14 baps
16 fatted
19 any
20 alive
21 bar
22 heifer
23 best
24 one
25 revelation
28 I am no longer

Down:
1 celebration
2 den
3 saw
4 staff
5 PTO
6 on
10 gas
11 father
12 inheritance
13 edible
15 psyche
17 arise
18 famine
23 bathe
25 ran
26 ego
27 pa

Acknowledgements & reading list

Key*: *Title* (publication/release date) author; **content title**

p10 *Exercises in Style* Raymond Queneau (published in French by Editions Gallimard 1947); English translation by Barbara Wright (John Calder Ltd 1958)

p11 *La Disparition* Georges Perec (Gallimard 1969); english translation *A Void* Gilbert Adair (Harville Press 1995)

p11 *La vie mode d'emploi* Georges Perec (Hachett Littératures 1978); english translation *Life: A User's Manual* David Bellos (Vintage 1987)

p11 *Se una notte d'inverno un viaggiatore* Italo Calvino (Einaudi 1979); english translation *If on a Winter's Night a Traveller* William Weaver (Vintage 1981)

p11 *Euonia* Christian Bök (Cannongate, 2001)

p11 *99 Ways to tell a Story* Matt Madden (Jonathan Cape 2006)

p11 *Oulipo Compendium* Ed. Harry Matthews & Alastair Brotchie (Atlas Press 1998 & 2005)

p12 *The Seven Basic Plots* Christopher Booker (Continuum 2004)

p12 *The Poets' Manual & Rhyming Dictionary* Frances Stillman (Thames & Hudson 1966)

p12 *The Ode Less Travelled* Stephen Fry (Arrow Books 2005)

p14 Luke 15:11-24 *New International Version* ©1973, 1978, 1984 by the International Bible Society

p14 Luke 15:11-24 *The Message* Eugene Peterson ©1993, 1994, 1995 NavPress

p15 Luke 15:11-24 *Authorised Version* ©2001 HarperCollins

p16 Luke 15:11-24 *English Standard Version* ©2004 American Bible Society

p16 *The Art of Fiction* David Lodge (Penguin 1992)

p16 *Vain Art of the Fugue* Dumitru Tsepeneag (1993), translated by Patrick Camiller (Dalkey Archive, 2006)

p19 **Greener Grass?** Voyage & Return noted in *The Seven Basic Plots* (ibid)

p29 **Epic Metaphor** *A Transport of Delight* lyric by Michael Flanders & Donald Swann; recorded on *At the Drop of a Hat* (1957 album)

p32 **Vealbeast** Overcoming the Monster noted in *Seven Basic Plots* (op.cit.)

p35 **Yoda** Character created by George Lucas for *Star Wars* (1977 movie)

p36 **Nigel Molesworth** Character created by Geoffrey Willans & Ronald Searle for *Down with Skool* (Parrish 1953) and *How to be Topp* (Parrish 1954)

p40 **Chaucerian** Inspired by *The Canterbury Tales* by Geoffery Chaucer (15thC), Everyman edition (1992)

p41 **New Sole, New Soul** Rags to Riches noted in *The Seven Basic Plots* (op.cit.)

p46 **Lord of the Rings** by J R R Tolkein, published by Geo. Allen & Unwin (1954)

p50 **Playing with Fire** The Quest noted in *Seven Basic Plots* (op.cit.)

p71 **Authorised Version** (op. cit)

p73 **Thesaurus Attack** Dr Peter Mark Roget devised 1805, first published 1852

p76 **Fault** Tragedy noted in *Seven Basic Plots* (op. cit)

p90 **Christian Vegetarian Society** (invented name); check all-creatures.org

p98 **Villanelle** *Do Not Go Gentle into That Good Night*, (1951) Dylan Thomas, included in *Collected Poems* (Everyman New Edition 2000)

p98 **Star Trek** Inspired by characters and dialogue in *Star Trek: The Next Generation* (Paramount TV, 1987-94), the film series from *Star Trek:*

329

p197 **Nightmare Song** From Iolanthe, lyrics by WS Gilbert

p199 **Amplified Version** inspired jointly (strange bed-fellows) by *The Amplifed Bible* Zondervan (1965) and *The Dead Parrot Sketch* by John Cleese & Graham Chapman in *Monty Python's Flying Circus* (BBCtv, 1969)

p209 **Bildungsroman** Novel of Coming of Age; inspired by many classic examples – *Candide* Voltaire; *Great Expectations* Charles Dickens; *A Portrait of the Artist as a Young Man* James Joyce; *The Catcher in the Rye* JD Salinger; *The Voyage of the Dawn Treader* CS Lewis

p213 **Catechism** Inspired by the theological Q&A *Westminster Shorter Catechism*

p224 **Bertie Wooster** Created by PG Woodhouse, first appearing (without surname) in *Extricating Young Gussie* – a story in the 1917 collection *The Man with Two Left Feet*

p226 **Reverse** Inspired by the entirely magnificent *Slaughterhouse-Five* by Kurt Vonnegut, Delaconte (1965) in which the narrator travels in time & Martin Amis' *Time's Arrow* Jonathan Cape (1991), written entirely in reverse chronology

p227 **Aporia** A classic example of this form of vague inconclusiveness expressed in literature is the 'To be or not to be' soliloquy in *Hamlet*

p240 **Metafiction** Other examples of self-aware fiction: *The French Lieutenant's Woman* John Fowles; *Lolita* Vladimir Nabakov; *Atonement* Ian McEwen; *Life of Pi* Yann Martell

p249 **Seagoon's Return** Inspired by *The Goon Show*, the BBC radio series, broadcast from 1951-1960 (233 episodes), written mostly by Spike Milligan, and regularly featuring the vocal talents of Milligan, Peter Sellers and Harry Seacombe

(cont from) of The Winchester Club in ITV's *Minder* (1979-1994).

p253 **P455w0rd 5t7l£** Also called 'leetspeak'

p263 **Public Information Film** Inspired by brief films made for the Central Office of Information, aimed mostly at children re safety, stranger danger, kerb drill (crossing roads) etc; and some contemporary adverts. An authoritative voice-over addresses on-screen characters, who respond mutely with theatrical gestures

p268 **Road Yellow Goodbye Brick** Lyrics from *Goodbye Yellow Brick Road*, top ten single written by Bernie Taupin & Elton John, performed by Elton John. Released 1973; reached No 2 in US, No 6 in UK. The road is the path of life followed by Dorothy and her friends in the 1939 film *The Wizard of Oz*.

p269 **Dr Seuss** Reflecting books by Theodore Guisel *The Cat in the Hat* (1957), *Green Eggs and Ham* (1960), *Fox in Socks* (1965) and *Oh, the Places You'll Go!* (1990)

p270 **Pinteresque** Characteristic of Harold Pinter, British playwright (1930-2008). Style and themes include menace, claustrophobic spaces, silences, pauses

p276 **144 Clichés** Inspired by the character CJ (Charles Jefferson) in *The Fall and Rise of Reginal Perrin* (op. cit.)

p288 **Scrabble Parable** Based on the Mattel board game invented by Alfred Mosher Butts in 1938 and developed by James Brunot in 1948

p299 **Bohemian Rhapsody** Lyrics by Freddie Mercury, released 1975. Reached No 1 in UK, No 9 in US. Re-released in 1991, following Mercury's death, reaching No 2 in UK

p296 **Under Milk Farm** Inspired by Dylan Thomas' 1954 radio drama *Under Milk Wood*, featuring dreams and thoughts of the inhabitants of a village while they sleep and wake. With two narrators, plus blind Captain Cat and Polly Garter, who mourns her deceased lover

p308 **Acrostic (Diagonal)** Inspired by chapter 51 of *Life: A User's Manual* by Georges Perec (fr: Hachette 1978; eng trans David Bellos, Collins Harville 1987)

p312 ABBA **songs: spoof title**, song title *Album*

I have his cash I have a dream *Voulez-Vous*

Moo Neigh, Moo Neigh, Moo Neigh Money, Money, Money *Arrival*

Step-Mama Mia! Mamma Mia! *ABBA*

Shame on You Voulez-Vous *Voulez-Vous*

Take a Chance on Me *ABBA*

This sinner takes it all The Winner Takes it all *Super Trooper*

Grooving Female Monarch Dancing Queen *Arrival*

Gimme, Gimme, Gimme (a man after midnight) *no album*

Knowing Me, Knowing You *Arrival*

Thank you for the Meusli Thank You for the Music *Thank You for the Music*

I to my Senses Came The Day Before you Came *no album*

Fen and O Fernando *Greatest Hits*

Ring Ring *Ring Ring*

Now Your Father Knows Does Your Mother Know? *Voulez-Vous*

Welcome You Waterloo *Waterloo*

Undone Lost Son Super Trouper *Super Trouper*

insert **Lostopoly** The 1935 Monopoly game was based upon Atlantic City, NJ. Acknowledgements to Hasbro, who bought the rights from Parker Bros. The familiar London version was originally marketed in the UK by Waddington's

Tube Map Respect and credit to Harry Beck for his clean, simple and elegant original design using horizontal, vertical and diagonal lines inspired by the style of electrical circuit diagrams

---

* **op. cit.** abbreviation of the Latin phrase *opere citato*, meaning 'as previously mentioned', referring to a book, film or album title already listed here

ibid. abbreviation of Latin word *ibidem*, meaning 'in the same source', referring to the previous entry

Index by section

Essentials

Alphabet Games

Alliteration

Keywords

Language

Pastiche

Style

Viewpoint

Wordplay

Index: title by alpha

340

Index: theme/content/origins by numeric/alpha

Lightning Source UK Ltd.
Milton Keynes UK
UKHW040648110419
340861UK00002B/63/P